Sport and Women

Although female athletes are successful in all types of sport, in many countries sport is still a male domain. This book examines and compares the sporting experiences of women from different countries around the world and offers the first systematic and cross-cultural analysis of the topic of women in sport.

Sport and Women presents a wealth of new research data, including in-depth casestudies of 16 countries in North and South America, Asia, Oceania, Eastern and Western Europe and Africa. In addition, the book offers comparative assessments of the extent to which women are represented in global sport and the opportunities that women have to participate in decision-making processes in sport.

The book illuminates a wide range of key international issues in women's sport, such as cultural barriers to participation and the efficacy of political action. It is therefore essential reading for anybody with an interest in the sociology, culture and politics of sport.

Ilse Hartmann-Tews is Professor of Sport Sociology and Gender Studies at the Institute of Sport Sociology and is currently Dean of the Faculty of Social and Cultural Sciences at the German Sport University, Cologne. **Gertrud Pfister** is Professor at the Institute of Exercise and Sport Science at the University of Copenhagen and was President (now Vice-President) of the International Society for the History of Physical Education and Sport.

International Society for Comparative Physical
Education and Sport
Series Editor: Ken Hardman
University of Manchester
Other titles in the series include:

Sport and Physical Education in China
Edited by James Riordan and Robin Jones

Sport and Physical Education in Germany
Edited by Roland Naul and Ken Hardman

Sport and Women

Social issues in international
perspective

Edited by Ilse Hartmann-Tews
and Gertrud Pfister

Routledge
Taylor & Francis Group

LONDON AND NEW YORK

ISCPES

International Society for Comparative Physical Education and Sport

First published 2003
by Routledge
11 New Fetter Lane, London EC4P 4EE

Simultaneously published in the USA and Canada
by Routledge
29 West 35th Street, New York, NY 10001

Routledge is an imprint of the Taylor & Francis Group

Typeset in Garamond by Taylor & Francis Books Ltd
Printed and bound in Great Britain by TJ International Ltd,
Padstow, Cornwall

British Library Cataloguing in Publication Data
A catalogue record for this book is available from the British Library

Library of Congress Cataloging in Publication Data
Sport and women : social issues in international perspective / edited
by Ilse Hartmann-Tews and Gertrud Pfister.
Includes bibliographical references and index.
1. Sports for women–Cross-cultural studies. 2. Sports–Social
aspects–Cross-cultural studies. 3. Sports–Sex differences–Cross-
cultural studies. I. Hartmann-Tews, Ilse. II. Pfister, Gertrud.

GV709 .S66   2003
796'.082–dc21   2002073982

ISBN 0–415–24627–X (hbk)
ISBN 0–415–24628–8 (pbk)

Contents

Illustrations

Tables

Figures

Contributors

D. Margaret Costa is Professor of Kinesiology and Director of Interdisciplinary Studies at California State University, Long Beach, USA. Her current research is on the international sporting woman with emphasis on women from developing countries. She has published 'Cultural Diffusion in Brazil: Sports and Other Pastimes' in *Brazil 500 Years: Crossing Borders From Cabral to the Third Millenium* (2000), supported by the United States' Department of Education Fulbright Commission. Her latest book review is of Maartin Van Bottenburg's *Global Games*, published by the Journal of Sport History.

Nicole Dechavanne is Senior Lecturer at the Institut Universitaire de Fomation des Maître Physical Education (IUFM) in Paris (since 1991). She was president and national coach of the Fédération Française d'Education Physique et de Gymnastique Volontaire (FFEPGV). In 1998 she was elected as a member of the Comité National Olympique et Sportif Française (CNOSF) and in 2000 as Foundation President of the Association 'Femmes, Mixité Sport'.

Kari Fasting is Professor at the Department of Social Science of the Norwegian University of Sport and Physical Education in Oslo, Norway. She became the first elected Chair of this institution and served as Rector from 1989 to 1994. She is Past President of the International Sociology of Sport Association (ISSA) and is currently the Vice-President of the Executive Board of Women's Sport International (WSI). Her main research is gender and sport. She has published widely on different aspects related to women, exercise and sport. At present she is involved in collaborative research in the area of sexual harassment.

Ludmila Fialová is an Associate Professor at the Charles University, Prague, Czech Republic and is working in the Department of Psychology, Pedagogy and Didactics at the Faculty of Physical Education and Sport. Her most recent books include *Body Image as a Part of the Self-Concept* (Karolinum, 2001) and *Didactics of School Sport* (with Antonin Rychtecky, Karolinum, 2000). She is the Scientific Secretary in the Czech Kinanthropologic Society. Her research is in the area of body concepts, health and sport, especially amongst women.

Rubiela Arboleda Gómez is a teacher and research assistant at the Instituto Universitario Educación Física y Deporte at the University of Antioquia in Medellín, Colombia. She graduated in Physical Education and Anthropology and has a Masters degree in Contemporary Social Problems. Her research focuses on body culture and semiotic with a special interest in the relation between sport, gender and social behaviour. Her most recent research deals with somatic culture in different human groups. She has several publications on the relation of body and culture and she is member of the *Somatic Culture Research Group*.

M. Ann Hall is a Professor Emeritus at the University of Alberta in Canada. She serves on the editorial board of several academic journals, and is co-editor of the 'Sport and Culture' book series published by the University of Minnesota Press. Her most recent books include: *The Girl and the Game: A History of Women's Sport in Canada* (Broadview Press, 2002); *Honoring the Legacy: Fifty Years of the International Association of Physical Education and Sport for Girls and Women* (with Gertrud Pfister, Smith College, 1999), and *Feminism and Sporting Bodies: Essays on Theory and Practice* (Human Kinetics, 1996).

Ilse Hartmann-Tews is Professor of Sport Sociology and Gender Studies in the Institute of Sport Sociology, and is currently Dean of the Faculty of Social and Cultural Sciences at the German Sport University, Cologne. She serves on editorial boards of several academic journals and is member of the Extended Executive Board of the International Sociology of Sport Association (ISSA) and member of the Board of Directors of the European College of Sport Science (ECSS). She has written extensively on sports development in a comparative perspective and on gender issues in sports. Her ongoing research focus is on social construction of gender in the sport media, gender imbalances in decision making positions in sport and issues of gender mainstreaming.

Fan Hong is Reader in the Department of Sports Sciences at De Montfort University in England. She was an editor of the *Chinese Journal of Sports Culture and History* in the 1980s. Her main research interests are in the areas of body, gender and sport with particular reference to China. Her most recent books in English are: *Sport in Asian Society: Past and Present* (co-edited with J.A. Mangan, Cass, 2002), *Freeing the Female Body: Inspirational Icons* (co-edited with J.A. Mangan, Cass, 2001) and *Footbinding, Feminism and Freedom: The Liberation of Women's Bodies in Modern China* (Cass, 1997). She is a member of various renowned editorial boards and sport commissions.

Denise E. M. Jones is a Senior Lecturer at the University of the Western Cape in South Africa. She completed her Ph.D. on *Gender, Sport and Power: The Construction of Identities as Sportswomen in South Africa* (2001) at the Netherlands Research School for Women's Studies. She received the

National Sports Council's award for her contribution to women and sport in South Africa. She has served as an elected member of Women and Sport South Africa (WASSA) and is an editorial member of the International Council for Sport Science and Physical Education (ICSSPE). She has written a policy document entitled *Women and Girls get Active* (1997), has an entry on 'South Africa' in the *International Encyclopedia of Women and Sports* (with Jennifer Hargreaves, 2001) and a chapter entitled *In Pursuit of Empowerment: Sensei Nellie Kleinsmidt, Race and Gender Challenges in South Africa* (with J.A. Mangan and Fan Hong as editors, 2001).

Machiko Kimura is Professor at the Nara University of Education in Japan. She is Commissioner of the Sports Sector in the Science Council of Japan, and co-editor of the Japanese Journal of Physical Education, Health and Sports Science. Her most recent books are *Taiikukakyoiku o manabuhito no tameni* (For Students of Physical Education) (co-edited with Atsuo Sugimoto, Kyoto: Sekaishisosya, 2001) and *Sportsbunka no Genzai* (Sports Culture at Present) (Nara University of Education, 1998).

Sascha Alexandra Luetkens studied Sports Science, English and Spanish philology at the University of Cologne and German Sport University Cologne, Manchester Metropolitan University (UK) and Universidad de Sevilla (Spain). She is Research Assistant at the Institutes of Sociology of Sport and Leisure Studies at the German Sport University Cologne and part time lecturer in Gender Studies. Her research focuses on national and international sports development and youth research (gender approach). In the context of research projects, she advises regional sports and youth organisations on sports development. Her most recent publication is *Berichterstattung und Wissensmanagement im Sportsystem* (Surveillance, Monitoring and Knowledge-Management in the Sport System) (in collaboration with C. Breuer, V. Rittner and F. Herb, Cologne, 2002).

Prisca Massao graduated with a Bachelor of Education in Physical Education at the University of Dar-es-Salaam and a Master's degree in Sport Sociology at the Norwegian University of Sport and Physical Education. Her masters thesis was titled *Women in Sport: Feminist Analysis of the Sport Development Policy of Tanzania.*

Ludmila Mourão has been teaching since 1985 and is a Research Assistant at the Department of Physical Education, Gama Filho University, in Rio de Janeiro, Brazil. Her doctoral study was in the area of Gender and Sport, specifically on *Social Representation of Brazilian Woman in Physical Sporting Activity* (1998). Her research is related to gender, body and society with a main focus on the analysis of Sport Events. Her most recent publication, co-authored with S. Votre is 'Ignoring Taboos: Maria Lenk, Latin American Inspirationalist', in *Freeing the Female Body: The International Journal of the History of Sport* 18, 1: 196–218 (2001).

Gertrud Pfister is Professor at the Institute of Exercise and Sport Sciences at the University of Copenhagen. She serves on editorial boards of several academic journals, is co-editor of three book series and holds a number of international offices including Vice-President of the International Society for Sport History and Convenor of the Committee of Consultants of IAPESGW. She had 'guest professor' status at several universities (among others Queens University, Kingston, Canada and University Playa Ancha, Valparaiso, Chile) and has given numerous keynote presentations at international congresses. Recent authored books are *Sport im Lebenszusammenhang von Frauen* (Schorndorf: Hofmann 1999), *Frauen und Sport in der DDR* (Köln: Strauß 2002). She is co-editor of the *International Encyclopaedia of Women and Sport* (New York: Macmillan 2001).

Núria Puig is Professor for Sociology of Sport at the Institut Nacional d'Educació Física de Catalunya (INEFC) in Barcelona. She has a Ph.D. in Political Sciences and Sociology (Paris, 1980) and a Ph.D. in Philosophy and Sciences of Education (Barcelona 1993). She has published in different languages. Her main areas of research are Socialisation, Sport Organisations and Sport and Space. She serves on the editorial boards of several academic journals. She is a member of the International Sociology of Sport Association and the Asociación Española de Investigación Social aplicada al Deporte.

Gloria Vallejo Rendón is a teacher and research assistant at the Instituto Universitario Educación Física y Deporte of the University of Antioquia in Medellín, Colombia. She graduated in Music Education , specialising in Music and Pedagogy of Dancing at the German Sports University, Cologne; she has a Masters in Linguistics. Her recent research deals with the relationship of sport and music focusing on non-verbal communication and terminology in the fields of instrumental music execution and sport training (gender perspective). She has several publications on the relation of body and culture and she is member of the Somatic Culture Research Group.

Susanna Soler is a member of the research group Attitudes and Values in Physical Education and Sport at the 'Universitat Autònoma de Barcelona' and collaborates with the Women and Sport Study Group (G.E.D.E.) at the INEFC Barcelona, Spain. Her most recent research is on sport history in Catalonia and the development of women soccer players' training. She is involved with several projects on values in physical education in primary schools in Barcelona, and especially in coeducation. She collaborates as a teacher in different courses in continuing education training.

Shona M. Thompson is a Senior Lecturer at the University of Auckland in New Zealand. She serves on the editorial board of several academic journals and is currently editing a book which collates research on women in sport in New Zealand. Her recent book, *Mother's Taxi: Sport and Women's*

Labor (State University of New York Press, 1999) is based on research in Australia, recording experiences of women, who are wives and mothers of sport players and also those who are sport-playing club members.

Sebastião Votre is a research assistant at the Department of Physical Education, Gama Filho University, Rio de Janeiro, Brazil. He has a Ph.D. in Socio-linguistics. Recently published texts include 'Ignoring Taboos: Maria Lenk, Latin American Inspirationalist', in *Freeing the Female Body: The International Journal of the History of Sport* 18, 1: 196–218 (2001) (co-authored with L. Mourão), and 'On Athleticism in the Victorian and Edwardian Public School: A Semiotic Analysis of J.A. Mangan's Approach to Historical Knowledge', in *Culture, Sport, Society* 4 (2001).

Anita White is a Visiting Professor at Loughborough University, UK, and an international consultant in sports policy and sports development. She is an acknowledged leader in the Women and Sport Movement both in the UK and internationally, and advises several national and international organisations on women's sports development. Recent publications include *The Politics of Sports Development: Development of Sport or Development through Sport?* (with Barrie Houlihan, Routledge, 2002) and *From Windhoek to Montreal: Women and Sport Progress Report 1998–2002* (with Deena Scoretz, Sport Canada, 2002).

Foreword

Ilse Hartmann-Tews and Gertrud Pfister

There have been several international calls for action to increase the representation of girls and women in sports-related physical activity and provide greater opportunities for appropriate participation in decision-making processes. The extent to which these actions have had an impact on the situation of girls and women in sport is difficult to determine, mainly because there is a dearth of substantiated information on impacts in different countries. To date there has been no systematic international or cross-cultural analysis about opportunities for, and constraints on, participation in sport, about the influence of different structural and cultural phenomena and no authentic documentation to evaluate the effects of political action. These are gaps in knowledge that this book intends to fill.

The content of the book is international, analysing trends in countries from North and South America, the Middle East, Asia and Oceania, in Africa and West and East Europe. The selection of countries is reflective of geographical representation, different socio-economic, cultural contexts and political structures. It will help to gain a deeper understanding of the peculiar features of each country and of social issues in women and sport, which are of central concern in different countries. At the same time it will provide authentic material for critical comparative analysis and test the generality of statements about common patterns of development and gender issues in sport in different cultures.

The book brings together authors that have first hand experiences and scholarly knowledge of the situation of girls and women in physical education and sport. Although all chapters are written against the background of a shared analytic framework, they are characterised by individual styles, they reflect the diversity of cultures of science and sometimes even political constraints. All of this makes each of the contributions an invaluable piece of a mosaic still to be unearthed.

The book has a contextualising introductory chapter on the analytical background of international and comparative research and the underlying theoretical framework of a constructivist gender studies approach. The main contents of the book are individual chapters on sixteen countries. The final concluding chapter draws all the threads together in comparative/cross-cultural contexts. It focuses on the general findings with a special orientation to cross-cultural trends and the recognition of idiosyncratic developments, 'those that are tied up with specific cultures' and appreciates examples of 'good practice'.

Series editor's preface

Ken Hardman

The International Society for Comparative Physical Education and Sport (ISCPES) launched this book series in conjunction with E. & F.N. Spon and Routledge in 1999 with the first title *Sport and Physical Education in China* (Riordan and Jones, 1999: E. & F.N. Spon). The concept for the series originated in a perceived need to rectify the dearth of published literature in the international, comparative, trans-national and cross-cultural domains of sport and physical education. The concept was linked with the intention of moving international and comparative studies beyond description through disseminating analytically interpreted information and fostering critical awareness and understanding. Hence, in keeping with the ISCPES mission of developing international and comparative study through support and encouragement of those seeking to initiate and strengthen research and teaching programmes in physical education and sport throughout the world, the primary purposes of the titles in the series individually and collectively are to extend knowledge and stimulate comparative and reflective understanding of national systems and thematic and topical issues.

Structurally, the series is divided into two types of text: volumes, which essentially adopt an 'area' (i.e. mono-national) focus, and volumes which address 'problems' (i.e. topics or themes) in international and/or cross-cultural settings. Thus, the first two published titles in the series, *Sport and Physical Education in China*, followed by *Sport and Physical Education in Germany* (Naul and Hardman, 2002: Routledge), focused on national systems. This third title, *Sport and Women: Social Issues in International Perspective*, in specifically addressing this gender-related topical theme, is the first volume to take a 'problem' study approach. Like its two 'area' text predecessors, the template for the content of this 'problem' study volume facilitates comparative awareness of situations and developments in a differentiated array of countries and cultures and provides an analytic dimension rather than a mere descriptive narration of systems and issues, which are pervasively important in global and cross-cultural contexts. At the same time, these situations and developments are subject to culturally specific 'local' (national and/or community) interpretations, policies and practices, which have variously been shaped by a range of historical, ideological, political, economic and social factors. Inevitably, therefore, similarities, variations and differences are encountered at these 'local' levels. The informed contributions, which form the content and which provide the international and comparative perspectives contained within this third volume, accord with the intention that all titles in the series present explanations and/or interpretations. In this way each volume represents a significant contribution to the progression of comparative, cross-cultural and trans-national studies.

Each text can be used on an individual/separate basis to extend knowledge and understanding. Equally, the volumes can be taken together as an integrated basis for informed comparisons, whether of national systems or thematic issues, thereby serving the overall purpose of contributing to critical awareness and analysis amongst confirmed and potential 'comparativists', academics, professionals and young scholars at undergraduate and postgraduate levels. The facilitation of acquisition of critical and analytical skills and deeper insights into national systems and thematic issues in a variety of geo-demographic, political, economic and sociocultural settings is indicative of the ISCPES quest for development and enhancement of the international and comparative genre in sport and physical education related studies. This book series is a significant element in this quest.

Acknowledgements

Good ideas need individuals who are ready to work for it and commit energy, time and resources. Ken Hardman, former President of the International Society for Comparative Physical Education and Sport (ISCPES) and Editor-in-Chief of the Series has been central for the success in compiling this book and the editors express their deep appreciation for the work he has done. He not only played a vital role in the conception of the idea but committed inestimable energy in language control and comments on the contents.

We are indebted too to Sascha Alexandra Luetkens who played a central role at the operational basis in Cologne. Her managing abilities and obliging communications secured that (most) of our authors kept perfectly to the schedule and accomplished all the missing bibliographical material just in time. We very much appreciate her collaboration.

In addition we thank the 'Club of Cologne' for its sponsorship of a meeting of contributors and editors in Cologne 2001, a meeting, which intensified communication about the contents of the book and assisted in securing additional authors.

Last but not least we want to express our thanks to all the authors who helped to make this book an important building block in the broader feminist comparative research cycle.

1 Women and sport in comparative and international perspectives

Issues, aims and theoretical approaches

Gertrud Pfister and Ilse Hartmann-Tews

Women in sport: still marginalised?

Physical activities are always intertwined with the structures, norms and ideals of a society, and they always mirror that society's gender order and gender hierarchy. Therefore, in many countries all over the world and in all phases of history, women have played a specific, but often marginal, role in traditional games, dances and physical activities.

What is the situation today? Using the Olympic Games as an example, we observe that women are increasingly being admitted to more and more previously designated 'male' types of sport – even soccer, ice hockey, weightlifting and pole-vaulting are now included in the women's programme (Pfister 2000). This development gives rise to the issue as to whether the long-standing demand for equal access and equal opportunity for women and men in sport has finally been met. However, women in 'male' sports still represent a tiny minority of young athletes and, as far as is known, women and girls in many countries of the world are engaged in physical activities and sport to a much smaller extent than boys and men (see the contributions in Christensen *et al.* 2001). Nonetheless, questions surrounding the issue still remain. Are there countries where women form the majority of those active in sport? Do girls and women everywhere prefer the same types of physical activities and sport and the same sport providers? Do female elite athletes worldwide enjoy the same support as their male counterparts? And, while decision-making committees still seem to be in the hands of men, is this true for all countries throughout the world?[1]

We know about the tendencies mentioned above from data, which are available in many countries. However, the statistical data are taken from different sources and are of varying quality; moreover, they are gathered for different reasons and by different methods. They may range from the membership statistics of sports federations to public opinion polls, but their value is often limited. In addition, in some countries, a considerable amount of research about women and sport has been conducted, taking into consideration the background of active participation in sport, the reasons for the gender hierarchy in sport and the social context of sports practice. But in many parts of the world there is scarcely any scholarly interest in this topic.[2] Furthermore, there is a general lack of reliable, accessible and comprehensive surveys of the situation of women in sport, and even if information about women's role in sport and its organisations is available, language barriers are a major obstacle in preventing the dissemination of knowledge beyond a country or at least beyond a language group.

We know from various sources that in many countries women have undertaken different kinds of initiatives in sport with different objectives: The extent to which these initiatives have had an impact on the situation of girls and women in sport, the nature of these impacts and whether they have been positive has not yet been adequately determined, mainly because there is a dearth of substantiated information on the situation of girls and women in sport in different countries. If we wish to evaluate the effects of political action and discuss the question of whether and how these activities can be transferred to other countries, we need verifiable documentation on the initiatives and best practices in various areas as well as in different countries.

There are so many blank spots on the map of women's sport that it is impossible to discern a clear overall picture, to learn from each other or to conduct inter-cultural comparisons. Up to now, no one has undertaken a systematic international or cross-cultural analysis, which takes into account not only the participation and situation of women in sport as well as their opportunities and problems, but also the influences of their social environment and of different structural and cultural factors ranging from religion to the labour market.

Knowledge and understanding: the objectives of the book

The primary intention of this book is to fill the gaps mentioned above and answer the questions raised. The aim is to collect systematic information, to analyse backgrounds and causes, to identify connections between participation in sport on the one hand and gendered structures and hierarchies in society on the other and to find explanations for the gender differences and hierarchies in the world of sport. Hence, the main objective of the book is to contribute in a systematic way to the general knowledge and awareness of the situation of women in sport in different countries. It will help to gain a better understanding of the particular features of each country and of issues, which are of central concern in different countries.

Detailed knowledge about how sport is organised in different countries, who participates and what projects and programmes have been set up, together with a regular and intensive exchange of information, is as important today as it ever was. For one thing, supra-national co-operation in an increasingly integrated Europe, and indeed worldwide, is only possible if the structures and conditions in the different countries, the different 'sports cultures', are taken into consideration. Here, the specific situation of women in sport must be accounted for in all debate, initiatives and co-operation agreements. For another, in the context of globalisation processes, it is not only the ideologies and practices of modern sport that are spreading throughout the world but also the gender order. This makes it especially important to identify and document the typical patterns of structures and cultures existing in the different countries both in sport and outside it. On this basis, it is then possible to discuss and decide upon the transfer of projects and programmes to Third World countries. Last but not least, we want to provide authentic material for critical comparative analysis.

The contents of the book are multi-national and international in scope, with analyses of trends in countries from North and South America, Asia, Oceania, Eastern and Western Europe and Africa. The countries were selected according to criteria of geographical representation as well as according to their different socio-economic and cultural contexts and political structures. At the same time it was considered important to include countries that have demonstrated positive advocacy and action on equity issues with regard to the representation of girls and women in sport. The choice of countries also depended on the availability of information as well as the existence, the interest and the commitment of potential authors. Women and sport still seem to be a non-issue in many areas of the world.

Bearing these criteria in mind, the following countries were included: Brazil, Canada, Colombia, the Czech Republic, China, France, Germany, Iran, Japan, New Zealand, Norway, South Africa, Spain, Tanzania, the United Kingdom and the United States.

Through the diversity of the countries selected, insight is provided into a broad spectrum of organisations, practices and ideologies prevalent in sport; the diversity also enables identification of correlations between women's sport and social systems. In this respect the contributions may serve as a basis for cross-cultural studies and, beyond this, generate ideas for further, more detailed and more comprehensive comparisons.

Methods: framework and guidelines

A precondition of undertaking an analysis of the situation of women in sport beyond national boundaries and, as a second step, drawing up inter-cultural comparisons is that information from the different countries and/or cultures is available. For this reason we proposed to the authors beforehand an underlying concept, namely Judith Lorber's theory of gender, and chose this as the theoretical background of the contribution as well as the starting point for guidance on. On the basis of this gender theory, it was possible to reduce the enormous number of questions relating to women's sport to the relevant issues and fit them into a concise set of questions, which was then passed on to the authors in the form of guidelines. Thus, the book does not contain a random collection of articles, which have little relation to each other owing to the different interests and competence of the authors. What has been attempted here is the collection of reliable and comparable information from the different authors on the same subjects and issues. In doing so, it was also important to agree on a definition of sport – a difficult undertaking since, although the word is commonly used in many countries, there are terminological variations and/or differences in meanings. Sport in the context of this book relates to the same comprehensive understanding of sport as it is defined in the European Sport for All Charter, i.e. in the sense of free, spontaneous physical activity engaged in during leisure time including competitive sports and various other physical activities. It includes not only sport as such (competitive games and sport), but also, and especially, multifarious forms of recreational physical activities, ranging from playing games and outdoor activities to health-related physical activities and aesthetic movement.

We asked all authors to provide insight into the organisation and structure, the trends and dynamics of sport in their countries, focusing the gender issue along a shared framework of key questions. They focused on central structural elements as well as on significant international issues of women in sport, for example the system of sport (voluntary sector, public sector, commercial providers, etc.) and the representation of girls and women within these structures (special organisations for girls and women, sports that are dominated by men or women, etc.); women in decision-making committees of sport organisations and institutions and models of advocacy (percentages of representation, strategies to increase the number of female leaders, etc.); support of top-level athletes; and, finally, 'best practices' with regard to the 'empowerment' of girls and women in sport. In addition, the authors were asked to reflect on the impacts of culture and society as well as of conditions of life and gender roles on the sporting biographies of girls and women and to provide explanations for the gender differences on the basis of the scientific knowledge available in their respective countries.

Through intensive editing and supplementary enquiries we were able to ensure that this framework of reference was made use of in each of the national contributions as far as this was possible on the basis of the information available. All in all, the process of editing and the continual revision of the findings extended over a period of many months, but the time and energy spent are justified by the wealth and the authenticity of the data and insights gathered, especially as many of them emanate from countries about whose sports organisations and practices scarcely anything was known in the West up to the present. The contributions in this book lend themselves to first cross-cultural comparisons, offering numerous possibilities of gaining fresh insights as well as providing starting points for further-reaching research work.

Aims, problems and theories of cross-cultural studies

Cross-cultural approaches help not only to overcome ethnocentric points of view and awaken more understanding for the great diversity of physical cultures but also to understand and explain the connections between sport, gender and society.

Using cross-cultural studies, we can among other things explore:

- the interaction of cultural influences (religion, values, norms, etc.) and – more or less universal – structural gender hierarchies;
- the interaction between the gender order on the one hand and the organisation and the practice of sport on the other;
- the significance of social structures for women's sport in different cultures and also opportunities for women to deal with or perhaps even change these structures;
- the role of socialisation and education in people's active participation in sport;
- 'best practices' – their benefits and costs as well as their efficacy and their limitations;
- sport policy and its influence on sport providers and participation in sport.[3]

Cross-cultural studies confront researchers with particular problems with regard not only to the equivalence of symbols, meanings and institutions but also to data collection and interpretation. One of the greatest problems in this respect is ethnocentricity, which can influence the entire research process from the very first approach to the issue right up to the conclusions drawn from the findings. But apart from these problems, intercultural comparisons are based on the same research principles, the same theories and the same methods that are used in the social sciences generally (Allardt 1976; Ragin 1989; Øyen 1990).

Comparisons are made up of the search for similarities, variations and differences in the systems or subsystems under investigation. Similarities can verify hypotheses and theoretical concepts, and are related to structural links. By contrast, differences are much harder to explain and in inter-cultural comparisons must be attributed to specific factors in the different cultures. It is for this reason that cross-cultural studies are often described as 'natural' experiments (Nowak 1989).

In the controversy over cultural relativism and universalism in cross-cultural studies, we assume that there are both universal as well as culturally rooted patterns of behaviour and thinking, structures, values and ideologies. If we believe that human thoughts and actions are totally dependent on the cultural context, it would be impossible to understand them from 'outside'. If, on the other hand, we put on 'universalising glasses', we would be blind to culture-related patterns of behaviour and thinking. Navigating the straits between the Scylla of cultural relativism and the Charybdis of universalistic approaches, we must be careful not to use categories and theoretical concepts, which are valid only for industrial countries (e.g. Trommsdorff 1986). Analogous to the linguistic distinction between phonemic and phonetic, the terms 'emics' and 'etics' have been used for the local versus the universal approach in cross-cultural studies. 'Emic' interpretations of gender may be based on culture-specific myths and/or religions, whereas 'etic' approaches may focus, for example, on the global argument of the 'unequal' distribution of power and resources. Chinese constructions of gender as a balance between *yin* and *yang* is an 'emic' approach, which cannot be understood using Western ways of 'logical' thinking. On the other hand, the gendered division of power seems to be an universal basis for the hierarchy between men and women. But it has to be taken into consideration that seemingly universal categories like power may also have culture-specific components and meanings. This has been shown, for example, by Lenz and Luig (1990), who have tried to identify the structures of power in non-patriarchal societies.

Without an appropriate theoretical framework, cross-cultural studies can offer nothing more than impressionistic interpretations. On the one hand, theoretical concepts provide the criteria and categories for the questions to be asked and the methods to be used as well as for the interpretation of the results. On the other hand, as already mentioned above, theories rely on comparisons since it is only through comparisons that correlations and explanations can be demonstrated to be generally valid (Nowak 1989). Universal perspectives such as in Marxism, the systems theory or in modernisation or globalisation theories are based on cross-cultural comparisons (for example, Allardt 1976; Nowak 1989: 40ff; Galtung 1990). In recent years, however, universal theories have been increasingly subjected to criticism, with accusations ranging from reductionism to ethnocentrism, or have at least been faced with demands for modification, such as taking into consideration the complexity of social reality.[4] However, the more complex the issues are, the less likely it is that a single interpretation model can be applied to explain them. As for the contributions to this book, we propose a theoretical approach to gender, which not only allows cross-cultural comparison but also allows us to integrate other theoretical approaches, like concepts of socialisation or the gendered division of labour.

This approach should provide the tools for answering these questions as well as for giving interpretations and explanations.

Gender as a social construct

The enactment of gender in sport and the gendered structures of sport can be best described using a constructivist approach to gender.

At present there is general agreement among scholars of gender studies that gender is a complex construct with different dimensions ranging from genetic sex to sexual orientation, gender roles and images, and gendered display (see Hirschauer 1994). Gender is based on the body as a biologic entity (and we do not deny the reality of bodies) – but gender is culturally transformed in a life-long process with ambivalences and contradictions (Lorber 1994: 31; see also Featherstone *et al.* 1991). In recent years Lorber's main thesis about the social construction of gender has been supported by the studies of other authors from other scientific fields. Hirschauer (1994), for instance, has interpreted gender as a system of knowledge, and the French science reporter Natalie Angier (2000) has demonstrated how the signs of the body and the biological 'facts' are used to reinforce the prevailing gender ideology.

Gender always has an individual and an institutional side. 'The social reproduction of gender in individuals reproduces the gendered social structures; as individuals act out gender norms and expectations in face-to-face-interaction, they are constructing gendered systems of dominance and power' (Lorber 1994: 7).

The gender order

Gender as an institution structures societies and organises daily life (Lorber 1994: 15). Social responsibilities and duties are allotted according to the major categories of gender, age, class and ethnic origin, the categorisation being legitimised by the dominant norms and values and carried out by institutions such as religion and science, law and administration, school and – last but not least – the media. In all these domains gendered scripts are produced which influence thinking and behaviour. This holds true for all societies, although the contents of the script may change from country to country.

The gender order is based on and legitimised by the symbolically conveyed duality of gender, which corresponds to thinking in binary patterns. Man and woman are constructed as exclusionary categories (Hagemann-White 1984; 1993). A person can be only one gender, never the other or both; and reality is constructed according to the dichotomy and polarity of female and male. Gender duality is not a universal concept, but we can assume that in the wake of globalisation, in all countries surveyed in this book old and new elements of this symbolically conveyed duality of gender interconnect.

The organisation of the labour market is another basis and also the product of the gender order (Beck 1996; Delphy 1998). The decisive factors here are, firstly, the responsibility of women for children and, secondly, the economic structure of modern societies, which can be characterised as a dual economy, i.e. combining paid work outside the home and unpaid work – mostly done by women – in the household (Rabe-Kleberg 1987; Knapp 1989). The gendered division of labour is, according to Ulrich Beck, 'the foundation as well as a product of industrial society'. But the gendered division of work can also be found in non-industrial societies with little differentiation of tasks and with no segregation between production and reproduction.

The social construction of gender produces a hierarchy and legitimises marginalisation and unequal treatment of women:

> It is the man's body, its sexuality, minimal responsibility in procreation, and conventional control of emotions that pervades work and organisational processes. Women's bodies – female sexuality, their ability to procreate and their pregnancy, breast-feeding and child care, menstruation and mythic 'emotionality' – are suspect, stigmatised, and used as grounds for control and exclusion...to function at the top of male hierarchies requires that women render irrelevant everything that makes them women.
>
> (Lorber 1994: 283)

Doing gender

Apart from the institutional aspect of the social construction of gender, there is an individual aspect to be taken into consideration. Gender is not something we are or have but something we produce and do. 'Gender is constantly created and re-created out of human interaction, out of social life, and it is the texture and order of that social life...it depends on everybody constantly doing gender' (Lorber 1994: 13). Gender is a performance, and a performance which is produced according to specific scripts dependent on culture.

People are categorised as belonging to social groups and also to one or other of the sexes by means of outward features such as dress, hairstyle, the way they move or their body language – and as a rule this happens unconsciously. Even though what is considered typically male or female changes according to the cultural context, it is always more or less strictly defined. One of the most important gender markers is clothing, since this makes gender difference clearly visible. The example of clothing demonstrates not only that gender symbols are embedded in culture and thus, not immutable but also that there is no logical connection between the sign, i.e. clothing, and its meaning, i.e. gender. Thus, in one society it is the men who 'wear the trousers', both literally and figuratively, whereas in other cultures trousers are worn exclusively by women, but then there is no power connected with these female trousers (Lehnert 1997). Any refusal to be categorised with regard to sex meets with severe disapproval. We only need to think of our own uneasiness at not being able to recognise clearly the gender of the person we are speaking to.

Doing gender in sport

Since sport is physical activity, and involves the presentation of the body and the demonstration of the physical, it appears to provide convincing evidence of the gender duality and of the 'natural' hierarchy of the sexes. This message is especially powerful because of the globalisation of sport and its worldwide attractiveness. But we have to take into consideration that the definitions and social arrangements, as well as the associations and evaluations, which are connected with sporting activities are created through discourse and constructed socially (Hartmann-Tews 2000). On the one hand, sports are constructed and labelled as male or female; on the other hand, women and men develop preferences for certain sports in accordance with gendered social norms, values and expectations (Messner and Sabo 1990; Pfister 1999). Gendered 'sports culture', which is specific to each sport but which differs from country to country, is created not only by tradition and the image of a sport, but is performed by the participants and corresponds to their self-images. Gabriele Klein has described this phenomenon, taking football and gymnastics in Germany (1997) as examples:

> The body images and attributes ascribed to women who play football and women gymnasts, for example, differ fundamentally from one another, the one group being strong, self assertive and part of a team; the other frail, almost anorexic and individualistic.
>
> (Klein 1997: 146)

The 'gendered images' of sports are different in different cultures and different periods of time. Sport, however, is a social sphere in which gender cannot only be produced but also 'deconstructed' and changed. Whereas earlier studies investigated the conflicts, which female athletes in 'male' sports faced in their roles as women, it has been emphasised in a number of more recent studies that by taking up sports such as body-building or boxing women are putting up resistance to the gender order, and that, as a result, it might be possible to detect and perhaps even change the construction of gender, at least in cultures where women are accepted in these types of sport (see for example Hall 1996; Heywood 1998). Doing gendered sport is learned in socialisation processes, and we define socialisation as 'self-training in and through social practices'. Here not only parents and peers but also the school and the media are important.

In the contributions to this book special emphasis is laid on the institutional side, that is, on the gendered sport system with its structure, its hierarchies of power, its messages and ideals and its economy.

Lorber's concept: a framework for inter-cultural comparisons

A major problem connected with theories of gender is the reinforcement of gender duality. Research, for example, which perceives and interprets attitudes and behaviour of men and women against the backdrop of gender duality, reproduces the symbolic order of the differences between the sexes (Delphy 1998). A way out of this dilemma seems to be Lorber's proposal that gender should not be thought of as an entity but as a construction and combination of various components. The multiplicity of the interdependent and interacting categories allows us to identify different patterns of gender, which are typical for a particular culture. The following different components of gender at the institutional and individual levels can be used as 'looking glasses' for the identification of inter-cultural similarities or differences. Lorber proposes, among others, the following categories:

Gender statuses are the socially recognised genders in a society and the connected norms and expectations as well as the evaluations, which lead to gender hierarchies. Even if the gender order in Western societies is based on two genders, the degree of deviance, e.g. the acceptance of homosexuality, differs greatly, even among the countries included in our book. Gender statuses are reproduced and legitimised, among other things, through sporting practices and images, but sport – for example, top performances by women – can also challenge the gender order. In addition, sport reinforces the gender duality because sport knows only two sexes, and everybody has to fit into this dichotomy. In addition, types of sport are defined as 'male' or 'female' and evaluated accordingly, but the definitions of 'male' and 'female' sports vary in different cultures and in different periods of history. Football, for example, is a male preserve in many countries but a female sport in the USA.

The gendered division of labour means that different work and tasks are assigned to the different genders, that work is evaluated according to the sex of the worker and that the division of labour and gender statuses reinforce each other. We have already mentioned the importance of the division of labour as a basis of the gender order in industrialised societies. There is, however, a broad variation regarding the gendering of work and the employment of women in the countries surveyed in our book. In addition, the gendered division of labour determines the opportunity which women and men have to participate in sport.

Gendered personalities are the imagined traits and behaviour patterns of both sexes according to the existing stereotypes. In most cultures more or less fixed beliefs about the 'natures' of women and men exist, but the traits, which are looked upon as female or male are culture-specific. In modern China, for example, women are looked upon as strong and persistent and hard-working, whereas in other countries the myth of women as the weaker sex is still powerful. The 'personalities', which are produced and needed in sport or in different types of sport can support or change socially constructed gendered personalities. 'Strong' women like boxers and body builders can challenge the stereotypes of women as the weaker sex.

Gendered sexual scripts are the norms governing sexual behaviour. With regard to the regulation of sexuality, huge differences exist, for example, between Christian and Muslim societies. Christian societies deal with sexuality via an internalisation of prohibitions, Muslim cultures via a segregation of men and women or, rather, an exclusion of women from public life. Sexuality plays an important role in discourses in and about sport and different types of sport: Does 'doing sport' in tight-fitting clothes convey sexual messages? How do Muslim women deal with a dress code which is looked upon as immoral in Muslim countries? What are the reasons for the 'sexualisation' of female athletes in the mass media?

Gendered ideology legitimises gender statuses and prevents resistance by 'normalising' the gender order. Although gender ideology frequently uses biology as legitimisation, the variations of gender ideologies can range from a socialist claim of emancipation to the subordination of women according to religious dogma. Sport ideologies and gender ideologies are closely connected. Sporting performances seem to legitimise the superiority of men. And the myths about the 'natures' of the two genders have always provided strong arguments for the exclusion or the integration of men or women in certain types of sport.

Gendered imagery is the symbolic presentation of gender in culture, especially in language, but also in the arts, science and the media. We have already described above how symbolically conveyed gender duality structures societies and is embodied in individuals. Sport is a powerful symbol and an enactment of differences, particularly of gender differences, and sport plays an important part in the mass media. Sport, especially sport in the media, 'constructs men's bodies to be powerful, women's bodies to be sexual' (Lorber 1994: 43). Sport, however, is a social sphere in which gender cannot only be produced but also changed.

Girls and boys, women and men appropriate the gender arrangements of their culture and develop gender images and identities. At the individual level, too, gender is composed of different components, among others the sex category (which is assigned at birth), gendered identity (the individual interpretation of the gendered self), gendered sexual orientation (sexual desires, practices, identifications) and gendered display (the presentation of the gendered self).

The social and the individual components of gender are closely intertwined and also connected with, and influenced by, numerous other categories like race, religion or social class as well as achieved statuses such as level of education, profession, material and/or financial resources. The complex and multidimensional construct of gender proposed by Lorber can be used to describe the different components of gender and the gender order in different countries. It makes clear that a decrease in gender differences in one category does not automatically change the structures in other areas. A high rate of women's employment, as is to be found in former socialist countries, does not automatically change a woman's role in the family. However, there are numerous interactions between the various components. The gendered sexual scripts, for example in Islamic cultures, have a powerful influence on women's work, on family structures and also on gender display. Intensive research and theoretical considerations are necessary before we can identify causes and effects and, as a whole, a 'configuration' of gender in different cultures.

Lorber's categories as tools

Lorber's approach can provide instruments and strategies for cross-cultural comparisons. The components of gender can be used as categories, which help to identify similarities and differences in the gender order, in the individual appropriation of gender and also in the connections between sport and gender. These categories can be used as a thread, which helps to organise the findings and fit the pieces of the puzzle together. Lorber uses these components to paint a coherent picture of gender as a social construct, which also can be applied to sport as a social subsystem. The gender order of a society and individual 'doing gender' are closely intertwined with the structure of sport and the conditions of doing sport in different countries. However, gender and sport form different patterns depending on manifold variables, like tradition, the economic situation, the role of top-level sport, the ideologies and beliefs connected with sport, the aims and contents of physical education, sport policies and, last but not least, the organisation of sport. Other determining factors are the rituals and conditions of everyday life, like time schedules, climatic features, the environment, the economic situation of the population and also the costs involved in practising sport. Moreover, all these factors influence men and women to different degrees and in different ways.

If one were to use all the categories presented by Lorber for an in-depth analysis of gendered sport structures and/or individual 'doing gender' in sport, this would mean setting up several research projects in each country involved. This would be both a great opportunity as well as a challenge – and fruitful not only for scientific progress but also for the various areas of sports practice.

The theoretical approach presented here is not necessarily connected with evaluations, which are always in danger of being ethnocentric. But, of course, all considerations of gender also lead sooner or later to evaluations, and these demand political action. We hope that this book will not only contribute to scientific discourse but will also have practical consequences.

Notes

1 If we look at the IOC under-representation of female leaders becomes obvious. Online. Available HTTP: [http://www.Olympic.org/uk/organization/commissions/women] (14 February 2002).
2 This can be seen when doing research in relevant data bases like in SIRC. Online. Available HTTP: [http://www.sportquest.com] (14 February 2002).
3 See especially Lonner/Berry 1986; Reimann 1986; Øyen 1990; Ragin 1987; 1989; Scheuch 1990.
4 Nowak 1989; cf. also post-structuralist approaches such as Lemert 1992; Weedon 1997. See especially Butler 1990; for 'post-post-modernism' see Walby 1992.

Bibliography

Allardt, E. (1976) 'Vergleichende Sozialforschung und die Analyse des Sports', in G. Lüschen and K. Weis (eds), *Die Soziologie des Sports*, Darmstadt: Luchterhand.

Angier, N. (2000) *Frau – eine intime Geographie des weiblichen Körpers*, München: Bertelsmann.

Beck, U. (1996) *Risikogesellschaft. Auf dem Weg in eine andere Moderne*, Frankfurt am Main: Suhrkamp.

Bertaux, D. (1990) 'Oral history approaches to an international social movement', in E. Øyen (ed.), *Comparative methodology: Theory and practice in international social research*, London: Sage.

Butler, J. (1990) *Gender trouble: Feminism and the subversion of identity*, London: Routledge.

Christensen, K., Guttmann, A. and Pfister, G. (eds) (2001) *International encyclopedia of women and sport*, New York: Macmillan Reference USA.

Connell, R.W. (1987) *Gender and power: Society, the person and sexual politics*, Cambridge: Polity Press.

Delphy, C. (1998) *L'ennemi principal. Économie politique du patriarcat*, Paris: Syllepse.

Douglas, M. (1974) *Ritual, Tabu und Körpersymbolik: Sozialanthropologische Studien in Industriegesellschaft und Stammeskultur*, Frankfurt am Main: Fischer.

Featherstone, M., Hepworth, M. and Turner, B.S. (1991) *The body: Social process and cultural theory*, London: Sage.

Flax, J. (1987) 'Postmodernism and gender relations in feminist theory', *Signs* 12, 2: 621–8.

Galtung, J. (1990) 'Theory formation in social research: a plea for pluralism', in E. Øyen (ed.), *Comparative methodology: Theory and practice in international social research*, London: Sage.

Hagemann-White, C. (1984) *Sozialisation: Weiblich – Männlich?* Opladen: Leske + Budrich.

—— (1993) 'Die Konstruktion des Geschlechts auf frischer Tat ertappen? Methodische Konsequenzen einer theoretischen Einsicht', *Feministische Studien* 11, 2: 68–78.

Hall, M.A. (1996) *Feminism and sporting bodies: Essays on theory and practice*, Champaign, IL: Human Kinetics.

Hargreaves, J. (1994) *Sporting Females: Critical issues in the history and sociology of women's sports*, London: Routledge.

Hartmann-Tews, I. (2000) 'Forschung in Bewegung: Frauen und Geschlechterforschung in der Sportwissenschaft', in A. Cottmann, B. Kortendiek and U. Schildmann (eds) *Das undisziplinierte Geschlecht*, Opladen: Leske + Budrich, 17–34.

Heywood, L. (1998) *Bodymakers: A cultural anatomy of women's body building*, New Brunswick, NJ: Rutgers University Press.

Hirschauer, S. (1994) 'Die soziale Fortpflanzung der Zweigeschlechtlichkeit', *Kölner Zeitschrift für Soziologie und Sozialpsychologie* 46, 4: 668–92.

Jagose, A. (1996) *Queer theory: An introduction*, New York: New York University Press.

Klein, A.M. (1993) *Little big men: Bodybuilding subculture and gender construction*, Albany, NY: State University of New York Press.

Klein, G. (1997) 'Theoretische Prämissen einer Geschlechterforschung in der Sportwissenschaft', in U. Henkel and S. Kröner (eds), *Und sie bewegt sich doch! Sportwissenschaftliche Frauenforschung, Bilanz und Perspektiven*, Pfaffenweiler: Centaurus Verlagsgesellschaft.

Knapp, G.-A. (1989) 'Arbeitsteilung und Sozialisation: Konstellationen von Arbeitsvermögen und Arbeitskraft im Lebenszusammenhang von Frauen', in U. Beer (ed.), *Klasse Geschlecht: Feministische Gesellschaftsanalyse und Wissenschaftskritik*, Bielefeld: AJZ-Verlag.

Kuhn, A. (1983) 'Das Geschlecht – eine historische Kategorie?', in I. Brehmer *et al.* (eds), *'Wissen heisst leben…' Beiträge zur Bildungsgeschichte von Frauen im 18. und 19. Jahrhundert*, Frauen in der Geschichte IV, Düsseldorf: Schwann.

Lehnert, G. (1997) *Wenn Frauen Männerkleider tragen: Geschlecht und Maskerade in Literatur und Geschichte*, München: Deutscher Taschenbuch Verlag.

Lemert, C. (1992) 'General social theory, irony, postmodernism', in S. Seidman and D.G. Wagner (eds), *Postmodernism and social theory: The debate over general theory*, Cambridge, MA: Blackwell.

Lenz, I. and Luig, U. (1990) *Frauenmacht ohne Herrschaft: Geschlechterverhältnisse in nichtpatriarchalischen Gesellschaften*, Berlin: Orlanda Frauenverlag.

Lonner, W.J. and Berry, J.W. (eds) (1986) *Field methods in cross-cultural research*, London: Sage Publications.

Lorber, J. (1994) *Paradoxes of gender*, New Haven, CT: Yale University Press.

Lowe, M.R. (1998) *Women of steel: Female bodybuilders and the struggle for self-definition*, New York: New York University Press.

Luig, U. (1990) 'Sind egalitäre Gesellschaften auch geschlechtsegalitär?' in I. Lenz and U. Luig (eds), *Frauenmacht ohne Herrschaft: Geschlechterverhältnisse in nichtpatriarchalischen Gesellschaften*, Berlin: Orlanda Frauenverlag.

Messner, M.A. and Sabo, D.F. (eds) (1990) *Sport, men, and the gender order: Critical feminist perspectives*, Champaign, IL: Human Kinetics.

Nowak, H. (1989) 'Comparative studies and social theory', in M.L. Kohn (ed.), *Cross-national research in sociology (as an analytic strategy)*, London: Sage.

Øyen, E. (ed.) (1990) *Comparative methodology: Theory and practice in international social research*, London: Sage.

Pfister, G. (1999) *Sport im Lebenszusammenhang von Frauen: Ausgewählte Themen*, Schorndorf: Hofmann.

—— (2000) 'Women and the Olympic Games', in B.L. Drinkwater (ed.), *Women in sport*, Oxford: Blackwell Science.

Rabe-Kleberg, U. (1987) *Frauenberufe – zur Segmentierung der Berufswelt*, Bielefeld: B. Kleine.

Ragin, C.C. (1987) *The comparative method: Moving beyond qualitative and quantitative strategies*, Berkeley, CA: University of California Press.

—— (1989) 'New directions in comparative research', in M.L. Kohn (ed.), *Cross-national research in sociology (as an analytic strategy)*, London: Sage.

Reimann, H. (1986) 'Der interkulturelle Vergleich in der Frauenforschung', in H. Reimann (ed.), *Soziologie und Ethnologie: Zur Interaktion zwischen zwei Disziplinen*, Opladen: Westdeutscher Verlag.

Scheuch, E.K. (1990) 'The development of comparative research: Towards causal explanation', in E. Øyen (ed.), *Comparative methodology: Theory and practice in international social research*, London: Sage.

Trommsdorf, G. (1986) 'German cross-cultural sociology', *The German Journal of Psychology* 10: 240–66.

Walby, S. (1992) 'Post-post-modernism? Theorizing social complexity', in M. Barrett and A. Phillips (eds), *Destabilizing theory: Contemporary feminist debates*, Cambridge: Polity Press.

Weedon, C. (1997) *Feminist practice and poststructuralist theory*, Oxford: Basil Blackwell.

Willms-Herget, A. (1985) *Frauenarbeit: Zur Integration der Frauen in den Arbeitsmarkt*, Frankfurt am Main: Campus Verlag.

2 Women and sport in Norway

Kari Fasting

Development of sport: general features

Norwegians are known for being an active population. Outdoor life is an important part of the culture, and in many places Norwegians will use a part of their weekend for cross-country skiing during the wintertime and walking/hiking during the rest of the year. Norway has a population of 4.5 million. In 1999, the 12,242 sports clubs had as many as 1,836,000 members (NOCCS 1999a), representing a high proportion of the population.[1] Compared with many other countries, organised sport in Norway has traditionally not been sex-segregated. In the 1920s there were a few sports clubs for women only, but that has never been the norm. Today sports clubs solely for women are not a common feature. Article 8 in the Act no. 45 of 9 June 1978 on Gender Equality, states that 'Any association shall be open to women and men on equal terms', but continues, 'The injunctions of the first paragraph do not apply to associations where the main object is to promote the interests of one of the sexes'. The article means that all sport clubs should be open to both women and men. However, it would probably not be illegal to have sports clubs for women only because women are the under-represented gender in sport.[2]

Sports clubs, sports associations at district level and federations in Norway were until a few years ago organised in and by an umbrella organisation called The Norwegian Confederation of Sport (NCS). In 1996 this organisation merged with the Norwegian Olympic Committee (NOC) to form what is now called the Norwegian Olympic Committee and Confederation of Sports (NOCCS). Besides the number of clubs mentioned above, the organisation consists of nineteen sport districts which in the main conform with the borders of the Norwegian counties. In addition, fifty-seven different sports associations are members of the NOCCS. For the largest sports associations, like for example the Norwegian Football Association and the Norwegian Ski Association, there also exist specific sport districts, which have the same geographical borders as the general sport districts. They are named 'football district' or 'ski district' and prefaced by the name of the geographical district, as for example the Akershus ski district.

In 2001, the Norwegian state spent 824 million Norwegian kroner from the State lottery (equivalent to US $90 million, or 104 million euro) on sport. Local sports clubs received 82 million Norwegian kroner, primarily dedicated to children and youth (16–19 years of age) sport. Ninety million Norwegian kroner were earmarked for local sport facilities with the aim of strengthening the opportunities for children and youth to participate in sport and physical activity. Top-level sport also receives money directly from the state. In 2001 this amounted to 44 million kroner. Compared with earlier years, there is a decrease in money given to larger sport facilities and international championships and competitions (37 million Norwegian kroner). In contrast with the situation in neighbouring Sweden a specific proportion of state money for sport has never been for women's sports in general.

Norway has a very high proportion of voluntary organisations per inhabitant, and the largest of these is the NOCCS. In spite of the public money spent on this organisation, it has traditionally been relatively independent of the state. Though it is difficult to compare with the past, recently there seems to have been a greater interest both from government and parliament in the way public money has been spent in sport. Indicative of this development is that for the first time in history the Royal Ministry of Cultural Affairs (under which sport belongs) has presented reports, both in 1991–2 (Report to the Storting, no. 41 1991–2) and in 1999–2000 (Report to the Storting, no. 14 1999–2000), relating to parliament's participation in situations, challenges and future of sport and physical exercise in the country. The last report was titled *The Changing of Sports*, with the subtitle *the federal government's relationships to sports and physical activity*. Another trend is that the state now earmarks more funds than in previous years; this can be seen in the figures presented earlier. Based on the 1991–2 report, some funds were allocated to increase the recruitment of female coaches and administrators. This is the only time any state funds have been earmarked for women in sport. Examples of themes or areas for suggested support are: disabled sport, research and developmental work and work on ethics and anti-doping initiatives. Girls and women receive little mention in the later report compared with the first one in 1991–2. The latter could be said to have a gender perspective, while the report of 1999–2000 can be characterised as gender neutral.

In addition to outdoor activities and practising and competing in a sport club, a third means has been developed very successfully in recent years for Norwegians who want to exercise. This is the so-called private sector. In all major and many smaller Norwegian cities and towns, there are private training centres and/or studios. One of these, SATS, is a large franchised chain, which recently has taken over many independently operated centres. SATS was bought up by foreigner investors some years ago, and is now owned by a company known as Fitness Holding World. The goal for SATS is to improve people's everyday lives through physical activity. Today SATS has

150,000 members, of which 70 per cent are women. The private training centres and studios in general seem to have more female than male members, the main reason for which is probably the fact that these centres offer child care and are flexible, a factor which seems to be important for many women today; they can practise alone, or take classes in aerobics, yoga, kick-boxing, step, step/strength and so on.

Participation of girls and women in physical activities and sports outside school

There are two main ways of acquiring knowledge about girls and women's participation in leisure-time sport, and numbers and figures from both of them are presented here. One way is to present results from nationwide surveys about participation in sport and physical activities; the other way is to look at membership statistics in the NOCCS. Both methods have their limitations: there are different samples and measurements (surveys), and double or maybe triple memberships in the sports organisations. Comparisons between the different data are also hampered by the fact that the age limits defining a child, a youth or an adult may differ. With this in mind, a start is made with results from some national studies about involvement of children and youth in physical activities and sport.

Participation of girls and young women

More than half of all Norwegian girls participate regularly in one or another form of exercise and sport. Boys were slightly more active than girls in one major study from 1997, which included about 5,000 young people in grades 6, 8 and 10 in the elementary school. The study showed that 52 per cent of the 11 year-old girls, 66 per cent of 13 year-olds, and 63 per cent of 15 year-olds participated in some form of exercise or sport at least twice a week. The equivalent figures for boys were 58 per cent, 73 per cent and 70 per cent. The differences between girls and boys diminished with exercise participated in only once a week. Using this measure, about as many girls as boys participated in sport, but boys seemed to exercise more often than girls (Wold *et al.* 2000). In relation to gender, it is worth noticing that the difference between girls and boys was almost the same for all three years. The same study showed that there was an increase in the number of 11–15 year-olds who participated in exercise and sport in the mid-1980s. This development now seems to have stopped, particularly among the 15 year-olds, and among girls. According to this longitudinal study, 15 year-old girls have developed more sedentary lifestyles during the last ten years. For example, the number of 15 year-old girls watching television four hours or more every day has increased from 6 per cent in 1989 to 22 per cent in 1997 (Wold *et al.* 2000: 42).

Another study (MMI undersøkelsen 1998, in Report to the Storting no. 14, 1999–2000) showed that the number of girls and boys that participated and competed in a sport club in 1998 decreased from the 8–12 year age group to the 16–19 year age group. The difference between the sexes is largest for the age group 8–12 and smallest for the age group 16–19 (Report to the Storting no. 14 1999–2000: 25). Notably, many more boys (more than 70 per cent) than girls (less than 50 per cent) are recruited into sport at an early age.

In 1992, 1996, 1998 and 2000 the Norwegian Market and Media Institute (MMI undersøkelsen 2000) conducted nationwide studies among children and youth (age 8–24 years) about their participation and involvement in sports clubs. These studies showed that boys practised more and competed more in sport clubs compared with girls in all four years investigated. When the year 2000 is compared with 1992, fewer girls and fewer boys than previously participated in sports clubs.

Of interest here is whether these patterns accord with the official membership statistics for girls and boys up to 17 years of age provided by NOCCS (1980–99).[3] From NOCCS data it is obvious that more boys (58 per cent) than girls (42 per cent) were members of a sports club in 1999, and that the gap between girls and boys has not diminished since 1980. Compared with 1980, this difference has increased from 74,666 to 91,141 more memberships among boys in 1999. The increase among girls from 1980 to 1999 was 28,810, while boys memberships increased by 45,285. To this it should be added that marginally more girls than boys make up the Norwegian population, and that boys in 1980 had more memberships than girls. However, organised sport is a popular activity among Norwegian girls: according to the nationwide study mentioned earlier, 73 per cent of the age group 8–24 years said that they either were or had been a member of a sport club (MMI undersøkelsen 1996: 11).

Which sports are most popular among girls, and can one notice any changes in the popularity of some sports over the last few years? From the above mentioned MMI studies among 8–24 year-olds in 1992, 1996, 1998 and 2000, more boys than girls played soccer during each year, but the opposite was the case for team handball. Martial arts were most common among boys during the first three investigation years, but the differences between the girls and boys were no longer obvious in year 2000. The girls dominated in equestrian sports (horseback riding), gymnastics and dance in all four years, while the boys dominated in tennis and badminton in the three first years but not in 2000. It seems that the difference between girls and boys is diminishing in some sports, but this is related more to girls participating in 'boys' sports rather than boys taking up the more traditional 'girls' sports.

Longitudinal studies of membership patterns also provide information about the popularity of different sports. Among girls under 12 years of age, by far the most popular sport in 1999 was soccer, followed by team handball, gymnastics, skiing, dance and swimming. For girls between 12–16 years of age it is still soccer which is most popular, followed by handball, equestrian sports, skiing and dance. For boys under 17 year of age the largest sports in 1999 were soccer, skiing, team handball, track and field and swimming. When the two age categories are combined we find that for girls below 17 years of age, the five most popular sports in 1999 were soccer, gymnastics, team handball, skiing and dance. Since 1985 there have been significant changes within these sports.

Team handball has been relatively stable, but soccer and dancing have increased quite dramatically. Gymnastics and skiing, on the other hand, have lost many young girls as members. Since 1985 a broad range of new sports have been introduced to girls, including motorcycle riding, budo, American football, billards, kick-boxing, climbing, boat racing, softball/baseball, triathlon, frisbee, rugby and snowboarding. Among these, budo is by far the largest with 3,230 female members under 17 years of age.

What is most interesting in the figures presented above is that soccer, which until 1975 was 'the male sport' in Norway, now has become the most popular and largest sport among girls (53,367 female players under 17 years of age in 1999). There are probably multiple reasons for this. It may be explained partly by women's position in Norwegian society in general (and this may be linked to Norwegian legislation for equal rights), and also related to the fact that the Norwegian Football Association itself has since 1975 worked systematically at recruiting and keeping girls in soccer.

Participation of adult women

National studies of participation in physical activity among adult women and men in Norway show inconsistent results both in relation to the amount of activity and according to differences between the sexes. The reason for this inconsistency is first of all due to differences in the way participation in physical activity has been measured. A study of living conditions of Norwegians found that 54 per cent of the population (16–79 years of age, N=871) participated in some form of physical activity at least once a week (SCB 1997). In contrast to earlier studies, this study found few differences between women and men. When the threshold for being active is set at 'exercising at least once a week', Norwegian women exercise less the older they become: while more than 70 per cent of 16–24 year-old women exercise at least once a week, only about 60 per cent of the age group 25–44 years old and less than 50 per cent of the women aged 45–66 years do so. In the group of 67–79 year-old women, only 40 per cent admit to being active that regularly (SCB 1997).

Another study from the same year found that 55 per cent of the men and 61 per cent of the women answered positively to a question concerned with frequency of exercise for a minimum of at least twenty minutes per week (walking, jogging, bicycling, swimming etc.) (National Council on Nutrition and Physical Activity 2001). One further study, from 1997, confirmed that Norwegian women seem to be more active than their male counterparts. Among the women in this study, 68 per cent exercised at least every second week, compared with 62 per cent among the men (Breivik and Vaagebø 1998). Further analysis showed that the difference was due primarily to the age group 30–9 years. In this group only 54 per cent of the men compared with 63 per cent of the women exercised regularly at least once every second week (Breivik and Vaagebø 1998: 13). The last study mentioned, from 1997, has been conducted every other year since 1985. It has surveyed the Norwegian population with exactly the same questions. In looking at the results from 1985 until 1997, it turned out that until 1993 men were more active than women. From that year on, more women than men have been active. It is difficult to explain why this change happened particularly that year. However, the development must be looked upon as a result of the Norwegian state's policies on equal rights between women and men. In contrast to many other studies, women's participation in some physical activities increased after the age of 29 years (Breivik and Vaagebø 1998: 13). When interpreting this figure, it is important to keep in mind the broad definition of being physically active (i.e. every second week) taken as a base in the study by Breivik and Vaagebø (1998).

Another study has indicated that hard physical exercise (defined as an index of four factors: type of activity, intensity, frequency and duration) is more common among men than women (Søgård *et al*. 2000: 4).

In the 1997 study mentioned above (Breivik and Vaagebø 1998), the survey also queried whether there was any difference in activity level among women and men who had children living at home. The hypothesis was that when a family had a child the amount of leisure physical activity would be reduced, and that this would affect women more than men. The results showed that both genders, with children at home, reduced their activity level after 29 years of age, but there was no significant difference between women and men. The same study also showed that the motives for exercising have been pretty much the same since 1991. The motives differ however, in relation to age. 'Health concerns' are most commonly mentioned among 40 and 50 year-olds, 'fun' is the main reason for the young people (15–24 years of age), and 'energy production' and 'stress reduction' are the most important motives among the 30–40 year-olds. Women scored higher than men on motives related to 'increasing energy mentally and physically', 'stress reduction', 'health concerns', 'keep the weight down', 'increase self-esteem', and 'appearance'. Men scored higher than women on motives related to 'competition', 'excitement' and 'challenge' plus 'fun'. These gender differences in motives are mirrored in the types of activities that Norwegian women and men participate in during their leisure time. More women than men participate in activities in which there is no competitive aspect, such as different kinds of aerobics and walking. Men, on the other hand, are more involved in activities with speed and excitement. Besides jogging and skiing, men dominate in football and ice hockey. Bicycling, strength training and swimming seem to be more gender-neutral activities among the Norwegian population. The most popular physical leisure activity among Norwegian women is walking as exercise (SCB 1997). According to this national survey, the four most popular activities women are actively involved in – presented for four different age groups – are, besides walking as exercise, bicycling, swimming and aerobics/gymnastics [http: //www.ssb.no/fritid] (24 June 2001)}.

After 44 years of age the participation rate for all four activities drops. This drop in activity for swimming and aerobic seems to start as early as aged 24. Walking as exercise (physical activity), however, increases first after the age of 16 to 24, but then after age 44 decreases again, while bicycling is relatively stable before it decreases after 44 years of age (see Figure 2.1).

The description of Norwegian women's participation in sport so far has been based on national surveys. Now results will be presented from organised sport by membership-figures in sports clubs taken from the official membership statistics of the NCS and NOCCS.

All differences between women and men become more marked in organised sport. Membership statistics show that in 1999 the NOCCS had 455,408 female club memberships among women above 17 years of age, compared with adult male club memberships, which were 796,530. Adult women, therefore, accounted for 36 per cent of the adult members in sports clubs (NOCCS 1999a: 34). Since 1980 the number of female and male membership has increased. The difference between women and men did diminish between 1980 and 1990, but has since then remained relatively

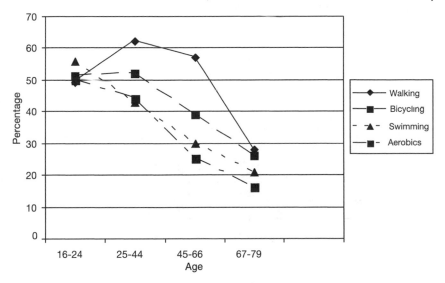

Figure 2.1 The percentage of physically active Norwegian women (at least once a month), who participate in walking, bicycling, swimming and aerobics, presented by age groups

Source: SCB online; available http: //www.ssb.no/fritid/1997

Note: N=871

stable (Annual Reports NCS/NOCCS 1980, 1985, 1990, 1995, 1999). In practice this means that 183,267 more women have joined a sport club since 1980, as against 186,733 for men. As with girls and boys, there is more potential for recruitment of women since there are as many or in fact more women than men in the adult population. One conclusion that may be drawn so far is therefore that organised sport has, during the last ten years, not been very successful in reaching membership equality between the sexes, neither among children nor adults.

In terms of women's participation in different kind of sport activity and changes in recent years, membership figures from the different sports reveal that the most popular sports among adult men are soccer, skiing, golf, shooting and walking. Among women, skiing is number one followed by gymnastics, soccer, team handball and walking. Figure 2.2 shows developments since 1985 among women in these sports and indicates changes over the years.

Sports clubs that increased the most among adult women are those that offer walking. Since 1990 the sport association for walking has increased markedly. Since 1990 there has been a peace march every year, registration for which brings automatic membership of the walking association. Soccer has remained relatively stable, and gymnastics, which formerly was a popular sport for women, lost many members from 1985 to 1990. This was probably due to the 'aerobic' wave that came from the USA, and together with it the increase in private training studios. Skiing also lost many members from 1990 to 1995, which may have something to do with the 'bad' snow conditions during recent years in many parts of Norway. It is, however, probably not the only reason. The Norwegian Ski Federation is known for its conservatism, and not for having taken special action in rela-

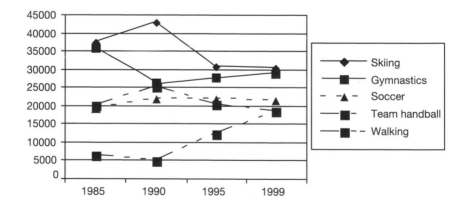

Figure 2.2 The development in membership in the largest sports in Norway among women over 17 years of age, 1985–99

Source: Annual Reports NOCCS 1985, 1990, 1995, 1999

tion to the development of women's sport, in spite of the fact that skiing has always been a very popular sport among Norwegian women.

Women in decision-making positions in the sport organisations

In terms of the number of women in decision-making positions in organised sport there are both employed and elected people in such positions. In 1997, women accounted for 46 per cent of those who were employed in Norwegian sports. There were only small differences between the different levels in the organisation. The Norwegian Olympic Committee and Confederation of Sports had the most women (53 per cent) and the sport districts the fewest (44 per cent) (NOCCS 1997b).

In looking at 'elected' women in decision-making bodies, it is important to be aware that the Norwegian Olympic Committee and Confederation of Sports has had a form of gender quota regulation since 1987. This regulation was sharpened in 1990, and taken into the Sports Law. Today's policy is characterised as follows:

> When electing or appointing representatives to councils, as well as members of boards, and committees in the NOCCS and the NOCCS's organisational branches, there shall be candidates/representatives of both sexes. The distribution of the sexes in the memberships of the individual organisational branches shall be a guide to the proportions, but apply to bards and committees etc, which consists of 3 or fewer members. The executive committee of the NCS may, in special circumstances, make exceptions to this provision.
>
> (NOCCS Law 1990, Paragraph 2–4)

The quota regulation concerning female representation seems to have had an effect, primarily among the special federations. The representation of females among executive board members at three different levels in the organisation from the years 1985, 1990, 1994 and 1998 are as follows:[4] female executive board members in the federations have increased from 15 per cent in 1985 to 30 per cent in 1998; in the Norwegian Olympic Committee and Confederation of Sports a total of 38 per cent of female representatives were on the board in 1998 (1994: 27, 1990: 38, 1985: 36 per cent); there is a decrease among the sports districts (1998: 38, 1994: 42, 1990: 43, 1985: 30 per cent), which is difficult to explain. In 1998 women accounted for 39 per cent of all the members in Norwegian organised sports (Annual Report NOCCS 1998: 33), and therefore it may be concluded that except for the special sports federations, women are equally represented at the executive boards in organised sports.

With regard to the most powerful positions, i.e. the chair or president of the executive committees, the positive picture of women's representation changes. The so-called 'glass ceiling' for women seems also to be operating in Norwegian organised sports. Out of nineteen sport districts, only two had female presidents in 1998, the same as in 1993. In the same year only four (7 per cent) of the fifty-five sports organisations had female presidents. This however represents an increase since 1993, when the total was only 2 per cent (Fasting 1996).

In a hierarchical organisation, normally fewer women are found in powerful positions the higher one becomes in that hierarchy; hence, one expects more female presidents at the lowest level in the organisations, i.e. in the sports clubs. This is indeed the case. The latest figures, from 1997, show that 17 per cent of the presidents are women. In spite of the quota regulation decided upon in 1991, the proportion of female presidents in sports clubs has only increased from 15 to 17 per cent during the last decade (NOCCS 1997b).

Even though these data demonstrate that men still have the most powerful positions in organised sports, in summarising the last ten years, women seem to have developed more and more influence in the sport organisations. There are more women today in decision-making positions than previously. Some have also passed through the 'glass ceiling'. As examples should be mentioned that one of the largest sport organisations, the Norwegian Amateur Track and Field Federation, now has for the first time a female president, and that the most powerful sports organisations of all, the Norwegian Football Association, employed a female Secretary General two years ago.

Programmes and action for promotion of girls and women in sport

Before the First World War, Norwegian sport was organised in two sports confederations: Norges Landsforbund and The Workers Sports Confederation (AIF). The latter had a political goal that promoted equal rights between women and men. For example, there was a women's committee appointed as early as 1935 (Lippe 1989). This was the first time that a specific sport policy was developed for women. Women's committees were appointed in all sports districts, and a women's network was established which also included local sports clubs. The goal was to involve more women in physical activity and to create social meeting places (Hovden 2000). Sport was looked upon as an important means to better the living conditions of women, create freedom for women and thereby create social change (Rafoss 1999). In 1946 the Workers Sports Confederation was merged with the other Norwegian Federation of Sport. The women's committee from the Workers Sports Confederation continued under the new umbrella organisation, but following different conditions. In 1947 there were women's committees in thirty out of thirty-six sports associations. By 1953 the number of women's committees had declined to eighteen, and at the 1953 General Assembly meeting the Women's Committee was abolished. However, it was intended that work with women's sport should continue under a new committee called the 'Committee for Instruction and Information'. Few measures were implemented by this committee to boost women's sport (NCS 1990).

'More sport activity for more women': The NCS's Women's Committee 1985–94

The unfairness and discrimination against women in sport were made visible through the media on many occasions in the 1970s. In the International Women's Year of 1975, the NCS started an educational programme: 'More sporting activities for more women'. As a part of this programme, a seminar was arranged in November of that year. After the seminar, the NCS executive board started discussing women and sport, but it was not until after the general sport assembly in 1984 that the mobilisation of women in organised sport led to concrete actions. Shortly after this meeting, the Norwegian Equal Status Council arranged a hearing about women and sport. The outcome of this was a project aimed at activating and educating women in sports organisations. The NCS appointed thereafter a Committee to review the organisation's commitment to women and sport. The task of this central women's committee was to 'appraise and draw up proposals or short-and long-term objectives and action plans to boost participation by women in organised sport' (NCS 1990). A plan of action from 1985–7 was adopted in 1984, followed by one from 1988–90. At the same time a consultant for women's sport was employed in the NCS administration. The long-term goal was that 'women and men should be assured of equal opportunities in practice for enjoying sport, taking on leadership assignments and holding offices' (Fasting and Skou 1994: 28). The purpose for establishing a Central Women's Committee therefore was:

- to legalise working with women's rights in the organisation
- to establish a formal network for women
- planning, initiating and coordinating activities especially for women

A network was established, and all sport associations and sport districts had been asked to establish a women's committee as early as 1985. It very soon proved to be difficult for some federations and districts to do this. As a substitute, some established a one-person committee, called a 'woman's contact' or a contact person for women's sport. In this introductory phase most of the individuals who were members of a women's committee were women, but there were also a few men. As an effect of the legislation from 1990 (mentioned previously) concerning equal representation, both genders should be represented in all women's committees, and a contact person for women's sport could be either a man or a woman.

The chair of the Central Women's Committee had since its establishment been a member of the Executive Board. This was a principle that was laid down in the first action plan: 'At least one member of the women's committee shall also be a member of the board at the same organisational level' (NCS 1990). The reason behind this was that it was thought to be important to have a direct line into the place of power, i.e. at the level of the executive board where the important decisions are discussed and decided.

The Women's Committee tried to take into account women's position in the society, their values and their culture. The main intention was to increase women's involvement in sport organisations at all levels and in all roles. The following measures were set up at the personal level:

- increase knowledge about the organisation and sport's policy
- increase consciousness of women's qualities and strength as well as the values of women's experiences and insight
- increase women's confidence in different situations
- increase women's self-confidence and give them courage to further work on new challenges
- set targets
- change attitudes about women's roles and remove barriers which prevent personal development

At the organisational level the following measures were taken:

- establish women's committees and contact persons at all levels to create a women's network
- provide information in order to change attitudes and remove barriers against raising women's status in the organisation
- make women's representation mandatory
- set aside money especially for the women's project

To reach the goals just mentioned it was necessary to give women more power and real influence at all levels in the sport system. Consequently, a developmental course for women only was developed. The course was called 'women can, will and dare'. It was designed to provide an increased insight into oneself – one's present status and one's potential development. The course aims to:

- give the participants insight into themselves and improve their self-confidence
- point out mechanisms which break down self-confidence
- give the participants increased speaking and presentation skills
- give the participants insight in how common goals can be achieved through networking

The course was also described as a 'training camp' to give:

- increased self-awareness
- increased self-confidence
- increased motivation to meet new challenges

When this course was started, the fundamental idea was that as more female leaders were brought in, more activities would have to be developed on women's premises. As a result, more female athletes and new female members had to be recruited into the organisation. Furthermore, to complete the recruitment circle, the basis for recruiting new female leaders would increase through the new membership.

The development and implementation of this course was the prominent activity of the Central Women's Committee. During the years 1985–89 thirty-four courses were completed, and about 2,500 women participated. Further training and educating teachers for this course was also an important part in this period. An evaluation of the course undertaken in 1989 tried to measure the effects on both the organisational and the individual level. The results showed that most of the women that had taken the course already had some positions in the organisation. Of those who did not have a position when participating in the course, 50 per cent were in position within two years afterwards. Before the course, nine women held a position in a sport association. After the course, this number had increased to fifty-five. In addition to these effects at organisational level, the course seemed to have major effects at personal level. Among these, many women reported better self-confidence and self-esteem after participation in the course (Drivenes 1990).

The second prominent activity was to hold annual or semi-annual meetings for the chair and members of the women's committees and the women's representatives in the sport associations and the sport districts. Another networking activity was nationwide meetings for female members of different executive boards and committees that also were held at least once a year. The last course that was developed was for women who did not exercise. This course was called 'Women in Shape', and its aim was to attract more women into actively doing physical exercise.

The Central Women's Committee started other activities primarily for three different groups: a coaching seminar for elite female coaches in 1988, a coaching school for women only in 1989 and 1990, and a forum for female top-level athletes, their administrators and support personnel. This forum met both in 1989 and 1990.

In 1989 it was decided to evaluate the core of this women's network, the women's committees in the sport districts and the sport federation. The main questions asked in the evaluation study were:

- who are the leaders of the women's committees?
- what have the women's committees done?

- how do the women's committees function?
- what characterises 'good' and 'bad', i.e. active and passive women's committees?
- what are the barriers and the predictors for good work?

The most important predictors for successful work on women and sport turned out to be:

1 the knowledge and the personal characteristics of the woman representative;
2 how the work was formally based and structured in the sport organisation;
3 the level of consciousness and common understanding in the sport organisation.

All these factors were also influenced by each other. Factor 2 was related to how the work for women and sport was rooted formally and informally in the organisation. The ideal seemed to be:

- representation on the executive board in the organisation
- secretary/consultant in the administration
- having a network, formally and informally

It seemed to be important that the organisation had knowledge about gender issues, and was conscious of the difference between male and female culture (factor 3). Knowledge in this area is mirrored in the degree of seriousness that the organisation put forward when working with women and sport. The study showed that the following four criteria demonstrated to which degree the work concerning women and sport was taken seriously and put into practice:

- if women were mentioned in the federation's or district's main plan of action
- if there existed a special plan of action for women and sport, and if this had been discussed and accepted by the executive board
- if the work for women and sport had it's own budget
- if the executive board had discussed women and sport at board meetings

One important point here (for the implementation of the plan of action) was funding. It turned out that there was not enough money to support the work of a women's committee. The organisation had to have some money to implement a plan of action. This money had to be taken from a larger budget, and it therefore demonstrated an organisation's priority and willingness to try to promote the work for women and sport (Fasting and Skou 1994).

Several conclusions could be drawn from this study. It is important that someone in the organisation, either a committee or a person, has the responsibility for developing women-related work. This can be a man, but he needs to have knowledge about gender issues and about the difference between female and male culture. The work on women and sport should be rooted in the organisation, both formally and financially. Consciousness-raising for both female and male sport leaders seemed to be important, at the same time as different courses and meetings for women only also were looked upon as very valuable. To have a separate budget for the promotion of the work with women and sport was of central importance in order to be able to change existing structures. Accordingly, to develop and carry through special plans of action to increase women's involvement in sport, resources were needed. But this was not enough. The work itself had to be taken seriously. It had to be given status and power. This was the reason why the contact person, or someone in a 'women's committee', also needed to be a member of the executive board, or another decision-making body.

In spite of these conclusions, the NCS General Assembly decided in 1994 to dissolve the women's committee at the same time as the position of the consultant for women's sport was withdrawn. The argument was 'full gender integration', which meant that the whole organisation should be responsible for the development of women's sport (Hovden 2000). It is, however, difficult to measure the result of this 'full gender integration', since there has been no formal evaluation. Nonetheless, it is a fact that the women's network in the organisation has disappeared, and except for one project (The Norwegian Women Project 1995–2000, mentioned below), no other major projects have been carried through by the NOCCS. Accordingly, it is difficult to see how the NOCCS has followed up its goals concerning equal rights for both genders.

The Norwegian Women Project 1995–2000

Another project – well-known internationally – has received a great deal of Norwegian media attention. The Norwegian Women Project (1995–2000), was financed primarily by the Norwegian government through the Royal Ministry for Cultural Affairs, which invested 7.5 million Norwegian kroner in the project. By way of comparison of financial scale, the Central Women's Committee yearly budget was between 700,000 and 1,200,000 Norwegian kroner, a budget that included the salary for the consultant in the administration who worked with women's sport. Another large difference between these two projects was that the former aimed at women in all roles and at all levels in the sport organisation, while the latter was concerned with mainly a small sample of Norwegian women in sport: female elite athletes. It was run by 'Olympiatoppen', a division within the NOCCS, representing all branches of top-level sports in Norway, and had a clearly defined purpose of concentrating exclusively on top-level sports. The main aims of the 1995–2000 Norwegian Women Project were:

- female athletes should win a total of 10–15 medals in the Nagano and Sydney Games together
- the percentage of women among leaders, coaches and other team supporters should be at least 20 per cent (NOCCS 1996)

For a country like Norway which has an equal rights law that demands that 'Each sex shall be represented with at least 40 per cent of the members when a public body appoints or elects committees' (Article 21, The Norwegian Act on Gender Equality; see Gender Equality Ombudsman 1978), this was not especially ambitious, particularly when one takes into account that the membership of women in the organisation was about 39 per cent. This argument is strengthened by the fact that at the Olympic Games in Atlanta in 1996, more female than male athletes represented Norway. On the other hand during the Lillehammer Olympic Games in 1994 there were only 3 women among the 74 leaders from the Norwegian sports federations (The Norwegian Women Project 1996). These negative statistics were also used as an argument for the whole project.

To reach the above mentioned aims the women Project was divided into five sub-projects. These were (1) the top level athlete project, (2) research, (3) motherhood and top-level sport, (4) network meetings for sharing experiences and training, and (5) development of leaders and coaches. There is no doubt that as a result of these sub-projects, the goal for the whole project was reached. The female athletes took a total of 11 medals in Nagano and Sydney. In Nagano there were 21 per cent accredited female leaders, coaches and support personnel, which increased to 22 per cent in the summer Olympic games in Sydney (Skirstad 2000).

There are large differences between the two projects that have been presented here. The work of the Central Women's Committee that existed from 1985 to 1994 can be characterised as having a more radical feministic perspective. It had a women's perspective, which was defined as follows:

- women's daily lives should be taken into account in planning and organising sport activities for women;
- women's knowledge and experiences must influence the organisation and be equally valued to that of men's;
- women should take responsibility for the development of their own activities (NCS 1990).

The Norwegian Women Project can at best be characterised as liberal feminism. Female elite athletes should have the same opportunities as male athletes, and they should be given the chances to reach the same performance level without being discriminated against. It is difficult to see that the project ever questioned the ideology of elite sport. It took into account the fact that women are different from men, but primarily in relation to biology. The sub-group 'motherhood and top-level sport' is an example of this. There has (as far as I know) never been any project or seminars in Norwegian sports about 'fatherhood and top-level sport'. It is difficult to know if this successful project will have any long-term effect on women's sport in general. The danger may be that it functions as a 'sleeping pillow' for the fact that there have been no other projects or special concerns for women in organised sports, if they are not elite athletes, since 1994.

Conclusion

First of all, probably as an effect of Norwegian equal rights politics in general, girls and women are almost as physically active in their leisure time as boys and men. The results from different studies, however, show inconsistent results depending on the measurement used. One nationwide study measuring physically status as active 'at least once every second week' shows that women since 1993 have been more active than men. It seems, though, that boys and men exercise more often than girls and women do. If we look at organised sports, i.e. membership in sports clubs, more boys than girls are recruited at an early age, and girls and women never seem to catch up. Boys and men not only practise more often than girls and women, they also compete more. It is also worth noting that the difference between boys and girls in memberships in a sport club seems not to have diminished since 1980. There has been an increase in membership of both genders, but more boys have become members of a sport club during these years in spite of the fact that there already in 1980 were more boys in the organisation.

These data mirror the traditional gender relations in society at large. Sport has always been very much connected to hegemonic and heterosexual masculinity. There has accordingly always been a strong relationship between men and sport. Sport was developed by, and for, men and has historically been directed by men. Important in this context is probably that the values embedded in sport, particularly in sport competition, have had such strong links to hegemonic masculinity such as competitiveness and high achievement motivation. The fact that Norwegian women participate more in exercise outside the sports club system, for example, can be interpreted in different ways. It may mean that organised sport either does not have sufficient potential activities for adult women, or that the offerings that they have are not attractive enough. Both of these views are probably true. Since the sport organisations are supported to a longer extent by the state, this may be looked upon as unfair. One conclusion that could be drawn is that in relation to membership in sport organisations, equal rights for both sexes have yet to be gained.

The traditional gender relations and gender order are also mirrored in the motivation for why women and men participate in exercise and sport, and in the specific sport activities that women and men are engaged in. Changes have occurred here over the last few years. First of all, girls and women seem to participate more than before in both 'new' and so called 'masculine' sports. This development has not taken place to the same degree for boys and men. One excellent example is the development of girls and women's soccer since 1975, which today is the largest female sport in Norway.

In order to foster a change in the culture of sport so that sport becomes more attractive for women, one means could be to have more women as members of decision-making bodies in the sports organisations themselves. This was one of the thoughts behind the quota representation rule that was decided upon by the Annual Meeting of the Norwegian Sport Confederation in 1990. As has been shown above, this seems to have had a positive effect, particularly in an increase in female executive board members in the sport associations. However, there is still a huge gap between women and men in relation to female chairs of sports clubs and female presidents of sport associations. In an interesting empirical study about power and gender in sport organisations, Hovden (2000) presents two different ideological patterns that were present among the executive board members that she observed and interviewed. She named these 'the market profile' (earning money, professionalisation, financing elite athletes) versus 'the caring profile' (taking care of the sports club members in terms of the positive contributions of sports to life). Many more men than women had a market profile. This profile also seems to be the dominant one. According to Hovden (2000) this may mean that one effect of more women in decision-making bodies is to keep the focus of sport organisations as potential sites for public welfare, a view that also may be looked upon as reinforcing the sport organisations' traditional understanding of themselves and their autonomy. If this turns out to be the case, more women will not necessarily bring in something very novel. On the other hand studies from other areas, for example of women in high-level positions in politics, have shown that women are carriers of 'new ways of thinking and doing', and only the future development of the gender of the power holders in organised sport will show whether or not this may be the case for sport too.

Notes

1   Some people have memberships in more than one sport club, and will be counted twice. The correct membership is therefore unknown, but it is lower than the figure presented here.

2   According to the author's knowledge there has never been a case where this paragraph has been used for a sport association. There may still exist a few sports clubs with only male members, but they are required to be open to female members also.

3   The official statistics from the Norwegian Olympic Committee and Confederation of Sports were until a few years ago always presented separately for girls and boys, women and men. Girls and boys are in these statistics defined up to 17 years of age, and women and men from 17 years of age. Since 1991, the statistics for boys and girls have been divided into two sub-groups, 0–12 years and 12–16 years.

4　The figures for the first three years are taken from Fasting (1996), while the 1998 figures are from Tollanes (2001), who at present works in the Norwegian Olympic Committee and Confederation of Sports.

Bibliography

Article 21, The Norwegian Act on Gender Equality 1978, Oslo: Gender Equality Ombudsman.

Breivik, G. and Vaagebø, O. (1998) *Utviklingen i fysisk aktivitet i den norske befolkning 1985–1997* (The development of physical activity in the Norwegian population 1985–1987), Oslo: Norges Idrettsforbund og Olympiske Komite.

Drivenes, I. (1990) *Kvinner kan-vil-tør' evaluering av kurset* (Women Can-Will-and-Dare, an evaluation of a development course), Oslo: Norges Idrettsforbund Kvinneutvalget.

Fasting, K. (1996) *Hvor går kvinneidretten?* (In which direction does the women's sport develop?), Oslo: Norges idrettsforbund.

Fasting, K. and Skou, G. (1994) *Developing Equity for Women in The Norwegian Confederation of Sports*, Oslo: Norwegian Confederation of Sports / Norwegian University of Sports and Physical Education.

Hovden, J. (2000) 'Makt, motstand og ambivalens. Betydninger av kjønn i idretten' (Power, resistance and ambivalence: The meaning of gender in sport), unpublished Phd.thesis, Institute for Sociology, University of Tromsø.

Lippe, G. (1989) 'Kvinneutvalg – organisering av kvinners særinteresser' (Women's committees – organising women's special interests), *Nytt om kvinneforskning* 13, 4: 34–45.

MMI undersøkelsen (1996) *Barne og Ungdomsundersøkelsen* (The Children and Youth Study of MMI), Oslo: Norges Idrettsforbund og Olympiske Komite.

—— (1998) *Barne og Ungdomsundersøkelsen* (The Children and Youth Study of MMI), Oslo: Norges Idrettsforbund og Olympiske Komite.

—— (2000) *Barne og Ungdomsundersøkelsen* (The Children and Youth Study of MMI), Oslo: Norges Idrettsforbund og Olympiske Komite.

National Council on Nutrition and Physical Activity (2001) *Fysisk aktivitet og helse, kartlegging* (Physical activity and health, survey), Oslo: SEF.

NCS (1990) *Women in Sport programme for 1985–1990*, Oslo: Norwegian Confederation of Sports Women's Committee.

NOCCS (Norwegian Olympic Committee and Norwegian Confederation of Sports) (1997a) *Annual Report 1997*, Oslo: NOCCS.

NOCCS (1997b) *Resultatrapport for Norsk Idrett* (Report of the results for Norwegian Sports), Oslo: NOCCS

NOCCS (1998) *Annual Report 1998*, Oslo: NOCCS.

NOCCS (1999a) *Annual Report 1999*, Oslo: NOCCS.

NOCCS (1999b) *Lov for Norges Idrettsforbund og Olympiske komite* (Law for the Norwegian Olympic Committee and Confederation of Sports), Paragraph 2–4, Oslo: NOCCS.

Rafoss, K. (1999) 'Nettball i Arbeidernes Idrettsforbund – idrett for kvinner eller kvinneidrett?' (Netball in the Workers Sport Federation – Sports for Women or Women Sports), *Heimen*, 36: 275–88.

Report to the Storting no. 14 (1999–2000) *Idrettslivet i endring, om statens forhold til idrett og fysisk aktivitet* (The changing of sports, the federal government's relationships to sports and physical activity), Oslo: Akademika.

Report to the Storting no. 41 (1991–2) *Idretten. Folkebevegelse og folkeforlystelse* (Sports. Popular movement and popular entertainment), Oslo: Akademika.

SCB (Norwegian Statistical Central Bureau) (1997) *Tables from a survey about the Norwegian population's living conditions*, http://www.ssb.no/fritid (24 June 2001).

Skirstad, B. (2000) 'More opportunities for women in top-level sport both as leaders and athletes', *Kunnskap om idrett* Oslo: Norges idrettshøgskole.

Søgård, A. J., Bø, K., Klungland, M. and Jacobsen, B.K. (2000) 'En oversikt over norske studier – hvor mye beveger vi oss i fritiden?' (An overview of Norwegian research – how much do we move in our leisure time?), *Tidsskrift for den Norske Lægeforening* 28, 120: 3439–46.

Tollanes, I. (2001) statistics received from Tollanes, who is a consultant in the Norwegian Olympic Committee and Confederation of Sports, Oslo.

Wold, B. *et al.* (2000) *Utviklingsrekk i helse og livsstil blant barn og unge fra Norge, Sverige, Ungarn og Wales. Resultater fra landsomfattende spørreskjema-undersøkelser tilknyttet prosjektet 'Helsevaner blant skoleelever: en WHOundersøkelse i flere land (HEVAS)'* (Developmental traits in health and lifestyle among children and Youth from Norway, Sweden, Hungary and Wales. Results from nationwide questionnaire connected to the project 'Health habits among school children: A WHO study in several countries'), Bergen: HEMIL-sentret, Universitet i Bergen.

3 Women and sport in the UK

Anita White

Sports development in the UK

Sports development in the UK is usually conceptualised as a continuum comprised of four stages of development: foundation, participation, performance and excellence. Foundation refers to the early development of movement literacy and physical skills upon which all later participation is based. Participation has traditionally applied to recreative activities undertaken primarily for fun, friendship and fitness. Performance signifies a move from recreative to competitive sport where people more seriously seek to improve their performance. Excellence is about reaching the highest standards in top-level sport. This model of sports development, conceptualised and promoted by the Sports Council in the late 1980s and 1990s has been used as a framework for planning sport by both public and voluntary sectors (Houlihan and White, forthcoming). The Council of Europe also accepted it as a means of promoting a common European framework for sports development (Council of Europe 1992).

The sport system in the UK

The sport system in the UK is complex. Although the UK has a unitary rather than a federal system of government it incorporates four home nations (England, Scotland, Wales and Northern Ireland). Within each of these nations and at UK level there is a mix of governmental, quasi-governmental, voluntary and commercial organisations that are concerned with sport policy, development and provision. At UK central government level the Department of Culture, Media and Sport (DCMS) has main responsibility for sport policy although Education and Environment departments also have an interest. The main sport development agencies at the national level are the five 'quasi-governmental' Sports Councils (UK, England, Scotland, Wales and Northern Ireland). They are funded directly by the DCMS or their Government Office and also have responsibility for the distribution of Lottery funds to sport. The English Sports Council is now known as 'Sport England' and the UK Sports Council as 'UK Sport'. At local government level local authorities make a substantial contribution to the provision of facilities and sports opportunities for their communities. Turning to the voluntary sector, the National Governing Bodies (NGBs) of sport are responsible for the administration of their respective sports. Many of these were established in the nineteenth century and are led by voluntary commit-tees. However the larger NGBs, such as the Lawn Tennis Association and the Rugby Football Union, employ professional staff, own their own facili-ties and profit from the staging of events. The smaller NGBs tend to be more dependent on the Sports Councils for funding. The main non-govern-mental organisations at national level are the Central Council of Physical Recreation (CCPR) and the British Olympic Association. There are also a number of sport related organisations that make a significant contribution to the sport system such as Sports Coach UK (formerly known as the National Coaching Foundation) and the Youth Sport Trust. Though some NGBs (such as the Football Association) are heavily involved in commercial activity, it is privately run facilities and clubs that form the biggest part of the commercial sector.

Relating the sports system to different stages of the sports development continuum, it is clear that different agencies are important at different stages. At the foundation stage, schools are the key agency in providing a sound physical education for all young people coupled with opportunities to participate in extra-curricular sport. Participation opportunities are provided by voluntary and commercially based clubs and local authorities. Although not a statutory requirement, all local authorities provide leisure facilities and services, and most communities have access to public sports halls, swim-ming pools and playing fields. Within the voluntary sector there are sports clubs in a wide range of different sports, and also significant private provi-sion through commercial fitness and health clubs. Performance development is provided primarily through clubs and county sports associations affiliated to NGBs, with some universities and colleges also providing good coaching and competitive opportunities for their students. Sporting excellence is nurtured primarily by the NGBs through national training squads, and in the major professional sports through premier league clubs. National Lottery funding to sport, introduced in 1996, has had a significant impact on the level of support provided to elite sportsmen and women.

Girls and women in the sport system

How is girl's and women's sport catered for within the sport system described above? To what extent are girls and women included in main-stream provision, and what remains of single sex traditions?

For the purposes of this chapter, physical education (PE) may be defined as the activity which goes on in physical education lessons and classes within the schools and colleges (see Kirk 1992 for a full discussion of the social construction of the definition of PE in post war Britain). PE is considered by sports organisations as an essential foundation for future participation and excellence in sport. It is in school PE lessons that young people should acquire fundamental movement competencies and sport skills. The UK has had a long tradition of sex-segregated PE, as the work of both Sheila Fletcher and Sheila Scraton illustrates (Fletcher 1984; Scraton 1992). Men and women PE teachers were trained separately in sex-segregated colleges until the 1970s, a situation that preserved gender duality within the profession and practice of physical education. Traditionally, secondary school girls and boys were taught different activities in separate classes. Team games comprised the largest part of the PE curriculum, with girls playing hockey, netball and tennis and boys playing soccer, rugby and cricket. The PE curriculum for girls was also likely to include dance. As important as the activities taught were the cultures of femininity that pervaded the way PE was taught and the values of the female PE profession (Scraton 1992). Even though men and women trainee teachers now follow co-educational courses, the school physical education curriculum still tends to reflect a traditional gendered approach with predominantly sex-segregated classes in secondary schools. However, the trend is towards co-education, more choice of activity for students (for example, allowing girls to learn soccer and boys to dance) and greater flexibility in delivery of the curriculum.

A similar trend towards mixed provision and organisational structures can be seen in the governing body sector where men's and women's NGBs for cricket, soccer, squash and hockey have all amalgamated in the last twenty years. These amalgamations have taken various forms with different consequences. In some cases, such as football, the long established and powerful Football Association took over or incorporated the much smaller Women's Football Association in 1993. In other sports such as hockey it has been more a marriage of equal partners. The All England Women's Hockey Association had been established for over 100 years and amalgamation with the equally long established Hockey Association in 1997 was carefully negotiated with the constitution of the emergent 'English Hockey Association' designed to ensure women's presence on the Board. Many regarded this amalgamation as an ideal one, but in fact a report to the Sports Council in 1995 highlighted the clash of cultures and differences in management philosophies between the men's and women's associations in both hockey and squash (Abrams *et al.* 1995) While every one of these amalgamations is different, and women in the organisations have different views on the costs and benefits of joining the men, the general pattern emerging is that women have sacrificed autonomy and control over their sport, but gained financial advantages and access to facilities, coaching and sponsorship. In terms of the culture of the new organisations formed from the take-overs and mergers, it seems that male models have prevailed.

An exception to this general trend towards a pattern of mixed governance of sports is the sport of netball. The All England Netball Association estimates it has nearly 4,000 clubs and 3,000 schools in affiliated to it with

57,000 individual members. Though the organisation is open to men and there are some male umpires and coaches, netball remains a largely female-defined sport played by women and governed by women.

Soccer dominates the club sector, and although there has been a large growth in girls and women's soccer in recent years, the sport is still male-dominated. However, in all the traditional male team sports of rugby, soccer and cricket, clubs are now slowly responding to demand from girls and young women and making better provision for then to join clubs and play the sport. In other sports like tennis, athletics and swimming, clubs have traditionally been mixed.

The Women's Sport Foundation (WSF)

Alongside this long-established tradition of voluntary sports clubs and governing bodies, an organisation dedicated solely to women and sport, the Women's Sport Foundation (WSF), was set up in 1985. Its aim was to promote the interests of all women in and through sport and to gain equal opportunities and options for all women. It was formed by a group of women working in sport who were concerned about the male domination of sport in the UK and the discrimination and inequalities faced by women. A small organisation, with limited financial resources, its influence in its early days was mostly in raising awareness of issues and challenging the male sports establishment. By 1990 it had gained legitimacy through recognition and funding from the Sports Council, and through the 1990s it has worked with various agencies to mainstream gender equity. There have been some interesting studies of the influence and effectiveness of the WSF. Brenda Grace (1995, 1997) conducted a case study of the WSF for her Masters thesis, and identified three key themes of the organisation: first, its ambivalent relationship with mainstream feminism; second, the politics of sexuality; and third issues of difference. Ann Hall (1997) conducted a comparative analysis of the WSF and other women's sport advocacy organisations and highlighted similar issues. Notwithstanding these issues and tensions, Jennifer Hargreaves (1994) comments that 'the WSF has done a tremendous amount to keep the campaign for women's sport constantly alive; to stimulate interest in women's sport; to nurture talent; to educate and inform'. She concludes that the WSF 'has provided an indispensable forum for the empowerment of women and sports' (Hargreaves 1994: 288), but adds that it needs to go further in contributing to the transformation of sport itself.

Women and sport policy

The first significant state policy development in Women and Sport in the UK was the publication by the Sports Council of the document 'Women and Sport: Policy and Frameworks for Action' in 1993. Along with policies for people with disabilities and black and ethnic minorities, it was based on the two key principles of sports development and sports equity defined as follows:

> Sports development is about ensuring that pathways and structures are in place to enable people to learn basic movement skills, participate in sports of their choice, develop their competence and performance, and reach levels of excellence.
> Sports Equity is about fairness in sport, equality of access, recognising inequalities and taking steps to redress them. It is about changing the structure and culture of sport to ensure it becomes equally accessible to everyone in society whatever their age, race, gender or level of ability.
>
> (Sports Council 1993: 3)

The policy development process and the concept of sports equity is described in an article written in 1994 (White 1997) but it is no coincidence the Sports Council developed this policy at the time the Women's Sports Foundation was becoming increasingly active as a lobbying and advocacy organisation. Many of the individuals who were leading the women's sports movement in the UK were influential in the framing of the policy, which had the over-arching aim of increasing the involvement of women and sport at all levels and in all roles. It was a comprehensive policy embracing all four stages of sports development, women as a human resource, organisational responsibility and communication, and it subsequently informed the drafting of the Brighton Declaration on Women and Sport in 1994. The Brighton Declaration, endorsed by 280 delegates from 83 countries at the first World Conference for Women and Sport, now has worldwide currency as an international statement of principles for women's sport development (UK Sports Council 1998).

Participation of girls and women in sport outside school

Women's participation

There are a number of surveys of sports participation in the UK, the best known of which is the General Household Survey (GHS) carried out on a regular basis by the Office of National Statistics. It is based on a representative sample of the general population and provides a wide range of information about adults aged 16 and over. The most recent survey was carried out between April 1996 and March 1997 and involved 15,696 people. Survey questions on sports participation have taken a standard form since 1987, which allows comparisons to be made over time.[1]

Extrapolating the statistics on gender from these surveys, we find an overall increase in the percentage of women in the population participating in sport between 1987 and 1996 (a rise from 34 to 38 per cent) but a decrease in men's participation from 57 to 54 per cent during the same period. The sports in which women participated most frequently (i.e. at least once a month) in 1996 were swimming (17 per cent) keep fit/yoga (17 per cent) and cycling (8 per cent) The comparative percentages for men are cycling (15 per cent) swimming (13 per cent) and keep fit (7 per cent) (Sport England/ UK Sport 1999a).

This trend towards a narrowing of the gender gap in adult participation can be attributed partly to the investment in public swimming pools and sports halls over the last 30 years. A survey of the use and management of these facilities (Sport England 1999a) shows that in the 1960s men accounted for 71 per cent of users and women only 29 per cent, but by the 1980s the gap had narrowed considerably (55 per cent men and 45 per cent women), and by the 1990s women's participation had overtaken men's (42 per cent men and 58 per cent women).

Girls' participation

It is reasonable to assume that participation habits and patterns may become established early in life, and so to complement the surveys on adult participation, the Sports Council and Sport England have commissioned surveys of young people's participation in sport both in and out of school lessons. Similar surveys were conducted in 1994 and 1998 covering a representative sample of 6–16 year-olds (Mason 1995; Sport England 2000b). The findings of the 1999 study give the following picture of girls' participation in sport outside school lessons and how it has changed since 1994.

In 1999 the most popular sports for girls were swimming (52 per cent), cycling (50 per cent), roller blading (28 per cent) and walking/hiking (24 per cent), while for boys the most popular sports were cycling (54 per cent), swimming (50 per cent), football (43 per cent), and roller blading (26 per cent). In extra-curricular sport, the percentage of girls involved increased from 36 to 42 per cent between 1994 and 1999, while for boys the percentage increased from 39 to 49 per cent over the same period. Boys' membership of sports clubs outside the school increased from 49 to 56 per cent between 1994 and 1999 while girls' membership showed little change from 35 per cent in 1994 to 36 per cent in 1999. Football clubs are at the top of the league in terms of providing for young people, but their membership is dominated by boys: 32 per cent of boys belong to football clubs compared to only 3 per cent of girls. Swimming is the second most popular club sport for young people with 13 per cent of girls as club members compared with 9 per cent of boys.

The conclusion to be drawn from these studies is that though there is evidence of a narrowing of the gender gap in adult participation, this is not mirrored in the participation patterns of young people. Attitudinal findings from the 1999 Young People and Sport Survey support the premise that girls and boys develop different attitudes to PE and sport very early in life. More boys say they enjoy sport both in and out of school lessons than girls do. Boys define themselves as 'sporty types' more than girls. Girls care less about being successful at sport than boys, but they mind more about getting cold, wet, sweaty and dirty (Sport England 2000b).

Women in high-performance/top-level sport

Turning to high-performance sport, there are relatively few opportunities for women to make a living as sports professionals. Men's soccer is extremely popular in the UK with the top players commanding huge salaries and transfer fees, but the women's game has been slow to develop in comparison with other countries. Sue Lopez (1997) in her book 'Women on the Ball' charts the failure to develop the women's game in England. One of the themes running through her book is the relationship of the women's game to the male administration of football through the Football Association (FA). Going back to 1921 when the FA banned women's teams from playing on the grounds of their affiliated clubs, there has been continued male dominance of the game where women have always had to seek approval and support from the male establishment to develop the women's game. England did not qualify for the Women's World Cup held in the USA in 1999, and though the current administration seems more committed to women's football, it will take time to make up for the years of neglect.

The other major team sports of cricket and rugby also provide professional opportunities for men but not for women. In golf and tennis there are better opportunities for women though their earning power is not as great as men.

One of the major changes to the funding of high performance sport in the UK was the introduction of the National Lottery in 1996, with sport receiving between £250–£300 million per annum. Initially this money was divided between capital investment in community facilities and support to 'world-class athletes'. The support to world-class athletes went partly to the governing bodies of sport, but also directly to those athletes who were considered potential medal winners in major international sports competitions such as the Olympics. Britain's performance in the Sydney Olympics was much improved from previous years, partly as a result of this investment. The men brought back thirteen medals and the women brought back nine. Current funding by UK Sport to UK and British athletes favours men, reflecting their medal winning potential. As of January 2001, there were 232 female athletes in 30 sports receiving £563,000 per annum, and 373 male athletes in 32 sports receiving £883,000 per annum. The reasons for more male athletes receiving financial support than female athletes can be explained by the greater number of sports, events and competitions available to men, and the better development opportunities for boys and men to put them in the 'potential medal winner' category. So while the funding criteria are the same for men and women, when these criteria are applied, the outcome is that more men than women access funding for top-level sport at UK level.

A slightly different picture emerges at England level, where the Sport England Lottery Fund supported women's cricket, rugby and golf in 2000, but not the parallel men's sports. This was partly because the men's sports were funded commercially and so were not eligible under the 'demonstration of financial need' criterion. Thus at England level the allocation of public funds has compensated to some extent for the lack of professional opportunities accessible to sportswomen in the major team sports.

Women in decision-making positions in sport

Moving on to women in decision-making positions in sport, and despite the strong policy statements on this issue, the overall trend is towards a decrease in women's influence in the boardroom and presence as top-level coaches. With a few notable exceptions, most senior positions in NGBs are held by men, as are the powerful positions in professional sport including football ownership and management. The same pattern is seen in coaching. As an illustration, there has been an overall decline in the percentage of women coaches to the British team at Summer Olympic Games over the last twenty years; from 9 per cent in Moscow in 1980 to 7.6 per cent in Sydney in 2000 (WSF: personal communication). The drive to improve top-level sport in the UK and the appointment of highly paid performance directors with Lottery money has attracted many good candidates, mostly from overseas, and nearly all of them men.

The proportion of women members on the Sports Councils where appointments are made by the Minister of Sport demonstrates a better gender balance. For example, UK Sport had seven women members on a board of nineteen in 2000. Women have also become more visible and audible in the media over the last ten years with several leading women television presenters and increasing numbers of sports journalists, albeit that in order to progress their careers they have to focus mainly on men's sport. The recreation management profession is still largely male-dominated, but in the newer, related field of sports development women and men are more evenly balanced.

Summing up these patterns and trends, we can see that both commercialisation and the quest for medals have led to a decline in women's involvement and influence at the top level. However there is a greater involvement of women at public policy levels in the Sports Councils, and some inroads have been made into the mass media. Despite some outstanding women leaders in basketball, hockey and rowing, to name but three sports, there has been little change in the voluntary governing body sector. The growing field of sports development is attractive to women, and women are successful in it, but sports development jobs are often low in status with limited career advancement opportunities.

In all three of the areas discussed above – participation, high-performance sport and decision making – women's involvement in sport is strongly mediated by socioeconomic status and ethnicity. Just as a clear gender order is apparent in sport as a whole, based crudely on a gender duality in which sport is valued as a masculine activity, when one examines women's sport one finds a predominantly white, middle-class sporting culture.

Ethnicity

A recent survey on Sports Participation and Ethnicity, conducted by the Office of National Statistics on behalf of Sport England, enables comparisons to be made between participation rates of men and women from different ethnic groups and national averages (Sport England 2000c). The survey was based on a random sample of 3,084 adults 16 and over from non-white ethnic minority communities interviewed in their homes between June 1998 and March 2000. Respondents classified themselves as 'Black Caribbean', 'Black African', 'Black Other', 'Indian', 'Pakistani', 'Bangladeshi', 'Chinese' and 'Other non-white'. Participation in sport is defined as having taken part in sport or physical activities, excluding walking, at least once in the previous four weeks (Sport England 2000c). The overall participation rate for all ethnic minority groups is 40 per cent, compared with a national average of 46 per cent. For men the comparative percentages are 49 per cent and 54 per cent, while for women they are 32 per cent and 39 per cent. Taking the data on women, analysis by ethnic group shows that some groups participate more than the national average of 39 per cent, some a little less and others substantially less. Black Other (45 per cent) and Other (41 per cent) participated more, but Black Caribbean and African (34 per cent), Indians (31 per cent) and Bangladeshi (19 per cent) participated less. Referring to the kinds of sport, keep fit/ aerobics/ yoga and swimming were the most popular activities.

The survey throws up some interesting findings on those sports where the participation rates of particular ethnic groups exceed the national average. Running and jogging are much more popular with Black African women (11 per cent) than the national average (2 per cent). Weight training is more popular with Black Caribbean women (7 per cent compared with 3 per cent). Self-defence and martial arts are more popular with Chinese women (3 per cent compared with >1 per cent), basketball is more popular with Black Caribbean women (3 per cent compared with >1 per cent), and cricket is more popular with Bangladeshi and Pakistani women (2 per cent compared with >1 per cent) (Sport England 2000c: 23). These findings suggest that different cultural identities find expression in those sports that have a history and tradition in the parent culture. It would be interesting to know what meanings these women give to their participation in these sports and how they became involved. Reasons given for not taking part in sport are predictable with women more likely than men to give 'home and family responsibilities' as the main reason (Sport England 2000c: 30). The study is a useful one because it provides, for the first time, some detailed empirical evidence on ethnic minority participation in sport. However, more in-depth qualitative studies are needed to help us understand the dynamics of ethnic minority participation or lack of it. One such study, which explores the relationships and contradictions between faith, Bangladeshi/Indian culture and Western culture, is Hasina Zaman's work with Muslim pupils and former pupils from a school in the East End of London (Zaman 1997).

As regards top-level sport, there are no systematic studies that identify the numbers of women involved from different ethnic groups. However, a number of black women athletes are household names such as Fatima Whitbread and Tessa Sanderson (both Olympic Javelin throwers), Judy Simpson (pentathlete) and more recently Denise Lewis (gold medallist in the heptathlon at the Sydney Olympics and runner-up in the BBC Sports Personality of the Year competition in 2000). The success of these women probably serves to reinforce stereotypical ideas about the racial superiority of black people in sport, and it has been argued (Lovell 1991) that racial stereotyping facilitates the integration of Afro-Caribbean women into British sporting cultures while militating against the integration of Asian women. Certainly there is a good deal of evidence that the labelling of black girls and boys as 'naturally gifted at sport' means that teachers and others have high expectations of their success in sport and channel them towards sporting success rather than academic achievement (Cashmore 1990). Some of these high-profile women athletes have become involved in sports leadership on retirement from top level competition. Judy Simpson is President of the Women's Sports Foundation and a member of the UK Sports Council, and Tessa Sanderson is a Vice Chair of Sport England. Politicians have been keen to hold them up as exemplars and to be photographed with them as if to demonstrate that sport is truly integrated and an arena where black women can succeed as performers and leaders. However, their high-profile positions mask an overall dearth of black women in sports leadership and an almost total absence of Asian women in high-profile leadership roles.

Social class

After accounting for age and sex, social class is the most significant factor in predicting levels of participation in sport (Sport England 1999b). Despite overall increases in both overall participation and women's participation, comparative analysis of GHS data show that differences of level of participation between the higher and lower socio-economic groups grew between 1987 and 1996. It seems that despite the expansion of facilities for indoor sport and the increases in participation which ensued, social class remained a pervasive factor in women's sport participation. In some ways this is not surprising given the historical development of sport in Britain and the way in which social class differences and relations are so soundly embedded in sporting practice (Hargreaves 1994). The education system also has done much to reinforce these differences (Scraton 1992). Girls from middle-class families are more likely to be encouraged to participate in out of school sport than girls from working-class families, and working-class girls leave school earlier and start their own families earlier than their middle-class counterparts. Many working-class girls are socialised to take on caring responsibilities and domestic chores in the home, whereas their brothers' relative freedom from these expectations gives them more leisure time to play sport (Coakley and White 1992). In their study of women's sports participation in Sheffield, Green *et al.* (1987) found that it was usual for working class men to control the leisure activities of their wives, girlfriends and daughters, and women often lacked both money and transport to participate in sport outside the home.

The history of women in top-level sport in the UK is not surprisingly underpinned by social class relations, with most of the pioneers of sport in the nineteenth and twentieth centuries coming from upper and middle-class backgrounds. Writing about the expansion of women's leisure and the development of competitive sports for women, Jennifer Hargreaves describes how upper-class women in the early nineteenth century took up sports such as archery and croquet, but always in ways which did not undermine or challenge traditional ideologies of 'femininity'. Sportswomen were expected to behave in exemplary fashion and display feminine traits. In the middle and later 1800s more middle-class women took up sports like cycling and swimming, but their working-class sisters were excluded from participation both by cost and by attitudes towards them. Writing about the interwar years (1918–39), Hargreaves highlights the achievements of a number of outstanding sportswomen in asserting themselves and challenging conventional definitions of femininity, but concludes that it is difficult to assess the extent to which they influenced ideas about female athleticism. She concludes that most sports remained exclusive to upper and middle-class women, and even since that time have remained resistant to democratisation (Hargreaves 1994).

Hargreaves' claim is borne out by data collected on top level athletes (English Sports Council 1998) which show clear social class biases with far greater representation from the higher socioeconomic groups. Not surprisingly, few women from working-class backgrounds become sports leaders at other than community levels.

Programmes and action

Over the last ten years or so, as awareness of women and sport issues has grown, there have been many initiatives taken in the public, private and voluntary sectors to promote sport for women and girls. These initiatives fall into two broad categories: special measures for developing women and girls' sport, and mainstreaming gender equity within sports development programmes.

Some of the early work on increasing participation by women was carried out by the Sports Council in the 1980s under the banner of their 'National Demonstration Projects'. These were innovative projects set up in partnership with a variety of agencies designed to develop new ways of working with 'target groups' (of which women were one). The projects were closely monitored through action research, and lessons learned were used in future policy and programme development (Sports Council 1991). Two of the fifteen projects focussed specifically on women. In the Norwich project, a development worker was employed by the local authority with a remit to work solely with women. The Women's Institute project worked through the Cambridgeshire branch of the Women's Institute – a large voluntary organisation with social and educational objectives – to promote outreach work with women in rural areas. Both of these projects were concerned with grassroots sports development and the lessons learned have influenced sports development since (Sports Council 1991: 19–21). One of the major lessons learned was the importance of promoting activities through existing women's groups rather than through traditional sport structures. A second was the need to recognise diversity among women and to listen to what women themselves wanted. This led to the provision of a wide variety of different sports opportunities at times that fitted with the other demands in women's lives. Third, the appointment of development workers with a specific remit for promoting women's participation in the local community proved its worth, and in the late 1980s and early 1990s many local authorities made these kinds of appointments, often part funded by the Sports Council in their region.

Other initiatives at local level include the formation of sports clubs. Jenny Hargreaves (1994) writes about two interesting examples of this kind of development: the Newham Women's Football Club and the Queens of the Castle netball club. In both cases women set up these clubs in opposition to the dominant models of football and netball prevalent at the time. The Newham Women's Football Club wrote into its constitution that women should run the club and have absolute control over its affairs. This is in contrast to other developments in football, where most development of the women's game occurs under the aegis of men. At Newham, members were supported to go on refereeing and coaching courses as well as on assertiveness training to assure the next generation of women leaders. The club also adopted tactics on a positive style of play in contrast to the negative and defensive tactics prevalent in the men's game, and they negotiated the lease of their own ground from the local authority rather than having to share pitches with men's teams. The Queens of the Castle netball club was in an inner urban area of London with a mostly working-class membership and a high proportion of black players. They believed mainstream netball was too 'straight-laced', and so attempted to create their own radical club culture with flamboyant playing kit and a politicised approach to being in touch with young working-class London women.

The idea of creating new sports groups, run by women for women, has been a fairly popular way of challenging dominant male sporting ideology and practice. The idea is not new: indeed the women-only 'Pinnacle' mountaineering club was founded in 1921 as a result of a shared feeling among women climbers that they would have better opportunities to lead and participate if they were 'sans homme' (Pilley 1989).

At present the 'Running Sisters' network, though perhaps less ideologically motivated than the clubs mentioned above, aims to put women of all ages and abilities in touch with women in the same area who would like to run/ jog together. It has 5,000 members nationwide and links experienced runners (Big Sisters) with inexperienced runners (Little Sisters) to help them train for races. More importantly it puts women runners, or would-be runners, who live in the same neighbourhood in touch with each other so they have the social support and security of running together rather than alone (http://www.sbu.ac.uk/sally/sisternet.shtml).

Local authorities have also recognised the value of running 'women-only' sessions in public leisure facilities. This has been particularly useful in providing a safe and private environment away from 'the male gaze' where women can swim or exercise together without embarrassment or awkwardness. The legality of holding women-only sessions has been challenged by some men under the terms of the Sex Discrimination Act (1975) and local authorities, wary of prosecution, have to demonstrate equal provision for men. Consequently the practice of running such sessions is decreasing, despite their success in attracting new women participants.

Among voluntary groups, the Women's Sports Foundation has been active in promoting women and girls' sport in a number of ways. Apart from a few years when it attracted commercial sponsorship from to run an awards scheme for girls, it has been largely dependent on working in partnership with mainstream sports organisations and on funding from the Sports Council. Since its formation, the WSF has been a constant advocate for women's sport, commenting on issues of the day, drawing attention to inequalities, developing resources, and providing information and advice. It publishes a quarterly newsletter featuring issues, events, and interviews/ profiles of sportswomen and women leaders. Furthermore, the WSF has developed a Curriculum Guide for Schools on Women's Sport, posters, videos, fact sheets on topics such as sexual abuse, research and writing on women's sport, women in the Olympics and the female athlete triad. It has also developed a leadership course, 'Women Get Set Go', and has recently launched an initiative with the National Coaching Foundation and the governing bodies of football, rugby union and league and cricket to develop more women in high-performance coaching. Working strategically with Sport England, the WSF has developed a 'National Action Plan for Girls and Women in Sport' (Sport England 1999b) which provides a framework for the coordination of the action and efforts of different agencies.

Despite the efforts of organisations such as the WSF to raise the profile of women's sport, the sports media still give scant coverage to women's sport and to sportswomen's achievements. Since 1998 the *Sunday Times* has run a 'Sportswoman of the Year' Award in conjunction with the CCPR. Because this award is run by the *Sunday Times*, it is not covered by rival newspapers, but it does get a certain amount of television coverage and the awards ceremony is a fine celebration of women's sporting achievements. Awards are given in a number of categories including student, PE teacher, team, inspiration, lifetime achievement and administrator/coach, as well as overall Sportswoman of the Year.

Other commercial sponsorship has been forthcoming from Nike for the 'Girls in Sport' project in partnership with the 'Youth Sport Trust'. It is 'a school based project aimed at assisting teachers to develop forms of Physical Education and sport that will enable more girls to lead active lifestyles now and in the future' (Institute of Youth Sport / Youth Sport Trust 1999). The project has been monitored by the Institute of Youth Sport at Loughborough University and its interim report confirms the existence of gender discrimination and sexist attitudes, identifies the need for urgent reform of physical education for girls, describes action plans and intervention strategies tried by the schools in the project, and evaluates their impact on pupils' attitudes and beliefs. The project is still in its early days, but it is a good illustration of the mainstreaming approach to gender equality by attempting to change existing practice within existing structures.

The approach of the Sports Councils has also been primarily one of mainstreaming, following the policy developed by the GB Sports Council in 1993. Subsequent strategies published by the English Sports Council and Sport England Lottery Fund have included specific gender equity aims and targets (English Sports Council 1997, Sport England Lottery Fund 1999). Sport England seeks to influence the development of sport through its relationships with partners in the commercial, voluntary and public sectors. Although it does this partly through advocacy and persuasion, its policies and strategies are seen to have real teeth when funding is dependent on the compliance of the applicant with equity conditions. Since Sport England became a distributor of National Lottery funds to sport in 1995, it has implemented criteria making organisations that operate discriminatory membership schemes ineligible for funding. Private clubs in the UK are outside the scope of the Sex Discrimination Act and some of them have discriminatory membership arrangements. Most notable of these are some golf clubs, which do not allow women full membership or voting rights. Some refused to change their constitutions, and thus have been denied Lottery funds for capital development. Others were prepared to change. Two very long-established and well-known clubs have recently changed their policy on women's membership, notably the Leander Rowing Club and the Marylebone Cricket Club, and it is no coincidence that their ineligibility to be recipients of Lottery funds while under the old regime, and the subsequent adverse publicity associated with this, not to mention financial expediency, helped hasten the changes. The targets in the Lottery Strategy for the ten years from 1999–2009 are explicit on gender, and their implementation should ensure some redress in the balance of funding that goes to sport for women and girls (Sport England 1999b: 31, 44).

Sport England has also recently toughened its stance towards governing bodies of sport by insisting on equity plans with targets and timescales as a condition of grant aid. This is a 'carrot and stick' approach, as governing bodies are provided with training and resources on equity planning (Sport England 2000a). Nevertheless the tougher stance taken by Sport England has not made it popular among sporting organisations resistant to change and who do not see the need to involve more women as participants, performers and leaders.

The other main way in which Sport England is mainstreaming gender equity is through its major programme development in the three 'Active programmes': Active Schools, Active Communities and Active Sports. These new programmes have equity principles built in from the outset, which should prove a much more sound basis for development than trying to add gender to existing programmes. For example, an element of Active Schools is the Coaching for Teachers programme, and over 50 per cent of participants are women teachers. Active Communities will work with women at community level in a bottom-up approach to development, and Active Sports requires local partnerships between governing bodies and local authorities to come forward with plans that take account of current inequities, targets for their reform and actions to achieve those targets.

Notwithstanding the good intentions, special initiatives and bureaucratic measures that are being put in place, it will still take a lot of work to change attitudes and bring about fundamental change to the sport culture in the UK. However, a mix of special measures and mainstreaming is probably the best way to challenge the existing gender order that continues to celebrate men's sport above women's sport, and to give men greater opportunities than women to become involved in sport.

Other issues

The main social issues around the influence of ethnicity and social class on the gendered practice of sport in the UK within the context of strong historical traditions of male dominance of sport have been explored, but there are three important issues that have been omitted from the text so far.

One is the integration and development of sport for women with disabilities. It is often said that women with disabilities face double discrimination, and there is no doubt that in paralympic sport, athletes who have sustained spinal injury through accident and armed combat (who are mostly men) have a higher status than some other categories of disability. At the time of writing we do not have good data on the participation of men and women with disabilities in sport.

Another issue absent from the text is that of sexuality. Like many other societies, British sporting culture assumes compulsory heterosexuality at least on the part of men, and is ambivalent about lesbians in sport. Gill Clarke (1997) has written persuasively about the lives of lesbian PE teachers, but hers is the only significant scientific research on this issue in Britain.

Other concerns about the practice of women's sport are sexual harassment and abuse. There have been several high-profile cases of sexual abuse in the UK, the most notorious of which was the conviction in 1995 of Paul Hickson, a swimming coach who was also British team coach at the Seoul Olympics in 1988, for assaulting eleven female swimmers, including the rape of two of them, between 1976 and 1991. The British researcher and activist Celia Brackenridge has done much to draw attention to the issues of sexual harassment and abuse, and has developed useful theoretical frameworks for analysis of these phenomena as well as policy and programme advice on dealing with harassment and abuse (Brackenridge 1997, 2001).

Evaluation

Evaluating the main problems and achievements of sport for women in the UK, it is clear that a strong gender order persists which is grounded in the historical traditions of sport as a male preserve. Sport is still experienced by many, whether participants or consumers and spectators, as a site for the expression of heterosexual masculinities. While women's participation in sport has increased over recent years, their involvement in top-level sport is limited and their influence in sports leadership is diminishing. Social class and ethnicity continue to have a pervasive influence. The globalisation and commercialisation of male sport is far more significant to the sporting world than any increases in the involvement of women in sport. Public opinion remains obsessed with football and the performance of national teams in the major men's sports.

Despite this gloomy picture (from the perspective of a sports feminist) there are some more encouraging signs. Though the legal framework is weak, the UK has strong policies on gender equality and although they may be resented by some, they are beginning to be implemented more rigorously by the Sports Councils. The current political climate, with the Labour government's commitment to social inclusion, is helpful in this regard (see Houlihan and White, forthcoming). Other cause for some optimism is the challenges to the gender order that have been manifest in the increasing participation of women in traditionally male sports like rugby, where determined women have broken down barriers and begun to create a new order assisted by enlightened men. And the UK has some strong women leaders in sport who are becoming increasingly influential and respected by the male sporting establishment. Overall, the challenge remains to accelerate the process of change to the culture of sport and the way that gender is lived through sport so that more women can gain fulfilment through sport in the future.

Note

1   See Sport England (1999), 'Sport Trends in Adult Participation in Sport in Great Britain 1999', for trends in overall participation, participation in different sports, and participation by age, gender, socio-economic group, ethnic group and region.

Bibliography

Abrams, J., Long, J., Talbot, M. and Welch, M. (1995) *Organisational change in national governing bodies of sport: Report to the Sports Council*, Leeds: Carnegie National Sports Development Centre, Leeds Metropolitan University.

Brackenridge, C. (1997) 'Sexual harassment and sexual abuse in sport', in G. Clarke and B. Humberstone (eds), *Researching women and sport*, London: Macmillan.

—— (2001) *Spoilsports: Understanding and preventing sexual exploitation in sport*, London and New York: Routledge.

Cashmore, E. (1990) *Making sense of sport*, London and New York: Routledge.

Clarke, G. (1997) 'Playing a part: The lives of lesbian physical education teachers', in G. Clarke and B. Humberstone (eds), *Researching women and sport*, London: Macmillan.

Coakley, J. and White, A. (1992) 'Making decisions: Gender and sport participation among young British adolescents', *Sociology of Sport Journal* 9,1: 20–35.

Council of Europe (1992) *European Sports Charter*, Strasbourg: Council of Europe.

English Sports Council (1997) *England, the sporting nation: A strategy*, London: English Sports Council.

—— (1998) *The development of sporting talent 1997*, London: English Sports Council.

Fletcher, S. (1984) *Women first: The female tradition in physical education 1880–1980*, London: Athlone Press.

Grace, B. (1995) 'Women, sport and the challenge of politics: A case study of the Women's Sports Foundation (UK)', unpublished Masters thesis, University of Alberta.

—— (1997) 'Researching a women's sport organisation', in G. Clarke and B. Humberstone (eds), *Researching women and sport*, London: Macmillan.

Green, E., Hebron, S. and Woodward, D. (1987) *Leisure and gender: A study of Sheffield women's leisure experiences*, London: Sports Council/ESRC.

Hall, A. (1997) 'Feminist activism in sport: A comparative study of women's sport advocacy organisations', in A. Tomlinson (ed.), *Gender, sport and leisure: Continuities and challenges*, Aachen: Meyer and Meyer.

Hargreaves, J. (1994) *Sporting females: Critical issues in the history and sociology of women's sport*, London and New York: Routledge.

Houlihan, B. and White, A. (forthcoming) *The politics of sports development: Development of sport or development through sport?*, London and New York: Routledge.

Institute of Youth Sport/Youth Sport Trust (1999) *The Nike/YST Girls in Sport Partnership Project: Interim report*, Loughborough: Loughborough University.

Kirk, D. (1992) *Defining physical education: The social construction of a school subject in post war Britain*, London: Falmer.

Lopez, S. (1997) *Women on the ball*, London: Scarlet Press.

Lovell, T. (1991) 'Sport, racism and young women', in G. Jarvie (ed.), *Sport, racism and ethnicity*, London: Falmer Press.

Mason, V. (1995) *Young people and sport in England, 1994*, London: Sports Council.

Pilley, D. (1989) *Climbing days*, London: Hogarth Press.

'Running Sisters' Network *Sisternet*, http://www.sbu.ac.uk/sally/sisternet.shtml (December 2001).

Scraton, S. (1992) *Shaping up to womanhood: Gender and physical education*, Milton Keynes: Open University Press.

Sport England (1999a) *Best value through sport: Survey of sports halls and swimming pools*, London: Sport England.

—— (1999b) *National Action Plan for Women's and Girls' Sport and Physical Activity*, London: Sport England/Women's Sports Foundation (WSF).

—— (2000a) *Making English sport inclusive: Equity guidelines for governing bodies*, London: Sport England.

—— (2000b) *Young People and Sport. National Survey 1999: Headline findings*, London: Sport England.

—— (2000c) *Sports Participation and Ethnicity in England. National Survey 1999/2000: Headline findings*, London: Sport England.

Sport England Lottery Fund (1999) *Investing for our sporting future: Sport England Lottery Fund Strategy 1999–2009*, London: Sport England.

Sport England/UK Sport (1999a) *Sport trends in adult participation in sport in Great Britain 1987–1996*, London: Sport England/UK Sport publication.

—— (1999b) *Trends in adult participation in sport in Great Britain 1999*, London: Sport England/UK Sport publication.

Sports Council (1991) *National demonstration projects: Major lessons and issues for sports development*, London: Sports Council.

—— (1993) *Women and sport: Policy and frameworks for action*, London: Sports Council.

UK Sports Council/International Working Group on Women and Sport (1998) *Women and sport. From Brighton to Windhoek: Facing the challenge*, London: UK Sports Council.

White, A. (1997) 'Towards gender equity in sport: An update on Sports Council policy development', in A. Tomlinson (ed.), *Gender, sport and leisure: Continuities and challenges*, Aachen: Meyer and Meyer.

Zaman, H. (1997) 'Islam, well-being and physical activity: Perceptions of Muslim young women', in G. Clarke and B. Humberstone (eds), *Researching women and sport*, London: Macmillan.

4 The inclusion of women into the German sport system

*Ilse Hartmann-Tews and
Sascha Alexandra Luetkens*

The development of the German sport system and the exclusion of women

The early comprehensive writings on physical education for youth, notably by Johann Christoph Friedrich GutsMuths (1793), aimed at young citizens' education but focused solely on boys to the exclusion of girls. GutsMuth's 'system' of physical education had a marked influence on Friedrich Ludwig Jahn, who at the beginning of the nineteenth century developed a patriotic form of German gymnastics (*Turnen*). Jahn's underlying purpose in translating his concept of gymnastic exercises into, and through, *Turnen* was as an expression of nationalism and as a means to overcome the feudal order that had divided Germany into a patchwork of antagonistic states. Despite a Prussian imposed 'Ban' from 1820 to 1842 emanating from conflictual political events of the day (Naul and Hardman 2002), *Turnen* saw a rapid upswing during the ensuing decades. The establishment of physical education and gymnastics was accompanied by the foundation of *Turnvereine* (gymnastics clubs), with multi-functional character. Their central aim was to provide the material basis for gymnastics[1] and to enable young men to do physical exercises. Additionally, they became a place to celebrate community as well as to convey social responsibility, solidarity and patriotism.

Given Jahn's patriotic goals and emphasis on military preparedness, the exclusion of women seemed self-evident and nobody bothered to explain or justify it. It was embedded in a general resistance against the physical education of females based on moral, medical and aesthetic arguments. Thus, exercises for girls were restricted to free but limited range of movements and dances in order to make them healthier and more attractive, and to strengthen their capacity to bear strong children. In the course of the nineteenth century, there was increasing concern about the effects of industrialisation and urbanisation on girls' and women's health, which led to a lively debate over female physical education. Few girls, however, benefited from this movement, and those that did were predominantly from the middle classes. Physical education for girls was only gradually introduced into schools (far later than physical education for boys), first in higher education (1894) and then, after the turn of the century, in elementary schools.

In the early years of the twentieth century, modern sport entered the German scene and attracted the upper classes. Besides differences in the concept of physical activities, the central ideas of gymnastics and of sport were competition and increase in performance levels. These reference points became the general action orientation of clubs and can be seen as the driving force to codify sporting activities, to establish rules of competition, to create clubs and associations, and to integrate these into national federations. At the end of the nineteenth century and beginning of the twentieth century, gymnastics and sports began to take the clear shape of a social system with distinguishing social and material structures (Hartmann-Tews 1996: 60ff).

With few exceptions, German sports organisations were sexually integrated, which tended to place women under men's supervision. In spite of a range of barriers, women's sections of men's gymnastics clubs and even a small number of sports clubs exclusively for women were created. However, the concern for preserving health, beauty and morals set limits on the sporting activities of women, who in addition were especially restricted by their clothing (corsets, long skirts, narrow blouses). The aftermath of the First World War brought profound political, economic and social change, including some change in gender relationships. The most important impetus was the women's right to vote, legally implemented in 1919. Among other things a new 'modern' ideal of femininity was proclaimed, a more athletic type with short hair and clothes that gave more freedom of movement. Participation in sport was rising constantly, but fierce controversy over female participation in competitive sport still prevailed: medical experts especially argued against it as they feared a masculinisation of the female body and diminishing fertility of female athletes (Pfister 2002: 168–70; Pfister 2001).

The National Socialist ideology of the 1930s recast masculinity and femininity as the polar opposites they were thought to be in the nineteenth century. Physical education during the Nazi regime became a central pillar to prepare men for their 'predetermined biological role' as fighters and women for their role as mothers. The ideology of physical superiority, which was based on biological and racist ideas, led to an extreme cult of masculinity and at the same time to the provision of so-called healthy and 'appropriate' exercises for girls and women. Although National Socialist ideology had originally been opposed to competitive sport for women, the regime supported female athletes in a number of ways and the 1936 Olympic Games witnessed a most successful German team of female athletes.

After the devastation and deprivation of the Second World War, organised sport in Germany had to regain recognition and acceptance. The former ideal of 'train the fittest', which prepared male youth for military service, could no longer be the frame of reference. Thus the foundation of new organisational structures in the divided country of West Germany (Federal Republic of Germany) and East Germany (German Democratic Republic) was celebrated as a new beginning.[2]

General features of the German sport system today: voluntary, public and private sector sports provision

The federal structure of Germany, consisting of sixteen constituent Länder (states), is reflected by the structure, organisation and division of responsibilities in the field of sport (see Figure 4.1). In accordance with the constitutional maxim that the interest and rights of the individual are to be exercised and fostered in free, autonomous organisations, German sports policies have been based on the principle of independence and self-responsibility; thus sports organisations have autonomous control of their respective domains.

There are three discernible central sectors within the sport system: the public, private and voluntary sector.

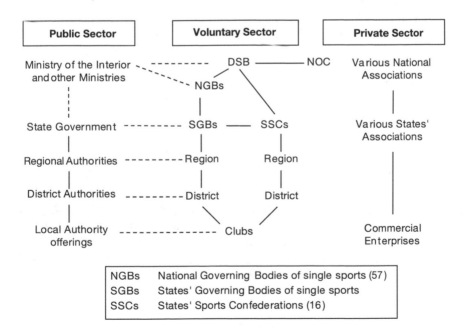

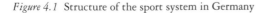

Figure 4.1 Structure of the sport system in Germany

Public (governmental) sector

The Federal Government, the Länder States and local authorities provide the legal and material basis for the development of sport. They support the activities of sports organisations in the voluntary sector in those cases where the latter's staffing and financial resources are inadequate. All public promotion is in accordance with this principle of subsidiarity. The autonomy of sport with regard to governmental policy is well reflected by the fact that the constitution in Germany does not explicitly assign responsibilities for sport to the Federal Government; consequently there is no Federal Ministry of sports that is authorised to control the matters of sport and implement a general sports policy. Instead, there are a variety of ministries both at Federal level and at Land level that fulfil their supportive action, including the Federal Ministry of the Interior that claims responsibility for elite sport only.

In accordance with the Constitution, sports development is seen as part of cultural development. As the sixteen constituent Länder of Germany hold supremacy in cultural affairs and physical education at school, they are responsible for the development of sport. Sports policies, including the promotion of programmes to foster sport for women, vary considerably within the sixteen Länder, depending on the parties in government, the Ministry that claims responsibility for sport, and the size and strength of the voluntary sector sports federations.

The public sector's sports offerings comprise a large variety of provisions that are predominantly financed by municipal authorities. They include physical education at schools and universities, youth centre programmes, financing of swimming pools, and co-operation with charities, churches and unions. Although there is no representative and comprehensive data on the users' profile, it seems that the proportion of women is rather high compared with the membership data of the voluntary sector (Hartmann-Tews and Petry 1994).

Voluntary (non-governmental) sector

The sport system in Germany is characterised by a strong and highly organised voluntary sector that consists of numerous clubs and federations. The German Sports Confederation (Deutscher Sportbund, DSB) is the umbrella organisation of approximately 87,000 voluntary associations at grass roots level, comprising a membership of 27 million people – 39 per cent of them female (DSB 2001a: 98). The DSB was founded in 1950, albeit when there was still a strong mistrust of organised interests. It claims to represent sport in general, that is, it encompasses elite sport and sport for all. All members are independent as far as their organisation, finance and activities are concerned and the DSB has no right of interference in these matters. Its aim is to coordinate all necessary joint measures for the promotion of sport and physical recreation, and to represent the mutual interests of its member organisations at all governmental levels and the general public. The

National Olympic Committee (NOC) for Germany is an independent and autonomous non-governmental sports organisation. It promotes the Olympic idea and carries out the tasks entrusted by the IOC to the NOCs.

The most central group of members of the DSB are organisations that provide a legal frame, material and human resources to participate in sport (National Governing Bodies of Sport (NGBs), Sports Confederations, gymnastics and sports clubs; see Figure 4.1). These are:

- 57 National Governing Bodies for single sports, as for example the German Football Federation, Federal Federation of German Weightlifters and German Track and Field Federation. The National Governing Bodies represent and organise the activities of their respective sports and have subdivisions at the level of the sixteen constituent states (Länder), at regional, and at district level.
- Sixteen Sports Confederations of the constituent states (Landessportbünde) – the Sports Confederation of Nordrhein-Westfalen being the largest and the Sports Confederation of Mecklenburg-Vorpommern being the smallest. Each of these sixteen Confederations embraces all governing bodies of single sports and all gymnastics and sports clubs at Land level. They represent the interests of all gymnastics and sports clubs beyond the interests of individual disciplines and, therefore, serve different ends to those of the governing bodies of sport. Their activities in the area of mass sport are multifarious and they have become known as the driving force for the implementation of sport for all and, within this policy, the inclusion of women into sports.
- 87,000 gymnastics and sports clubs that provide material and social resources to participate in sports at the grassroot level. The majority of sports clubs are small in size: one-third includes less than 100 people and only 6 per cent of all clubs have a membership of more than 1,000 people. Surveys among sports clubs indicate that they offer a broad variety of physical activities and 240 different sports. However, most of the clubs offer one sport only, and only 10 per cent provide more than four sports (Heinemann and Schubert 1994).

Private (commercial) sector

Private sector sport is a more recent phenomenon of the late twentieth century and is characterised by a wide variety of commercial institutions. Research and marketing data suggest that this sector comprises a range of various forms of supply and programme content, including fitness centres, leisure centres (offering badminton, racket, squash, sauna and wellness classes), and institutions for dancing, martial arts and horseback riding.

In 2000, there were 6,500 fitness and sport centres and 4.6 million people registered according to the German Sport Centre Association (Deutscher Sport Studio Verband), corresponding to about 5.7 per cent of the population. The overall percentage of female membership is about 55 per cent (Kamberovic and Kretzschmar 2001; Veltins Sport Studie 2000; Schubert 1998; Zarotis 1999). Comprehensive data on the commercial fitness and sport market are not available; however, comparative data indicate that at present Germany depicts the greatest European fitness market when related to membership figures (Deloitte & Touche 2001: 8).

Female inclusion in German sport

Sport and physical activity, especially leisure sport, has become increasingly more important in the lives of German girls and women. This process is well reflected in the increasing inclusion of girls and women into the German sport system over the years, both mirrored in growing participation rates and in the variety and number of sports and physical activities they are actively involved in. Both developments are closely related to new body and youth ideals prevalent in the middle-class lifestyles of modern German society.

Participation of girls and women in sport and physical activities

General survey data

General survey data and membership statistics concerning female sport participation allow the following conclusions to be drawn:

- the proportion of girls and women who regularly participate in sport has been constantly growing faster than that of boys and men in almost all age-groups;
- significant gender differences related to participation rates in sport exist in adolescence and post-adolescence, both inside and outside organised sport;
- following a lifespan perspective, the relative growth of women's participation in sport and physical activity is continuously increasing with age. According to survey data, 'male dominance' in sport participation is reversed for the elderly: 18.9 per cent of women asked report regular involvement in sport compared with only 16.3 per cent of the men; this is not true, though, for female inclusion in sports clubs;
- according to recent survey data, most female sport participation in Germany is realised in informal environments.

Recent research data confirm that most adults (men as well as women) participate in sport on an informal basis (see Breuer and Rittner 2002: 105; Hübner 2001: 79). Some 54 per cent of regularly active sportswomen asked in the 2001 population survey reported that they do their main sport in a non-organised form, i.e. outside of any kind of institution (compared to 57 per cent of men), about 28 per cent participate in sports clubs (compared to 31 per cent of men), and approximately 14 per cent of women reported they participate in sport in a commercial institution (compared to 9 per cent of men) (Breuer and Rittner 2002).[3] National survey data, which refer to sport participation rates in general, indicate that on average, only 25.9 per cent of men and 21.8 per cent of women asked regularly participate in sport/physical activity, i.e. at least once a week (DIW 2000). Compared with participation rates in the voluntary sport, the figures are not only much lower, but the gender gap appears to be much narrower.

Participation rates for adults show the general tendency of a relative decrease of sport involvement for both men and women with growing age (DIW 2000; DSB 2000, 2001b). Data show that gender differences concerning sport participation are biggest during adolescence and post-adolescence, both inside and outside organised sport, and are almost brought into line in the age group of 45–54 year olds (20.8 per cent men to 20.2 per cent women). In the group of 55–64 year-old individuals, the generally observed tendency of male dominance is reversed: 18.9 per cent of women asked, report regular involvement in sport compared with only 16.3 per cent of men (Breuer forthcoming, referring to DIW 2000). A longitudinal approach to the development of sport participation of the German population indicates that between 1985 and 1999 the proportion of women involved in sport on a regular basis has increased more than that of men. Furthermore, the relative growth in the group of women continuously increases as they become older: for the group of 16–24 years old, the figure is +2.6 per cent, while for women aged 45–54 years the figure is +60.4 per cent (ibid.).

Membership statistics

(A) INCLUSION OF GIRLS AND WOMEN IN GERMAN SPORTS CLUBS

Apart from national and regional survey data, the DSB membership statistics provide useful information on the inclusion of people into organised sport over the years. However, the data need to be interpreted with caution, because double/multiple and passive memberships are not taken into consideration, and thus the figures may be exaggerated (see Reents 1993; Breuer 2000).

Inclusion into sports clubs has always been characterised by social stratification. Sports clubs have always been more attractive for young people than for elderly people, for boys and young men than for girls and women, and for people from the middle and upper classes than for people of the lower classes. This typical feature of the traditional sports club has been changing constantly over the past five decades. Growing numbers of adults and senior citizens as well as girls and women have entered sports clubs. The number of female members in the voluntary sector has increased continually during the past fifty years: whereas in 1950 only 10 per cent of the membership were girls and women, in 1970 this proportion was 26.8 per cent, increasing to 34.1 per cent in 1990, and to 39.1 per cent in 2001 (see DSB 1990, 1999, 2000, 2001a, 2001c). The profile of sports clubs in the 1950s was that of a male and youth-dominated field of competitive sports activities. The rise in number of clubs and membership, related to an active sport for all policy and changing life styles in Germany, has changed this profile to a less youth-, less male- and less competitive-oriented profile of sports clubs (Hartmann-Tews 1996).

However, there are marked differences in participation between the sexes. The gender gap is greatest amongst 15 to 18 years old adolescents: 63 per cent of male adolescents are a member of at least one sports club, but only 41.7 per cent of female adolescents are members (DSB 2001c). Furthermore, sport participation in the voluntary sphere decreases dramatically by about 20 percentage points on average for both sexes when reaching post-adolescence: only 40.9 per cent of the male and 23.4 per cent of the female population is engaged in a sport club after leaving school (DSB 2001c). The general decrease of membership afterwards is larger for men than for women. As a consequence, the gender gap is narrowing slightly. This picture changes again dramatically when looking at senior citizens (60 years and older): only 8.8 per cent of the female population of that age group is organised in a sport club, compared with 22.8 per cent of the male population (DSB 2001c).

Several studies indicate that social stratification significantly influences the patterns of sport and physical activities of children/adolescents. The lower the education level, the less is the inclusion into voluntary sports clubs (Berndt and Menze 1996: 389–90). Furthermore, an intersection of gender with social strata is obvious as the gender gap increases continuously with a decreasing level of education. Thus the impact of social stratification on the involvement in sport is higher with girls and women than with boys and men (Berndt and Menze 1996). Looking at the participation rates of ethnic groups and migrants, girls and women are far less involved in physical education and sports than boys and men. Kleindienst-Cachay (1998) highlights the triple negative effect on being non-native, a woman and of low social strata. At present, single programmes at regional level have been designed and implemented in order to have this doubly discriminated-against group of women integrated, not only into the sport system but into German society in general.

(B) WOMEN IN DECISION-MAKING POSITIONS IN THE VOLUNTARY SPORT SECTOR

The German sports system is far from being a 'gender neutral' domain. This is obvious when taking a close look at the situation of women in leadership and decision-making positions in the voluntary sport sector. While there has been a substantial increase in female membership (from 10 per cent in 1950 to 39 per cent in 2000), there is no equivalent inclusion of women into decision-making positions and coaching. On average only 20 per cent of honorary decision-making positions are held by women. The proportion of women is highest within the Executive Board and Standing Committees of the DSB (24 per cent), followed by the Executive Boards of the State Confederations (23 per cent) and gymnastics and sports clubs (21 per cent). It is lowest on the Executive Boards of the National Governing Bodies of Sports (10 per cent). Beside such general data, we have to take into account huge differences within each segment, for example within the NGBs or the State Confederations. Representation of women on the Executive Boards of the State Federations varies from 11 per cent (Hessen) to 40 per cent (Saxony-Anhalt). Representation of women on the Executive Boards of NGBs varies from 0 per cent for one-third of all NGBs (basketball, rowing, badminton, soccer) to 40 per cent (roller skating) (DSB 2001a).

This general feature of under-representation of women in leadership positions, i.e. a vertical stratification, is accompanied by data showing a horizontal segregation. Women are responsible in limited functional spaces. Women are in charge of positions concerning 'women' (100 per cent) and 'youth' (40 per cent), but none of them is responsible for 'finance/funding' and 'leisure sport' (Hartmann-Tews and Combrink 2001). A similar tendency holds true for the NGBs: if females are in decision-making positions they are responsible for women's issues (100 per cent), but no female board member is responsible for top level sport and competition (NOK 2001).

All data available on this issue clearly show a vertical and horizontal stratification, a feature that might be characterised as restricted inclusion: there has been a remarkable inclusion of women into gymnastics and sports clubs at grassroots level, as witnessed in increasing female membership, but their access to leadership positions is still restricted in number and to selected spheres of influence.

(C) INCLUSION OF GIRLS AND WOMEN IN THE PRIVATE SECTOR

The increase of fitness and health-related commercial enterprises is remarkable. Within ten years, the number of fitness and health centres associated with the DSSV rose from 4,100 (1990) to 6,500 (2000) and the number of members from 1.7 million to 4.6 million people, corresponding to about 5.7 per cent of the population (DSSV 2001). The overall percentage of female membership is higher than in voluntary sector traditional sports clubs and is estimated to be approximately 55 per cent (Kamberovic and Kretzschmar 2001; Veltins Sport Studie 2000; Schubert 1998; Zarotis 1999). With regard to the fitness and health centres, around 15 per cent are women-only centres, which are characterised by a higher proportion of fitness/aerobic courses on offer, while the area with training and weightlifting equipment is smaller in size than in mixed sex studios (Kamberovic and Kretzschmar 2001; Kamberovic and Schwarze 1998: 56).

The attraction of fitness centres especially for women, seems to be partly related to the great flexibility concerning time tables (which allows women with families to use them for physical acitivity), but also to the existence of offerings which more appropriately meet their needs and interests (see Schubert 1998; Brinckhoff and Sack 1996: 50).

With regard to young people, gender relations are reversed when compared with sports club membership: more girls and female adolescents (22 per cent of this group) are members or regular visitors of private institutions like horseback riding or dance schools (compared with only 15 per cent of the boys and male adolescents). However, great differences exist within the group of female youths according to social strata (indicator 'level of education'): girls/female adolescents with high educational levels (grammar school pupils) are at the highest level with 27 per cent of all female grammar school pupils participating, as opposed to only 21 per cent and 17 per cent of girls with middle or lower education respectively (see Berndt and Menze 1996: 366).

(D) FEMALE ATHLETES IN TOP-LEVEL SPORT

The constantly growing proportion of girls and women in sport and physical activities is reflected in elite sport as well. In the 1992 Olympics in Barcelona, there were 168 female athletes in the German team (29 per cent of the team): in the 1996 Games (Atlanta) the proportion had grown to 35 per cent (194 women top athletes), and in the 2000 Games (Sydney) 44 per cent (187 women athletes) (NOK 2001). Moreover, the success rate of female athletes in the area of elite sport is at least as high as that of their male colleagues. In Atlanta, 60 per cent of all German medals were won by female athletes, although they represented only 35 per cent of the German team; in Sydney their success rate was 37.5 per cent even though they were represented in a lesser number of events than their male colleagues.

Gendered sports and motives

While women and girls have entered many areas of sport which traditionally were 'male domains', such as soccer, boxing, bodybuilding and weightlifting, there are still differences between the sexes concerning their participation profiles. In describing typical 'female' and 'male' sports, there are two ways of looking at the data: the first is to refer to absolute figures of membership data; and the second is to refer to relative figures, to the proportion of female/male membership.

The top five sports preferred by girls and women are gymnastics (3.4 million female members), tennis (0.8 million), soccer (0.8 million), horseback riding (0.5 million) and track and field (0.4 million). The top five sports preferred by boys and men according to absolute figures are soccer

(5.4 million male members), gymnastics (1.4 million), tennis (1.2 million), shooting (1.2 million) and sport fishing (0.6 million) (DSB 2000).[3]

The preferred top five sports according to the highest female proportion are sport acrobatics (72 per cent), gymnastics (71 per cent), horseback riding (70 per cent), modern pentathlon (69 per cent) and dancing (64 per cent) (DSB 2000). These are sports and activities which include a certain affinity to an aesthetic-compositional component. The preferred top five sports according to the highest male proportion are chess (94 per cent), aerosports (93 per cent), sport fishing (92 per cent), soccer (87 per cent) and pool/billiards (87 per cent) (DSB 2000).

A slightly different picture is drawn when referring to survey data and preferred activities independent of club membership. Participation rates for women are highest in general physical exercise, running, swimming, walking/hiking and bicycle riding; participation rates for men are highest in soccer, running, bicycle riding, fitness and swimming (Breuer and Rittner 2002: 89). There is a surprisingly high degree of homogeneity between the sexes according to their preferred sports and physical activities. At the same time, soccer remains a male domain while physical exercise remains a female domain. However, two aspects seem to dominate for both sexes: first, a tendency to individualised sports, which can be engaged in informally and do not need an organisational framework; and second, physical activities with health and/or wellness orientation.

Motivation to participate in sport varies along age and gender. The central interest of adolescents (age 13–19 years) to take part in physical exercises seems to be 'fit for fun', because 'to have fun' and 'to keep oneself healthy and fit' are the most important motives for them (Baur and Burrmann 2000: 77). Nevertheless, gender differences prevail: girls and female adolescents report 'physical well-being', 'to shape one's figure' and 'to relax' as most important motives; boys and male adolescents, on the other hand, most frequently stress the importance on 'performance' ('to further ones performance', 'to test performance limits', 'to compare oneself with others'), 'thrill' and 'suspense' (Baur and Burrmann 2000: 77). Their domain is game sports (especially soccer) and they have affinity for sports including body contact and a competitive aspect (see Rittner *et al.* 2002; DSB 2000, 2001b, Berndt and Menze 1996: 369–411; Brinkhoff and Sack 1996: 120; Brinkhoff 1998: 131).

In adulthood, these gender-related motives are more or less prevalent: while 'performance' generally is of main importance for men, 'body shaping' and 'psychological experience' are dominant for women, motives closely related with the 'outer appearance' and 'body consciousness' (BAT 1994: 25; Institut für Demoskopie Allensbach 2001: 4; 1998: 37ff.; Zarotis 1999: 99, 107, 113). For adults another motive becomes important, namely a 'health-oriented' lifestyle. This orientation remains of essential importance until late in age for both sexes (Schubert 1998: 39; Denk and Pache 1996: 104).

Policies of public and voluntary institutions

Sport for All policy and the inclusion of women in the voluntary sector

Competition, performance and improvement are traditional values and orientations of the sports system in general, and of sports clubs in particular. One implication of this value system is a limited inclusion of people into gymnastics and sports clubs. Clubs used to be more attractive for young people than for elderly people and more attractive for boys and men than for girls and women. This is well reflected in the membership statistics of the DSB, which indicate for the 1950s a male proportion of membership of 90 per cent and a dominance of young people of approximately 70 per cent (Hartmann-Tews 1996: 103ff).

In spite of this tradition, the DSB adopted an active Sport for All policy right from the beginning in the mid-1950s and developed an enormous range of public campaigns to attract people who formerly had not (regularly) taken part in sport (adults, women, senior citizens) and convince them about the benefits of taking part in physical activities. A central driving force for this strategy can be identified in the fact that after the Second World War organised sport in Germany had to regain recognition and acceptance. Physical education and sport had been instrumentalised to serve Hitler's regime and could no longer be the frame of reference. Thus, the foundation of the DSB was celebrated as a new beginning with new organisational structures, which became a breeding ground for the development of Sport for All initiatives. The challenge of sport policies was to establish leisure sport activities and physical recreation right beside the traditional structures of performance and elite sport (Hartmann-Tews 1996).

To foster this intended move from an exclusive to an inclusive policy strategy, the DSB implemented new structures and started massive campaigns to attract more people to participate in sports and to join clubs. The implementation of Sport for All has been a success story for the voluntary sector, and the inclusion of women is a central part of this development. A central pillar of this success was the establishment of a Women's Committee within the DSB right from the outset in 1951. The Chair was represented on the Executive Board of the DSB including voting rights. The Women's Committee held regular general meetings once a year, initiated courses for instructors on women's sport, including methodological aspects and biological/psychological bases. Hence, there was an awareness of 'women's sport' and the necessity to support the development of inclusion of girls and women, but resistance and restrictions to women's participation were manifold. As an example, girls and women were discouraged from playing soccer, which was still deemed unfeminine as late as 1955. In the 1950s and 1960s, the German Football Association strictly implemented its decision that clubs were not allowed to let women's teams use the soccer pitches. It was not until the 1970s that the Association reversed this decision and began to accept women's soccer, which up to today is far less financially supported than men's soccer, despite the female team winning the European championships five times and competing in the World Championships final in 1995.

In the late 1960s, there was a sense of a new era about to dawn in German society and in the sport system. The political order of society, traditional values and the gender order were put to question and the voluntary sector of sport adopted a more explicit policy of supporting gender equality. In 1970 the DSB established various departments run by volunteers and assisted by paid staff. 'Women's Sport' was one out of seven departments and the head of this department is Vice-President by statute. In addition a resolution was passed that all member federations should establish committees of women's sport and foster the inclusion of women in leadership positions. The DSB department as well as standing committees on women's sport within the federations became the nucleus of a variety of action and participation programmes for girls and women, of information leaflets and courses for female volunteers, of co-operation with ministries, scientists and politicians to foster knowledge on barriers of women's participation in sports.

Twenty years later, the DSB took stock of its policy and had to realise that besides a considerable increase in female membership (from 2.8 million in 1970 to 8.7 million in 1990), the female proportion in leadership positions lagged far behind their proportion in membership. In 1990 the DSB department 'Women's Sport' was renamed 'Women in Sport' in order to more adequately reflect the tasks of the department and avoid traditional stereotyping of women's and men's sports respectively female/male physical activities. In the same year, the DSB passed a resolution of women's promotion including the aim that the proportion of women in the Executive Board and Central Committees of the DSB should rise to at least 25 per cent within the next five years. Five years later it passed a resolution that the proportion of women on all committees should reflect their proportion in membership (DSB 2001a).

The list of resolutions, actions, initiatives and programmes is impressive, but confronting these with the most recent data on female representation in leadership positions, it becomes obvious that 'talking action' was not followed by 'taking action'. The under-representation of women in leadership positions especially of NGBs and the Olympic sports led the German NOC to launch a 'Plan for Action for the Promotion of Women in Sport' in 1996. This action plan is closely related to the principles and final objectives of the 105th meeting of the IOC and the Declaration of Brighton in 1996, in which the NOCs of the associated countries were urgently requested to elevate the proportion of women in the decision-making positions of the sport up to 20 per cent by 2005. The German NOC wants to make a recognisable contribution towards this objective, 'without committing rigid quotas themselves' (NOK 2001). It adopted a guideline for women's deputizing which goes even further than the IOC: women shall be represented at least according to their membership proportion in the Executive Boards of the DSB and its member organisations (BMI 1999: 63).

A variety of measures are being taken to make this resolution a success: (a) member organisations have to report the present status of the representation of women in decision-making positions annually to the NOC; (b) women are to be preferably chosen as lecturers and/or moderators in meetings, symposia and other activities; (c) efforts are to be made to increase the number of female staff in decision-making positions in elite sports; (d) in developmental aid service, more women examiners will be sent by the German NOC; (e) publications by, and about, women will be promoted by the NOC and its member organisations; and (f) specific projects for the promotion of women will be initiated (NOK 2001).

Public policy in favour of women and gender studies in sport

The situation of girls and women in sport is a topic and subject of a variety of social actors in politics, science and sports organisations. Over the last decade the interplay of forces led to a growing awareness of gender inequalities in sport. The creation of new positions and the election of new representatives foster the intention and realisation of gender equity. Some of these changes are worth highlighting.

In the mid-1980s, the Minister of Science and Research in Nordrhein-Westfalen (based on a strong social democratic tradition) started a programme to implement professorships for women's studies at universities and colleges of higher education and to finance research on women's issues. Within ten years, 35 professorships were established covering sociology, pedagogy, history, arts, languages, urban development and, almost last but not least, a professorship in women's research in sports science in 1996 at the German Sports University in Cologne. At that time very few researchers took interest in women's studies in sport and the education of physical education teachers, and sports scientists generally neglected the role of gender and the effects of a social gender order.

The establishment of a professorship in gender studies at the German Sports University was intended to institutionalise research and teaching in this field of study and to give it a prominent status in the range of sport science and physical education.[4] The effect was twofold: on the one hand, beside introducing students to gender studies and raising their levels of awareness about gender inequalities, research was intensified that helps to shed light on the processes and mechanisms that reproduce gender inequality; on the other hand the establishment of an academic position in women's and gender studies in sport had a radiating effect on the acceptance of the topic and implementation of gender equity.

Embedded in a favourite political climate, networks became stronger, inter-sectional cooperations became more official, and politics and the voluntary sector seem to realise the importance of gender equity programmes in sports. The Federal Institute of Sport Science (a subsidiary institution of the Federal Ministry of the Interior, dedicated to support elite sport and research) started a series of symposia in cooperation with the NRW Ministry of Culture and Sport and the DSB on the situation and role of female athletes in elite sport. The same NRW Ministry supported a five-year-programme to give 'Girls and Women in Sport a better chance to participate' and initiated symposia, workshops and research in a variety of fields.

Evaluation

Evaluating the main problems and achievements of the inclusion of women into sport in Germany, it becomes clear that a strong gender order persists underneath a surface of enlightened decision making (male) actors. While women's participation in physical activities and sport has increased over recent decades, their involvement in decision-making positions is far behind this representation and media coverage of women's sport and competitions has remained marginal. There is an encouraging political climate in favour of gender equality but the legal framework is weak and gender main-streaming policies have still to be developed and implemented. Increasing participation of girls and women in traditionally male sports like boxing and rugby is transforming the gendered images of individual sports and challenging the traditional gender order. At the same time, commercialisa-tion of high-performance sport is reinforcing gendered stereotypes especially via marketing strategies.

All the bits and pieces of the analyses reveal that the gender order is borne by social actors who produce social structures that frame the action of other social actors. Doing gender is a stabilising factor and difficult not to do. Changing the traditional gender order needs social structures that provide a binding framework of gender mainstreaming that systematically integrates gender equality into all organisations, policies and cultures.

Notes

1   The term gymnastics may be misleading for some readers as it is a translation of *Turnen*.
     The Deutsche Turner Bund organises and comprises physical activities that include
     gymnastics in its proper sense but also a variety of other physical activities on a leisure
     sport basis.
2   The two nations were reunited as the Federal Republic of Germany in 1990. Data and
     analysis of inclusion of girls and women into sport will focus on the development in West
     Germany until 1990 and in the united FRG from 1990 onwards.
3   The gender-sensible analysis of the survey data is unpublished material. The results are
     part of a 2001 representative telephone inquiry on the sport-related behaviour of the
     population in Nordrhein-Westfalen, carried out in two model communities (the city of
     Essen and the rural area Rhein-Sieg-Kreis) with a sample of n=3,023 and n=5,773
     respectively.

4   The German Sports University is the central academic institution in the field of sports science, with about 6.500 undergraduate and graduate students: www.dshs-koeln.de/geschlechterforschung.

Bibliography

BAT Freizeit-Forschungsinstitut (1994) *Sport – Aktivitäten, Interessen und Motive*, Repräsentativbefragung in der Bundesrepublik Deutschland, Hamburg: BAT Freizeit-For-schungsinstitut.

Baur, J. and Burrmann, U. (2000) *Unerforschtes Land: Jugendsport in ländlichen Regionen*, Aachen: Meyer & Meyer.

Berndt, I. and Menze, A. (1996) 'Distanz und Nähe – Mädchen treiben ihren eigenen Sport', in Ministerium für Stadtentwicklung, Kultur und Sport des Landes NRW (ed.), *Kindheit, Jugend und Sport in Nordrhein-Westfalen. Sport in Nordrhein-Westfalen*, Düsseldorf: MSKS NRW.

BMI (Bundesministerium des Inneren) (ed.) (1999) *Neunter Sportbericht der Bundesregierung*, Bonn: BMI.

Breuer, C. (2000) *Zur Aussagekraft der Mitgliedsstatistiken der Landessportbünde für die Sportplanung*, http://www.dshs-koeln.de/soziol/statistik.pdf (12 October 2000).

Breuer, C. (forthcoming) 'Sozialer Wandel und Sportengagement im Lebenslauf', in H. Allmer (ed.), *Sport und Bewegung im Lebenslauf*, St. Augustin: Brennpunkte der Sportwissenschaft.

Breuer, C. and Rittner, V. with Herb, F. and Luetkens, A. (2002) *Berichterstattung und Wissensmanagement im Sportsystem*, Köln: Sport & Buch Strauss.

Brinkhoff, K.-P. (1998) *Sport und Sozialisation im Jugendalter*, Weinheim und München: Juventa.

Brinkhoff, K.-P. and Sack, H.-G. (1996) 'Überblick über das Sportengagement von Kindern und Jugendlichen in der Freizeit', in Ministerium für Stadtentwicklung, Kultur und Sport des Landes NRW (ed.), *Kindheit, Jugend und Sport in Nordrhein-Westfalen. Sport in Nordrhein-Westfalen*, Düsseldorf: MSKS NRW.

Deloitte & Touche GmbH (2001) *Der Deutsche Fitness & Wellness Markt*, Düsseldorf: Deloitte & Touche GmbH.

Denk, H. and Pache, D. (1996) *Bewegung, Spiel und Sport im Alter – Band 1: Bedürfnissituation Älterer*, Bundesinstitut für Sportwissenschaft, Köln: Sport & Buch Strauss.

DIW Berlin (2000) *SOEP 1984–1999 und Cross National Equivalent Files. Projektgruppe Sozio-oekonomisches Panel (SOEP)*, Berlin: DIW (Deutsches Institut für Wirtschaftsforschung).

DSB (Deutscher Sportbund) (1990) *Deutscher Sportbund 1986 – 1990. Bericht des Präsidiums*, Frankfurt am Main: Limpert.

—— (1999) *Jahrbuch des Sports 1999*, Frankfurt am Main: Limpert.

—— (2000) *Bestandserhebungen 2000*, Frankfurt am Main: Limpert.

—— (2001a) *Mitmachen. Mitdenken. Mitlenken. 50 Jahre Frauen im Deutschen Sportbund*, Frankfurt am Main: Colour Connection GmbH.

—— (2001b) *DSB Presse*, no. 39 (25 September 2001).

—— (2001c) *Bestandserhebungen*, http://www.dsb.de (21 January 2002).

DSSV (Deutscher Sport-Studio Verband e.V) (2001) *Eckdaten der deutschen Fitness-Wirtschaft*, http://www.dssv.de/welcome_eckdaten.html (28 November 2001).

Hartmann-Tews, I. (1996) *Sport für alle!? Strukturwandel europäischer Sportsysteme im Vergleich*, Schorndorf: Hofmann.

Hartmann-Tews, I. and Combrink, C. (2001) 'Ehrenamt im Wandel. Analyse der Geschlechterverhältnisse in den nordrhein-westfälischen Sportfachverbänden und ihren

Sportjugenden', Research Application, Köln: German Sport University (unpublished manuscript).

Hartmann-Tews, I. and Petry, K. (1994) 'Individualisation and changing modes of consuming in sport: Some gender aspects', in A. Tomlinson and L. Lawrence (eds), *Gender, leisure and cultural forms*, Brighton: CSRC.

Heinemann, K. and Schubert, M. (1994) *Der Sportverein: Ergebnisse einer repräsentativen Untersuchung*, Schorndorf: Hofmann.

Hübner, H. (2001) *Sporttreiben in Mannheim – Ergebnisse der empirischen Studie zum Sportverhalten*, Münster: Lit.

Institut für Demoskopie Allensbach (2001) *Fit durch Sport*, Allensbacher Berichte 2001, no. 8.

Kamberovic, R. and Kretzschmar, Y. (2001) *Eckdaten 2000 der Fitness- und Racket-Anlagen in Deutschland*, Hamburg: Deutscher Sportstudio Verband e.V.

Kamberovic, R. and Schwarze, B. (1998) *Deutsche Fitness Wirtschaft. Daten – Fakten – Zahlen – Prognosen*, Hamburg: Deutscher Sportstudio Verband GmbH.

Kleindienst-Cachay, C. (1998) 'Breitensport im Sportverein – Erwartungen und Wünsche ausländischer Frauen und Frauen unterer sozialer Schichten', in Ministerium für Stadtentwicklung, Kultur und Sport (ed.), *Zwischen Utopie und Wirklichkeit: Breitensport aus Frauensicht. Eine Dokumentation. Materialien zum Sport in Nordrhein-Westfahlen 47*, Wuppertal: MSKS NRW.

NOK (2001) *NOK Aktionsplan zur Förderung von Frauen im Sport* (04.11.2000), http://www.nok.de (21 January 2002).

Pfister, G. (2001) 'Germany', in K. Christensen, A. Guttmann and G. Pfister (eds), *International Encyclopedia of Women and Sports*, New York: Macmillan References.

—— (2002) 'Sport for women', in R. Naul and K. Hardman, *Sport and Physical Education in Germany*, London: Routledge.

Reents, H. (1993) 'Zahlen lügen nicht! Zur Problematik der Mitgliederbestandserhebung des DSB und der Landesverbände', *Olympische Jugend* 38, 10: 12–14.

Rittner, V., Breuer, C. and Luetkens, A. (2002) 'Die Verantwortung des Staates für den Sport. Kommunalpolitik als Schlüsselproblem der Sportentwicklung', in Club of Cologne (ed.), *Sonderausgabe zur 2. Konferenz des Club of Cologne, Thema Jugendsport* (25.09.2001 Dorint Hotel Köln), Köln/Bielefeld: Club of Cologne.

Schubert, M. (1998) *Zur Nachfragestruktur in kommerziellen Fitness-Anlagen. Ergebnisse einer empirischen Untersuchung*, Hamburg: DSSV e.V.

Veltins Sport Studie (2000) *VELTINS Sport Studie 2000* (in Kooperation mit DSB), Meschede: C. & A. Veltins GmbH & Co.

Zarotis, G.F. (1999) *Ziel Fitness-Club: Motive im Fitness-Sport*, Aachen: Meyer und Meyer.

5 Sports development and inclusion of women in France

Nicole Dechavanne and Ilse Hartmann-Tews

The formation of a sport system and female inclusion in the nineteenth and twentieth century

Stereotypes: the role of the doctors

A run by young shop-girls, organised in Paris in 1903, amused the news-papers. 2,500 'young messenger-girls or older female runners' ran from the Tuileries Gardens to Nanterre. They could hardly make their way through the middle of the many spectators who were 'curiously' interested by this event. Jeanne Cheminel, a finery maker, won the competition, accomplishing the 12 kilometres in 1 hour and 10 minutes. This poorly-prepared run had a rather disastrous effect on the development of female sport. The organisers of the event did not understand that the athletes' lack of preparation and the spectators' taste for sensationalism and promiscuity would be harmful to women (Eyquem 1944: 25). At the beginning of the century it was forbidden for women to participate in sport. It was not only considered dangerous, because women were not seen to have the physical potential to face competition in sport, but it also constituted an element of immorality. Exhibitionism was deemed not appropriate for women, for whom it was essential to remain modest: 'We oppose the introduction of physical education of girls because it is based on indecent and deliquescent attitudes…Let us take care not to make our daughters comedians' (Dehoux 1947: 72).

However, some doctors advised women to practice gymnastics. Future mothers were encouraged out of their passivity because strength and a good state of health were necessary qualities for good motherhood: 'Women are not made for fighting but for procreating' (Boigey 1922: 220). In fact, everybody believed that women's primary function was procreation and that physical education would be the best way to give them a solid constitution for a more fertile life and a healthier maternity (Tissié 1919: 3). Female physical activity was especially restricted by their clothing and tight corsets. The fight against these obstacles started at the beginning of the twentieth century, but the small freedoms of movement that were then granted to young women were to be used in their primary mission. Participation in sport was harmful to images of femininity. Motherhood was seen as being women's predominant function but it was also expected that they have grace and charm (Démeney 1920). Respective discourses which were both emancipatory and conservative lasted until the Second World War. They were emancipatory because they encouraged girls to be more active but, at the same time, they were conservative because they reinforced the traditional social construction of femininity and gender-adequate movement and body culture.

The first organisations

Despite this discouraging atmosphere for female sport, it nevertheless took place through the efforts of some pioneers. At the end of the nineteenth century we can see the first structures of a sport system, mainly constituted by state supported voluntary clubs. Predominantly led by patriotic zeal, several gymnastic clubs (*sociétés de gymnastique*) spread from the east of France all over the country. The names of these clubs indicate their patriotic roots: 'La Française', 'La Patriote' or 'La Vailante'. They aimed to foster discipline, manliness and strength. In 1873 the first national federation of these clubs was founded, the French Federation of Gymnastics (Union des Sociétés Françaises de Gymnastique, USFG).

At the same time, and in contrast to these politically motivated and military oriented '*sociétés de gymnastique*', the English sport model of sports spread over the country, supported by Pierre de Coubertin who played a most important role in shaping the French sport system. He fostered the introduction of athletics and ideas about educating young males to become gentlemen, characterised by moral strength, discipline and striving through athletic competition. The spread of English sports was accompanied by an intensive process of institutionalisation and finally led to the establishment of the Federation of Athletics (Union des Sociétés Françaises des Sports Athlétiques, USFSA) in 1887.

Pierre de Coubertin, president of the International Olympic Committee, contended that the Olympics would never admit women to competition, and many medical doctors still had reservations about any sort of women's sport. Alongside this ideology, sports organisations and clubs were adamant in their refusal to accept women. These included the powerful French Federation of Athletics and the French Federation of Gymnastics. As a result, women founded their own organisations. In 1899, the teachers' club seated at the Voltaire gymnasium in Paris created a female section. In this same year a club emerged in Lyon called 'Wild Roses', followed by the foundation of clubs offering women a specialised 'female gymnastics' inspired by the works of Demeney and Irène Popart (Arnaud 1996: 154). In 1912 these different groups founded the French Association of Female Gymnastics (Union Française de Gymnastique Féminine, UFGF).

Some women had already attracted attention through their success in sport, particularly in parachuting, mountaineering and cycling (Laget and Mazot 1982). In 1912 the first female multi-sports club, 'Fémina Sport', came into being in Paris. Its big rival, 'Académia Sport', followed in 1916. These clubs joined together and founded the French Federation of Female Sport Associations (Fédération des Sociétés Féminines Sportives de France, FSFSF) in 1917, directed by Alice Milliat, a brilliant oarswoman. This association supported the participation of female athletics in the Olympic Games and organised French championships for women in many disciplines, such as cross-country racing, athletics, football, rowing, swimming and hockey. It also published a review called *Sport Women*.

Female sport developed on the fringes of male sport because the powerful Federation of Athletics (USFSA) was not inclined to pay attention to, or even accept, women's participation in sport. Female sections, however, were established within some clubs of the Federation of Athletics. Pierre de Coubertin proposed that these female sections be moved to the Federation of Female Gymnastics instead of joining the French Federation of Female Sport Associations, which favoured women's participation in the Olympic Games. Women continued to organise themselves and to pursue their interest in sport, despite strong resistance, and women's sport organisations grew rapidly from two clubs in 1916 to seventy in 1921 (Terret 2001: 434).

Under Alice Milliat's initiative the 'International Female Sport Federation' was created in 1921, comprising of Great Britain, Italy, Spain, the USA and Czechoslovakia. Its main objective was to organise the female Olympic Games that eventually took place in Paris (1922), in Sweden (1926), in Prague (1930) and in London (1934). These games were a spectacular success, so much so that the IOC, under the direction of Pierre de Coubertin, had to take note. Consequently, some athletics competitions were opened to women at the Olympic Games of Amsterdam in 1928 (100m, 800m, high jump, discus, 4x100m). With the struggles of the International Female Sport Federation partly won, it was disbanded in 1936.

It appears significant to note that, while France is indeed the country of Pierre de Coubertin who was opposed to female's sport for so long, it is also the country of Alice Milliat who set up structures making it possible to stand up to the IOC and to promote female sport at national and international levels (Leclercq 1999).

Features and policies of the French sports system

The organisation of sport is predominantly based on state supported and directed clubs, federations and confederations. Since 1940 the sport system has gradually become the focus for state intervention. This is well documented through various decrees and laws, especially in 1975 (Loi Mazaud), 1984 (Loi Avice) and 1992. The Ministry of Youth and Sport (Ministère de la Jeunesse et des Sports) is responsible for the development and support of

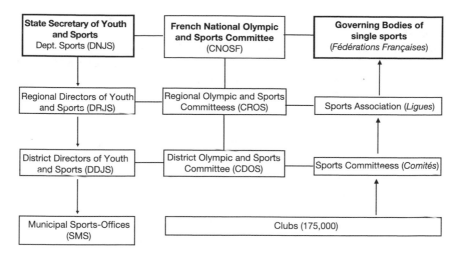

Figure 5.1 Structure of the sport system in France

sport and physical education in general. This responsibility encompasses the supervision and control of all sports organisations, including the appointment of Technical Directors of the National Governing Bodies (NGB) of sport by the Ministry of Youth and Sport. The structural features of the French sport system reflect the administrative structure of the state.

The National Olympic and Sport committee (Comité National Olympique et Sportif Français, CNOSF) is the umbrella organisation for approximately 175,000 associations at grass-roots level, comprising about 14 million people. This macro-organisation was established in 1972 as a merger of the National Olympic Committee (Comité National Olympique) and the National Sports Committee (Comité National du Sport) The CNOSF represents four different groups:

- National Governing bodies of Olympic Sports (Fédérations Sportives Olympiques)
- Federations/National Governing Bodies of non-olympic sports (Fédérations Sportives Non-Olympiques)
- Federations/National Governing Bodies of multi-sports-associations that organise a variety of physical activities related to special groups, such as workers, people with disabilities etc. (Fédérations Multisports et Affinitaires)
- Federations/National Governing Bodies of sport at schools, colleges and universities (Fédérations Scolaires et Universitaires)

The voluntary sector's vertical structure of representation corresponds with the administrative structures of the state. All clubs at grass-roots level are represented at departmental level in committees, at regional level in associations and at national level in federations. In addition to the representational structures of clubs–committees–associations–federations, the CNOSF has established administrative units to represent the interests of the voluntary sector in cooperation with state administration at all levels. These are the Olympic and Sports Committees at regional level (CROS) and at departmental level (CDOS).

In France, the structure of the sport systems strongly reflects support for the Olympic ideal. The central idea of Pierre de Coubertin – to strive for excellence in sport – remains unanimously the central reference point for sports clubs. They more or less follow the so-called '*modèle Coubertinien*', characterised by a strong orientation towards competition, performance and excellence. Thus they are exclusive in their recruitment of members by attracting primarily young people and males (Leblanc 1992: 94ff). Within this context most of the federations implemented strategies of social closure that excluded all sorts of leisure sport activities or physical recreation (Hartmann-Tews 1996: 200ff).

In the 1960s and 1970s French policy was characterised by General de Gaulle's project to restore the nation's greatness. As a part of this project, de Gaulle wanted to improve the international image of French sport. He supported the voluntary sport sector in their pursuit of excellence and made physical education in schools a significant part of the ideal of 'excellence for all'. Two central strategies were used to put these ideas into effect: (1) the establishment of clubs and federations at all levels of the education system in order to include as many young people as possible and provide an efficient way to search for new talent; and (2) strong financial support for federations of Olympic sports.

Changes in governments and social conditions led to new policies in the 1980s, with the expectation that sports federations should promote general welfare and foster the European Charter of Sport for All. Madame Avice – who entered the Ministry for Youth and Sport in Mitterand's government in 1983 – was the first politican to support the inclusion of women in sport. The inclusive policy was quite new for the federations that had previously been solely striving for excellence and supporting the model of Coubertin. In effect, they were neither willing nor prepared for Sport for All activities, or for the inclusion of the lesser talented and those who wanted to take part in physical activities for reasons other than high-level competition, such as for reasons of health, fitness and fun. They acted hesitantly, and only a few federations developed a policy to promote sport for all and for the inclusion of women. The Multi-Sports Federation were the first to take up the idea of Sport for All and became a trailblazer of this movement.

Given the state agencies' growing interest in fostering Sport for All, they developed two strategies. First, the Ministry increased public funding to support the establishment of public sport centres, providing a variety of leisure sports which in turn attracted more and more people to take part in physical activities. Second, it used its huge state-intervention potential and made some of its financial support of the federations dependent on their success in developing inclusive strategies. Under this policy, voluntary sport sector federations were manoeuvred into a difficult position and sooner or later had to give up their traditional stance of exclusiveness and striving only for excellence. Nowadays, they are part of the cultural programme of many regions and have become a central provider of sport for all programmes.

Participation in sport

Physical education at school

Gender stereotypes occur very early and physical education in schools plays a vital role in the social construction of gender. The curricula of physical education and sport in schools and colleges encourage male involvement as they are dominated by competitive and team sports (Hartmann-Tews 1996: 208).

Boys from 11 to 16 years old are the most enthusiastic about participating in sports, and they prefer football and team sports. Girls from 17 to 19 years are the most uninvolved in physical education and sport in school, and prefer swimming and dancing. Boys have better results in PE than girls. Regardless of the examination methods, girls get marks that are, on average, one point lower than those of boys.

Co-education is becoming prescribed for PE lessons, although this has happened a little later compared to other subjects. This complicates the teaching, as girls are more likely to play contact sports such as rugby than boys are likely to practise expressive sports. At the same time PE teachers are more used to teaching team and competitive sports than they are teaching leisure and expressive physical activities.

It becomes obvious that girls' retreat from PE happens during adolescence, when sport at school constitutes a proof of virility for boys yet creates a paradoxical situation for girls. The challenge for girls is that, as athletes, they must constantly prove that they remain women in spite of being physically active.

General survey data

Due to the diversity of methods and survey data, it is difficult to present reliable figures and especially to make comparisons. Only two sources of survey data, from the early 1970s and late 1980s, can be compared directly as they use the same questionnaire. One source are surveys from the Ministry of Culture that allow us to compare participation data from 1973 and 1981. The other are surveys from CESP (Centre d'Études des Supports Publicitaires) that allow comparisons between data from 1984 and 1990 (Faure 1984; *La lettre de l'économie du sport* 1990: 4).

Data from the 1970s indicate that participation rates in France increased about 13 per cent from 1973 (34 per cent) to 1981 (46 per cent). The inclusion of a broader range of people was mainly due to an impressive increase in the number of people participating in gymnastics, '*éducation physique*' and jogging, whereas individual sports continuously attracted less people (Faure 1984; Thomas 1983).

As our historical background would suggest, women are less likely to participate in physical exercises and sport, and the data indicate an overall difference of 13 per cent between male and female participation. However, there are no major differences between men and women with respect to the increase in participation rates. While participation of males increased from 41 per cent (1973) to 52 per cent (1981), participation of females increased from 28.0 per cent (1973) to 40 per cent (1981). A closer look at the kinds of exercises and sport that are practised reveals that women are far more likely to participate in gymnastics, '*éducation physique*', fitness exercises and jogging than in team sports and martial arts. This tendency also holds true for men but is less dramatic compared with the women (Ministère de la Jeunesse et des Sports 2001).

While the 1970s are characterised by an overall increase in participation by people of both genders, data from the 1980s indicate a continued increase in women's participation while men's participation rates stagnated. Comparisons made between the two surveys from CESP (Centre d'Études des supports publicitaires) show that women's participation increased from 36 per cent (1984) to 40 per cent (1990) while men's remained at 54 per cent (La lettre de l'économie du sport 1990: 4).

This data, as well as other surveys, indicate that involvement in sport is highly stratified: participation in physical activities and sport is for the young, males and the middle/upper classes. More recent data support these trends but also reveal interesting variations concerning gender and age. The 1994 national survey on sport and health (Eval 1996) confirms the general gender-gap in participation rates but indicates that this gap narrows with age (Table 5.1).

In addition, the data support the notion of gendered modes of participation. After leaving school, young women abandon clubs and turn to less organised sports participation. Their motivations for doing physical activi-

Table 5.1: Physical activity in France by sex, age and regular physical activity

	Men		Women	
Age groups	Physically active (%)	Regularly physically active (%)	Physically active (%)	Regularly physically active (%)
15–24 years	63.2	48.0	49.2	41.4
25–39 years	61.9	47.7	53.4	41.9
40–59 years	50.3	36.6	43.2	34.4
60–74 years	21.9	13.5	22.4	18.7

Source: Eval (1996)

ties are predominantly aesthetic concerns, whereas males are more motivated by competition and adventure. Health and pleasure are motivations that are shared equally by both sexes.

Membership in clubs and federations

Besides the data from national surveys, membership numbers for clubs and federations are published annually by the Ministry of Youth and Sports. These figures are of limited reliability as some federations only register members who have a license, i.e. those who are entitled to participate in competitions. Other federations are more generous with their calculations because part of the financial support from the Ministry is related to the size of their membership. The increased membership in voluntary sector clubs and federations over the last years has been impressive. In 1970 members numbered approximately 5,5 million, of which 24 per cent were women. By 2000 memberships had increased to 14 million with females comprising approximately 29 per cent (Ministère de la Jeunesse et des Sports).

The percentage of women varies amongst the different types of clubs and federations. It is highest in *gymnastique volontaire* (93 per cent), horse riding (60 per cent) and gymnastics (60 per cent). Multisport federations, swimming and volleyball have a gender ratio of 50/50. On the other hand there are single sport federations like football, rugby, boxing and cycling in which female memberships are no more than 10 per cent.

High-level sport

In 1998 females represented 30 per cent of the national lists of high level athletes. The proportion of female athletes in the French Olympic delegation increased from 13.5 per cent in Montreal 1976 to 20.6 per cent in Los Angeles 1984, 30 per cent in Barcelona 1992 and 38 per cent in Sydney 2000. In Atlanta, more female than male athletes were medal-holders (17 per cent of the female team and 11 per cent of the male team). In Sydney, 9.3 per cent of the female delegation were medal-holders compared to 12.2 per cent of the male delegation.

As far as reimbursement of expenses, lodging and team-building conditions and medical follow-up are concerned, it seems that women's teams do not receive the same attention and support as the men's. Currently, there are debates about the awarding of different prizes and bonuses for men and women in competitions. It is time that each federation took a close look at these inequalities in treatment. The disrespect shown to female elite sportswomen has significant consequences for the career of each athlete. Female athletes are less present in the media, they have more difficulties in negotiating contracts, have less support from sponsors and they are forced to stop their sport careers earlier than males (Carpetier 2001).

It is particularly interesting to note the large differences between the sexes in their ways of being physically active and their reasons. Alternative forms of physical practice seem to be specifically female, which has the capacity to transform sport. The effects of 'competition' are mitigated by other values, such as communication, pleasure and health. This can be seen in women's pursuit of daily activities as well as their input in high-level sports. Women's tennis and football, for example, reveal strategic qualities and team spirit which refreshes the sport spectacle. Through women's involvement, 'sport' diversifies, is extended to include participants of retirement age, moves from the clubs and away from being exclusively about competition. It develops a sociability that is less built on opposition and more on 'playing with rather than against', and thus raises the issue of how sport should be defined.

Access to responsibility

French women's representation in leadership positions in sport is worse than their representation in politics. This holds true for elected and technical officials in the sport federations, and for high-ranking administrative positions in the Ministry for Youth and Sport. Administrative positions in the Ministry for Youth and Sport remain largely occupied by men. There are 22 Regional Centres of Physical Education and Sport (CREPS) responsible for the education of PE teachers, research and top-level sport, and only 14 per cent (3) of their directors are women.

After the Sydney 2000 Olympic Games, new elections took place in the sport federations. Now there are four female presidents (5 per cent) including the governing bodies of horse riding, cross-country, sport for deaf people and 'physical training in the modern world', a federation based on sport for all. Three women also joined the Directors' Board of the National Olympic Committee, representing horse riding, cross-country and golf. Even if the CNOSF intended to be more ambitious, this is indeed slow progress, going from zero to three women members on the Executive Board, and from 1 per cent to 5 per cent of women presidents of governing bodies.

However, there is no change to the male domination of the Olympic and Sports Committees at regional and departmental levels (CROS, CDOS). There are no female presidents of the CROS, and only 6 per cent of the CDOS are women. The situation is the same for the National Technical Directors of the National Governing Bodies, who are responsible for all technical and operational aspects of the competitive sports and the top-level athletes. There is only one female NTD (Triathlon Federation) and only 15 per cent of technical officials are female. The list of judges and high-level referees includes 45 women out of a total of 549, which is 8 per cent. Thirty-one federations out of 56 do not have any women in these positions.

Changes to provide women with better access to positions of responsibility and leadership seem to have only just begun. Expectations are great and each individual breakthrough is appreciated as a victory. The main reasons for their exclusion are historical and social. Sport and the public sphere have been male domains, while family and the private sphere have been traditionally reserved for women. The end of the twentieth century witnessed an increased number of women in traditional male domains. Thus we see, for example, that during the local elections:

> a majority of the French want their mayor to be a woman, a majority thinks that management by women would improve the policy in almost all sectors of municipal intervention (environment, culture, budget, security) – except in transport and obviously in sport, last protected male hunting grounds.
>
> (*Le Monde* 10/1/2001)

Attitudes and behaviours are strongly determined by stereotypes of typical female/male activities, responsibilities, attitudes and competencies. Decision making is still seen to be a male competency and (even) women in most milieus share this opinion. Excluded from public life for so long, women often do not feel able to take responsibilities. They do not dare and may need to be reassured of their competence before entering and becoming committed to the field of competitive sport. Some women tell of having to first prove themselves before gaining confidence.

Towards the future: possible changes

Female involvement in physical activities and sport has significantly development over the last 20 years. With this stocktaking, two approaches can be suggested. One is to wait until the social relations change and expect a change of stereotypes to follow, the second is to give this process an accelerating push.

It seems that France has begun to move since 1998. Since her appointment as Minister for Youth and Sport, Mme. Buffet has installed a dynamic policy favouring women and sport. A female technical adviser was appointed in the cabinet and another woman is in charge, as Director of Sport, to initiate and co-ordinate actions carried out to promote women. National sessions were organised in May 1999. A network of regional female collaborators has been established, and several innovative decisions have been made (subsidies of sport, statute of high level sport, media prices, and so on). An important step forward seems to have been the extension of §8 of the Law on Sport:

> The approval [of a sports association] is in particular based on the existence of statutory regulations that guarantee the democratic functioning of the association, the transparency of its management and the equal access of women and men to its leading positions.
>
> (Loi Avice §8)

The French National Olympic and Sport Committee (CNOSF), following the orientations of the IOC, has created a Commission for Women and Sport which took an active part in the World Conference organised in Paris in 2000. It proposes to change its statute so that five positions on the board of directors are reserved to women. The CNOSF goes even further and is developing strategies for equal opportunities (CNOSF 2001).

At the same time it seems that women are also taking their own destinies firmly in hand. Several associations have been created and 'Femmes, Mixité, Sports', founded in 2000, is expected to co-ordinate these initiatives, to build a network for women and to keep watch on discrimination in areas related to sport. In this very favourable climate many actions have been started and are already modifying the perception of women's sport. However, the most difficult thing remaining is to convince the journalists to pay attention to women's sport and look at it differently. The success of female champions certainly has a positive effect.

Various policies are being debated or have recently been implemented. New ways of financing sport are already being designed to support initiatives favouring women's sport on the local, federal and national levels. These efforts, however, remain insufficient and must be expanded. Cases of discrimination should be revealed and denounced. It would be desirable to establish a systematic investigation to better understand the open and hidden discrimination practises. Gender equity in leadership positions and the implementation of more rigid measures (for example, quotas) are on the agenda. A particular focus concerns the technical support team. Different support systems for national teams have been proposed, replacing single coaches with a team who share responsibilities, allowing more opportunity for women to balance time for occupations, volunteer work and families.

It seems crucial to recruit women, to create networks from which women can be asked to become involved, to help them to take the first steps then to follow their progress and involvement. The organisation envisaged by the commission of the CNOSF is heading in this direction and the association 'Femmes, Mixité, Sport' also poses this mission for itself. Attracting women to their cause consists of showing them how personal fulfilling such commitments can be, in terms of friendships, progress, teamwork and the discovery of new endeavours to enrich their lives. Media portrayals of personal successes would help to entice other women. Showing happy, dynamic and balanced female sport directors, who are accepted in society and also appreciated in their families, should provide motivation for these vocations.

In general, all these actions have been initiated by groups of women. However, it is quite obvious to us that women's greater participation in decision-making positions and equality with men is a human rights claim for enhanced personal fulfilment, and the design of participatory democracy at all levels. Men who hold the majority of power must be persuaded to collaborate in this social change.

As a conclusion: the specificity of France

The history of women's access to sport is a history of conquest, like that of their right to vote and the recognition of gender equity. France, however, the country of humans rights, shows a certain lag in the progress of female representation compared to other European nations. The right to vote was granted to women only in 1944, and today we see that women's presence at the top of the sport hierarchy is still just beginning. Before Mme. Buffet, only two previous ministers were interested in the development of women's sport: Mme. Avice, who initiated a re-thinking of traditional values and set up new structures, and M. Bambuck, who unfortunately did not have time to continue the first initiatives taken.

It seems that, in France, a specific culture of relations between the sexes has developed. 'France is the culture of conversation, of seduction, the experience of co-education. France is able to negotiate a good relationship between difference and equality, which does not occur in other countries' (Ouzouf 1999: 20). Women are more attached to the concept of complementarity, of co-operation with the other sex, than they are to the firm insistence on equal right for women, which could too easily lead to the kind of labelling that is negatively associated with feminism.

This situation partly explains the persistence of the problems of co-education at school. When the body is concerned, efforts to respect equality and difference at the same time cause real headaches. It is a difficult task to resolve equality with difference. This may also partly explain the absence of women in leadership positions, because it is difficult for a woman who has grown up in France to enter into competition with the other sex. What is to be done? Wait until the competitor is convinced about female qualities and leaves his place! The association 'Femmes, Mixité, Sports' created in 2000 favours collaboration with men. In France it seems beyond anyone's imagination to create social places for only one sex, and the use of the term '*Mixité*' in the title is deliberate, providing space for a mixture of different cultures.

Within Europe, France is geographically and culturally located at the intersection of north and south. It holds the 'egalitarian' claims of the north and, at the same time, the southern attachment to specifically female roles. Today, France seems able to bring the north and the south of Europe a bit closer together. Its candidature for the organisation of the EWS (European Women Sport) was accepted and it now prepares to receive the European Conference on Women and Sport in 2004. Let us assume that we are then going to speak about men and the need for them to promote women in sport. French women have already instigated the foundation of an international association 'Woman, Sport, Culture, the Mediterranean Sea', created in 2000 and sited in Antibes. So, let us hope that this mediation role will be advantageous to international exchanges and that a model of collaboration between men and women will develop which holds new possibilities for expression for both sexes.

Bibliography

Arnaud, P. (1996) 'Le genre ou le sexe? Sport féminin et changement social', in P. Arnaud and Th. Terret (eds), *Histoire du sport féminin*, Paris and Montréal: Ed. L'harmattan tome.

Boigey, M. (1922) *Manuel scientifique d'éducation physique*, Paris: Ed. Masson.

Carpetier, C. (2001) Dossier 'Le sport de haut niveau', *Femix sports infos* 2001, 2, Femmes, Mixité;, Sport Paris.

CNOSF (2001) *Séminaire du CNOSF: Acces des femmes aux postes de décision*, Paris: CNSOF.

Davisse, A. and Louveau, C. (1998) *Sports, écoles, société: la différence des sexes*, Paris: Ed. L'harmattan.

Dehoux, L. (1947) 'Initiation à la gymnastique esthétique', *Revue des jeux scolaires et d'hygiène sociale*, April.

Démeny, G. (1920) *Education et harmonie du mouvement*, Paris: Ed. Alcan.

Eval, Y. (1996) 'Enquête "sport et santé"', *Actualité et dossier en santé*, March, 14.

Eyquem, M.T. (1944) *La femme et le sport*, Paris: Ed. J. Susse.

Faure, J.-M. (1984) 'Les pratiques sportives', in Institut Nationale de la Statistique et des Etudes Econnomique (INSEE) (ed.), *Données sociales*, Paris: INSEE.

Hartmann-Tews, I. (1996) *Sport für alle!? Strukturwandel europäischer Sportsysteme im Vergleich: Bundesrepublik Deutschland, Frankreich, Großbritannien*, Schorndorf: Karl Hofmann.

Hébert, G. (1919) *Muscles et beauté plastique féminine*, Paris: Editions Vuibert.

(1990) *La lettre de l'économie du sport 1990*, Paris: Editions sport.

Laget, S. and Mazot, J.P. (1982) *Le grand livre du sport féminin*, Belleville sur Saone: FMT éditions.

Leblanc, M. (1992) *Le club de l'an 2000*, Paris: INSEP.

Leclercq, A. (1999) *Historique de la participation des femmes aux jeux Olympiques modernes et aux grandes compétitions internationales*, Paris: CNOSF, Assises Départementales femmes et sports.

Ministère de la Jeunesse et des Sports (2001) *Stat.info 1*, Paris: Ministère de la Jeunesse et des Sports.

Ozouf, M. (1999) *Les mots des femmes, essai sur la singularité française*, Paris: Ed. Gallimard.

Terret, T. (2001) *France*, in K. Christensen, A. Guttmann and G. Pfister (eds), *International Encyclopedia of Women and Sports*, New York: Macmillan Reference.

Thomas, R. (1983) 'Milieu social relations et pratiques sportives', in R. Thomas (ed.), *La relation au sein des A.P.S.*, Paris: Vigot.

Tissié, P. (1919) *L'éducation physique et la race, lieu et maison?*, Paris: Flammarion.

6 Women and sport in Spain[1]

Núria Puig and Susanna Soler

Translated from Spanish by Richard Rees

Introduction

The organisational framework of sport in Spain

Sport in Spain, since the transition to democracy that began in November 1975, constitutes a complex network of organisations in which the public, voluntary and commercial sectors[2] are all involved. Figure 6.1 provides a synthesis of this organisational framework on the local, provincial, regional (i.e. autonomous) and state levels.

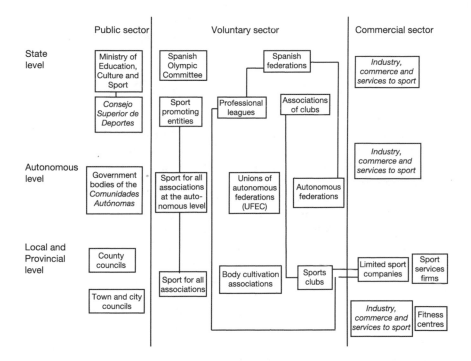

Figure 6.1 Structure of the sport system in Spain

Source: Puig *et al.*, forthcoming

Public organisations constitute a coherent network whose powers are established by law.[3] The town and city councils, in accordance with the 1978 Spanish Constitution, are responsible for making sport accessible to the entire population. The state organisations have responsibilities of a general nature (planning of sport facilities, research programmes, overall coordination and so on) and of international representation. Their regional/autonomous[4] counterparts are responsible for everything related to implementing policies within their jurisdiction. And both provide support for the programmes devised by the municipalities. The public sector as a whole occupies a position of hegemony in the sport system, as it does in other spheres of social life. This phenomenon may be explained in terms of the social-historical context of the country, which has been late to develop a civil society able to organise itself with the focus on meeting democratic, egalitarian objectives (Burriel and Puig 1999; Puig *et al.* forthcoming).

Since 1979, the year in which the first democratic municipal elections after the Franco era took place, the town and city councils have facilitated access to sport. The programmes they have developed are considered to be the main cause of the increase in indices of sport participation since 1975 (García Ferrando 1997).

Sports clubs constitute the basis of the voluntary sector. A total of 48,563 clubs are shared out unevenly between the Autonomous Communities (Burriel and Puig 1999: 199). On average, there are 1.2 clubs per 1,000 inhabitants, a relatively low figure compared to the high indices of membership of organisations in other European countries (Heinemann 1999). Each club may be assigned to one or several governing bodies at autonomous level (autonomous federations, which in turn are linked to the governing bodies at national/state level). At this level, there is no umbrella organisation which coordinates all these governing bodies. That makes the voluntary sector very divided and dependent on the public one (Puig *et al.* forthcoming).

In the sphere of sport linked to the world of federations, hiking associations should be singled out by virtue of their great importance, particularly in Catalonia, Madrid and the Basque Country. Hiking is characterised by a set of cultural traits and governed by organisational principles very different from those of other sports (Puig *et al.* 1999).

On the fringe of federated sport organised in the voluntary sector, 'sport for all' organisations have recently emerged. At state level these are represented by the Entes de Promoción Deportiva. The purpose of these organisations is to ensure that the entire population has access to sport.

Lastly, there are also voluntary organisations that foster body care through the use of naturalistic methods, physical activities and alternative medicines. These organisations have their own communication channels and are thoroughly dissociated from the sport movement, with which they have nothing in common.

In short, voluntary sport organisations constitute a complex mix in which federations and clubs geared towards competition, hiking associations with their own dynamics and a set of organisations (sport for all, body care and so on) disassociated from the structures of federated sport coexist.

Finally, mention must be made of commercial organisations which are conditioned by the laws of the market. Since sport in Spain has become a consumer commodity the number of commercial organisations of all kinds has grown, and one wonders what effect their emergence in the sport panorama will have on the voluntary movement (Campos 2000; Dehesa 2000; Heinemann 1994).

Women's sports organisations

According to the information at our disposal, at present there are no sport organisations exclusively for women in Spain, at least at the state and autonomous/regional levels. On the other hand, a constantly increasing number of women's sections has been and still is being created in existing sport organisations, or programmes addressed specifically to women are being set in motion.

In contrast to this present situation, at the turn of the twentieth century, and almost simultaneously with women's initial engagement in sport, a number of women's clubs as well as public organisations were founded with the aim to foster sport for women. When the Civil War ended in 1939, these initiatives were quashed and in their place, in 1941, the Sección Femenina was entrusted with the task of developing women's sport. This was the women's branch of the Falange (Falange Española Tradicionalista de las Juventudes de Ofensiva Nacional Socialista), the fascist organisation whose purpose was to inculcate the ideology of the new regime into the Spanish people. Due perhaps to an increasing rejection of this organisation in the last years of Francoism, the idea of 'specifically female' organisations was seen as something contrary to the interests of women in democracy. On the following pages we provide a brief overview of this process.

The history of Spain, particularly during the nineteenth and first half of the twentieth centuries, according to Pierre Vilar (1947), is the history of two Spains. One was liberal, secular and even anticlerical sometimes, federalist, which was open to Europe and with a thirst for modernisation; the other was reactionary, Catholic, centralist, which was opposed to influence from abroad, and rooted in tradition. Both represented very different sectors of society and, depending on changing political circumstances, their margins of expression varied considerably. These two radically opposing stances in Spanish society affected the stereotypes associated with gender and, by extension, the greater or lesser acceptance of equality between men and women. The Civil War (1936–39) was the tragic outcome of this confrontation.

Despite the variations these circumstances might have generated, the overall situation of women in the period to which we refer was of clear inferiority to men, a situation reinforced by strong social and institutional pressure to maintain the status quo and a legal system that left women completely dependent on men (Nash 1999). Even so, in the period prior to the Civil War there were occasions during which women were able to express their claims for equality and the right to fully participate in collective life.

The first women's sports club was most probably the Fémina Natación Club, founded in Barcelona in 1912 (Segura 2000). Its purpose was recreational and hygienist. Although we do not know its total eventual membership figures, we do know the reasons why the club was created:

> The idea to found this Society...was born from young ladies' increasing enthusiasm for swimming and our observation that some of them had reached such levels of prowess in the sport that they could even compete with some swimmers of the male sex.
>
> (Segura 2000)

A more progressive ideology informed the activities of the Club Femení d'Esports (Feminine Sports Club), founded in 1928 on the initiative of women intellectuals of the bourgeoisie whose aim was to foster sport among young women of the middle and lower classes. The club set out to 'modernise young Catalan women according to feminine, not feminist, criteria' (Gusi 1991: 7). Although the role of motherhood was still considered very important, they rejected the image of the docile, submissive woman in favour of the woman who would play an active role in public life. There is documentary evidence of the fact that the club caused a major social impact, and the founders 'converted it into a political platform, in the broadest sense of the term, with the aim of incorporating the needs and desires of women into the general social debate' (Segura 2000). The female membership of the club reached a total of 1,200.

The Civil War put an end to these activities, and the task of the Sección Femenina was to foster sport in accordance with the stereotyped image of women, whose only purpose in life was to be a good wife and mother. Reactionary Spain had won the war. The victors' ideal woman is perfectly portrayed in the following fragment:

> The model advocated was that of a devoted housewife, for whom the kitchen, washing and ironing held no secrets, an efficient administrator of her husband's salary and dedicated to looking after her children, far removed from culture, needing to know only what was strictly necessary to be a good wife and mother.
>
> (Sánchez 1990: 29)

Physical education 'was understood as a way of inculcating discipline and fortifying morals, never as a way of fostering all the personal capacities of women...' (Fiol and Salva 1979). It was required to contribute to the 'morphological and functional improvement of women in relation to their specific biological function' (Fiol and Salva 1979). Sports and physical activities were encouraged that would apparently fulfil these criteria: gymnastics, folk dancing, volleyball, basketball, team handball, swimming, tennis, skiing, mountain climbing and hockey. On the other hand, women were banned from cycling, boxing and certain disciplines of track-and-field, since those kind of sports were considered unsuitable/inappropriate for them (Grup de dones vinculades a l'esport, 1977: 414; Puig 1987; Puig *et al.* 1989).

Women's participation in sport

An analysis of Spanish women's participation in recreational and top-level sport reveals a phenomenon that is somewhat paradoxical. All surveys conducted on the sporting participation patterns of the population show that gender constitutes an independent variable fundamental to an understanding of these patterns. This variable repeatedly reveals 'different forms to relate oneself with sport' (García Ferrando 1997: 216). That is, as Spanish women have gradually gained access to sport, far from reproducing masculine behaviour patterns, they have modelled it according to other parameters; they have created their own sport culture. While they project onto this culture values acquired during their socialisation process, the creation of these spaces and times of women's sport has led to the emergence of other ways of understanding and engaging in sport. The situation of women in sport is not only a place where gender-associated hegemonic stereotypes are reproduced, but also a space of confrontation and creation of new forms of relationship.

Women's participation in leisure sport

According to the survey by García Ferrando (1997), 48 per cent of Spanish men and 30 per cent of Spanish women engage in one or more sports.[5] Ever since statistics have been available, more men than women have been sport participants. Between 1968 and 1995, figures show a rise in participation of 30 per cent among all the Spanish men and 25 per cent among all the Spanish women (Consejo Superior de Deportes 2000: 23). Regarding spectatorship, the differences are also significant, 73 per cent and 53 per cent respectively, while 13 per cent of men and 5 per cent of women regularly attend sporting events. However, more interesting than the quantitative differences are the qualitative ones. Many indicators reveal the different ways in which men and women engage in sport.

The most popular sports in Spain according to gender (percentage of the total number of practitioners[6]) are, for men: (1) soccer (56 per cent), (2) cycling (30 per cent), (3) swimming (28 per cent), (4) basketball (14 per cent), (5) jogging (13 per cent), (6) tennis (13 per cent), (7) track and field

(11 per cent), (8) hiking (10 per cent), (9) pelota (*frontón*) (9 per cent), and (10) fishing (8 per cent). For women the top ten sports are (1) swimming (42 per cent), (2) aerobics, rhythmic gymnastics and dance (27 per cent), (3) fitness gymnastics (25 per cent), (4) cycling (22 per cent), (5) jogging (13 per cent), (6) tennis (11 per cent), (7) basketball (10 per cent), (8) volleyball (7 per cent), (9) track and field (9 per cent), and (10) skiing (5 per cent) (Mosquera and Puig, 1998, based on García Ferrando 1997).

The greatest differences are observable in the competitive sports and opinions of them. Twenty-eight per cent of the men engaged in sport take part in competitions, as opposed to only 8 per cent of the women. Similar figures are repeated in the case of federation licence holders (29 per cent of the men and 8 per cent of the women) and membership of sports clubs (26 per cent and 17 per cent respectively). In the case of non-competitive sport, however, the ratio among sport practitioners is reversed: 50 per cent of men as opposed to 82 per cent of women. Such differing behaviour patterns according to gender in the sphere of competitive and organised sports suggests that the presence of women is different in each of the three sectors of which the Spanish sport system is composed, i.e. the public, the voluntary and the commercial sector (see Figure 6.1).

Women are least integrated into the voluntary sector, constituted of clubs and federations. Not only are they fewer in number according to membership, but also, in many cases, above all in that of elite sportswomen, the prevailing patriarchal system places serious obstacles in the way of their incorporation. As mentioned above, on average only 17 per cent of women are members in a sports club (García Ferrando 1997). This figure may be further qualified in terms of geographical areas and types of clubs. A survey conducted by Antonio Moreno in Barcelona indicates that 27 per cent of club members were women (Heinemann *et al.* 1997). However, this figure varies greatly depending on whether the clubs are large or small ones. The bigger the club, the greater the presence of women. Thus, in clubs with a membership of over 1,000, 37.7 per cent are women, dropping to 20 per cent in clubs with fewer than 100 members. Furthermore, 37.5 per cent of clubs with fewer than 300 members have no women among them (Heinemann *et al.* 1997: 47–8). In the city of Seville, where small clubs predominate, women account for 25 per cent of membership and a quarter of the clubs have no female members (Escalera *et al.* 1995: 45). Similarly, in Galicia in the north-west, women account for only 19 per cent of club members (Gambau 2001): 33.5 per cent of all Galician clubs have a percentage of less than 20 per cent of women members, and some of those clubs have no women members at all.

A number of factors may be put forward to explain the low number of women club members. In general, clubs provide services geared towards traditional and/or competitive sports (Moreno 1997; Puig *et al.* 1999). We have already identified the sports favoured by women, and most of the Spanish clubs have not yet provided facilities in correspondence with these new trends. Furthermore, clubs are organised in such a way as to require a certain degree of involvement in club life, which may constitute a factor of dissuasion for many of those women who are deeply committed to their families and/or professions. Since many women have to organise their time in accordance with the needs of the rest of the family, they seek a more flexible offer, and this is provided only by the big (more professionalised and commercialised) clubs or the commercial sector in its own right.

Indeed, the commercial (and in part the public) sector is much more attractive to women than to men. Thus, while only 4 per cent of sportsmen use commercial gyms (fitness studios), the percentage rises to 12 per cent in the case of sportswomen (García Ferrando 1997: 153). Although this is the sector for which least empirical information is available, both the views of people linked to the sector and the partial research conducted hitherto indicate that women constitute its clientele *par excellence* (Buñuel 1992).

By means of promoting programmes, the public sector has managed to attract many women and all those groups integrated into neither the voluntary nor the commercial sectors (García Ferrando 2000). Its strategies have varied greatly. After the first democratic municipal elections, indiscriminate campaigns were launched to attract boys, girls and young men. In those cases, where a statistical count has been made of participation, the proportions are about 58 per cent male (of all ages) and 42 per cent female participants (García 1999). Since then awareness has increased of the need to provide programmes specifically adapted to each social group, particularly adult women (García 1999). Where these programmes have been introduced, the opinions given by the promoters are very positive. Unfortunately, however, at present we have no statistical data at our disposal as evidence of this.

Finally, this assessment of women's engagement in recreational sport would be incomplete without reference to differences in terms of socioeconomic status. These differences are enormous and reveal the power of this variable as a strong discriminatory factor in the determination of the population's sporting behaviour. Thus, the survey conducted in 1995 by García Ferrando on the sporting habits of the Spanish people reveals that 56 per cent of women professionals, technicians and students engage in sport, compared with only 23 per cent of housewives aged between 16 and 54 and 10 per cent between 55 and 65 (García Ferrando 1997: 220–1) recorded for the farming community and retired people. This information, however, groups all active sportswomen together without taking into account the relative regularity of engagement. In the absence of research and following the theories of Bourdieu, women who engage most often and enthusiastically in sport probably belong mainly to the first group, since besides financial capital they would also have sufficient cultural and social capital at their disposal to enable themselves to organise and manage their time better. The reader will recall that at the beginning of this section we pointed out that without taking differences in age and socio-economic status into account, the number of women who engage in sport amounts to 30 per cent of the female population. Thus, although we have managed to detect a number of common traits that allow us to speak of a female sport culture, we must never overlook the fact that major differences exist within this culture.

Women's participation in top-level sport

From the data referring to women with a federation licence or who participate in competitions as presented in the previous section it is clear that far fewer women than men are active in top-level sport. The difference is much bigger here than in the field of recreational/leisure sport, and it also varies depending on the kind of sport in question (García Ferrando 1997: 63). Very few women engage in aviation sports, motor racing, billiards, bowls, boxing, competition cycling, pigeon breeding, soccer, motorcycle racing, pétanque or rugby. Participation is more equal in the case of track and field, basketball, handball, winter sports, fencing, golf, swimming, skating and tennis, whereas in gymnastics and volleyball the number of women's licences surpasses that of men's. The lesser presence of women in the world of federated sport is also reflected in their participation in Olympic games. Table 6.1 shows Spanish Olympic participation according to gender: an overall total of 86 per cent men and 14 per cent women (Consejo Superior de

Table 6.1 Spanish participation in the Olympics according to gender

	Men (per cent)		Women (per cent)		Totals
Paris 1900	6	100	0		6
Ambers 1920	63	100	0		63
Paris 1924	118	98	2	2	120
Amsterdam 1928	85	100	0		85
LosAngeles 1932	5	100	0		5
London 1948	71	100	0		71
Helsinki 1952	32	100	0		32
Melbourne 1956	6	100	0		6
Rome 1960	153	93	11	7	164
Tokyo 1964	58	95	3	5	61
Mexico 1968	151	99	2	1	153
Munich 1972	132	96	5	4	137
Montreal 1976	120	92	10	8	130
Moscow 1980	163	94	10	6	173
Los Angeles 1984	190	91	19	9	209
Seoul 1988	257	87	40	13	297
Barcelona 1992	503	78	141	22	644
Atlanta 1996	307	76	97	24	404
Sydney 2000	224	72	89	28	313
Totals	2644	86	429	14	3073

Source: Compiled from data of the CSD (Consejo Superior de Deportes 2000: 33)

Deportes 2000). Nevertheless, the number of Spanish women participants has gradually increased, and made a sharp upward jump in the Barcelona Games, rising from 13 per cent of the Seoul 1988 delegation to 22 per cent in Barcelona 1992. According to analysts, at the Barcelona Games Spain featured in the bottom half of the list of women participants from the developed countries (Sánchez Bañuelos 1992: 139). In Atlanta 1996 and, above all, Sydney 2000, it moved up to the top half.

Although women are far less present in top-level sport than men, their achievements – at least in terms of Olympic medals – are proportionately superior to those of their male counterparts. The differentiation in this respect between the Sydney results and those of all the previous editions together may be seen in the following: While up to Atlanta 1996 a total of 2,420 men (87.6 per cent) and only 340 women (12.3 per cent) participated in the Games, a total of 194 men (84.7 per cent) as compared to 35 women (15.2 per cent) won a medal. In Sydney 2000, a total of 224 men (72 per cent) participated in the Games and 7 of them (63.6 per cent of medal winners) won a medal, while only 89 women (28 per cent) participated, but 4 of them (36.3 per cent of medal winners) won a medal (Consejo Superior de Deportes 2000: 33–4, http://www.ado.es/Sydney2000/espanolesensydney.php3 [October 2001]).

What reflections can be made on the situation of women in top-level sport? The first aspect to be stressed is the fact that the patriarchal structures of Spanish society are further intensified in this sphere, and in a wide variety of ways. Despite progress that has been made here, of which empirical evidence exists, women's top-level sport is generally the history of a constant struggle to attain equality with men. The problem becomes even more acute in those sports regarded as male: in these cases, the difficulties and rejection that women encounter are bigger still (Martín 1993). In general terms, if a club is short of money the first to suffer are women teams and athletes. Technical support (trainers, masseurs and so forth) are either restricted, or else, the least qualified personnel is assigned to women's teams. Priority is invariably given to men. On the other hand, those women who carry their gender identity according to parameters far from what is considered 'feminine' are often subject to humiliation. Although women who claim their rights are a 'nuisance', men feel duty bound to satisfy their claims. This situation is underpinned by both the media, where women's sport 'has no face', as María Eugenia Ibáñez and Manuela Lacosta (1998, 1999) have meticulously shown, and the domestic tasks that for the most part still in responsibility of women. In this context, Cristina Mayo, coach of an elite women's handball team, commented in 1992 that the few married top-level sportswomen had to cope with a greater-than-usual load of household chores: they have to do more washing and cook according to the strict diet recommended for their sporting activities (Mayo 1992: 126–7).

However, such blatant discrimination, which must be denounced and combated, does not entirely account for the situation of women in top-level sport. The aforementioned women's sport culture also provides a suitable theoretical perspective to understand another dimension of it. If we analyse women's attitudes and *modi operandi*, we note that they generate a system of rules and values and a world of their own symbolic representations that may be clearly differentiated from those of men. Women respond differently to victory; they have other scales of values; they are more self-demanding; and they have such a high degree of motivation that they have managed to overcome the obstacles that had hitherto denied them access to the sporting elite. Indeed, this set of factors may even serve as an explanation for the better results they obtain. On the one hand, they have to surmount a greater number of barriers in order to be selected, and on the other, once selected, their positive attitudes drive them on to constantly do better. In a study on top-level sportswomen, highly paradoxical results were obtained that, in a way, corroborate the above (Puig 1996). Both men and women were asked to describe the greatest hindrances they had encountered to their sporting careers, and strangely enough, although empirical evidence and everyday experience suggested that men enjoyed more institutional support than women, statistically it turned out that the greatest hindrance as far as women were concerned was women themselves (lethargy, insecurity, lack of dedication), while for men it was the institutions. Although it might be perplexing that women do not seem to perceive the extent to which they are influenced by the fact that they work in an environment which is unfavourable to them, it is possible that their capacity for self-criticism helps them to be more demanding and attain a higher level of achievement than men.

Ultimately, it is essential to differentiate between gender-associated stereotypes, which configure a system of beliefs according to which some sports are suitable for men and others suitable for women, and what people actually do in specific situations. In other words, although the world of top-level sport is dominated by a system of patriarchal rules discriminating against women, none of the studies consulted suggest that the environment/social setting affects women in their day-to-day activities or gives rise to a conflict of roles (García Ferrando 1987, 1996; Martín 1993; Puig 1996; Martín and Puig 1996). If they have taken sport as their main socialisation environment, this is because the compensatory factors outweigh the difficulties they encounter. In top-level sport exactly as it is, they have found a space for self-fulfilment, for satisfaction and for the construction of their gender identity, an identity that in most cases does not coincide with the hegemonic stereotype.

Women in decision-making positions

In 2000, for the first time in the history of Spain, a woman, Pilar del Castillo, was appointed Minister of Education, Culture and Sport. Does this mean that Spanish women occupy significant decision-making positions in sport?[7] The answer is no.

Regarding the world of sport, the presence of women is inferior to their presence in the labour market in general. In Spain women involved in the labour market account for 35 per cent of the total, a figure much lower than that of other European countries as it is given in all statistics about the labour market in Europe. The figure for working women in sport is lower still: in 1991 the ratio was one woman to four men (Martínez del Castillo 1993: 110).

While in all cases the number of women is comparatively less than men, in federated sport it is even smaller, a fact corroborated by the many qualitative analyses we have found. Mercè Curull, general director of sports in Catalonia between 1998 and 2000, describes her entrance into the world of sport as follows: 'My feelings were very mixed...I felt alone, abnormal...rather like a Christmas decoration...surrounded by men, a circle of men that became tighter and tighter, leaving me outside, I had to elbow my way in...' (Curull 1999). Let us now examine the situation of women in decision-making positions.

The International Olympic Committee July 1996 recommendation that by 2000 at least 10 per cent of decision-making positions should be occupied by women has borne little fruit. We shall begin our analysis with the voluntary sector, which embraces federated sport.

The number of woman federation presidents in Spain has always been very small, and has not changed in the last ten years. In 1993 there were two women presidents, and in 1999 one woman in this position. The number of woman directors increased in those sport federations in which the number of federated women was greater, but only rarely are they in the majority.

The most complete study we have found on this issue is the one conducted by the Comissió Dona i Esport (2000) (Commission of Women and Sport) – as part of the Catalan Olympic Committee (COC)[8] – on women who occupy positions of authority in Catalan sport federations, in the Unió de Federacions Esportives Catalanes (UFEC) (Union of Catalan Sport Federations) and in the Executive Committee of the COC.[9] Referring to the situation in October 2000, in total there are only two women federation presidents, one woman was in the Executive Committee of the COC, and there was no female representative in a decision-making position on the board of directors of the UFEC. Women occupying less important positions of responsibility in federations accounted for 9 per cent of the total; 39 per cent of the federations had no women at all in a decision-making position, in 26 per cent of cases the presence of women varied between 1 and 10 per cent, and the figure of 10 per cent of women in decision-making positions was surpassed in only 32 per cent of federations.[10] Of the twenty-nine Olympic sport federations, only twelve surpassed the 10 per cent target, and most women occupied positions on the technical committees lowest down on the decision-making scale.

Who are these women? Almost one-third of them are university graduates who work full-time. Almost 40 per cent of all are former sportswomen who had actively taken part in international competitions. Only 21 per cent consider the fact of being women as having hindered their decision-making work, although 83 per cent believe that there is need for action to increase the number of women in these positions. They are conscious about the fact of being few in number. In order to achieve this they propose the following: to establish quotas,

> to increase the level of social awareness in general and of women in particular; to occupy positions gradually demonstrating their abilities and taking more initiatives sucessively; to liberate women from family responsibilities; to get more further education; to be more present in the mass media....

> (Comissió Dona i Esport 2000: 14)

We have little information concerning decision-making positions in other sectors. All in all, however, it seems that among people with higher education qualifications the differences between men and women are smaller. Thus, according to a survey conducted on all those people who graduated in sport sciences from the INEF-C of Barcelona between 1981 and 1997, one woman per 2.5 men works (Puig and Viñas, 2002). The presence of women is higher in number in the field of teaching,[11] lower in organised sport and in relation to the total number of women graduates, their numbers equal those of men in managerial positions.

The major presence of women in the field of teaching (physical education and training) comes as no surprise, since it is a phenomenon common to many countries. Teaching in a secondary or primary school is a decision-making position because the teacher has an autonomy in managing his or her tasks. However we are also familiar with the problems this profession has had to face as it has become increasingly feminised: it has lost social status and salaries have been progressively reduced. Furthermore, we are not surprised to note that the world of federated sport is practically a closed shop for women, independent of their qualifications and titles. On the other hand, it is interesting to note that women are involved in sport management, a sphere which has traditionally been considered reserved for men. While it is true that, according to information available to us, their salaries are lower, we believe that their significant presence in management may be a sign of changes taking place favourable to the presence of women in the services sector in general, by virtue of their special aptitudes, for example, empathy, the capacity for teamwork and communication skills (Piazza 1999; Puig 2002).

The promotion of women's sport in Spain

Throughout the democratic period so far, no public state institution has developed any sport programme designed specifically for women. On the other hand, there have been more general programmes contributing positively to fostering women's engagement in sport.

During the 1980s, a less competitive sport model was developed in Spain geared towards improving health, body care and enjoying physical activity. A major contribution to this model, which responded more appropriately to the interests and tastes of most women, was made by the 'sport for all' publicity campaigns and the corresponding facilities provided by town and city councils. Nevertheless, in the initial years it was mainly the commercial sector that provided this sport model. It was not until the last decade that the public sector has started to foster and disseminate this model by providing facilities and activities to the population. It has been verified that the offer of these activities in the public sector presents high indices of women's participation (García Ferrando 1997).

Specific initiatives addressed to women have also been set in motion by institutions such as the Diputación de Barcelona (Barcelona County Council), a supra-local authority that cooperates with and assists the municipalities. The Sports Department of this organisation has fostered a number of women and sport programmes through subsidies assigned municipalities in the province of Barcelona. Furthermore, in 1997 the Plan of Equal Opportunities for Women was drawn up, followed in 1998 by the Programme of Sport Integration, in collaboration with the Grup d'Estudi Dona i Esport (GEDE) of the INEF-C-Barcelona. The programme was elaborated for this group, and addressed to adult women. It implements policies that take into account the needs and specific conditioning factors of this group (García 1999).

Although the territorial federations have not devised a comprehensive programme of sport for women, certain individual federations, such as the Catalan Handball Federation and the Catalan Five-a-Side Soccer Committee, have begun to lead the way by setting projects in motion to foster women's teams and prepare coaches, train the players and attract new participants. Changes along these lines are also reflected in some modifications to out-of-school sport regulations, above all because of social pressure. Thus, while in 1990 in Catalonia mixed five-a-side soccer or roller hockey teams were not allowed in out-of-school competition, by 1991–92 the demand had increased to such an extent that women's and mixed teams had to be admitted to competitions (García/Asins 1995: 35).

However, one of the factors that might have the biggest indirect impact on and contribution to equal opportunities in sport is, undoubtedly, the 1990 Spanish education law, Ley de Ordenación General del Sistema Educativo (LOGSE) which has been progressively enacted all over Spain during the last decade. Twenty years ago, in 1970, when the Ley General de Educación (General Education Law) was in force, mixed education had become officially recognised. Nevertheless, sharing the same classroom did not necessarily mean an equal treatment of both sexes, since the recommendations governing physical education for girls differed from those for boys. The current law advocates a non-discriminating multi-functional physical education model. Consequently, in the official curriculum there are no aspects that explicitly discriminate between the sexes (García and Asins 1995: 25), for one of the principles taken up by the law is the concept of coeducation which implies the need for equal participation on the part of both sexes.

Although efforts are being made to reach an educational model without the stigma of sexual stereotypes, nobody is ignorant to the difficulties involved, no matter how much the laws may have changed. The *Diseño Curricular Base* (Directives for Teaching) (1989) points out about the influence of social models for men and women on learning, which may be transmitted through what is known as the 'hidden curriculum'. Furthermore, trainee teachers are not provided with all the necessary resources they need to face the difficulties involved in co-education (Vázquez *et al.* 2000).

On the situation of women and sport in Spain: a tentative interpretation

Having given an overview on women and sport in Spain, we now proceed to propose how, in our view, the situation should be interpreted. We consider it of fundamental importance to analyse women's incorporation into sport as the process of creation of a feminine sport culture. For Montse Martín (1999: 28 ff.), who bases her analysis on Bourdieu's concepts, people engaged in sport create a *field* characterised by interaction, diversity and conflicts generated by the different forms of *capital* (economic, cultural, social and symbolic) they possess, which are specific to each situation. Each field is unique; hence the fact that women create fields different from those of men in the spheres of both recreational and top-level sport.

This perspective has allowed us to see the changes that have taken place in the Spanish sport system. Had we not monitored the spaces and times of women's sport, we might have continued to fall into the trap of considering that sport is still federated sport. Women's incorporation into the world of sport, parallel to the construction and functioning of the welfare state, has been accompanied by the multiplication of organisations and ways of understanding and practising sport. They have built and reproduced their gender identity differently from men.

It is also important to understand why we regard women's sport culture positively. In this context, we base our evaluation mainly on the feminist theories of difference that inform feminist action in Spain and Italy.[12] The constitution of a women's sport culture does not mean that women restrict themselves to reproducing the hegemonic stereotype of femininity, thereby consolidating situations of inequality and even of oppression *vis-à-vis* men. On the contrary, it means projecting values and *modi operandi* more in keeping with women's desires and needs in society. Moreover, to think in terms of a women's sport culture is to break away from binary categories of thought (Pfister 1997) and to specifically analyse women's contribution to social life without taking the male world as the only parameter of analysis.

Nonetheless, and this is the second aspect to be taken into consideration, we must not ignore the fact that relative to other areas of Spanish public life, women's presence in sport is very small. Furthermore, in federated sport many signs still persist of rejection or undervaluing of the feminine presence. Thus, while we observe that women engage enthusiastically in top-level sport, obtain proportionately better results than men and build their own gender identity therein, in this field serious obstacles still exist in the way of their full recognition and equal treatment. From the theoretical point of view, we must not forget that women's sport culture must be analysed in the context of a patriarchal society.

The third important element to be considered is the difference between the hegemonic feminine stereotype that the Franco regime attempted to impose in Spain and the 'true' personality of women. Stereotypes are often confused with behaviour patterns and ways of being. In the Spanish case, this would be a serious error. Pierre Vilar's thesis, according to which there are two Spains, is a useful instrument with which to correct this misconception. The Franco regime was the outcome of victory on the part of reactionary, traditionalist Spain and meant the frustration of many of women's aspirations. But as we pointed out earlier, there is also a liberal, progressive Spain to which many women have contributed who are also a point of reference for many of us.

Finally, in a comparative context, Puig has pointed out elsewhere (2001) that northern and southern Europe underwent essentially different industrialisation processes. As a consequence of this, a small to medium-sized business system still prevails in Spain, in which the borderline between domestic and productive tasks is difficult to establish. Many women work in the family business without being officially registered as employed, which explains in part why the rate of female employment in Spain is lower than in other countries. On the other hand, a woman's contribution to the family economy is far greater and valued far more positively than that of a woman who occupies a low-paid, undervalued position in a firm. From this we deduce that though a country's rate of female employment may be low, this does not mean that women are less important socially, even in the sphere of public life.

Regarding sport, when it comes to assessing the situation of Spanish women we believe that both quantitative and qualitative evaluations have to be taken into account simultaneously. Indeed, we must stress the fact that women's sport culture has had an impact on Spanish sport, a fact that the cold figures we presented in this chapter certainly cannot fully measure.

Notes

1 This project enjoys the support of the INEF-Catalunya, Barcelona, which has funded the English translation and authorised Susanna Soler to participate in the project as part of her doctorate studies.

2   The public sector constitute governmental organisations, the voluntary sector non-profit and non-governmental organisations, and the commercial sector for-profit and non-governmental organisations. Each of these sectors embraces very different types of organisations.

3   Spain is a country where the public sector has a great influence in the sport since the article 43.3 of the 1978 Constitution states that the public powers will promote physical education and sport. Besides, there exists also a national Sport Law passed in 1990 which substituted the one of 1980. Finally, almost all the autonomous governments have a specific law in this field. As it can be seen, the intervention of public sector is so great that some authors speak about 'publification' of sport (Camps 1996). For more information see Puig *et al.* (forthcoming).

4   Spain is a federal state divided into seventeen autonomous regions called Comunidades Autónomas (CCAA).

5   García Ferrando takes the definition of sport given by the European Charter of Sport 1992. According to this document, sport includes a wide range of organised and unorganised physical activities conducted at competition or leisure level. The survey was conducted on a population between 15 and 65 years. The frequency of practice includes people practicing once a week or more.

6   The sum of the percentages is greater than 100 because the questionnaire allowed for more than one answer.

7   By decision-making positions we mean both those associated with voluntary organisations, for example as board member of a federation, and those associated with a professional activity.

8   The COC was founded in 1989 and is still trying to secure official recognition by the IOC.

9   Between February and October 2000 there was a total of fifty-nine of those women, of whom half answered the questionnaire they were given.

10 It strikes us as significant to point out that the federations that head the list of this group are the following: the Catalan Federation (CF) of Cerebral Paralysis (60 per cent feminine presence); the CF of the Mentally Retarded (38.5 per cent); the CF of Lifesaving (43 per cent); the CF of Gymnastics (55 per cent); the CF of Rowing (33.4 per cent); and the CF of Water-Skiing (33.4 per cent).

11 This is corroborated by the 1991 survey, according to which 33 per cent of people working in physical education were women as opposed to 66 per cent men (Martínez del Castillo *et al.* 1991).

12 For further information on the application of the theories of difference to the study of women and sport, see Martín (1999) and Puig (forthcoming).

Bibliography

Buñuel, A. (1992) *La construcción social del cuerpo: prácticas gimnásticas y nuevos modelos culturales*, Madrid: Editorial de la Universidad Complutense.

Burriel, J.C. and Puig, N. (1999) 'Responsabilidades y relaciones entre el sector público y el privado en el sistema deportivo', in J. Subirats (ed.), *¿Existe sociedad civil en España? Responsabilidades colectivas y valores públicos*, Madrid: Estudios de la Fundación Encuentro.

Campos, C. (2000) 'El consumo de deporte', in *La gestión de las instalaciones deportivas: el reto del siglo XXI (6° Congreso de Actividades Acuáticas)*, Barcelona: SEAE.

Camps, A. (1996) *Las federaciones deportivas en España*, Madrid: Civitas.

Comissió Dona i Esport (2000) 'Situació de la Dona Directiva a les Federacions Esportives Catalanes', unpublished research, Barcelona: Comité Olímpic de Catalunya.

Consejo Superior de Deportes (2000) *El deporte español ante el siglo XXI. Resúmenes, cifras y propuestas*, Madrid: Ministerio de Educación y Cultura.

Curull, M. (1999) 'Posicionamiento de las mujeres frente a los organismos deportivos. Presentación', paper delivered at the III Fórum Olímpico 'Las mujeres y el movimiento olímpico: presente y futuro', Barcelona, November.

Dehesa, A. de la (2000) 'El sector deportivo: entre lo atlético y el sportwear', paper delivered at the Congreso de la Asociación Española de Investigación Social Aplicada al Deporte, Granada, October.

Escalera, J., Diaz, A.L. and Martinez, J.G. (1995) *Asociacionismo deportivo en Sevilla*, Sevilla: Ayuntamiento de Sevilla, Instituto Municipal de Deportes.

Fiol, J.M. and Salva, F. (1979) 'La educación de la mujer propugnada por Sección Femenina en Baleares a través de sus actividades (1939–1970)', unpublished manuscript, Barcelona.

Gambau, V. (2001) 'Estudio de la organización de los clubes deportivos en Galicia: un análisis empírico', doctoral thesis in preparation, Instituto Nacional de Educación Física, Universidad de La Coruña.

García, M. (1999) 'Posicionamiento de las mujeres frente a los organismos deportivos', paper delivered at the III Fórum Olímpico 'Las mujeres y el movimiento olímpico: presente y futuro', Barcelona, November.

García, M. and Asins, C. (1995) 'La coeducació en l'Educació Física', in A. Rivas (ed.), *Quaderns per a la Coeducació*, 7, Barcelona: Institut de Ciències de l'Educació de la Universitat Autónoma de Barcelona.

García Ferrando, M. (1987) 'La mujer en el deporte de alta competición: conflicto de roles y adaptación al modelo deportivo dominante. El caso del atletismo español', in B. Vázquez, *Mujer y deporte*, Madrid: Ministerio de Cultura & Instituto de la Mujer.

—— (1996) *Los deportistas olímpicos españoles: un perfil sociológico*, Madrid: Ministerio de Educación y Ciencia & Consejo Superior de Deportes.

—— (1997) *Los Españoles y el Deporte 1980–1995*, Valencia: CSD & Tirant lo Blanch.

—— (2000) 'La gestión del deporte en el ámbito municipal: de la promoción a la fidelización del cliente', paper delivered at the Congreso de la Asociación Española de Investigación Social Aplicada al Deporte, Granada, October.

Grup de dones vinculades a l'esport (1977) 'La dona i l'esport a Catalunya', in *Jornades catalanes de la dona, maig 1976*, Barcelona: Documentación y Publicaciones generales S.A.

Gusi, O. (1991) 'El paper de la dona en l'esport d'alt nivell al llarg del segle XX', unpublished research, Barcelona: Institut Nacional d'Educació Física de Catalunya.

Heinemann, K. (1994) 'El deporte como producto de consumo', in *Apunts. Educació Física i Esports*, 37: 49–56.

—— (ed.) (1999) *Sports clubs in various European countries*, Schorndorf: Hofmann & Schattauer.

Heinemann, K., Puig, N., López, C. and Moreno, A. (1997) 'Clubs deportivos en España y Alemania: una comparación teórica y empírica', in *Apunts. Educació Física i Esports*, 49: 40–62.

Ibáñez, M.E. and Lacosta, M. (1998) 'Informació esportiva: només per a ells', in *Génere i informació*, Barcelona: Institut Català de la Dona & Ajuntament de Barcelona.

—— (1999) 'Tratamiento hombre/mujer en los medios de comunicación', paper delivered at the III Fórum Olímpico 'Las mujeres y el movimiento olímpico: presente y futuro', Barcelona, November.

Martín, M. (1993) 'Les esportistes d'alt nivell a Catalunya', unpublished research, Barcelona: Direcció General de l'Esport.

—— (1999) 'Making sense of the first stage in the history of women's rugby in England (1978–1985): Difference and multiplicity in gender and rugby', unpublished MA in Sport, Culture and Development, Roehampton Institute.

Martín, M. and Puig, N. (1996) 'Las deportistas de alto nivel que practican deportes llamados masculinos en Cataluña', in R. Sanchez Martin (ed.), *La actividad física y el deporte en un contexto democrático (1976–1996)*, Pamplona: Asociación Española de Investigación Social Aplicada al Deporte.

Martínez del Castillo, J. (1993) 'La construcción económica y social del mercado deportivo de trabajo', in *Apunts. Educació Física i Esports*, 32: 106–17.

Martínez del Castillo, J., Puig, N., Fraile, A. and Boixeda, A. (1991) *Estructura ocupacional del deporte en España. Encuesta en los sectores de entrenamiento, animación, docencia y dirección*, Madrid: Ministerio de Educación y Ciencia & Consejo Superior de Deportes.

Mayo, C. (1992) 'Problemas prácticos de la mujer deportista', in B. Vázquez (ed.), *El ejercicio físico y la práctica deportiva de las mujeres*, Madrid: Ministerio de Asuntos Sociales & Instituto de la Mujer.

Ministerio de Educación y Ciencia (1989) *Diseño Curricular Base*, Madrid: M.E.C.

Moreno, A. (1997) 'Clubes deportivos en la provincia de Barcelona', doctoral thesis in preparation, Institut Nacional d'Educació Física de Catalunya, Universitat de Barcelona.

Mosquera, M.J. and Puig, N. (1998) 'Género y edad en el deporte', in M. García Ferrando, N. Puig and F. Lagardera (eds), *Sociología el deporte*, Madrid: Alianza Editorial.

Nash, M. (1999) 'La construcción de los roles de género: las mujeres en la España contemporánea', in M. Nash (ed.), *Rojas. Las mujeres republicanas en la Guerra Civil*, Madrid: Taurus.

Pfister, G. (1997) 'Integration oder Segregation – Gleichheit oder Differenz. Kontroversen im Diskurs über Frauen und Sport', in U. Henkel and S. Kroner (eds), *Und sie bewegt sich doch! Sportwissenschaftliche Frauenforschung – Bilanz und Perspektiven*, Pfaffenweiler: Centaurus-Verlagsgesellschaft.

Piazza, M. (1999) 'Dal lavoro di cura al lavoro professionale. Sinergie, contaminazioni, perversioni', in *Il libro della cura di sé degli altri del mondo*, Torino: Rosenberg & Sellier.

Puig, N. (1987) 'El proceso de incorporación al deporte por parte de la mujer española (1939–1985)', in B. Vázquez (ed.), *Mujer y deporte*, Madrid: Ministerio de Cultura & Instituto de la Mujer.

—— (1996) *Joves i Esport*, Barcelona: Generalitat de Catalunya, Secretaria General de l'Esport.

—— (2001) 'Differenz und Geschlechterbeziehungen im Sport', in K. Heinemann and M. Schubert (eds), *Sport und Gesellschaften*, Schorndorf: Hofmann.

—— (2002) 'Weibliche Differenz im Sport. Die Situation der Frauen im Sport zu Beginn des neuen Jahrhunderts', in *Sportwissenschaft 1*, 48–67.

Puig, N., García Bonafe, M., Masnou, M., Ríos, M. and Salvadó, A. (1989) 'Frauen und Sport in Spanien. Vorschlag für einen Forschungsgegenstand', in C. Peyton and G. Pfister, *Frauensport in Europa. Informationen-Materialien*, Ahrensburg: Verlag Ingrid Czwalina.

Puig, N., García, O. and López, C. (1999) 'Sports clubs in Spain', in K. Heinemann (ed.), *Sports clubs in various European countries*, Schorndorf: Hofmann & Schattauer.

Puig, N., Sarasa, S., Junyent, R. and Oró, C. (forthcoming) 'Sport and Welfare State in the process of Spanish democratisation', in K. Heinemann (ed.), *Sport and the Welfare State*, Schorndorf: Hofmann & Schattauer.

Puig, N. and Viñas, J. (2002) *Mercat de treball i llicenciatura en educació física a l'INEF-Catalunya, Barcelona (1980–1997)*, Barcelona: Diputació de Barcelona.

Sánchez, R. (1990) *Mujer española, una sombra de destino en lo universal. Trayectoria histórica de Sección Femenina de Falange (1934–1977)*, Murcia: Publicaciones de la Universidad de Murcia.

Sánchez Bañuelos, F. (1992) 'La participación femenina en el programa ADO '92', in B. Vázquez (ed.), *El ejercicio físico y la práctica deportiva de las mujeres*, Madrid: Ministerio de Asuntos Sociales & Instituto de la Mujer.

Segura, I. (2000) *Calendari de dones esportistes, 2000*, Barcelona: Generalitat de Catalunya & Institut Català de la Dona.

Vázquez, B., Fernández, E. and Learreta, B. (2000) *Educación Física y Género. Modelo para la observación y el análisis del comportamiento del alumnado y del profesorado*, Madrid: Gymnos ed.

Vilar, P. (1947) *Histoire de l'Espagne*, Paris: Presses Universitaires de France.

7 Women and sport in the Czech Republic

Ludmila Fialová

Sports development in the Czech Republic

The organisation of the sport system

During the past ten years the Czech Republic has undergone radical political, economic, socio-cultural changes that are related directly or indirectly to the field of sport. Until 1989 the sports policy was based on legislation, was administered entirely by the state, and controlled by the universal physical education organisation 'Czechoslovak Association of Physical Education' (ČSTV – Československý svaz tělesné výchovy).

The desire for democratisation, pluralism and decentralisation in the last decade was the basis of the expression of protest against this universal organisation. The law of a centralised organisation of physical education and sport was abolished in 1990. A new division of agencies covering sports activities provided by the state on the one hand, and on the level of clubs or associations on the other, came into existence. At the same time a newly constituted commercial sector started to penetrate into the sport system. Nowadays, sport is organised at state, at voluntary, as well as at private (commercial) levels. This status, however, is not yet fully established and is still in progress.

At present the number of sports that have their own associations is at least 1.5 times larger than ten years ago. The rise of new associations and voluntary sector associations serves as an indicator of decentralisation and individualisation. About 5,500 former sports unions and clubs that existed within ČSTV up to 1990 were transformed, and their number has increased to more than 12,000 (Slepičková 2000).

Sports policy: state support of the sport

In 1999, the government introduced a new legislative concept of state policy concerned with physical education and sport. The Ministry of Education, Youth and Sports (MEYS) plays the most important role. The Section for Youth and Physical Education, headed by the Deputy Minister,

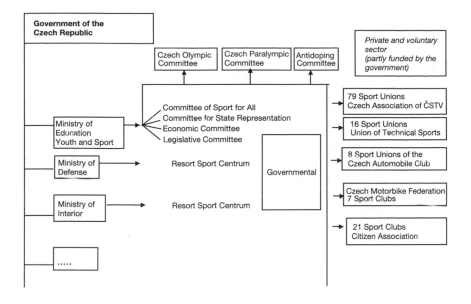

Figure 7.1 Structure of the sport system in the Czech Republic
Source: adjusted according to Táborský 1997

is responsible for state administration. The Ministry executes the following activities: public administration (management, methodology and grant policy, regulation, scientific research), attention to sportsmen/women and teams representing the Czech Republic (talent development, sports centres, education of experts), financing of physical education and sport (not only at school level, but in general). The Minister of Education, Youth and Sports makes decisions on any recommendations from the expert consultative body, the Sport and Physical Education Council, which comprises four committees:

1 Committee of Sport for All
2 Committee for State Representation
3 Economic Committee
4 Legislative Committee

One of the four deputies of the Minister is the Deputy Minister for Youth and Sports. The Department of Physical Education and Sport consists of two sections:

• the section of sport for all (four members)
• the section of high-performance sport (five members; see Figure 7.1)

Physical education and sport (in regard to function) is also part of the responsibility of the Chamber of the Czech Republic. The Committee for Science, Education, Culture, Youth and Physical Education has twenty-two members, and the Subcommittee for Physical Education is composed of twelve members. Czech sports organisations and the Czech NOC are independent and work on a democratic base; that is, they are non-governmental organisations with their own regulations, but they are partly supported by the state.

At present, the national programme of the development of sport for all is being created and the principles of support of state sport representation (top-level sport) have recently been outlined. These activities should be completed with a bill of protection and support of sport. The main goal of the programme of the development of sport for all is to foster active engagement in various forms of sport over the full life span, and with the largest number of people possible, especially children and youth (MEYS 1999). The programme documentation contains no section specifically devoted to women.

The new legislation should assure safety in and through sport against negative consequences and creation of clear conditions for sports development. In developed European countries, public administration has a big influence on creating basic conditions for sport for all, and this influence is increasing in the Czech Republic (Slepičková 2000). Nonetheless, administrative support of sport has not yet become systematised, rather it is incidental, and in the area of autonomy it is non-committal. There are no organisational structures or budget rules that should secure sport at this level. This area is still developing.

In regard to funding, sport in the Czech Republic is financed from different sources. Most of funding (59.3 per cent) comes from expenses of family budgets on sport, including membership fees as well as expenditure on equipment, tournament money and transport depending on the individual sport. Another large proportion comes from public monies, i.e. the state budget (4.7 per cent), local budgets (13.8 per cent), and profits from sport lotteries (2.3 per cent). Other sources especially for top-level sport include organised sport (club sources with 5.8 per cent and sports federations/clubs sponsorship with 1.3 per cent), the support of large companies, i.e. sponsorships (12.4 per cent), television and other media taxes for sport reports and broadcasting (0.6 per cent), and advertising through agencies (0.4 per cent) (Novotný 2000).

At present, the public sector budgets and the general financial situation of families have deteriorated because of the overall situation of the state economy. The support of sport in areas with a high-level index of unemployment and in the countryside is rather small. Families with children are particularly disadvantaged, as they have to cut down on their general expenditures including sport.

The most important sports organisations[1]

Czech Association of Physical Education (Český svaz tělesné výchovy, ČSTV)

The Czech Association of Physical Education is the largest sports organisation, constituting sport and tourism associations of nation-wide standing as well as sports organisations and sports clubs. The main objective is to support (also financially) sport, physical education, tourism, and also official sport's representation (by programmes, policies, facilities etc.). At the end of 1999 the ČSTV embraced seventy-nine sports unions and 7,530 sports clubs with almost 1.2 million members (MEYS 1999). The conception of activities and structure complies with European standards of non-governmental confederation of physical education and sports organisations. The ČSTV has been an ENGSO member since 1992. Most members involved in this association are men (71.5 per cent; ČSTV 1997).

Czech Association of Sport for All (Česká asociace sportu pro všechny, ČASPV)

The Czech Association of Sport for All was established after the separation of a significant part of original divisions of basic and recreational sport from ČSTV for ideological reasons, i.e. because of the development of commercial sport and a number of material reasons. Today, about 225,000 members employed in more than 2,100 clubs are involved in the centralised organisation ČSTV (MEYS 1999). The ČSTV is financed by governmental institutes and private sponsorship. The Association supports sport for all without any kind of talent, age and social restriction and also offers equal opportunities to participate in sport to non-members. Sports on offer include recreational sport, general gymnastics, aerobics, rhythmic gymnastics, yoga, health physical education, outdoor activities, exercises for parents with children and so on. The majority of the members are women (160,316 female members, 68 per cent; ČSTV 1997).

Czech Sokol Organisation (Česká obec sokolská, ČOS)

The Czech Sokol is the oldest gymnastic organization and incorporates the Sokol sports clubs and regional sports organisations. Today there are more than 1,000 regional organisations with around 171,000 members. As in the past, ČOS aims its activities mainly on sport for all bases. It also affiliates sports clubs, which participate in different competitions and events organised by the sports clubs of other organisations. The majority of members are adult women (32.9 per cent) and men (27 per cent; ČOS 1999). This organisation provides fifty-six different kinds of sports, and most members work in the Department of 'General Development' contributing to general education. Sokol Festivals have a long tradition (starting in 1882 with 720 gymnasts and 3,420 spectators) introducing mass public performances by

Sokol members. In the year 2000, some 21,000 gymnasts performed in twelve mass compositions at the thirteenth Sokol Festival.

In 1993 the World Sokol Federation was established. At present eight major national Sokol organisations in the world are affiliated members: Czech Sokol organisation, American Sokol organisation, Sokol in Slovakia, Slovak Gymnastic Union Sokol of the USA, Sokol Community Abroad, Slovenian Sokol Union, Sokol Australia and Czech-American Working-men's Sokol.

Association of School Sports Clubs (Asociace školních sportovních klubů, AŠSK)

The Association of School Sports clubs is the youngest, still developing sports organization. The AŠSK tries to involve the maximum number of young people in sport. Currently, school sports clubs collaborate with more than 2,100 different schools and offer an opportunity to participate in sport to more than 209,000 children. The AŠSK organises regular physical activities for those children and adolescents who do not practice high-performance sport. About 25 per cent students of secondary schools and 30 per cent pupils of elementary schools are members of the clubs (MEYS 1999).

Czech Association of Tourism (Český klub turistů, ČKT)

The Czech Association of Tourism is a famous institution with a long nationwide tradition dating back to the nineteenth century. Sport is provided especially for the older age category. There are 649 clubs with 41,200 members. They are financed by governmental institutes and private sponsorship.

With regard to membership in the biggest sport organisations – ČSTV, ČASPV and ČOS – sports clubs operating within sports organisations involve the greatest number of members: there are 2,164,539 members (1,239,842 adults and 909,726 youths) in twenty-six associations, and the members are affiliated in 119 unions and 19,873 clubs (MEYS 1999; ČSTV 1997; ČOS 1999). Czech sports clubs have a long historical tradition and are well organised. They have autonomous authority to evaluate and consequently replace officials, coaches or referees, who do not show an appropriate level of qualification. Additionally, they provide specialised courses and training programmes to improve individuals' levels of competence.

There is no overall guide umbrella organisation. The voluntary sector includes different organisations, which have affiliate voluntary members. The commercial sector in the Czech Republic is a recent development and the lack of established tradition brings many problems in relation to material background, professional licensing as well as the educational training of staff members. State and private sectors usually collaborate for mutual benefit. Fitness centres, tourism accommodation and saunas, however, operate on a commercial basis and thereby providing some financial support for sports associations' activities.

Participation in sport of girls and women

Sport for girls and women: a historical approach

Organised sport in the Czech Republic has a long and well-established place in society. Starting around the middle of the nineteenth century, and from the very beginning, women were invited to join all forms of activities provided. After the formation of the Sokol in 1862, a sports institution for girls was founded in 1863. In 1869, the Sports Club for Women and Girls was founded in Prague, the first chairwoman of which was Sofie Podlipská. In those days about sixty girls and women met regularly in the Sokol gymnasium in Prague (ČOS 1998a). In the Czech Republic, women were engaged in gymnastics right from the outset, at that time separately from men.

Women's sport at the end of the nineteenth century was also perceived as a social problem. Although some people considered there were some positive features of women's sport (as for example the appearance of the performers wearing long skirts during competition, the attraction of women's sport for spectators, and so on), unfortunately the opposite view also prevailed, testimony to which is a description given in one of the oldest Czech sports magazines, *Cyklista* (1893):

> Two sport events were held in Baden and in Brno and we feel really embarrassed that events of this kind took place. We faced performances of women. We are really sorry that there were clubs in Austria performing the same programme, and there is no doubt the only goal was to obtain entry fees from spectators eager for sensation as it was clear that performances of this character were absolutely useless.
>
> (Dvořáčková 1979)

At the end of the nineteenth century, Czech women were actively involved in skating, cycling and tennis (Dvořáčková 1979) and sports magazines of the time referred to their active participation. The first public performance of 867 women was held at the fourth Sokol Festival in 1901 (ČOS 1998a). The increasing power of the women's section in the Czech Sokol Organisation resulted in the establishment of an independent women's committee in 1911 (ČOS 1998a). A proposal of equal membership according to gender was accepted in the Sokol after the First World War, and hence women became equal to men (at least as far as voting rights were concerned). Recognition of women's rights on adequate levels of representation was seen in appointments in accordance with the number of female members in all important organisations (Waic 1997). The first female ČOS leader was elected in 1919, and since that year the Sokol management and executive board has always involved one man and one woman. Women were represented by women at every organisational level (for example, women chiefs), although not in the field of education in Sokol and not as mayors (Waic 1997). Gymnastics and sport became popular amongst women, as was proven at the Sokol Festival in 1920, when thousands of women also performed their compositions.

The goal of the Sokol idea and of Sokol activities was, and still is, 'a healthy beautiful human body, a harmonious development of the total personality with a well rounded, firm character, truthful and just, people that are strong, beautiful, good and honourable' (ČOS 1998b). The Sokol idea is based on strict adherence to principles of freedom, democracy, equality and justice for all. These principles are further enhanced by the idea of Sokol brotherhood, representing a conscious abandonment of privileges based on birth, wealth or education. The sense of Sokol brotherhood is not to demand equality, but to give it. Freedom in Sokol is combined with voluntary discipline. Sokol membership, on the other hand, is voluntary and all decisions are made on a democratic and conscious base. Most work by Sokol officers, instructors and committee members is performed voluntarily, without any remuneration, following the motto of Sokol activity: 'Neither for profit nor for glory' (ČOS 1998b).

Participation of girls and women in leisure sport today

In 1998 the total number of members in sports organisations was more than two million, or 20 per cent of the population. Amongst adults, 15–20 per cent of the population participate in organised sport. The commercial sector has been developing in the most dynamic way over the last decade, 2–3 per cent of athletes use the services of fitness centres (Rychtecký 2000). However, the number of participants in the private sector is limited by financial constraints. This is particularly true for families with children. Most adults, up to 70 per cent of the active sportsmen and sportswomen, practise their sport individually in a non-organised form (outdoor sports such as cycling, tourism and skiing) and/or at home (such as aerobics, ergometring and home gymnastics).

According to Teplý (1997), 35 per cent of adults (30 per cent of men, 40 per cent of women) do not participate actively in sport. Some 40 per cent of active sportspeople prefer non-competitive forms of sport. Men are interested mostly in individual sports (57 per cent) and ball games (49 per cent), and women in walking, riding a bicycle, skiing (51 per cent) and gymnastics (50 per cent).

Czech society does not perceive the necessity of establishing any special institutions for resolving the situation of women. Men and women have had equal opportunities to study, to participate in sport and to choose their leisure activities for a long time. At present, there are no special institutions for women in sport. Certain sports activities are done especially by women, but they are open to men as well; correspondingly, more and more sports are being opened for women (such as football and boxing). However, there are no sports federations or clubs in the Czech Republic designated only for girls and women. Female participation rates are lower in sports clubs with main focus on performance and competition. Differential participation patterns are demonstrated by Teplý (1997): in competitive sports, 13 per cent of women (38 per cent of men) and in other sports 51 per cent of women (30 per cent of men) are actively involved.

In the private sector there are some programmes, provided on a paying basis, which are predominantly for women. Participation in these is usually open to men as well, but the account for less than 5 per cent of all participants. In the main, female gymnastic instructors work in this area. The motivation is usually related to a desire for 'looking good' and image enhancement. For example, there are weekend programmes which include exercises, sauna, lectures on cosmetics or specialist lectures about nourishment. On the same commercial basis 'active holidays' are also offered; most often these are of a week's duration and include physical activities intended to reduce weight. Ninety-nine per cent of the participants are women. The programme usually includes exercising with music, swimming, hiking or cyclo-hiking, special lectures about nourishment, clothing, cosmetics, measuring of hyperdormic fat, active bodily mass and dietary eating. In April 2002 the Nike Women's Run 2002 took place, one of few sport actions designed only for women.

When examining sports participation among school children (and also out-of-school activities), only small differences between boys and girls are found when relating to content and intensity of physical activity, and not to the total amount of physical activity. The extent of decrease of female participation in sport increases with age. This is influenced, to a considerable degree, by the fact that young women are busy with their profession, and also have to take care of both children and household. Consequently, adult women do not have enough leisure time and often do not feel like participating in sport.

According to the COMPASS II study (Coordinated Monitoring of Participation in Sports; see Allin *et al.* 1999)[2] the relative number of Czech girls and women in the irregular (i.e. more than twelve, but less than sixty occasions per annum) and/or occasional (i.e. more than one, but less than twelve occasions per annum) participation category is higher than the number of Czech men. At the same time, participation is higher amongst women in the field of other physical (non-sport) activities (such as gardening, family trips, walking the dog and so on) (Rychtecký 2000).

Among the adult population, the differences in categories of competitive, organised and intensive sporting activities are augmented and more obvious than with the youth. With increasing age, more women leave competitive sport than men. Furthermore, the participation of women in non-organised sport decreases more than that of men. The difference between girls and women, on the one hand, and boys and men on the other, can clearly be seen in the membership in sports clubs: adult men are represented in sports clubs twice as much (21.7 per cent) as women (9.3 per cent; Rychtecký 2000).

When examining physical activities, we must distinguish those organised activities primarily offered by sports clubs and other institutions, and non-organised, leisure activities. The prevailing typical sports for boys in the Czech Republic are soccer, volleyball, tennis, swimming and basketball. Among girls the favourite sports are aerobics, volleyball, swimming and tennis. Girls also mention other regular healthy activities practised from mild to middle intensity (Rychtecký 2000).

Among adults, the preferences according to the kinds of sports are rather different. Besides traditional sports such as soccer, swimming, volleyball and basketball, other very popular activities are recreational sports such as walking, jogging. Among the activities that are practised most often are cycling and mountain bike riding, practised by men (13.8 per cent), boys (8.9 per cent), women (8.6 per cent) and girls (11.4 per cent) (Rychtecký 2000). This type of sport has been developing in a dynamic way and expanded to all age categories. Among physical activities outside the sphere of sport, working in the garden, strolling with a dog, exercising and muscle training at home and family trips to the countryside are also very frequent. Compared with men, women participate in many more activities in the area of 'sport for all' (mainly aerobics, gymnastics, yoga and activities including above all various forms of exercising, especially with music) (Rychtecký 2000).

The interest of women in aerobic and fitness activities can be explained by their focus on their body image which is an important part of self-image. The influence especially of gender and physical activities on level of satisfaction with the body and health behaviour is considerable. Czech women value single aspects of their body image more than men; they occupy themselves more with their body and are more conscious of their body problems (Fialová 2001). Women pay more attention to health, appearance and figure and believe that they can control these more than men.

Women of all age categories are less engaged in sports clubs activities than men (see Figure 7.2). The gender gap narrows in two periods (age 20–24 and 50–54 years). The course of women's membership development shows, with few exceptions, a downward trend: with increasing age the number of the female members who take part in club activities falls. Among men this relationship is not so evident. This may be connected to the fact that men are more often involved in this process as passive members – for example, as functionaries. The biggest differences according to gender are in the age group 35–39. This is a period when most women have to look after their children and household, in addition to being a time when women are returning to work. Consequently, they have no time for other activities. A further decrease in membership occurs for both men and women after the age of 50.

An international comparison of participation in sports (see Rychtecký 2000 referring to COMPASS II 1999) reveals that participation of Czech

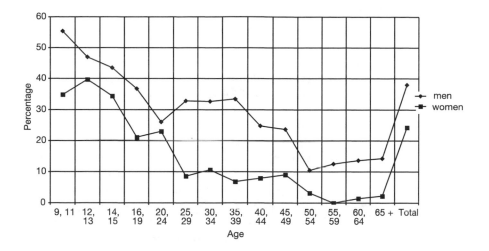

Figure 7.2 Membership in Czech sports clubs according to gender and age of respondents

Source: Rychtecký 2000

respondents in non-organised sports activity is comparatively high. On the other hand, a high number of Czechs do not participate in sport at all. About 34 per cent of Czech women do not engage in physical activity at all. That the numbers of persons active in sport is not so high as it appears to be according to some studies shows up in a survey of physical activities by parents (fathers and mothers) of Prague secondary school students (Mrazek *et al.* 1998). The findings reveal that according to opinions expressed by pupils only roughly 10 per cent of mothers and 17 per cent of fathers currently practice sport.

Women's and girls' access to high-performance sport

Sports schools and sports clubs develop talent regardless of gender; no discrimination against women in the preparation of representatives has been found. Historically, Czech women have achieved outstanding sporting achievements. Among the most well known are Věra Čáslavská, who won four gold medals in gymnastics in the 1968 Olympic Games in Mexico and Štěpánka Hilgertová, who won the wild water gold medal in Sydney 2000. Thirty-four women in eleven disciplines represented the Czech Republic in Sydney (ninety-two men represented the country in seventeen disciplines). The lower number of female representatives is mainly due to the qualifying limits and a wider number of sports open for men (fighting sports, strength sports). Czech male representatives in the 2000 Olympics were more successful than the female (seven/one medals, thirteen/four positioned to sixth place).

Women in decision-making positions in organised sport

Management and decision-making positions are in male hands. Within the Czech government, there used to be no women (women had, however, founded a 'shadow government'). In the 2002 government there are two women ministers. The aims of 'Women in Sports' (Oslo 1991, cited in Klementová 1998) are, therefore, not fulfilled systematically in the Czech Republic. The number of women in high decision-making positions at all levels of sport in the Czech Republic does not correspond to the relative proportion of female representatives in sports.

The main aim of Czech sport organisers (national programme of the development of sport for all – see Slepičková 2000) is to achieve equal participation and equal rights. Therefore, everyone should have the same opportunity to influence and inherit the same responsibility for sports development.

According to professional estimates, in the Czech Republic only around 20 per cent of the personnel who manage sporting institutions are women (Klementová 1998). In top functions this number is even lower (ČSTV 1999). The highest female proportion of representatives in decision-making positions is found in rhythmical gymnastics (80 per cent) and in the Czech Aerobics Federation, which has 40,000 participants, 500 instructors, referees and coaches. Most of them are women; even the president of this organization is a woman.

No female representatives in decision-making positions were found in the board room (general meeting, conference, convention) of three sports associations out of forty-three organisations (ice-hockey, canoeing and basketball) (Klementová 1998). An appropriate representation of women in the highest authorities can only be found in the Czech Handball Federation (thirty women and seventy men in 1993, and 57:144 in 1998).[3] The Czech Association of Sport for All was the only organisation with a prevailing number of female representatives at the highest level of authority, seventy-five women to fifty men in 1993 and 65:58 in 1998. This organisation also includes the Czech Aerobics Federation in which twenty-eight women and two men work at the highest authority level. There were female representatives on executive boards of sixteen out of thirty-eight organisations. Women worked in the presidium in four of nineteen organisations, though only one had a female president (Klementová 1998).

Programmes/activities to support girls and women in sport

The Working Group on 'Woman and Sport' in the Czech Olympic Committee (presided over by N. Vlasáková) has been working for the last ten years. Its major objective is to study the activities of women in sport in the Czech Republic. However, according to its findings, up to now no systematic gender differences between men and women in sport were found, because formerly this was not an aspect of the analysis, i.e. the category of gender had not been used systematically in those analyses. Therefore, no division is made according to the male and female groups. Consequently, no action plan concerning women's activities has been developed; regulating for example quotas for how many women should work in any sphere in the Czech Republic.

In 1988, the Czech Republic arranged for the first time a conference concerning women's sport. Up to then, no special meetings and conferences on the topic of women and sport had been held. About 140 people (approximately 70 per cent of whom were women) participated in this conference, which mainly aimed at sport administrative workers and coaches. Similar small conferences are now arranged regularly (Vlasáková 2000).

However, the demand for raising scientific information on the issue women and sport was not accepted as a priority. This situation was not even changed in 1996, at the 'National Conference on Sport' in any of the relevant 'round table' meetings. Only in 2001, one session was scheduled to address the issues. Women's sport is widely considered to be an integral part of sport in general. According to the official standpoint, women in the Czech Republic have equal conditions, opportunities and problems to men. Women in the Czech Republic, however, are insufficiently represented in leading functions and in the main spheres of societal areas: politics, economics, culture and sport. Nevertheless, no special research on this issue has been carried out yet.

In 2001 the MEYS founded a new centre for 'women in science'. Scientific work by women is to be supported at institutional level by this centre, which is funded by the Ministry. Up to now, not many women have been involved and the work is still in its beginning. Thus, for example in the field of social science (including ten disciplines), currently only three women are involved. For the sub-area of 'sport and leisure activity', Ludmila Fialová is the first woman to be involved.

Social structure and its influence on participation in sports by girls and women

The social position of women in the Czech society is determined first of all by the high level of employment, which is nearly the same as that of men during the last twenty years. The last social investigation (Machonin and Tuček 1996) found that 50 per cent of mothers of the oldest generation remained at home and did not work, the figure for mothers of the middle generation was 28 per cent, and only 9 per cent of the mothers of the youngest generation stayed at home without going to work. Unlike other countries, the majority of women work full-time in the Czech Republic. The number of working hours is similar to the working time of men: 40 per cent of women work more than fifty hours per week (47 per cent of men); 15 per cent work more than forty-three hours (22 per cent of men); a quarter of women (17 per cent of men) estimate their working time at forty-one to forty-three hours; the remaining number of women work less than forty-one hours (14 per cent of men) per week (Machonin and Tuček 1996).[4] The second shift represents mothers that spend about twenty-seven hours on household/domestic work per week. Men are estimated as spending fifteen hours each week on household tasks.

The income differences for men and women in the main job are big; nevertheless, the situation has improved over the last ten years. In 1984, 94 per cent of women were in the lowest three income groups; in 1993 the proportion was 10 per cent smaller (Machonin and Tuček 1996).

The gendered segregation of work was established in the past and has not changed much. Sociology experts do not expect big changes as far as the situation of women is concerned for objective reasons (stability of the work market, division of work between men and women, the level of education) and subjective reasons (silent general agreement of the population with the given division of roles). However, the dominance of men does not lead to discussions and conflicts. It should not be forgotten that women play an important role in cultural life: the number of women is, and has always been, greater if readers, visitors to theatres, concerts, exhibitions and so on are taken into account.

The life circumstances of women can help to explain the above described gender differences in sport. The obstacles that usually constrain development of women's sports are most often the lack of free time and the low importance given to sport, among others. Even though leisure sport is practised by most women, not many of them do participate in the leading positions of organised sport. It is time-consuming work for them, without the opportunity to gain any money. Therefore, it has become a tradition that men take over leading positions in the sport organisations. Like in other countries, one can assume that there are many other reasons for male dominance in decision-making committees of sport.

Despite the problems of leisure time and financial resources it would be important to motivate Czech women to be active in sport. According to Hainer and Kunešová (1997, n=3,386), about 20 per cent of the women in the Czech Republic are obese (BMI>30) and 54 per cent of women are overweight (BMI>25). Compared with other European countries, in the Czech Republic population obesity appears more often among women than among men.

Main problems of sports development in relation to women's participation

Women have made significant contributions to science, technology, societal developments, culture and in areas of human endeavour, and they have a proven record within all kinds of job and in almost every profession. In Prague for a short period of time there was a woman head of an important political party, and a woman director in the latest up-to-date hospital, as well as successful internationally renowned female managers.

Women have also achieved many outstanding results in sport, not only as athletes but also as coaches, referees, medical assistants and event organisers. Many of these achievements are in addition to fulfilling work duties, after work domestic responsibilities and bringing up children. However, the living conditions mentioned above prevent an upswing of women's sport. In addition, the material conditions have to be taken into account.

Facilities and equipment for sporting activities are not good in the Czech Republic compared with surrounding countries. The situation may well change when the state of the country's economy improves. At present, the main area of concern is within the technical area, such as constructing new cycle routes because their current status does not correspond to the increasing interest in cyclo-hiking. Additionally, there is a critical lack of public open playing fields, and there is also a marked lack of individual all-year-round activity programmes, which are common and accessible in developed countries.

Actual tasks that would help the development of women's sport in the Czech Republic include a consideration of the following:

1   To increase the number of women coaches and women advisors in decision-making and administrative authorities.
2   To increase the level of scientific information about women in sport.
3   To devote special attention to attracting women, their preparation for and to encourage them to remain in leading positions and governing functions.
4   To develop a differentiated sports programme offer according to gender differences (women have different interests, motivation, their own body culture and so on).

A woman as mother and tutor influences future generations, their values, preferences and behaviour. Therefore, investment in the education, culture and leisure activities of women is at the same time an investment in the health and desirable lifestyle of future generations. Greater support for women in the Czech Republic could be realised by state politics, by offering more opportunities to women (especially in decision-making positions), and by removal of differences between men and women in incomes and employment positions. These and other developmental changes are needed to improve social relations in a transformed society.

Notes

1   Other important organisations in the sphere of sport not mentioned here are the YMCA (Young Men's Christian Association) and YWCA (Young Women's Christian Association), Asociace tilovýchovných jednot a sportovních klubù (Sport Unions and Sports Clubs Association (ATJSK): zero unions, eighty clubs, 20,547 members), the Autoklub České republiky (AČR (Autoclub of the Czech Republic) with eight unions, 505 clubs and 83,454 members), Česká skateboardová asociace (Czech Skateboard

Association (ČSA): zero unions, 412 clubs, 14,000 members), Česká støelecká federace (Czech Shooting Federation (ČSF): zero unions, 801 clubs, 19,990 members).

2   COMPASS II (Coordinated Monitoring of Participation in Sports, cf. Allin *et al.* (1999)) is an international and comparative research study. Participating countries were Sweden, Finland, Netherlands, United Kingdom, Ireland, Spain, Italy, and the Czech Republic. This statistical survey was carried out in 1999–2000 in the Czech Republic by the sampling quota method according to demographical structure of the Czech population (Rychtecký 2000).

3   In the Czech Republic, next to the internationally known team-handball there exists another form known as Czech handball. The figures refer to the Czech handball.

4   Although the legal amount of working hours in the Czech Republic should not exceed 42 hours per week, the mentioned amount of working hours was given by the questioned individuals.

Bibliography

Allin, P. *et al.* (1999) *Sport participation in Europe. COMPASS II 1999*, London: UK Sport.

ČOS – Česká obec sokolská (1998a) *Praha, pohyb, Sokol* (Prague, Movement, Sokol), Praha: ČOS, Ústředcní škola.

—— (1998b) *Sokol past and present*, Praha: G´ART.

—— (1999) *Official Statistics*, Praha: ČOS – Česká obec sokolská.

ČSTV – Český svaz tělesné výchovy (1997) *Official Statistics*, Praha: ČSTV – Český svaz tělesné výchovy.

Dvořáčková, L. (1979) *Vznik a vývoj Českého sportu v letech 1880 až 1895 z hlediska soudobého tisku* (The origin and development of Czech sport in the years 1880 to 1895 from the point of view of the contemporary press), Praha: FTVS UK, diplomová práce.

Fasting, K., Pfister, G., Scraton, S. and Bunuel, A. (1997): 'Cross national research on women and sport: Some theoretical, methodological and practical challenges', *WSPAJ* 6, 1: 85–107.

Fialová, L. (2001) *Body image jako součást sebepojetí člověka* (Body image as a part of self-concept), Praha: Karolinum.

Hainer, V. and Kunešová, M. (1997) *Obezita* (Obesity), Praha: Servier.

Klementová, G. (1998) *Ženy ve vedení sportu v České republice* (Women in the management of sport in the Czech Republic), Praha: FTVS UK, diplomová práce.

Machonin, P. and Tuček, M. (1996) *Česká společnost v transformaci. K proměnám sociální struktury* (The Czech society in transformation: Changes in social structures), Praha: Sociologické nakladatelství.

Ministry of Education, Youth and Sport – MEYS (1999) *State policy concerning physical education and sports in the Czech Republic*, Prague: MEYS.

Mrazek, J., Fialová, L. and Bychovskaja, I. (1998) 'Sport, health and body concepts in central and eastern Europe: Students of physical education in Cologne, Prague and Moscow', *Journal of Comparative Physical Education and Sport* 20, 2: 52–62.

Novotný, J. (2000) 'Podpora sportu v ČR' (Granting sport in the Czech Republic), in P. Slepička and I. Slepičková (eds), *Sport, stát, společnost* (Sport, state, society), Praha: Phare Tempus.

Rychtecký, A. (2000) *Monitorování účasti ve sportu a pohybové aktivitě v České republice a v evropských zemích* (Monitoring of the participation in sport and movement activities in the Czech Republic and European Countries), Závěrečná zpráva pro Grantovou agenturu MŠMT ČR, Praha: UK FTVS.

Slepičková, I. (2000) 'Organizace sportu v České republice – spolková sféra' (Organisation of sport in the Czech Republic – societes and organisations), in P. Slepička and I. Slepičková (eds), *Sport, stát, společnost* (Sport, state, society), Praha: Phare Tempus.

Táborský, F. (1997) 'Sportovní reprezentace a stát' (Sport reprezentation and state), in P. Tilinger and T. Perič (eds), *Telesná výchova a sport na přelomu století* (Physical education and sport in interface of centuries), Praha: FTVS UK.

Teplý, Z. (1997) 'Zájem dospelé populace o různé formy telovýchovy a sportu' (Interest of adult population in various forms of sports), in P. Tilinger and T. Perič (eds), *Telesná výchova a sport na přelomu století* (Physical education and sport in interface of centuries), Praha: FTVS UK.

Vlasáková, N. (2000) 'Women and dport in Czech Republic', *Acta Universitatis Carolinae Kinanthropologica*, 2, 36: 5–10.

Waic, M. (1997) *Sokol v České společnosti* (Sokol in Czech society), Praha: FTVS UK.

8 Women and sport in Tanzania

Prisca Massao and Kari Fasting

Sports development in the country: general aspects

In Tanzania sport is organised just as hierarchically as it is in many other countries. Administratively, the most important unit is the National Sports Council (BMT), which is directly under the Directorate of Sport in the Ministry[1] concerned with sport. At the base of the hierarchical structure is the sports club (see Figure 8.1). There are thirty-two national sports associations in Tanzania, all of which are affiliated to the National Sports Council (Wigum and Leivaag 1983). Only one sports association is for women's sport alone – netball. Soccer was a male sports association until the late 1990s. Recently, women who play soccer have been struggling in order to be regis-

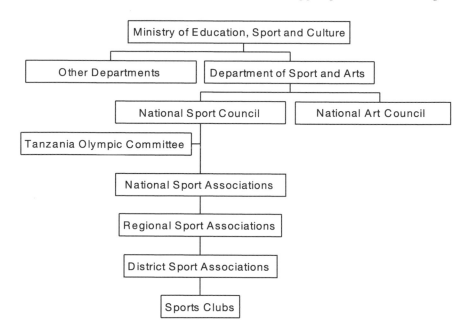

Figure 8.1 Structure of the sport system in Tanzania

tered as the Tanzanian Soccer Association for Women (TAWOFA), but not as a separate women's association. The goal is to become a part of the Tanzanian Soccer Association (FAT) (Massao 2001).

Although clubs are shown as the basic unit in the administrative structure of sport organisation, there exist many sports teams which do not belong to a sports club. These teams are organised locally in villages, work places, institutions, districts, and so on. Only a few teams and sports such as soccer and basketball have managed to form clubs, since clubs require a higher level of organisation in order to be registered. Clubs have more advantages in the sense that they are registered in the district, regional and national sport offices. This gives them more formal recognition, which again help them in the process of finding sponsorships. Most of the women's teams do not manage to reach the club registration stage because they do not satisfy the conditions that are needed, such as owning a training ground. Because of such demands, it has been difficult for women to form sports clubs in the country.

From historical records there is evidence that sport has been a gendered activity in Tanzania. In some areas of Tanzania, for example in the Lake Victoria region, there were inter-school competitions as early as the 1930s. During major public holidays, boys from schools and teachers colleges competed in competitive demonstration skills in physical training (drill) and traditional war dances, while girls had track events and gymnastics demonstrations (Nkongo 1979). The activities which demanded more physical effort and strength were assigned to boys, while the ones which demanded less physical strength and more aesthetic demonstration were assigned to girls.

In Tanzania there is just one sports organisation for girls and women only: the Netball Association. Netball is a girls' and women's only sport, introduced when Tanzania was under British colonial rule after the First World War. It was first established in schools, and later as a leisure activity in various institutions. After independence the Netball Association of Tanzania, known as CHANETA, was introduced in 1966 (Nkongo 1979). This has been a sports organisation for women, although CHANETA is not women-only by constitution. Women dominate CHANETA due to the fact that netball is a female sport. However, there are many male netball coaches.

Other women-only units in the sport system include the women's committees in the different sports associations. These committees were formed after the 1994 Resolution of the International Olympic Committee (IOC), which recommended that all National Olympic Committees and national sports associations should have a women's committee. Until 2000, only the Tanzania Athletic and Cycling Associations implemented this Resolution. These committees were formed in order to motivate and promote more girls and women in specific sports.

State intervention in sport in Tanzania has varied during the four decades since independence. The 1960s can be characterised as a revival period when the focus was to restructure the sport system to suit Tanzanian politics and environment after colonial times. The introduction of the National Sport Council was initiated at this time (1967). In 1970, the Tanzania secondary school tournaments (UMISETA) were introduced on an annual basis. The re-registration of the available sports associations and the new associations was also carried out in this period. The 1970s and early 1980s can be characterised as the peak phase of many sport activities.

Since independence in 1961, sport in Tanzania has mainly been organised and supported by the state and the public sector. The major supervising authority has been the Ministry responsible for sport. According to Nkongo (1979), in 1974 the Directorate of Sport and Youth put forward a proposal to train sufficient numbers of personnel for its departments from national to divisional levels by 1981. In the event, the proposal was not fully implemented by 1981; moreover, netball and specific plans for personnel to promote women's sport were not even contained within the proposal. This may well be one factor why women's sport in Tanzania continues to experience marginalisation even at the present time. No specifically trained personnel are available to promote women's sport in Tanzania, despite the knowledge that both cultural and structural factors place restrictions on women's participation in sport. The International Olympic Committee, under 'Olympic Solidarity', the British Council and a number of sports organisations have sponsored short courses of three to six months. In 1978, this programme of short courses resulted in the training of several sports coaches (Nkongo 1979). However, netball was not included in the programme even though it was the most popular sport for women in the country.

Up to the late 1980s, sport received much of its financial support from the government and public sectors, specifically central and local government, parastatals[2] and other institutions. Tanzania performed well in many African Games events including the East and Central African Games. At around this time many teams and clubs were formed in local communities, institutions and at places of work. It was also in this period (before the 1990s) when the netball league was popular in Tanzania, including teams from different parastatals such as the Tanzania Harbour Authority, Tanzania Postal and Telecommunication and various national banks, which involved their branches from different regions[3] of the country.

In the late 1980s and 1990s, during the political shift from a one-party to a multi-party system, and the economic emphasis on privatisation and trade liberalisation, many institutions including the sports system were decentralised. Commercialisation entered the sport system, involving profit motives such as are generally featured in professional sport (Ndee 1993). Under such circumstances, amateur sport had little chance to develop, and yet it is still amateur sport, which dominates Tanzanian sport. Sport began to receive less funding and support from the state. Districts, local governments, private organisations and people were required to fund and organise sport activities. The state supported only national teams and athletes for international tournaments such as the Olympic and Commonwealth Games, All African Games and so on. This support was given only shortly before tournaments. As a result, many of the national teams and individual athletes did not have enough time for proper preparation. Women's teams and athletes have been critically affected by this system to the extent that it is difficult to qualify for international tournaments. This critical situation contributed to a deterioration and poor performance of Tanzanian teams and athletes in many international sport competitions.

Women's sport was considerably affected. Until the 1980s, CHANETA used to organise tournaments at district up to national level. Netball was almost as popular for women as soccer was for men. Almost all primary schools in Tanzania had a netball court and the identification of good netball players began in primary schools. After the 1990s' economic liberalisation, all sports associations were required to find means of running their activities without dependency on government support. Thus, netball went into decline; there was a failure to organise tournaments and leagues, and even netball facilities deteriorated because many girls lacked the motivation and were not motivated by schools or by district, regional and national tournaments to play or be actively engaged in the sport.

Participation of girls and women in out-of-school sporting activities

Leisure sport in Tanzania has traditionally been a male and not a female domain of activity. It has been more common for men to go out in the evening to play for the local soccer team than for women to go out and play in the local netball team. In recent years, there have been fitness and training centres particularly in the cities focussing on health and fitness. When visiting these centres, it looks as if almost as many women as men are training there. However, by taking into account the average income of women in Tanzania, it is clear that only a few women from the upper class can afford to pay the training fees. The motivation for attending such centres is often related to weight control.

It is difficult to find any statistics about the participation of women and men in elite sport in Tanzania. Usually sports activity statistics are not presented separately for women and men. But there is some evidence available which shows differences between effort and motivation attached to boys compared with girls. One example here is the preparation of the junior Tanzanian soccer team accommodated at Makongo secondary school. The team represented Tanzania in the African Nations Junior Team Championships in 1997. The team members have an important motivational incentive through provision of a scholarship to study free at the Makongo secondary school. They are also provided with free accommodation at the school. No equivalent exists for girls in any sport despite the fact that there are some girls at the elite level who would benefit from such athletic scholarships.

Women in decision-making positions in sports organisations

There is a dearth of statistics about women in leadership positions in sport. However, there is some evidence which indicates that very few women hold sport leadership positions. Until 1999 there were only two national sports associations (CHANETA excluded) with women in top leadership positions: the National Sports Council and the Tanzania Amateur Athletic Association; both had a female vice chairperson (Shomari 1999). In 2001 another woman was employed in a leadership position in the National Sports Council. Clearly, to date the number of women in leading administrative positions in sport in Tanzania has been minimal. The first appointment in 1998 by the Directorate of Sport within the Ministry of Education, Sport and Culture of a woman to a higher leadership position at the Tanzania Sport Council, as Vice Chairperson, was received with scepticism by women with long experience in sport (Massao 2001). Some regarded the fact that women were appointed to leadership positions in sport as 'tokenism', since the women were not given key leadership positions, such as Chairperson or General Secretary of an Association. They believed that it was only in these top positions that women could participate effectively in influencing an organisation's decision-making. As a result, the appointment of these few female vice-chairs has not been regarded as a very effective step for women in the Tanzanian sport system in terms of decision making.

There has been a very small increase in leadership opportunities for women in sport during the last decade. One reason for this is that the women themselves do not regard taking on leadership positions in sport as something positive. In a recent study by Massao (2001), this kind of argument was expressed by several female participants interviewed. The study involved thirteen participants (10 women and 3 men) from different sports organisations. Some women in the study admitted that they had not taken a strong stance in terms of contesting male dominance in sport leadership.

According to Massao's (2001) findings, women in Tanzania cannot compete with men in obtaining leadership positions under the current sport system. The candidates' social and historical backgrounds in relation to sport seem to play a significant role in attaining leadership positions, especially in traditionally male-led organisations such as the National Sports Council (BMT), the Soccer Association of Tanzania (FAT) and the Directorate of Sport at the Ministry. Sport leadership was also found to be associated with economic and social status. Thus, low economic status also seems to reduce women's confidence in securing leadership opportunities in sports organisations. According to Coakley (1998), involvement in sport goes hand-in-hand with money, power and privilege. Women in Tanzania seem to lack money, power and privilege, especially in terms of leadership and training opportunities. Therefore, they lose faith in the public structures dealing with these sports institutions. The lack of funding and access to the higher stages of decision making have resulted in a tendency towards segregation and marginalisation. The women in the Massao's (2001) study had experienced marginalisation; they offered no possibility or hope of being allowed to take up leadership positions and had given up trying to contest for leadership, preferring instead to propose a quota system for sports leadership positions in order to narrow the gender gap.

The influence of the socio-cultural factors on girls' and women's sports participation

Socialisation

In Tanzania, as in many other countries, there is a larger proportion of children and youth than adults, who participate in sport. Most Tanzanian children and youth practise sports activities during their school-age years. There are several educational institutions tournaments conducted every year or every second year, which provide participation opportunities for most children and young people. These include UMISHUMTA for primary schools, UMISETA for secondary schools, SHIMIVUTA for ordinary learning organisations and Tanzania University Sports Association (TUSA) for universities and higher learning institutions. In relation to gender, it is quite common for most girls and women to drop out of sport after leaving school, especially primary school. Culturally, after leaving school most girls are expected to acquire or behave in accordance to traditional female gender roles of domestic chores rather than practising sports activities in their free time. Structurally, there are also very few public sports facilities outside the school or institutional environment for girls and women compared with men. While boys can continue to practise sport in public sports facilities such as soccer grounds after leaving school, it is not common for girls because there are no such facilities. Girls have either to organise themselves, or use sports facilities in the nearest institutions such as schools.

Most top-level athletes emanate from the school system. This is related to cultural and structural reasons. Not so many girls and women are motivated or encouraged to continue with sport even if they seem to have athletic talent.

Ethnicity

Ethnicity is not a particularly significant social structural issue in many of the public sectors, both in Tanzania and in many other African countries. However, in sport ethnicity patterns can easily be denoted. Ethnic group populations from the northern highlands and central regions of Tanzania, such as Arusha and Singida, are well known for their substantial numerical presence in track and field activities (Ndee 1993).

Race

Race is also a factor in Tanzanian sport. Although not so obvious to the Tanzanian public, there is some evidence that sports like cricket and golf are played by a few Indians and Europeans living in Tanzania, particularly those in the urban areas. There is no record of women as participants in these sports (National Sports Council Report 1999). The element of 'class' also seems to prevail in these sports. Most Indian and other foreigners are grouped in the higher social class level compared with the majority of Tanzanians.

Religion

Islam is highly significant as a religion in Tanzania, especially in the coastal regions. There is a common belief that Islamic restrictive constraints on dress codes inhibit most Muslim girls' participation in sport: exposure of parts of the body is contrary to Islam and sports clothes generally do not cover the whole body. Although no systematic specific study which analyses the way the Islamic religion has limited the participation of girls in sport has been undertaken in Tanzania, there is some evidence to support the efficacy of Islam in inhibiting female participation in sport. In a study which randomly interviewed some sports leaders in Tanzania in 1999, out of ten women interviewed only one was a Muslim (Massao 2001). As all the interviewees lived in Dar-es-Salaam, where most of the inhabitants are Muslim, this infers under-representation of Muslim women among female sports leaders.

Social class and education

For historical reasons, women in Tanzania have had less access to adequate education than men. Education has always been regarded as the key to a good life and advancement to a higher social class, whereas a career in sport has been regarded as a sphere of activity which does not need education. As most of the athletes and other practitioners, especially women, have a low level of education, they rarely manage to advance in their sports career and even the few educated women are not treated equally as their fellow men. Low or no priority is accorded to the education of the few women in sport or to educate special personnel for women's sport. This practice perpetuates the ideology that sport is the domain for the less educated, and continues the practice of social inequalities which are practised elsewhere in society (Massao 2001).

Marital status

Marital status is well known for intervening in sports participation for women in Tanzania. The continuation of a girl's participation in sport when she marries depends largely on support from her husband and her family in general. Most girls drop their athletic career because their husbands or partners do not want them to continue doing sport. Thus most women cease their sporting carrier either on marriage or giving birth. The women who do continue to participate in sport after marriage experience a deal of conflict stemming from both the sports structure and their families. The warm climate and lack of indoor training facilities are influential determinants on sports training, and morning and evening training patterns are the norm in Tanzania. This is also the time when most women are expected to be at home to serve their families, whether they are career women or housewives. The situation is worse for women with young children. The sport system has no service systems or programmes in place, such as moving sports facilities closer to women's residential areas, to assist in resolution of this problem. Sports-oriented Tanzanian women who were too busy with home activities and hence could not afford the time for necessary travel to engage in sport have proposed the provision of neighbourhood facilities (Leirvaag 1989). Most of the women are low-income earners and live in places with few or without any sports facilities for women.

From the perspective of the sport system, it is generally thought that it is supposed to be women's lack of serious commitment and effectiveness in sport if and when they do not attend sports practices as required (Massao 2001). Another factor is that married women are sometimes regarded as being too old for sports participation. Participation in sport is commonly regarded as an area of activity for children and young people, that is, for unmarried women (Leirvaag 1989; Massao 2001).

Programmes and/or actions for promotion of girls and women in sport

Governmental programmes (National Sports Development Policy)

Several state strategies have been formulated in order to increase the participation of women in sport. Among them was the 1995 National Sports Development Policy, which also focused on sport and physical activities for girls and women. The objectives of this policy were to make clear the need for sport promotion in Tanzania, and to develop sport in a more organised national framework. This included the clarification of the establishment of a range of networks for supporting sport in private, voluntary and governmental bodies. The policy also mentioned the need of sport for marginalised groups of the society, among them girls and women. To achieve this, the policy indicated the tasks to increase and improve female participation in sport. In a monitoring study on implementation by Massao (2001), these factors were placed into four groups:

1   promotion and education
2   training opportunities

3   leadership opportunities
4   women's sports associations

The policy also mentioned the organisations and institutions responsible for sports activities in the country and how they should work in order to improve the different aspects of the policies, such as women in sport. The Sports Department at the Ministry, the Tanzanian Sports Council and sports organisations are among the major implementers and monitors of this policy. In the study about the implementation of the policy the Directorate of Sport, the National Sports Council, the Soccer and Netball Associations and women's soccer were investigated.

Findings show that although the policy provided written encouragement about the efforts for women's sport, actual implementation does not occur in reality. Women in sport still experienced marginalisation and discrimination in leadership and training positions, let alone in general sports participation. The policy objectives concerning women as advocated have not been implemented effectively. The findings further reveal a number of factors continue to limit women's participation in sport (Massao, 2001):

- lack of specific programmes or projects to educate the public about the need of women to participate in sport and physical activities;
- fewer events or types of sports for women than for men (in terms of associations, competitions, teams, clubs etc.);
- fewer women than men in leadership position in sports organisations, which lead to gender imbalance in decision making;
- fewer training chances (scholarships), and thus fewer qualified sports women for leadership and managerial issues.

Although the government has shown concern about women in sport, there have been no really effective measures to deal with the problems, especially at the implementation level. One of the major findings in the study (Massao 2001) was the lack of funding particularly from central government to implement the sports development policy; this seemed to be the major limitation. Moreover, the policy did not show clearly the source of funds for most of its proposed activities such as the ones particularly concerning women. Herein lies a dilemma and challenge for most of the policy implementers.

Voluntary programmes (Sport for All Project)

The 'Sport for All Project' from the Norwegian Confederation of Sports had potential input into Tanzanian sport. It commenced with a pilot project in 1982–3, and officially was implemented in 1984. As part of Norwegian government development aid to Tanzania, it was one of the best-known programmes in supporting girls and women in sport in the country. From the outset, a focus of the project was to improve women's sport activities

(Wirsching 1988) and gender equality in all programmes. Findings of Tenga's evaluation study (1994) of the Training Programmes of the 'Sport for All Project' in Tanzania show that the participants who attended these training courses were almost equal in terms of gender (51 per cent women and 49 per cent men). However, their outreach in terms of gender is unknown, therefore, the extent to which these training programmes have helped to raise girls and women's awareness about sport has not been ascertained.

Other issues concerning Tanzanian women in sport

Due to economic hardship, the role of women in the society is increasingly changing and becoming more visible. Women are becoming more independent and the major families' breadwinners are no longer men only. This aspect has been explained (Massao 2001) as being related to the family context; women are becoming more and more 'fathers' of their families. As the economic difficulties are increasing in many African countries a single parent (husband) is no longer in a position to secure the family economically. So the traditional cultural perspective of the woman as a family caretaker and a man as an economic breadwinner, is gradually shifting as more women adopt the economic role of taking care of themselves and raising the family. As a result, women are also increasingly prioritising their activities, which give them higher economic gain and security. Sport has not been regarded as an activity that provides women with economic security as it is does for some male athletes. Sport for most Tanzanian women is still an extremely underpaid or unpaid activity.

In Massao's study (2001), most of the women interviewed expressed concern on the issue of irregularities which appear to exist in sports institution processes such as leadership, election and training opportunities. This discourages and prevents more girls and women from developing interest in a sports career, since not many women have achieved sufficiently in sport to act as role models for the younger generation. Therefore, it affects the training and leadership aspects in sport in terms of gender. Few women manage to cross the barriers to attain top leadership or training positions. Thus, in implementing the policy efforts of increasing the numbers of women in leadership and physical education, implementation should go deeper to monitor procedures and regularities which are used in leadership and training positions to see to what extent they can allow women to succeed.

Sports institutions in Tanzania still do not seem to have very positive relationships with the family institution. After marriage and during the maternity period, most women drop their sporting careers. However, there do seem to be some women who obtain support from their families in order to be able to participate in sport. Both traditions and the lack of a supportive sport system contribute to the problem, which may continue to make the implementation of sports development policy of Tanzania difficult.

Sexual harassment and assault seem also to happen in Tanzanian sport, although many of the sports leaders are not ready to admit it. In Massao's study (2001), several factors were mentioned as sources of sexual harassment in sport, such as physical attraction. This finding concurs with that of a study by Brackenbridge (2000), in which the 'attraction' excuse was also found. In Tanzania, silence has prevailed on this problem in order to protect some people and the sports institutions. As expressed by one of the women interviewed, a lack of knowledge of where female athletes can report harassment problems (which are related to an individual's privacy and issues of confidentiality) seems to exist among the female athletes. One consequence has been that some female athletes turn to the media because no systematic procedure exists to protect them in sport. Media attention, however, is also no guarantee of protection and/or support for the 'victim': the pervasive culture dictates that sexual scandals should not be made public through the media, although it has been admitted that female athletes are not informed as to how and where they might articulate such problems. The respect for coaches is such that any alleged sexual scandal involving them is covered up less they threaten to quit their job if 'harassment scandals' continue to be published.

Other factors, which encourage silence, are the un-assured confidentiality and the lack of opportunities for a fair resolution of the matter for the victim. The follow up of the few allegations claimed, discussed by some of the women interviewed in Massao's (2001) study, verify this. The risk is that young girls and women might quit or keep silent about the problem despite any disturbance experienced.

Conclusion

In Tanzania, most of the developmental measures do not reflect issues concerning gender and sport. How certain measures such as privatisation might and can affect the development of girls and women as a large group and sport as a long-term marginalised sector have been of little concern. Things like civil service reform have had a more negative effect on women than on men. Gender and sport, for example, have been left to chance under current economic reform. Privatisation of social institutions such as sport has been emphasised in order to reduce government's involvement. The sports sector has had to finance its own programmes, which has required turning to private donors and sponsors. However, private donors or sports promoters have become more interested in popular sport for business purposes. As a result, privatisation and economic liberalisation of a sector like sport has had a negative effect on women because most of women's sport does not attract as much attention as men's sport does. The groups with better resources have gained more by moving to the centre while those with limited resources have been pushed to the margins of the sports institutions because of the lack of state measures to protect them. The implication has been that groups like girls and women in sport continue to be marginalised; concomitantly, women and girls' sports activities continue to deteriorate.

Notes

1 Sport in Tanzania has been one of the areas moving from one ministry to another depending on political shifts or government reshuffles.
2 Parastatals means (in this chapter) the government monopoly organisations such as the National Bank, National Insurance, National Postal Corporation and so on.
3 A region in Tanzania is the second geographical and administrative unit in the country after nation.

Bibliography

Birell, S. and Theberge, N. (1994) 'Ideological control of women in sport', in D.M. Costa and S.R. Guthrie (eds), *Women and Sport Interdisciplinary Perspectives*, Champaign, IL: Human Kinetics Publishers.

Brackenridge, A. (2000) *Spoil sports: Understanding and preventing sexual exploitation in sport*, London: Routledge.

Coakley, J.J. (1998) *Sport in society: Issues and controversies*, Boston: Irwin McGraw-Hill.

Leirvaag, G. (1989) *Sport as a development aid: Theoretical considerations and results of fieldwork in Tanzania with particular reference to Mikoroshoni Women*, Oslo: Norges Idrettshøgskole.

Massao, P. (2001) 'Women in sport: The feminist analysis of the sport development policy of Tanzania,' unpublished masters thesis, Oslo: Norwegian University of Sport and Physical Education.

National Sports Council (1999) *A Report from National Sport Council about the approximate number of women in different sport associations*, Dar-es-Salaam: NSC.

Ndee, H.S. (1993) 'A tentative model of planning physical education for Tanzanian primary education', unpublished masters thesis, Stockholm: The Institute of International Education.

Nkongo, J.M. (1979) 'Factors influencing the development of physical education in Tanzania as compared to other African countries', unpublished doctoral dissertation, University of Manchester.

Ministry of Education and Culture (1995) 'Sera ya Maendeleo ya Michezo' (Sport Development Policy), in *Jamhuri ya Muungano Tanzania, Wizara ya Elimu na Utamaduni* (The United Republic of Tanzania, Ministry of Education and Culture), Dar-es-Salaam: Ministry of Education and Culture.

Shomari, C. (1999) 'Women's position in sport's decision making', speech at the National Leadership Workshop Zanzibar, Tanzania, October 1999.

Tenga, S.T. (1994) 'Sport for All Project in Tanzania: Evaluation of the training programmes in Dar Es Salaam region', unpublished masters thesis, Oslo: Norwegian University of Sport and Physical Education.

Wiigum, J. and Leivaag, G. (1983) *Rapport om Norges Idrettsforbunds Bistandsprosjekt 'Sport for All' i Tanzania 1982–83* (The Report about the Norwegian Confederation of Sport's project for development aid 'Sport for All' in Tanzania 1982–83), Oslo: Norwegian University of Sport and Physical Education.

Wirsching, I. (1988) *The Norwegian Confederation of Sports 'Sport for All Project'. Practical report*, Oslo: Norwegian Confederation of Sport.

9 Women and sport in South Africa

Shaped by history and shaping sporting history

Denise E. M. Jones

Introduction

Much has been written about the relationship between sport and politics in South Africa (SA). Unfortunately, the contributions of sporting females are largely invisible in these accounts. It is only since the late 1990s that scholars have begun to research the various histories around females and sport in SA. Through the work of Hargreaves (1997, 2000) more is known about the contribution to the anti-apartheid movement by Coloured[1] female sports-activists through their membership of the South African Council on Sport (SACOS). My account of the sporting career of a leading Coloured female in South African karate illustrates how the history of women and sport is both a history of the politics of the country, as well as a history of the restructuring and transformation of gender relations (Jones 2001a), while my analysis of 'gender, race, class and sport in the history of South Africa' (Jones 2001b) shows how the life circumstances of South African females impacted on the way they related to sporting practices at the time. Except for a report by the Sports Information and Sciences Agency (1997) and Burnett's (2001) analysis of the gendered representation of high performance sport in SA, little other quantitative research exists on the participation of females in South African sport. In contrast, the developments around women and sport in SA since the late 1980s have received a great deal of attention, because they coincided with the democratisation of South African society and the unification of different sporting cultures in the country. This chapter is an attempt to give an account of these developments against the backdrop of the history of sport in a racially divided SA. Where available, quantitative data will be included.

South African sporting females

Dikeledi Moropane is a twenty-three old African sporting female from an historically Black township in SA. Many sports were not offered at her school and Dikeledi only turned to track as a form of recreation when she found herself unemployed. Today she is a national 100 meter champion, having equaled the Olympic qualifying time. She has her sights set on the Athens Olympics. Dikeledi receives all the benefits afforded talented female and male athletes who are part of SA's elite sports development programme, referred to as 'Operation Excellence'. These include having all expenses covered as well as access to a doctor, physiotherapist, psychologist and free sports kit. As an African female athlete, Dikeledi carries additional pressures of being a role model, especially for thousands of Black female athletes, while simultaneously upholding cultural expectations around what it means to be an African woman (Roberts 2001).

For South African sportswomen, it is as much about differences between them as it is about dealing with gender inequality in the sports system. For example, unlike Dikeledi, Hestrie Cloete's talent as a high jumper was spotted at school level. At the age of twenty-three, this White-Afrikaans speaking sportswomen had won gold medals at both the World Athletics Championships in Canada and the Goodwill Games, as well as a silver medal at the Sydney Olympics. She is refereed to as 'Africa's queen of high jump' (Roberts 2001: 20) and has subsequently been given the coveted Abdou Diouf-Sport-Vertu Foundation award. Hestrie Cloete's talent is undeniable and her success in athletics is a celebration for all sporting females, but the differences between the opportunities which were available to her at school level compared to Dikeledi highlight the huge problems which females from historically disadvantaged communities still experience.

Nevertheless, Dikeledi is an example of the first generation of Black sporting females to be nurtured in SA since the democratisation of South African sport. Black women from her mother's generation did not have the resources or opportunities to develop their sporting potential. Many of them were involved in the broader struggle against apartheid and/or poverty. For them, participating in sport was not a priority, nor was there much of a need to consider how cultural expectations around appropriate ways of dressing the married female body might restrict their sporting careers. That still remains the task of Dikeledi's generation. This did not mean that Black women were not sports activists during the apartheid era. On the contrary, there were women, mostly of Coloured descent, who used sport to challenge apartheid and through the process realised the potential of sport as site of personal and group empowerment.

These sportswomen, many of whom were teachers, were amongst the most active supporters of the South African Council on Sport (SACOS) in its struggles against the apartheid government, especially during the 1970s and 1980s. They upheld the SACOS principle of 'no normal sport in an abnormal society', rejecting any (apartheid) government funding or joining government funded sports clubs, despite the negative effect this had on their own sporting development and that of the young sports-people whom they coached.[2] They were self-funded, and those who worked sponsored the kits and travel expenses of others. They established play-schools at practice sessions and matches so that space could be created for mothers to play their sport (Hargreaves 2000). They made do with few facilities compared to their White counterparts and other Black females who had joined sports organisations which were funded by the apartheid government. Their commitment, dedication and creativity were a source of inspiration to other Black sporting females at the time. Many participated in the sports unity process in the late 1980s and early 1990s. The work of sports activists such as these laid the foundation upon which the sporting females of the late 1990s like Dikeledi and Hestrie could build.

However, not all Black South African sportswomen played sport under the banner of SACOS. In fact, the power base of SACOS was to be found primarily amongst the Coloured population of the Western Cape Province and even here, despite remaining committed to the principles of SACOS, not all Coloured sports activists were SACOS members. Nellie Kleinsmidt, who was classified as Coloured by the apartheid government, was one such sporting female. Known as the Grandmother of karate in Africa, at sixty-two years of age, *sensei*[3] Nellie is regarded as the most senior female *karate-ka*[4] in SA. In Jones (2001a) I outline some of the discriminatory practices and race and gender-related struggles which she experienced as she pursued her karate career in a racially divided SA and achieved personal empowerment through and in her sport which is dominated by males. As a Black woman, her karate career and life were significantly shaped by apartheid legislation. At the time, racially discriminatory legislation divided the country into areas of occupancy and residency according to race.[5] All Black *karate-kas* were prohibited by law from practicing in White designated areas. The impact of various apartheid legislation, combined with the imposition of a sports moratorium by SACOS, negatively impacted on her sporting career. Despite these setbacks, in 1998, then in her late fifties, *sensei* Nellie earned her Sixth Dan Black Belt. She is greatly admired and respected by all female *karate-kas*, irrespective of race or ethnicity. This is also true of other sporting heroines, such as double gold Olympian Penny Heyns, who is a White-English speaking South African female.

> Women in sport in South Africa is one of the most volatile topics in the South African sporting arena. And when one thinks that it was a woman, Penny Heyns, who achieved South Africa's first double gold at an Olympics, one can be excused for asking why women have been ignored for so long.
>
> (Gilpin 1999: 146)

A former Olympic breaststroke champion, Penny Heyns retired from international swimming after the Sydney Olympics and has since been appointed to FINA'S athletes commission.[6] Not since Zola Budd's achievements in cross-country and track[7] has a White South African sporting female captured the imagination of the country the way Penny Heyns has done. She is remembered for her swimming successes and not for the opportunities the colour of her skin might have afforded her. It is more than seven years since she won double gold at the Olympics and more than a year since her retirement, yet Penny is still honored for raising the status of South African swimming. She is still considered to be a role model for South African female swimmers of all race groups. Her influence, it is claimed, has reached beyond the borders of South Africa (Ramsamy, President of the National Olympic Council for South Africa, cited in Roberts 2000).

These varied experiences of some of SA's sporting females raises questions not only around accessibility to necessary resources, opportunities and competencies, but also about difference and identity and how these shape the way females are able to relate to sport in SA today. The current developments and complexities can best be understood if examined against the history of the various liberation struggles in which South African women engaged and the implications thereof for their understandings of what equality (in sport) might mean for and to them.

Gender and sport in South African society

Equality, identity and differences

In pre-colonial society the social standing of a woman varied according to her age, marital status and her husband's rank. Colonisation introduced an intersection of gender with race and class. In addition to the general subordination of Black women to Black men and White women to White men, there was also a separation of White women from Black women as well as a separation amongst Black and White women themselves along class lines (Walker 1982). In the early 1900s all women had virtually no rights which were independent of men. Marital status determined the legal status of White women, while traditional marriages were not recognised by law. Apartheid policies which divided all South Africans into racially defined groups between the 1940s and 1990s further complicated the situation. Consequently, a woman would be defined as Black not White, and then more specifically as African, Indian or Coloured (Kadalie 1995).

The differences which exist between Black and White South African women can be traced to the different liberation struggles they fought during the late 1800s and early 1900s (Kadalie 1992). These can be divided into the suffrage movement fought for and by middle-class White women, mostly English-speaking women, and the resistance campaigns against the pass laws fought for and predominantly by African women. They were supported by Indian and Coloured women as well as some White women. The pass laws restricted the movement of African women in urban areas (Lewis 1993). The suffrage campaign was progressive for the early 1900s, yet it did little to improve the status of women as a group in SA. The majority of women were race-conscious rather than gender-conscious (Bertelsmann-Kadalie, 1989). They usually focused on issues around their own legal position and political equality. There was no consensus amongst suffragettes about the inclusion of Black women into the process.

Black South African women fought for seventy-eight years to attain basic human rights as citizens in the country of their birth (Kadalie 1992). Even after courageous protest actions from 1913 to the late 1950s, African females were eventually subjected to the same pass laws as their male counterparts. The anti-pass campaigns highlighted issues around identity and difference. Five issues are relevant to this discussion on women and South African sport, because they illustrate not only the way in which the gendered nature of roles were reinforced, but also how they intersected with cultural expectations about what constituted appropriate behavior for wives and mothers. In addition, they show how the demand for women's equality was placed firmly within, and then subordinated, to the transformation of the apartheid state.[8]

Firstly, the pass laws which, were first legislated in 1913, initially targeted African males. It was only in 1950 that they were extended to include African women. However, by adding women-related amendments to the 1930 and 1937 Native (Urban Areas) Acts, the White-controlled government emphasised sexual differences while simultaneously reinforcing the subordination of African women in relation to *all* men (Wells 1993). Secondly, although African women were more militant than their menfolk in tackling racial oppression, they were primarily defending their roles as mothers and homemakers. This enabled them to construct another identity as potential activists. Unfortunately, by appealing to their roles as wives and mothers they supported the values which shaped their oppression as women (Salo 1999). Thirdly, some African men resorted to cultural patriarchy when the militant identities of the women appeared to overshadow their identities as wives (Wells 1993). More than seven years after the formulation of SA's democratic constitution, the power of culture still shapes the way most South African women, especially married African women, are able to relate to sport.

A fourth issue was the dilemma facing many Black women regarding the prioritisation of their rights as women versus human rights (Beall *et al.* 1987). Unlike the (White) suffragettes, equality for Black women took on a special meaning within the national liberation struggle. Although the Federation of South African Women (FSAW), founded in 1954, cut across racial and class boundaries, race and gender were interpreted within the national liberation struggle for human rights. This highlights a significant difference in the notion of gender equality in South African society, including equality in sport. It was only in the early 1990s that South African women began their search for common ground in defining what equality, even in sport, might mean for them as a group without resorting to essentialism (Biehl 1993) or assuming the existence of cohesion over gender issues (Horn 1991). A fifth issue is that the FSAW was a women's movement with little focus on gender concerns. It called for equal, meaning identical, treatment with men before the law, while simultaneously focusing on the motherhood-identity (Albertyn 1994). This separated gender equality claims from economic and social equality, such as maternity benefits and crèche facilities. In the 1990s the concept of equality has changed little from the 1950s (Kadalie 1995).

The institutionalisation of gender in South Africa

The political activities in which South African women engaged from 1990–3 reflected numerous alliances which cut across racial and class boundaries. Their achievements included:

- the establishment of a Gender Advisory Committee;
- the launch of the Women's National Coalition;
- the establishment of a Commission on Gender Equality.

Since the 1994 democratic elections developments have included:

- the establishment of an office on the Status of Women in the President's office;
- a parliamentary committee on the improvement of quality of life and status of women;
- an extensive system of gender focal points within government departments and ministries.

(Msimang, 2000).

Although the inclusion of equality rights in South Africa's Bill of Rights was never under dispute, the form and status of these equal rights and what they meant for South African women still had to be negotiated in the mid-1990s (Albertyn 1994). Much attention had to be paid to the relationship between equal rights and customary law. Consequently, not enough could be given to other equally important issues, such as the wording of the equality clause, the status of affirmative action, effective enforcement mechanisms or the inclusion of a clause to ensure that equality overruled customary rights and claims to tradition. Despite the obvious successes, the institutionalisation of gender in SA raised a number of concerns for gender activists in the country.[9] For example, it is claimed that rights are indivisible (Biehl 1993). Since 1994 South African women have been granted equality with each other and with men, at both the constitutional and legislative levels. Yet the gap between the equality 'guaranteed' by the constitution and various legislation, commissions and policies at the broader societal level and the reality of women's lived experiences, still has to be negotiated and bridged (Kadalie 1995).

Sport in the history of South Africa

Sport and the South African government

Between the 1920s and 1930s, sport and politics became increasingly inter-linked (Odendaal 1988). For example, in 1926 the Liquor Act prevented the integration of ground and club facilities. It did not specifically target sportswomen and sportsmen, but it controlled the social environment in which sport is played.

Between the late 1940s and early 1990s, the ability of South African Blacks to construct identities as sportswomen or sportsmen was controlled at the institutional level of organized sport by apartheid legislation. There were eventually more than three hundred laws controlling nearly every aspect of the lives of Black South Africans (Odendaal 1995). This not only made it virtually impossible for Black and White sportspersons to play against each other or to mix socially without special permission, but also denied Blacks access to valued resources. It created different sporting identities which were primarily based on the colour of a person's skin.

Between the 1950s and 1980s there were changes in the apartheid-government's policy towards non-racial sport (Jarvie 1985). Fearing a complete boycott of South African sport by the international community, the policy statements on sport shifted from not allowing any inter-racial competition in the 1950s to the tolerance of multi-national sport competitions with the permission of the White-dominated government in the 1970s. This unfortunately did little to foster a national sports identity. It promoted alternative sporting cultures, each of which was shaped by access to valued resources. This complex situation was represented by a unique tripartite sporting structure comprising the government controlled sports organisations, the non-racial sports movement, and a group of Black sports people who confined their membership to Africans, Asians and Coloureds. In addition, there were Black sporting federations which had affiliated to White sports bodies (Roberts 1988).

From the 1940s, apartheid policy provided the framework for the structure, administration and practice of sport in the country. Although the sport unity process in SA began in the late 1980s, the objectives and operations of the Department of Sport and Recreation (DSR) reflected the apartheid policy of governance until after the first democratic elections in 1994. The post-apartheid DSR therefore inherited a tripartite system of sport together with approximately one hundred and fifty sports codes, each of which was governed by bodies representing the different racial groups, each with different sporting ideals. The various sporting cultures were racially hierarchical with Whites the most advantaged and Africans the most disadvantaged.

During 1994 and 1995 a new sports culture was developed for South Africa. The DSR was restructured and achieved status as an independent government department. The new Government of National Unity (GNU) appointed a Minister of Sport and Recreation.[10] These signified the importance attached to the role of sport in the reconstruction and transformation of the new democratic South Africa and in uniting a nation (Hendricks 2001). Sport was recognised as having a substantial role to play in the political future of the country, as it had done during the apartheid era (Booth 1998).

To this end, various sport and recreation policies were formulated and structures established at national, provincial and regional levels. In 1995 a draft White Paper on Sport and Recreation was circulated (National Department of Sport and Recreation 1995). The aim of the DSR, in conjunction with other national sporting structures, was to bridge the gap between the different opportunities available to Black and White sportswomen and sportsmen. The newly democratised DSR prioritised race above gender. It adopted a radical approach in transforming racial inequalities, but a liberal approach in dealing with gender inequalities in sport. Consequently, race and sport have periodically become a national problem, while gender inequalities remain a problem for women to resolve. For example, each sports federation is expected to formulate development programmes. The intention is that provincial and international teams will reflect the racial demographics of the country. This stance was emphasised by a resolution adopted in 1997 by the NSC to undertake a unity audit on racial differences in sports. In December 1998 the new government announced its intention to implement legislation which would mandate the selection of sports teams to ensure that black players were included.

The organisation of sport

In the 1990s various structures for the advancement of sport (and to a lesser extent recreation) included:

- the establishment of the National Sports Council (NSC) as the umbrella body for South African sport;
- the South African National Recreation Council as the umbrella body for recreation (SANREC);
- the National Olympic Committee of South Africa (NOCSA).

These were supported by national and provincial sport and recreation forums and councils and by structures for school and university sports, such as:

- the United School Sports Union of South Africa (USSASA)
- the South African Students Union (SASU)
- the Sport Information and Science Agency (SISA)
- the Sports Science Institute (SSI)
- the Western Cape Sports Academy (WECSA)

- The Sports Coaches' Outreach (SCORE). This is a non-profit, non-governmental organisation which provides opportunities for township children to acquire sports skills and leadership skills.

At a legislative level two sports-related bills were passed in 1998. This gave the Sport and Recreation Minister and his department more power to initiate and enforce change, rather than rely on a culture of goodwill (Hendricks 2000). The bills are the South African Sports Commission Bill (9B-98 1998; see Minister of Sport and Recreation 1998) and the National Sport and Recreation Bill (Gilpin 1999). Another key development was the establishment of the South African Sports Commission (SASC) in 1999. The Chief Executive Officer of the SASC is accountable to the Minister of Sport and Recreation who has significantly been able to maintain the Department of Sport and Recreation as his power base despite the formation of the Sports Commission.[11] It was within this climate in SA that a women's sports movement emerged in the early 1990s.

Women and sport in post-apartheid South Africa

Structures and policies

As the umbrella body for sport in SA at the time, the NSC created a structure in 1992 for promoting sport amongst females in the country. In 1993 an interim women's committee on sport was established in SA with the assistance of the Australian Sports Commission and the British Council on Sport (Hargreaves and Jones 2001). In 1994 this became known as the Women's Sports Foundation. With the restructuring of sport after 1994, the foundation lost its autonomy and in 1995 was replaced by a structure of the NSC and became one of its standing committees.

By December 1996, the NSC and the National DSR had jointly facilitated the formulation of a national strategy for Women and Sport South Africa (WASSA). Its mission is to ensure that women and girls have equal access to opportunities and support at all levels of sport (National Strategy 1997). In the meantime, the Western Cape DSR had formulated its provincial policy for women and girls in sport and recreation. It was launched in July 1997. In 1997 the NSC began the process of establishing women's sports desks in each of its affiliated sporting codes. In the same year WASSA was established in each of the provinces by the various Departments of Sport and Recreation. It is an all-female structure. Members are elected to serve on the provincial WASSA committees from where representatives are elected to serve on a National Advisory Council.

This level of detail is necessary for various reasons. Firstly, the process was consistent with the democratisation of South African society. Secondly, WASSA was the first structure ever to be established in SA for the sole purpose of promoting sport amongst women and girls. Thirdly, the election process in the establishment of WASSA was not without conflict as Black and White women had to find common ground after being racially divided by law. Fourthly, the establishment of the WASSA structures was partly funded by foreign investors who eventually became integrally involvement in the election process and in shaping many other issues around sporting females in the early development of the women's sporting movement in SA.

Physical education as life orientation

The status of physical education in South African schools reflects the complexities and conflict which characterise any education system in a process of transition. Physical education now forms one aspect of the learning area referred to as 'life orientation' (Solomons 1999). The focus of this learning area is to 'equip learners for meaningful and successful living in a rapidly changing and transforming society' (Sitzer 2001). Some schools have upheld the tradition of single sex classes, while others offer co-educational physical education. The subject is mostly taught by non-specialist physical education teachers. Workshops form the basis of life orientation training. Many specialist physical education teachers have been absorbed into the academic programme (Solomons 2002). There are numerous projects which have been instituted to supplement the physical education programme, especially in the Black townships and other areas previously marginalised during the apartheid era. One project which was initiated by the Departments of Education and Sport and Recreation is called 'stepping stones'. It develops competencies amongst unemployed young women and men who have completed their school careers, to teach sports skills at school level. They either assist in the physical education classes or with sports programmes after school.

Access to high-performance sports

As part of the restructuring of South African sport, an elite sports programme referred to as 'Operation Excellence' has been initiated under the auspices of NOCSA. The programme itself does not give preferential treatment to males or females. Once a talented sportsperson such as Dikeledi Morapane has been identified, she or he will be admitted to the programme where their sporting talent will be nurtured. It is therefore not at the institutional level where women and girls experience difficulties in accessing the sporting system, but at the level of the body where social stereotypes, religious beliefs and cultural norms still prevent many from pursuing a sporting career. Research findings indicate that cultural expectations about appropriate ways of clothing the married female body contribute in a significant way to the fewer numbers of African sporting females *vis-à-vis* their male counterparts competing in high-performance sport (Jones 2001b).

The cumulative effect of cultural constraints, gendered social roles and a serious lack of adequate infrastructures and resources, means that Black females, especially African women, have the most obstacles to overcome (Hargreaves and Jones 2001). The percentage of females representing SA in international competitions has shown no improvement since 1992 when SA was readmitted into the Olympic movement after its banning in 1968. Of the total number of South Africans competing at the Barcelona Olympics, only 30 per cent were female and these included three Black female athletes, namely, Rencia Nasson (fencing), Cheryl Roberts (table tennis) and Marcel Winkler (track). Only one Black woman represented SA at the Sydney Olympics in 2002, and she formed part of a mere 29 per cent of the South African females who qualified to compete (Burnett 2001). Female/male representation in national sports teams is equally gloomy. There are no females representing SA in rugby, golf or shooting, despite an Affirmative Action Policy (2000) which states that 'in the representative teams (from regional to national level) there must be at all times a 50 per cent representation of affirmative action groups'. Women only comprise 10 per cent of the national teams for rowing, 20 per cent for cycling and 60 per cent for swimming (Burnett 2001).

The White Paper on Sport and Recreation (National Department of Sport and Recreation 1997: 18) identifies women and girls as a special interest group alongside senior citizens, people with disabilities and 'worker sport'. It claims that gender equality and the right of women to participate in sport are of 'paramount' importance. It mentions 'encouraging national sports federations to devise training and development programmes to facilitate the participation of women' in sport. It refers to the removal of barriers which prevent women from pursuing careers in training, administration, coaching and management. However, it fails to offer any explanation of what it means by 'gender equality' and there is no mention of gender training. Gender equality has been interpreted as increasing the number of women and girls playing sport, not challenging male domination in decision-making positions.

Currently, the idea of addressing gender inequalities in sport is still limited to getting more women to participate in sport. In the late 1990s, leadership training in sport and recreation was offered by the DSR in partnership with the NSC and Recreation South Africa (RECSA). However, there was scant evidence to imply an understanding of the sport–gender relationship which should have been guiding sports policies and practices. Gender continued to be equated with women and gender inequality remained a 'woman's problem' – hers to experience and to transform.

Women and leadership

Despite the policies formulated and structures established for the promotion of sport amongst South African women, sport in the country remains gendered as male. Of the ten members on the executive committee of

NOCSA, only four are women. In 2001, two women and six men were elected to serve on the NSC, while only one of the nine provincial ministers for sport was a woman. Of the 140 sport federations who are affiliated to the NSC, only sixty-five had established women's desks, despite the national call for adopting gender equity strategies (Hargreaves and Jones 2001). Women do not play a significant role in decision-making positions in the national sport federations. Gymnastics is the exception with 70 per cent of women in leadership positions and 22 per cent in cycling (Burnett 2001).

Potential solutions

A liberal feminist approach to gender equality in sport in SA is problematic for two reasons. Firstly, the link with the equal opportunity model does not allow for the diversity which exists amongst South African females. The situation is further complexified by the enormous disparity in access to sports-necessary resources which still exists amongst South African women and girls.[12] The liberal approach presupposes the existence of a common notion of gender equality which is not a reality in SA (Albertyn 1994). Research done by Hargreaves (1997) and Jones (2001a) has revealed a willingness amongst South African sporting females to find spaces in which to pursue gender equality despite their diverse backgrounds. In addition, many women in the country would argue against an independent women's organisation because that would be something separate from struggles which affect their people as a whole, such as racism (Beall *et al.* 1987). It is possible that there are enclaves of South African sportswomen who are creating female-friendly environments for women and girls to enjoy the benefits of sports participation. They might, however, not refer to themselves as feminists. Identifying these feminist sporting groups in SA and/or establishing whether SA is ready for a more radical perspective to gender equality could be the subject of future research projects.

There is no simple solution to addressing gender inequalities in South African sport. What is clear is that a universal truth about South African women and sport does not exist. To move forward one needs to build on the progress made during the 1990s. In addition, it is necessary to acknowledge the connection which exists between forms of oppression and meanings attached to equality. Common goals need to be sought while simultaneously valuing diversity and constantly being sensitive to the way race, gender and class combine with structural constraints, social stereotypes and cultural norms to restrict the ability of women and girls to develop their potential as sporting females.

Notes

1 For the purposes of this chapter the terms black and white are used as mutually exclusive terms. Blacks refers to all those who are disenfranchised by the apartheid system and who were further classified as Coloureds, Africans and Indians. Where it is appropriate to

denote a particular category of race or ethnicity, then persons will be referred to specifically as Coloured, African, Indian, White-Afrikaans speaking, whichever is relevant. The first letter of the racial or ethnic grouping will be in capital letters.

2 Refer to Sacosport Festival (1988) and Roberts (1988) for insight into the role of the South African Council on Sport during the anti-apartheid struggle.

3 The term *sensei* is used in karate to refer to someone who has earned the right and accompanying respect to instruct others in karate.

4 The term *karate-ka* refers to all those who practice the sport of karate.

5 Refer to Ramsamy (1982) for more details regarding the impact of Apartheid legislation on Black sports-persons.

6 Penny Heyn announced her retirement at the Sydney Olympics 2000 after she competed in her last breaststroke race.

7 Refer to Guelke (1986) and Hargreaves (2000) for more details of the way Zola Budd's international sporting career was linked to the anti-apartheid movement. It also illustrates the relationship, at the time, between sport and politics. Zola Budd was very well known in athletics circles worldwide in the 1980s especially after the Mary Dekker episode at the American Olympics.

8 For a more detailed analysis of the link between identity, difference and meanings ascribed by South African women to equality, refer to Jones (2001b).

9 Refer to Bazilli (1991) and Liebenberg (1995) for discussions of the South African constitution from a gender perspective.

10 Refer to The Sports Movement of the Future (1992) for an account of the unity developments in South African sporting circles prior to the 1994 elections.

11 For an overview of the functions and structure of the South African Sports Commission refer to the document 'Taking sport into the future' (1999).

12 Refer to Hargreaves and Jones (2001) for more background on the way the legacy of apartheid still constrains the sports participation of the majority of South Africa women.

Bibliography

Albertyn, C. (1994) *Women and the transition to democracy in South Africa*, Johannesburg: University of the Witwatersrand.

Bazilli, S. (1991) *Putting women on the agenda*, Johannesburg: Ravan Press.

Beall, J., Hassim, S. and Todes, A. (1987) "'A bit on the side?": Gender struggles in the politics of transformation in south africa', *Feminist Review*, 33, Autumn.

Bertelsmann-Kadalie, R. (1989) 'The importance of feminism for the women's movement in South Africa', *Journal of Theology for Southern Africa*, 4: 48–52.

Biehl, A. (1993) 'Dislodging the boulder: South African women and the democratic transformation', in S.J. Stedman (ed.), *The Political Economy of Transition*, Boulder, CO: Lynne Reinner.

Booth, D.G. (1998) *The race game: Sport and politics in South Africa*, London: Frank Cass.

Burnett, C. (2001) 'Athena Nike was geen Suid-Afrikaanse Godin nie: Die Mite en Realiteit van geslagsgelyke sport', *S.A. Journal for Research in Sport, Physical Education and Recreation*, 23, 2: 7–22.

Draft White Paper on Sport and Recreation in South Africa (1995) Pretoria: National Department of Sport and Recreation.

Gilpin, T. (1999) *Match makers: A case for South African sport*, Cape Town: TED Gilpin.

Guelke, A. (1986) 'The politicisation of South African sport', in L. Allison (ed.), *The Politics of Sport*, Manchester: Manchester University Press.

Hall, M.A. (1996) *Feminism and sporting bodies: Essays on theory and practice*, Champaign, IL: Human Kinetics.

Hargreaves, J.A. (1997) 'Women's sport, development, and cultural diversity: The South African experience', *Women's Studies International Forum* 20, 2: 191–209.

—— (2000) 'Race, politics and gender: Women's struggles for sport in South Africa', in J.A. Hargreaves, *Heroines of sport: The politics of difference and identity*, London: Routledge.

Hargreaves, J.A. and Jones, D. (2001) 'South Africa', in K. Christensen, A. Guttmann and G. Pfister (eds), *International Encyclopaedia of Women and Sports*, New York: Macmillan Library.

Hendricks, D.J. (2000) Acting Director General, National Department of Sport and Recreation, South Africa, telephonic interview, 10 January.

—— (2001) 'Nation-building and the business of sport', *Perspectives – The Multidisciplinary Series of Physical Education and Sport Science*, 3: 65–76.

Horn, P. (1991) 'Post-apartheid South Africa: What about women's emancipation?', *Transformation*, 15: 25–39.

Jarvie, G. (1985) 'The political economy of White sporting practice in class, race and sport', in G. Jarvie, *South Africa's Political Economy*, London: Routledge.

Jones, D.E.M. (2001a) 'In pursuit of empowerment: Sensei Nellie Kleinsmidt, race and gender challenges in South Africa', in J.A. Mangan and F. Hong (eds), *Freeing The Female Body Inspirational Icons*, special issue of *The International Journal of the History of Sport*, 18, 1: 219–36.

—— (2001b) 'Gender, sport and power: The construction of identities as sportswomen in South Africa', unpublished doctoral dissertation, Utrecht University.

Kadalie, R. (1992) 'Role of women's organisations in transformation', working draft for: Ruth First Memorial Colloquium, Department of Anthropology, University of the Western Cape, South Africa, 17–18 August.

—— (1995) *Women in the new South Africa: From transition to governance*, Gender Equity Unit, University of the Western Cape, South Africa.

Lewis, D. (1993) 'The politics of feminism in South Africa', *Women's Studies International Forum*, 16, 5: 535–42.

Liebenberg, S. (1995) *The constitution of South Africa from a gender perspective*, Cape Town: The Community Law Centre.

Minister of Sport and Recreation (1998) South Africa Sports Commission Bill: B 89B – South Africa.

Msimang, S. (2000) 'African Renaissance: Where are the women?' *Agenda: Empowering Women for Gender Equity*, 44: 67.

National Strategy of Women and Sport South Africa (1997) Pretoria: National Department of Sport and Recreation.

Odendaal, A. (1988) 'South Africa's Black Victorians: Sport and society in South Africa in the nineteenth century', in J.A. Mangan (ed.), *Pleasure, profit, proselytism: British culture and sport at home and abroad 1700–1914*, London: Frank Cass.

—— (1995) 'The thing that is not round', in A. Grundlingh, A. Odendaal and B. Spies (eds), *Beyond the Tryline*, Ravan: Johannesburg.

Policy on affirmative action (1999) Pretoria: National Sports Council of South Africa.

Policy on women and girls in sport and recreation (1997) Cape Town: Department of Sport and Recreation – Western Cape.

Ramsamy, S. (1982) *Apartheid: The real hurdle*, London: International Defence and Aid Fund for Southern Africa.

Roberts, C. (1988) *SACOS 1973–1988: 15 years of sports resistance*, Cape Town: Havana Media.

—— (1993) 'Black women. Recreation and organised sport', *Agenda*, 17: 8–17.

—— (2000) *South African sports action*, December, 1–2, Cape Town: Havana Media.

—— (2001) *South African sportwoman*, 2: 1–19, Cape Town: Havana Media.

Sacosport Festival (1988) *A commemorative volume*, Cape Town: Buchu Books.

Salo, E. (1999) 'From woman to women: Feminist theory and the diverse identities of South African feminists', in K.K. Prah (ed.), *Knowledge in Black and White: The impact of apartheid on the production of reproduction of knowledge*, Cape Town: Centre for Advanced Studies of African Society.

Sitzer, J. (2001) 'Life orientation: A learning area in South African school curriculum', paper presented at the Southern African Congress in Sport Sciences, held at the University of Stellenbosch, South Africa, 5–9 November 2001.

Solomons, D. (1999) 'Good practices in physical education', in G. Doll-Tepper and D. Scoretz (eds), *Proceedings: World summit on physical education*, Berlin: ICSSPE.

—— (2002) Director: Subject Advisors, Western Cape Education Department, South Africa, Telephonic interview, 3 March.

SISA (Sport Information South Africa) (1997) *Research on the participation of women in sport in South Africa*, Pretoria: BMI-Sportinfo.

Taking sport into the future (1999) Pretoria: South African Sports Commission.

The sports movement of the future: The playground, emergence and policy of the National Olympic and Sports Congress (NOSC) (1992) Pretoria: National Olympic and Sports congress of South Africa.

Walker, C. (ed.) (1982) *Women and resistance in South Africa*, London: Onyx Press.

Wells, J. (1993) *We have done with pleading: The women's 1913 anti-pass campaign*, Johannesburg: Ravan Press.

White Paper on Sport and Recreation in South Africa (1997) Pretoria: National Department of Sport and Recreation.

10 Social issues in American women's sports

D. Margaret Costa

Sports development in the country: general aspects, central issues

The year is 2002 and the country is the United States of America, and in Women and Sport classes all across the nation, students are discussing the new 'firsts' from the 2002 Winter Olympic Games in Salt Lake City, Utah: the first African-American woman to win a Winter Olympic Games gold medal in a first-time competition for women, bobsledding. Why should race and gender continue to dominate any sporting discussion at the beginning of the twenty-first century? The answer is necessarily bifurcated. Although participation rates and media coverage of American women's sports have reached an all-time high, leadership opportunities for women are still relatively rare and girl's and women's participation opportunities do not mirror those of men.

What is the real status of the American sporting woman at the beginning of the twenty-first century? In an insightful article titled 'Gender Equity and the Black Female in Sport', Donna Lopiano, Executive Director of the Women's Sports Foundation, provided the statistics for American high school and collegiate sport participation:

- fewer than 35 per cent of all high school athletes are women;
- fewer than 34 per cent of all college athletes are women;
- male athletes receive $179 million more in athletic scholarships each year than their female counterparts;
- collegiate institutions spend 24 per cent of the athletic operating budgets, 16 per cent of their recruiting budgets and 33 per cent of the scholarship budgets on female athletes;
- fewer than 1 per cent of all coaches of men's teams and fewer than 46 per cent of all coaches of women's teams are female.

(Lopiano 2001)

A parallel report that included professional sports found that when leadership opportunities for American women were combined with participation rates and gender makeup of the industry, only the WNBA, headed by a woman, was found to be equalitarian. Furthermore the report found that there was a decline in the influence of women over most sports organisations. Only the US Olympic Committee and the NCAA, although not equalitarian by any measure, were found to have shown improvement in front-office representation of women (Lapchick 2001).

Historical synthesis of American women's sports participation

A brief history of American women's sports participation identifies the roots of the issues that envelope women's sports participation at the beginning of the twenty-first century. Prior to European colonisation of the United States, Native American women worked and recreated as they participated in the ebb and flow of tribal life. They danced, they played ball games, ran races, participated in rites of passage, and like women all over the world they bonded. Overall they were robust and healthy. The European women colonists came to America with different skills, interests and family compositions. Some were free. Others came as indentured servants. Lacking natural immunity to the diseases of their new homeland, many died and others suffered a variety of illnesses. Most of their lives were focused on survival. It was not until the third generation of offspring had become adults that any form of recognisable popular culture could be established. The Africans who came to America brought their games and dances with them. Although most were slaves they became important contributors to America's rich heritage of sports and dance. The Italians, the Germans, the Irish, the Polish, the Russians, the Chinese, the Japanese and the Latin Americans came. They all contributed.

By the mid-nineteenth century, American women were participating in sports and recreations according to socio-economic status. Industrialisation had served as a catalyst for the redefinition of the classes. The newly established middle-class women became the objects of social engineering, with leading medical authorities declaring women's bodies as dysfunctional. There were no such concerns for working women. Working women slaved 10–12 hours per day in garment factories and had little time or thought for recreation. Higher education became the hallmark of upper-class women with the establishment of Oberlin College in Ohio, the first coeducational institution in the United States. Upper-class women began attending the newly established women's colleges, beginning with Mount Holyoke College in 1836, Vassar College in 1861, Smith College and Wellesley college in 1875, Harvard Annexe (later known as Radcliffe) in 1879, Bryn Mawr College in 1888 and Barnard College in 1889. The socio-economic status of these students allowed them the freedom to participate in all manner of sporting activities. Such activities led President Calvin Coolidge to call the women's colleges 'hot beds of radicalism' (Coolidge 1921).

Nineteenth-century social engineering, aimed at the middle class, led to strict unhealthy dress codes that further restricted women's physical activity. It was generally believed that women would suffer from 'brain exhaustion' if they studied, and 'bicycle face' if they enjoyed recreational activities (Vertinsky 1994). It was the bicycle that liberated middle-class women from their corsets and gave them the freedom to make choices about their social activities. They could ride to the beach, the store, the theatre, or more importantly to a field hockey game or learn to play basketball at the YWCA.

In the first decade of the twentieth century, the newly invented sport of basketball swept across America with women and girls playing in the parks and play grounds as well as elementary schools, high schools and colleges. This plethora of competition was soon to recede to intramural activity. In 1912 a University of Chicago doctor declared that basketball led to enlarged overactive hearts (Costa 1987). The 1920s, the era of the flapper, may have showcased women's sexual freedom, but it also continued the social engineering of the nineteenth century. Non-feminine activities such as sport did not conform. Supporting the opposition to women's face-to-face competition were the women physical educators. Their control over women's sporting activities led to the slow and controlled development of women's sport in educational institutions during the first half of the twentieth century (Gerber 1974).

During that same time period, the early decades of the twentieth century, women's industrial league sports developed for working women. Hanes Hosiery, Coca Cola and Woolworth's were among the first business enterprises to sponsor women's teams. Babe Dedrikson, the greatest American athlete of the first half of the twentieth century, came to prominence as an employee of Employers Casualty Company (Dedrickson and Paxton 1955). Business and industry sponsored bowling, basketball, softball and track and field teams. Along with the Parks and Playground movements spawned by the economic recession of 1929, the Amateur Athletic Union provided girls and women with participation opportunities. There were thousands of teams and competitions. Women's sports outside of the educational setting were alive and well.

In the 1950s men came home from war and women were encouraged to retreat to domesticity. In the 1960s, fueled by the momentum of the civil rights movement, the first women's athletic revolution was born. Women athletes and coaches began taking responsibility for their competitions. By 1972 the stage was set for the passage of Title IX, the educational amendment to the Civil Rights Act of 1964. Requiring institutions that received federal funds to provide equal opportunity for participation in coaching, playing and officiating and equal access to facilities, Title IX increased the participation of women in sports from 74,239 in 1981 to 150,185 in 2000 according to the National Collegiate Athletic Association (Daprano and Titlebaum 2002).

Olympic participation by women has been the object of similar social engineering. Baron Pierre de Coubertin, *renovateur* of the modern Olympic

Games, believed that women would lose their femininity if they participated in sport (Leigh and Bonin 1977). Fortunately, the competitions were left to the local organising committees in 1900 and 1908 onward. Local organising committees initiated women's competitions in the socially acceptable sports of tennis and golf and swimming and 'feminine' gymnastics. In 1904 at the Games in St. Louis, the American organising committee did not allow women to compete although women's archery was a demonstration sport. Athletics for women was considered inappropriate. It was not until after the successful staging of various forms of Women's Olympic Games by the Feminine Sportive Federation Internationale under the leadership of Mme Alice Milliat (France) that women's athletics was offered in 1928. Because women moved to the infield to lie down after the 800 meter race in 1928, distances longer than 100 meters were not to be offered on the Olympic Programme until 1960 (Emery 1982). The 1932 Game of Los Angeles offered six athletic events. Two black women record holders, Louis Stokes and Tydie Pickett, were removed from the women's relay team after their arrival in Los Angeles (Costa 1992). Sixteen year later, Alice Coachman became the first African-American woman to win a gold medal in the Summer Olympic Games. Racism and sexism continued. In 1964, after the Japanese starting blocks proved to be an impossible fit, the American men's Olympic coaches forbade the use of the American men's starting blocks by American women Olympians, even though the male Olympians had offered their use (Costa 1992).

The continuous denial of equal opportunity for both women and black American Olympians was also spawned by American Olympic Committee President (later International Olympic Committee President), Avery Brundage (Leigh 1972). It was not until the Los Angeles Games of 1984 that American women Olympians received better but not yet equal treatment. The passage of Title IX is generally credited with the success of the American women (Schaap 1984). During the next two decades women received expanded media coverage and the number of competitions increased but control of the Olympic Games remain a male preserve. The only woman applicant to replace IOC President Juan Antonio Samaranch, Anita de Frantz, an African American and the only female member of the IOC Executive Board, was given little support for her bid. She was eliminated on the first round by the all-male nomination commission who nominated 14 males from the 48 names submitted by the national Olympic committees and by the international federations. Belgian Jacques Rogge took the helm in July 2001 at the 112th session of the IOC (Abrahamson 2001).

Social framework

Social engineering, attitudes towards race, gender, sexual preference and above all power and control continue to control girls and women's physical activities. Women's and girls' participation is strongly influenced by groups who use biologically based sex roles and socially constructed gender roles to define societal norms and sustain their influence. The hegemony theory of Antonio Gramsci provides the best explanation for the stratification of sport in American society. To hold power a ruling class must achieve hegemony over society, meaning its political, intellectual and moral authority or leadership must be predominant (Grossberg 1989). In the case of sport, male hegemony maintains its status through the subtle influence of ideology on the sporting masses. That ideology manifests itself in terms of body, gender, class, power, representation and subjectivity. When these ideological components are brought into play they serve as building blocks for the barriers to equality of competition opportunities for women and girls.

The United States of America is a consumer culture. Sport is organised according to the demands of that consumerism. Consumerism in turn reproduces images of masculinity and femininity that sustain asymmetrical gender relations in American society. Organisations, both public and private, control women's and girl's competitions. Female athletes are powerless outside of the organisational structure. Equipment, facilities and services are provided by those organisations which in turn have been penetrated by aggressive business interests. Participatory sport is commercialised.

Girls' fitness and health

Americans' fitness and health is watched over by two government entities, the President's Council on Physical Fitness and the Centers for Disease Control (CDC). Girls' sporting opportunities are organised by schools, parks and playgrounds, private clubs and sport specific associations. Women's sporting opportunities are organised by colleges, parks and playgrounds, private clubs and sport-specific professional and amateur associations.

Hundreds of articles deploring the decreased fitness of American children appear in daily newspapers across the nation. 'Fitness Crisis for American Kids', 'Schools Fail Kids by Cutting P.E.', 'Schools Skipping Gym Class', 'Jogging May Make You Smarter' are articles that represent the public concern for the assumed lack of fitness of American children. The organisations that sponsor these articles are as numerous as the articles themselves. The American Alliance for Health Physical Education Recreation and Dance is the umbrella organisation for the promotion of Health and Physical Education in the schools. Other groups include Afterschool Alliance, PBS TeacherSource, the American Association for the Child's Right To Play, the National Institute for Fitness and Sport, Fit 4 Life and the Centers for Disease Control. They all promote healthy lifestyles for the 50 million children that attend schools every day. What is the status of America's children? According to former US Surgeon General Dr M. Joycelyn Brothers, despite being the richest country in the world the United States ranks behind eleven other countries in how it takes care of its children (Burke 2002). A Center for Disease Control report states that 29 per cent of students nationwide in kindergarten through Grade 12 do not have physical education classes. Males are more likely than females to participate in vigorous physical activity, strengthening activities and walking or bicycling. White females are more likely to exercise than black females. Physical activity declines strikingly as age or grade in school increases (CDC 1997).

In 'Moving into the Future: National Standards for Physical Education, A Guide to Content and Assessment', a general description of each content standard is first presented, followed by presentation of the standards according to grade level: K, 2, 4, 6, 8, 10 and 12. Within each grade level, the standard is further defined, followed by a listing of the key points of emphasis for that grade level. Sample performance benchmarks, which describe developmentally appropriate behaviours representative of progress toward achieving the standard, are also presented. Lastly, a variety of assessment techniques appropriate for assessing student achievement of the specified content standard is described. The National Standards for Physical Education indicate that a physically educated student should show competency in many movement forms; an understanding of the development of motor skills and physical fitness; enjoyment of physical activity; and demonstrate responsible behaviours (Young 1997).

The Centers for Disease Control (CDC) promote Kids Walk-to-School programmes at the public out-of-school level. On 4 October 2001 David Satcher, Surgeon General and Assistant Secretary for Health of the Department of Health and Human Services, kicked off this event by joining groups of Maryland children as they walked to school. Besides promoting physical activity, the venture promotes safer neighbourhoods through increased social interaction. Other promotions from the Centers for Disease Control (CDC) include the National Bone Health Campaign, suggesting that powerful bones lead to powerful girls; PEP (Personal Energy Plan) a twelve-week self-directed healthy eating and physical activity programme; Ready. Set. It's Everywhere You Go; a physical activity campaign; and World Health Day: Move for health! (CDC 2002).

At the beginning of 1999, most states began feeling the impact of the second wave of baby boomers' children (children of parents born in the 1960s), classroom space at all levels of education became a premium. Baby boomers, wanting to secure college placement for their children, spent large amounts of their income on private tutoring services such as Hooked on Phonics and the Sylvan Learning Center. States began enacting standards for classroom subjects. As a result, emphasis on any activity that did not contribute to future college success, declined. In July 2001 the Council on Physical Culture of the American Alliance for Health Physical Education Recreation and Dance felt compelled to publish a position paper on the importance of school recess. Joined by the National Association of Elementary School Principals, the National Association for the Education of Young Children and the American Association for the Children's Right to Play, they emphasised that recess was an important component of a child's physical and social development. Recess was said to provide discretionary time where kids engage in physical activity of their choosing while learning lifetime skills of conflict resolution, cooperation, respect for rules and problem solving (COPEC 2001). Other entities such as the Afterschool Alliance heralded President Bush's initiative on after school programmes manned by volunteers from Americorps, Seniorcorps and Save the Children. Emphasising the need of low-income working families, the United State Congress re-authorised the Elementary and Secondary Education Act and recommended that $1.5 billion in 2003 and $1.7 billion in 2004 be spent on after school activities (Afterschool Alliance 2002a).

The issues remain the same. Physical inactivity is the major contributor to obesity in young girls. Obesity is a major risk factor for diabetes, hypertension, elevated cholesterol and early onset of osteoporosis. Girls are faced with attractive sedentary alternatives to physical activity. Watching television, playing computer games and chatting on the cell telephone are just a few of the unhealthy alternatives to physical activity.

Some schools are finding ways to control the rise in obesity. Schools are making exercise fun for girls. Physical education programmes now include inline skating, water sports, bicycling, rock climbing, kayaking and distance walking. Others are assigning exercise as homework and encouraging young girls to keep a journal of their physical activity. Classes take stairways rather than elevators. Girls learn to select food that is both tasty and healthy. Physical education is integrated into the classroom by encouraging girls to transfer what is learned in one setting to another setting. In the ideal school setting, social studies, language arts, mathematics and art, all integrate knowledge from the sport and physical activity realm. The Olympic Games, terminology used by different countries for sporting goods, calculation of heart rate both maximum and resting, calculation of the number of strides in the 100 metre competition, and appreciation of the colour of sports competition are examples of such integration (Elliott and Sanders 2002).

High school sports

Beginning in 1971, the National Federation of State High School Association (NFHS) kept statistics on the number of students participating in school athletics. In 2000–1 girls' participation rate increased by 60,662 to 2,784,154 over the previous year. Girls' participation was 70 per cent of that of boys. Basketball remained the most popular sport for girls (444,872 participants), outdoor track and field was second (415,666 participants), and then volleyball (388,518 participants), fast softball (328,020 participants), soccer (274,166 participants) and tennis (164,282 participants), followed by cross-country, swimming and diving, competitive spirit squads and hockey. The state of Texas had the largest girls' participation followed by California, New York, Michigan, Illinois, Ohio, Pennsylvania, New Jersey, Minnesota and Florida (NFHS 2002). Not all high school associations willingly supported increased equity for girls. In the 1990s there were twenty-four landmark court decisions in high schools and twenty-eight in high school and secondary school associations (University of Iowa 2002). Furthermore, the lack of equity in participation also fosters increased health risks. The Centers for Disease Control report that: only 19 per cent of all high school students report being physical active for 20 minutes or more in physical education classes; daily attendance in physical education classes declined from 42 per cent in the 1990s to 25 per cent in 1998; 25 per cent walk or bike to school; females are less likely to participate in vigorous physical activity, strengthening activities and walking or bicycling (CDC 1997, 2000).

Surrounding the Women's World Cup in 1999 was the explosion of opportunities for girls in team sports of soccer, softball, basketball and volleyball. The numbers soon declined, however. This explosion in access was not accompanied by a permanent demand for the acquisition of physical skills as a normal part of an average adolescent's girl's development. Several studies indicate that once puberty is reached, breasts become a focal point of adolescent girls and participation rates atrophy dramatically (Solomon 1999). Compounding the decline in participation rates of adolescent girls was the drop-out rate. The girls' drop-out rate, six times greater than that of boys, is further compounded when combined with the decline in participation that is associated with increase in age (Lopiano 2000; CDC 2000).

A more positive trend surrounded the University of Connecticut's win in Final Four basketball in 1995 and 2002. The agenda setting effects of the first success were studied by Sonski in 1996. The resulting increase in basketball participation by adolescent girls in Connecticut is credited to the media's power to shape public opinion. In a telephone poll, two-thirds of Connecticut's population reported following Connecticut women's basketball. Sonski theorised that agenda setting, the mass media's ability to shape public opinion, was as important in sport as it was in politics. As the women's coverage was presented and framed in a positive light in both hard news and sports news, women's sport became vital news. Both attitude change and attitude formation were found to be important to the redefinition of 'femininity' in relation to sports participation. More importantly, Sonski found that attitudes about women's sports competition were not rigid. They could be changed by positive media coverage (Sonski 1996). Sonski's analysis appears to be further supported by the previously mentioned NFHS 2002 report in which basketball was found to be the most popular girls' sport. A 1999 national survey showed that 12.67 million females aged six and over played basketball, a 12 per cent increase over two years. The number of girls registering for AAU tournaments exceeded that of boys. In 2001 602 teams competed for ten AAU Girls' Basketball Championship honours with an additional 199 teams playing in the AAU National Invitational Championships (Fiveash 2001). Agenda setting by the media really does pay off.

Opportunities for participation

Women's and girls' teams do not get the support that men's and boys' teams do. Although Title IX was passed thirty years ago in 1972, societal norms and values continue to be defined by dominant groups in some of America's major city parks. Although Los Angeles created the first municipal playground department in the United States in 1904, the region, southern California, was the site of two lawsuits filed by the American Civil Liberties Union on behalf of girls aged 5–18 years of age. In 1998 and 2000 the ACLU filed two lawsuits on behalf of girls seeking equal access to playing fields in Los Angeles and Montebello respectively. West Valley Girls' Softball was a twenty-nine-year league of 500 girls who were denied access to the same facilities as were made available to boys' baseball leagues. In this case the gatekeeper was the City of Los Angeles Parks and Recreation Department. Girls were temporarily allotted inferior and makeshift school fields to which they and their parents carried their own dirt in order to render them playable. The City not only provided permanent fields with appropriate amenities to the boys' teams, they also sponsored three leagues. Alleging gender-based discrimination, the ACLU expanded the case to all girls city-wide. The Los Angeles City Council finally responded by adopting a 'Raise the Bar' programme, a first step to providing equal access to participation opportunities and facilities for girls (ACLU 2001).

The second case involved access to public playing fields in Montebllo. A three-to-one ratio existed in the allocation of playing fields to boys and girls respectively. The 450 member twenty-year old Montebello Girls' Softball League was assigned only one playing field. The resultant crowding of the space, scheduling of the field ten times in one day, and increased risk of injury because of lack of warm-up and cool-down time also placed the players in physical jeopardy. Preliminary relief and a settlement agreement were approved by the court in 2000 (ACLU 2001).

Sport practice continues to reinforce societal roles. American culture demands heterosexualisation. Adolescent girls accommodate that demand by attempting to be popular with the most popular boys by overemphasising their femininity and de-emphasising those skills that may challenge boys, physically and emotionally. Participation in physical activity is encouraged for the wrong reasons. Cultural imperatives such as firm buttocks and lean thighs are often taken to extremes. Long hair is a premium among girl athletes. Being able to literally 'let their hair down' once the game is over is a means of legitimising femininity. The Sporting Goods Manufacturers Association has noted the growth in the female market and has accommodated products accordingly. Special batting helmets with holes in the back for ponytails have been produced (SGMA 2001; Solomon 1999).

The relationship between sport and adolescent health has different meaning for different girls. Graphic images of thin models continue to influence the perception of ideal body type. A Harvard School of Public Health study found that 47 per cent of girls in fifth through twelfth grades wanted to lose weight because their bodies did not mirror the shape marketed to them in magazines (Cheung *et al.* 1999). Other studies have found that body image is a major concern for girls as young as ten years old regardless of weight and pubertal development (Gowen 1998). Sports that emphasise slim bodies have a high occurrence of eating disorders in adolescent girls (gymnastics, diving, swimmers, figure skaters). Bulimia and anorexia are the most prevalent of weight-loss practices used by young female athletes, while excessive exercise, and laxative abuse are also common (McVey 1999).

Health risks in athletes may be a reflection of the cultural context in which they find themselves. The need to take chances and the need to display courage, shrewdness and strength of will are often part of the social milieu (American Academy of Pediatrics 1996). In an analysis of youth risk behaviour in grades 9 through 12 developed by the Centers for Disease Control and Prevention, it was found that athletes were less likely to use illicit drugs; highly involved female athletes (three sports) were more likely to use steroids, and to binge drink; both male and female athletes were less likely to be suicidal; and female athletes had more positive body images but were more likely to attempt weight loss (Women's Sports Foundation 2001a). Girls are still limited in their choices of sports participation and the notion that females exist for entertainment purposes still prevails. During the summer thousands of adolescent females attend female cheerleading camps held on college campuses across the nation. Cheerleading is still viewed as a supporting role to sports competitions that are mostly male dominated. Their revealing uniforms and provocative moves on the sidelines promote the image of cheerleading as non-serious entertainment.

Heterosexual sport has always been a male domain. The achievements of women athletes have been marginalised according to norms of femininity. Athleticism, although an accepted skill in the third millennium, is still accompanied by suspicion of a diversity that mainstream America is yet to embrace. Muscular bodies portray the image of control, independence and challenge to the heterosexual lifestyle. If women are muscular, the reasoning that follows is 'they must be different'. Furthermore the difference must be abnormal. When athletes happen to be lesbian, all of the ideological components of social stratification come into play: body, gender, class, power, representation and subjectivity. Their physical accomplishments are marginalised because they are different. Lesbians are demonised. Their occupation of 'athletic space' is questioned. In many instances lesbians have to be careful about their friendships, their team associations and their visibility. They are conditioned to abide by an unwritten set of rules that forbid them to call attention to their sexual preference. Homophobia is a social injustice that has yet to be fully addressed.

Another underrepresented, invisible group is disabled women and girl athletes. Once again, body, gender, class, power, representation and subjectivity are the components of social inequity. The United States has eight major sports organisations for the disabled athlete. Disabled athletes receive rare coverage in the media. Women and girl athletes who are disabled are often overly protected by their parents. Women with disabilities fare relatively worse in the arena of sports opportunities than their able-bodied sisters (Feminist Majority Foundation 2001).

At the beginning of the twenty-first century the differential distribution of sporting opportunities, prestige, privilege and power continues for women athletes. The fact that physical *in*activity is more prevalent among women than men, among blacks and Hispanics than whites and among less affluent than affluent people suggests that a massive national commitment to fitness is needed (CDC 1998). A positive trend has started. In 2000–1, 77 per cent of NCAA women athletes were white non-Hispanic, down from 78.1 per cent in 1999–2000. Badminton had the steepest per ethnic group increase, moving from 8.8 per cent Asian women participants in 1999–2000 to 33.3 per cent Asian women participants in 2000–1. The participation of white women in badminton also increased by approximately 30 per cent (NCAA 2002).

Title IX

Until the advent of the Women's National Basketball Association, the most popular professional women's sports have been individual sports, golf and tennis. In the last decade, institutions and organisations have been forced to 'voluntarily' participate in gender equity. During the last decade of the twentieth century, twenty years after the passage of Title IX, there were fifty colleges, eleven higher education athletic conferences and eight associations that voluntarily agreed to comply with Title IX regulations (University of Iowa 2002). The largest university system in the country, California State University, was one of the volunteers. After a lawsuit was filed by the California Chapter of the National Organisation for Women and it became obvious that the university would lose the case, a settlement was reluctantly reached. The term reluctantly is used here, because as a member of one of the Athletic Committee on one of the campuses, this author was told that the lawsuit was brought by 'a bunch of radical women lawyers who could not get a job anywhere else'. All of the twenty campuses were found to be out of compliance with Title IX and all agreed to come into compliance by the 1998–9 academic year (The Orange County Register 1993). In the settlement, the system agreed to provide women students equal athletic opportunities. By the 1998–9 academic year, the number of varsity sport slots that the system offered women athletes were to be equal to the percentage of women in the general student body within 5 per cent (Hollon 2002). Acosta and Carpenter (2000) have kept track of participation rates in higher education institutions since 1971. They agree that the rise in women's sports participation in higher education has been a result of the filing of Title IX and gender equity lawsuits. In 1999–2000, although 205 new women's teams were added, more than half were in the less prestigious Division II and Division III of the NCAA.

Basketball, volleyball, tennis, cross country, and soccer are the most popular sports, with soccer now being offered on 84 per cent of all campuses. Softball is next in popularity, and lacrosse and golf have shown marked increases. Again, media coverage played an important role in the success of women's basketball. In 2001, NCAA Division I women's basketball signed a $160 million eleven-year contract with ESPN to cover their tournament. More important than the money was the fact that ESPN agreed to broadcast all games (Women's Sports Foundation 2002).

Title IX continues to be a double-edged sword. Before its implementation, women held over 90 per cent of coaching jobs for women's sport. In 2000 of the 7,771 head coaching jobs of women's NCAA teams, only 45.6 per cent were women, down from 47.7 per cent in 1998. One hundred and seven of the 534 new jobs went to women in 1998–2000. Only 17.1 per cent of women's athletic programmes were under the direction of women in 2000; down from over 90 per cent when Title IX was enacted. Other positions such assistant athletic directors, sports information directors and head athletic trainers mirror the statistics for head coaches (Acosta and Carpenter 2000).

Social stratification represented above is compounded when money and race enter the picture. Male athletes still receive $179 million more in scholarships than women; collegiate institutions spend less than 40 per cent on athletic operating budgets, recruiting budgets and scholarship budgets for women athletes. African-American women athletes although well represented in the most popular sport basketball, have 10 per cent of college team slots. African-American women coaches represent 5 per cent of NCAA coaches and less than 1 per cent of NCAA administrators. African-American women also suffer from the sociological phenomenon of stacking in sports. They have highest rates of participation in basketball and track and field, and rarely captain teams or have positions in which they make decisions involving control and outcome (Lopiano 2001).

Professional sport

An attempt was made for women to have control over a women's professional sport, with the inauguration of the American Basketball League (ABL) and the Womens National Basketball League (WNBA) in 1996 and 1997 respectively. The ABL played from October until March, had a salary scale of $40,000 to $150,000 and was totally independent and self-supporting. The players had stock options in their organisations, played with the same sized ball as the men, used the same type of shots, shot clock, timeouts and quarters and played forty-four games per season (Kampfner 2001). Why did they fail? There was no agenda setting by the media. The media knew that the WNBA, the sister league of the NBA was about to be launched. As a result, they paid little attention to the ABL.

The ABL did not have sufficient financial backing. The WNBA had eleven sponsors and full financial backing of respective NBA franchises. Its season was during the summer months, June to August, so as not to compete with the men's competitions.

The WNBA and the NBA are the only professional teams that are close to gender and racial equity. This equality is the direct result of the way in which the WNBA was established. The Commissioner of the NBA insisted that the WNBA be an equal partner to their counterpart organisations in the NBA in that they were given equal access to the same facilities for practices and games; equal access to coaching, media representation, officiating and medical facilities; and most importantly a large share of revenue dollars (Costa, 2001). Twenty-seven per cent of WNBA players are from outside the USA, as compared to 11 per cent in the NBA. The WNBA has 45 per cent persons of colour and 85 per cent women in the League offices (Lapchick 2001).

The sport that represents true inequity is professional golf. From 1996 to 2000 the annual LPGA prize money rose from $26.5 million to $38.5 million while the PGA prize money increased from $69.1 million to $167 million. With the entrance of Tiger Woods, the greatest golfer of all times, the differences have increased dramatically between 2000 and 2002. Annika Sorenstam signed a three-year endorsement contract with an apparel company during which she could make up to 60 per cent of top male golfers' endorsements excluding Tiger Woods. He is estimated to have $100 million in endorsement contracts (PGA and LPGA 2002: see Table 10.1).

As of September 15, 2002 Serena Williams ($3,073,076) is well ahead of Lleyton Hewitt ($2,113,989) in professional tennis. Men's tennis has more depth with 50 players having earned more than $300,000. Seventeen players have earned more than $300,000 on the women's side (TSN.CA). The Australian Open and the US Open are the only Grand Slam tournaments to award equal prize money. In 2000 the highest paid women athletes were all tennis players: Martina Hingis ($11 million) Anna Kournikova and Venus Williams ($10 million) and Serena Williams ($7.5 million). Venus Williams signed a five-year $40 million endorsement contract with Reebok in December 2000 (Womens Sports Foundation 2002).

Table 10.1 Comparison of all-time LPGA winners with 2002 PGA winners

LPGA	All-time	PGA	2002
Anita Sorenson	$8,869,794.00	Tiger Woods	$2,685,500.00
Karrie Web	$7,709,707.00	José Maria Olazabal	$1,772,273.00
Betsy King	$7,200,744.00	Phil Mickelson	$1,715,863.00
Dottie Pepper	$6,658,613.00	Retief Goosen	$1,608,795.00
Julie Inkster	$6,638,337.00	Vijay Singh	$1,514,370.00
Beth Daniel	$6,483,278.00	Sergio Garcia	$1,420,180.00

Source: Statistics from LPGA and PGA Websites April 21, 2002

The new women's soccer league WUSA with salaries in the five figure range is hiring women for front office positions (Women's Sports Foundation 2001b). Other new professional leagues include United States Professional Volleyball (2002) with teams in Grand Rapids, St Louis, Chicago and Rochester; the Women's Professional Football League (2000); and Women's Senior Golf (2000).

There are over six million jobs in sports-related careers in the United States. The sports industry that is predominantly male does recognise that most sport-related purchase decisions in households are made by women, even though they are fewer than 20 per cent of participants. Women are also consumers of men's professional sports. Corporations are also using sports to sell to women (Eitling 2001). Although the number of women working in sports departments, writing about sports, broadcasting sports on television and radio has increased dramatically in the last decade, the number of women in management and editorial positions is still negligible. From 1991 to 2001 the number of women at small, medium and large newspapers was 13 per cent. The number of women sport editors was 1 per cent. Furthermore, women sportswriters enjoy a ten-year career span at best. If women are not reporting about women, then it is possible that women's sports may not be reported with a women's point of view (Eitling 2001).

Opportunities for American women and girls to compete and manage sports have increased in the last decade. Those opportunities are coupled with many challenges. Only with increases in grassroots programming, women mentoring women and girls, increased corporate sponsorship, marketing and promotion of women and girls sports at all levels, will the landscape change.

Bibliography

Abrahamson, A. (2001) 'Latest round of nominees for IOC lacks women', *Los Angeles Times*, 28 July: 1.

Acosta, V.R. and Carpenter, L.J. (2000) 'Women in intercollegiate sport: A longitudinal study twenty three year update 1977–2000', *Women in Sport and Physical Activity Journal* 9, 138: 1–3.

American Academy of Pediatrics (1996) 'Promotion of healthy weight-control in young athletes', *Pediatrics* 97, 5: 752–3.

Burke, K. (2002) 'An interview with Dr. Joycelyn Elders', 2002 Association Supervision and Curriculum Development interview at the 57th ASCD Conference, 9 March, San Antonio, Texas.

CDC (Centers for Disease Control and Prevention) (1997) *Guidelines for School and Community Programmes: Promoting Lifelong Physical activity*, U.S. Department of Health and Human Services, Atlanta, GA: CDC, March 1997.

—— (2000) *Promoting better health for young people through physical activity and sports: A report to the President from the Secretary of Health and Human Services and the Secretary of Education*, Atlanta, GA: U.S. Department of Health and Human Services, CDC.

CDC (Centers for Disease Control and Prevention: Nutrition and Physical Activity) (2002) *Physical activity topics*, U.S. Department of Health and Human Services, Atlanta, GA: CDC Division of Nutrition and Physical Activity.

Cheung, L., Gortmaker, S. and Colditz, G. (1999) *Exposure to the mass media and weight concerns among girls*, in Harvard School of Public Health, *Around the School*, Boston: HSPH.

Coolidge, C. (1921) 'Enemies of the republic: Are the reds stalking our college women?' *The Dilineator* 98: 4–5, 66–7.

Costa, D.M. (1987) 'It was no slam dunk, but loads of fun: Women's basketball in southern California 1900–1920', in J. Berryman (ed.), *Proceedings of the North American Society for Sport History*, Seattle: NASSH.

—— (1992) *Oral history interviews with various women Olympians*, Los Angeles: Amateur Athletic Foundation of Los Angeles Archives.

—— (2001) Interview with James Bakken, Manager for Group Sales, Los Angeles Sparks and Los Angeles Lakers, Staples Center, Los Angeles, 1 July.

Coubertin, Baron Pierre de (1912) 'Les femmes jeux olympiques', *Revue Olympic* July 1912, 79: 92.

Council on Physical Education for Children (2001) *Recess in elementary school*, National Association for Sport and Physical education, an Association of the American Alliance for Health Physical Education Recreation and Dance, Reston, VA: AAHPERD.

Daprano, C. and Titlebaum, P.W. (2002) 'Women's sports: Opportunities and challenges', *SportaPolis Newsletter*, 8: 1–5.

Dedrickson Zaharias, B. and Paxton, H. (1955) *This life i've led*, New York: Barnes.

Emery, L. (1982) 'An examination of the 1928 Olympic 800 meter race for women', in J. Berryman (ed.), *Proceedings of the North American Society for Sport History*, Seattle: NASSH.

Feminist Majority Foundation (2001) 'Disabled women in sport', in *Sports and the disabled*, Arlington, VA: FMF.

Gerber, E. (1974) *The American woman in sport*, Reading, MA: Addison-Wesley.

Gowen, L.K. (1998) 'Social victimisation, teasing and weight concerns in young adolescents', presented at the Stanford Center on Adolescence, 17 August, unpublished.

Grossberg, L. (1989) 'The circulation of cultural studies', in *Critical Studies in Mass Communication* 6, 4: 413–20.

Kampfner, J. (2001) 'The end of the American Basketball League', in *Sportsjones newsletters*, 24 August, 1–4.

Leigh, M. (1972) 'American women's participation in the Olympic Games', doctoral dissertation, Ohio State University.

Leigh, M. and Bonin, T. (1977) 'The pioneering role of Madam Alice Milliat and the FSFI in establishing international track and field competition for women', *Journal of Sport History*, Spring: 72–8.

McVey, R. (1999) 'Eating disorders and athletes', *Selfhelp Magazine*, 5: 1–4.

NCAA (2000–1) 'Sport-by-sport student-athlete ethnicity percentages', in *NCAA Research*, Indianapolis: NCAA.

—— (2002) 'Sport-by-sport participation and sponsorship – Womens sports 1982–2001', in *NCAA Research*, Indianapolis: NCAA.

NFHS (National Federation of State High School Associations) (2002) 'Participation sets record for third straight year', press release, Indianapolis: NFHSA.

Schaap, D. (1984) *The 1984 Olympic Games*, New York: Random House.

SGMA (Sporting Goods Manufacturers Association) (2001) 'U.S. sporting goods market outlook for 2002', Indianapolis: SGMA Press release.

Solomon, A. (1999) 'Girl power?', *The Village Voice*, 27 April: 1–2.

'CSU system gives boost to women' (1993) *The Orange County Register*, 21 October: 1.

Vertinsky, P. (1994) 'Women, sport and exercise in the 19th century', in M. Costa and S. Guthrie (eds), *Women and sport: Interdisciplinary perspectives*, Champaign, IL: Human Kinetics.

Welch, P. and Costa, M. (1994) 'A century of Olympic competition', in M. Costa and S. Guthrie (eds), *Women and sport: Interdisciplinary perspectives*, Champaign, IL: Human Kinetics.

Young, J. (1997) *National standards for physical education*, ERIC identifier: ED406361: ERIC Clearinghouse on Teaching and Teacher Education, Washington, DC: United States Department of Education, Office of Educational Research and Improvement.

Online sources

ACLU (American Civil Liberties Union), Baca *v.* City of Los Angeles and Romero *v.* City of Montebello (2001) http://www.aclu-sc.org/litigation/wmnsrghts.shtml (26 March 2002).

Afterschool Alliance (2002a) 'President Bush speaks to values of afterschool', http://www.afterschoolalliance.org (19 April 2002).

—— (2002b) 'Poll shows public concerned about effects of welfare on children, http://afterschoolalliance.org (19 April 2002).

Eitling, L. (2001) 'Missing in management', http://www.womenssportsfoundation.org/cgi_bin/iowa/issues/disc/article (9 April 2001).

Elliott, E. and Sanders, S. (2002) 'The issues: Children and physical activity', *PBS Teacher Source*, http://www.pbs.org/teachersource/prek2/issues (28 March 2002).

Fiveash, S. (2001) 'WBCA: AAU girl's basketball, bigger and better than ever', http://ct-starters.org/wbca01.htm, 1–4 (18 April 2002).

Hollon, S. (2002) 'NOW remain vigilant in pursuit of Title IX enforcement', http://www.now.org/nnt/08_95/titleix.html (6 March 2002).

Lapchick, R.E. (2001) 'Racial and gender report card', http://www.sportinsociety.org/rgrc2001 (28 March 2002).

Lopiano, D. (2000) 'Recounting our thoughts about girls and sports', http://womens sportsfoundation.org/cgi-bin/iowa/issues/part/article.html (19 April 2002).

—— (2001) 'Gender equity and the black female', http://www.womenssportsfoundation.org/cgi_bin/iowa/issues/disc/article (19 April 2002).

LPGA (2002) http://www.lpga.com/statistics/index.cfmwebsites (19 April 2002).

PGA (2002) http://www.golfweb.com/stats/index_r.html (19 April 2002).

Sonski, J. (1996) 'Huskymania and agenda-setting effects on girl's high school basketball', http://vax.wcsu.edu/mccarney/acad/sonski.html (19 April 2002).

The Women's Sports Foundation (2001a) 'Research report: health risks and the teen athlete', http://www.womensportsfoundation.org/cgi-bin/iowa/issues/body/article.html (19 April 2002).

—— (2001b) 'Sports careers for women', http://www.womensportsfoundation.org/cgi-bin/iowa/issues/body/article.html (19 April 2002).

—— (2002) 'Sports business', http://www.womensportsfoundation/womenssports/fitnessfact/figures/article (15 January 2002).

University of Iowa (2002) 'Gateway to womens sports: Web links to womens' sportslinks topics', http://bailiwick.lib.uiowa.edu/ge/category.html#CaseIndex (19 April 2002).

USTA website (2002), http://USTA.com/stats/default.sps (15 September 2002).

11 Girls' and women's sport in Canada

From playground to podium

M. Ann Hall

Like most countries, Canada's sporting ethos is based on the fundamental, yet sometimes contradictory, goals of participation and excellence. From children's play for fun on local playgrounds emerge the talented few who eventually reach national and international athletic stardom, even though the climb from playground to podium is often long and tortuous. For the past forty years and more, since Canadian governments became seriously involved in sport, they have struggled to find just the right balance between promoting mass participation in physical activity and sport among the populace, and at the same time developing a 'seamless' sport system in which the talented few can rise to the top and succeed.

Despite millions of tax dollars contributed annually to active living programmes and to amateur sport, as well as the endless government studies and reports each with a set of recommendations (rarely acted upon), there is a continuing decline in sport and physical activity participation among Canadians. At the international level, we are a visible sporting nation, although sometimes not as successful as we would like. For example, at the summer Olympic Games in Sydney, we placed seventeenth, measured both by medals and top eight finishes, which was a slide from our previous ranking of eleventh in 1996. By contrast, Canada's performance at the 2000 Paralympic Games was very successful, improving from seventh to fourth place (Canadian Heritage 2001).

Most Canadians, it seems, are content to be among the sedentary or to take the view that as long as our athletes 'do their best', winning medals is not necessarily all that important – except when it comes to ice hockey – which brings much hand wringing and national angst if we lose. Far more attention (among men anyway) is devoted to men's professional sports – especially ice hockey, baseball, basketball and Canadian football – with so-called 'amateur' sport a poor sister to the glitzy entertainment sector. Girls and women have until recently had access mainly to amateur sport, and at the international level they often perform better than their male counterparts. Now there are more professional sport opportunities for talented females, which has brought a new marketing of women's sport, especially team sports, and the making of female sports stars into commodities.

Organisation of amateur sport in Canada

The sport system in Canada has many elements (see Figure 11.1). On one level, there are the millions of individuals involved in sport – recreational participants, athletes, coaches, leaders, officials, administrators, and others – some of whom are paid, but many more play purely for the love of the game or volunteer their time and expertise. There are the communities where sporting events take place. There are the institutions and organisations with roles in the sport system, some single-sport (like Basketball Canada), others multi-sport (like the Coaching Association of Canada), some at the national level, others at the provincial/territorial or local level. These organisations receive financial support from governments according to the scope of their programmes and services. Finally, there are the corporate sector enterprises who also sponsor sport and sport events (Canadian Heritage 2001).

The framework for governing and managing amateur sport in Canada is based on a complex and decentralised system that cuts across sport organisations and jurisdictional lines. At the federal level, there is a Secretary of State for Amateur Sport, an elected politician of the governing Liberal party, who is responsible for administering the Fitness and Amateur Sport Act (passed in 1961), developing national sport policy and distributing funding (through a bureaucracy called Sport Canada). In most of the ten Canadian provinces and three territories, there is also an elected politician responsible for sport (and likely also recreation and tourism) along with a counterpart

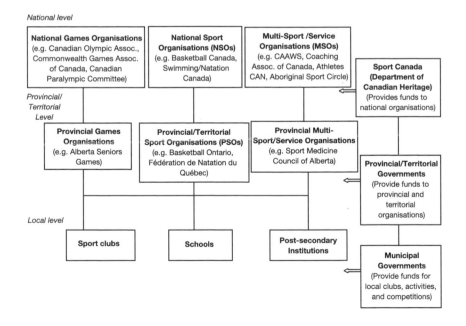

Figure 11.1   Structure of the sport system in Canada

bureaucracy to administer funding, policy and programmes. The direct and ongoing intervention of the state over the past forty years has resulted in a more corporate style of management within sport organisations and hence more paid professionals (and fewer volunteers) directing these organisations (Hall *et al.* 1991). Sport Canada has had a women in sport policy since 1986, and although there is no longer a special women's programme within the Fitness and Amateur Sport Branch, it continues to support initiatives designed to advance participation and leadership opportunities for girls and women in physical activity and sport through monitoring national sport organisations and providing funding for special projects.

In 2000–1, the federal government contributed $82.8 million to amateur sport through national sport organisations, multi-sport organisations, the athlete assistance programme, Canada Games, hosting major games and six national sport centres. There has been a steady increase in the level of funding over the past few years, and beginning in 2001–2, the federal government has promised to increase its sport budget by $10 million a year for three years, raising the annual commitment to $95 million. Similar funding programmes exist within the provinces and territories although they vary considerably. Ontario, for example, with a large population base and considerable wealth, spends several millions annually on amateur sport, whereas a tiny province like Prince Edward Island contributes less than $500,000. Yet compared to other state-supported programmes in similar countries (such as Australia), the overall government expenditures on amateur sport are small, especially in comparison to other social and cultural programmes. For example, Health Canada has $110 million in its current budget just to stop children from smoking. Increasingly, amateur sport organisations from the local to national level must find other ways to generate revenue whether through fund-raising schemes or corporate partnerships.

Although in the past there were sometimes separate sport organisations for women and for men, today virtually all national and provincial organisations, and certainly local clubs, do not segregate by gender. At the national level, there is one multi-sport organisation, the Canadian Association for the Advancement of Women in Sport and Physical Activity (CAAWS), which also has a few provincial counterparts, whose purpose is to advocate on behalf of girls and women in sport. These associations are discussed in more detail later in the chapter.

Participation of girls and women in physical activity and sport

Physical activity participation

Some thirty years have passed since the first serious efforts were undertaken by individuals, women's groups, government agencies, recreational bodies, educational institutions, and the like to improve gender equity in Canadian physical activity and sport. Where are we now? Despite ample evidence of increased interest and participation by females in certain sports, as well as renewed exercise and recreational physical activity among sectors of the population, far too many Canadian women (and men) are not active enough to benefit their health. For instance, according to the Canadian Fitness and Lifestyle Research Institute, some 60 per cent of young female adults (age 18–24 years), compared to 36 per cent of males in the same age group, do not engage in physical activity sufficiently frequent and intense enough to develop fitness. As age increases, the level of inactivity also increases such that at the upper age range (65 and over), 78 per cent of women (and 65 per cent of men) are insufficiently active (Canadian Fitness and Lifestyle Research Institute 2001).[1]

Sport participation[2]

Fewer Canadians are active in sports than was the case a decade earlier. This is true for both children and adults, and as always fewer girls and women play sport than do boys and men. In 1998, one-third (34 per cent) of the Canadian population (age 15 and over) participated in sport on a regular basis (at least once a week), down almost 11 percentage points from the 45 per cent reporting participation in 1992 (Sport Canada 2000: 9). There is an even more noticeable drop in the rate of adult females engaging in sport over this six-year period. In 1992, 38 per cent of Canadian women over fifteen years of age were regularly engaged in sport, but by 1998, this figure had dropped to 26 per cent as compared to 43 per cent for males (Sport Canada 2000: 11). Women's involvement in physical activity is more likely to take the form of individual fitness activities than organised sports. In 1998, only 19 per cent of Canadians aged fifteen and older belonged to a club, a local community league or other local or regional amateur sport organisation. On the other hand, women who do play sport tend to belong to a club or league. Of the 2.4 million Canadians who were registered members of national and provincial sport organisations, just under 30 per cent are female (Sport Canada 2000: 29–30). Finally, every study of sport involvement demonstrates that participation for both genders decreases with age, and increases with the level of education and household income (Sport Canada 2000).

Physical activity and sport among children

Children and adolescents with physically active parents tend to be more active than children with inactive parents. In 1998, just over half (54 per cent) of the estimated 4.1 million Canadian children aged 5–14 were regularly active in sport. Girls were less active than boys. While 61 per cent of boys were active in sport, the corresponding figure for girls was 48 per cent (Sport Canada 2000; Kremarik 2000). Children of both genders are getting increasingly less exercise as measured by being overweight, even obese. Between 1981 and 1996, the percentage of overweight girls between the ages of seven and thirteen went from 15 to 24 per cent (for boys it went from 15 to 29 per cent) (Picard 2000). Eating habits, long hours of watching television or playing video games, as well as insufficient exercise, all contribute to the growing problem. There has also been an erosion of school physical education both in terms of the amount of time devoted to it as well as the number of years it remains a compulsory subject.

Reasons for low participation among girls and women

Analyses of persistent physical inactivity by girls and women have become more sophisticated and far reaching during the last decade. Abby Hoffman, former head of Sport Canada and now Director General of the Women's Health Bureau in the federal government, argues that 'real gains will only be achieved if we take account of the social, cultural, economic and political realities of women's lives beyond sport, and if we endeavour to change those conditions beyond sport that limit sport involvement' (Hoffman 1995: 85).

Women's increased labour force participation, their domestic and family responsibilities, substantially lower incomes and a higher poverty rate all contribute to fatigue, stress and health-related problems. These are significant factors, although not necessarily causes, contributing to women's lower participation in physical activity and sport.

Patricia Vertinsky, who has researched the subject for many years, argues that even today the medical profession assists 'not only in rendering women dependent upon the health care system, but also in poisoning their concept of physical self by causing them to perceive their natural processes as deviant and problematic, thus thwarting a vigorous approach to exercise and competitive sport' (Vertinsky 1997: 3). Menstruation, pregnancy, childbirth and menopause have become increasingly medicalised, such that much of the professional and popular discourse on female health, exercise and sport is contaminated by a focus on women's reproductive function. For example, a recent article appearing in a local newspaper with the headline 'Bike riding may endanger women's sexual health' (*Edmonton Journal*, 31 May 1999) reported on genital numbness in women from recreational cycling; the fact that males also complained of penile numbness from the same activity was not significant. Cultural messages that overstate the negative rather than positive effects of exercise and physical activity on women's health continue to act as a deterrent to women's enjoyment and participation.

Early in adolescence, girls (most often white and middle-class) are socialised in ways that promote body-hating attitudes, which in turn distort their attitudes towards exercise and sport. 'It's fair to say', argues sociologist Helen Lenskyj, 'that by puberty most girls have learned that others evaluate them first and foremost in terms of their physicality and sexuality' (Lenskyj 1995: 6). Even though images of today's healthy, beautiful women allow for more muscularity and vigour, young women and girls are still bombarded through fashion magazines, advertisements and television programmes with models and bodies they simply cannot become. Some become obsessed with their bodies, and view them as segmented objects in need of repair – nose, breasts, face, bottom, legs, whatever – something overindulgent and misguided parents allow with increasing frequency (Humbert 1995). The pursuit of thinness leads to unhealthy eating at best and disordered eating at worst, sometimes unhealthy patterns of excessive exercise, and at the very least instils little appreciation for the joy of movement and physicality, what Helen Lenskyj calls 'physical illiteracy'.

It is also important to recognize, as do many others, that we cannot rely on the sameness of girls and women when discussing their bodies, their health, and their exercise and sport participation. For example, the rate of participation among women with disabilities is lower than that of able-bodied women due to inaccessible facilities, transportation problems and lack of programme information (Watkinson and Calzonetti 1989; Olenik *et al*. 1995). Aboriginal women, especially those living in rural and remote areas, are severely disadvantaged and marginalised. On native reserves with sporting facilities and programmes, far fewer girls and women compared to boys and men have access to these resources and opportunities (Paraschak 1995; Hargreaves 2000).

Increased participation in ice hockey and soccer

There are several sports that in recent years have seen large increases in the number of girls and women playing and competing, although in most cases their numbers still do not compare favourably with males playing the same sports. Ice hockey is a good example. According to the Canadian Hockey Association, 43,421 females were registered to play organised hockey in Canada in 2000, although the majority were in Ontario and Quebec. The growth since the mid-1980s, when less than 6,000 girls and women were registered, has been steady, which is not the case for males where some years have seen losses. Yet compared to the total number of males (approximately 500,000) playing hockey, there is still a long way to go (Christie 2000; Etue and Williams 1996; Theberge 2000).[3] Gender inequality persists at every level from ice time to clubs, leagues, championships and media attention. Still, in the more than one hundred years Canadian women have played the game, there have never been the same numbers, resources, programmes, administrative structures and media focus as there are today. Player registration and awareness of the national team soared after Canada won the first Women's World Championship sanctioned by the International Ice Hockey Federation in Ottawa in 1990. Canada won the next six world championships, always beating the United States in the gold medal game. In fact, one of the few times the United States defeated Canada was at the 1998 Nagano Olympics, where six teams competed for the gold medal. Given the disparity in teams from North America compared to those from Europe and Asia, there are some who think that women's hockey does not yet belong in the Olympics; nonetheless, it was again on the programme for the 2002 Winter Olympics in Salt Lake City, where Canada won the gold medal.

While Canada is known as a hockey nation, we are not particularly noted for soccer. Yet, among active 5–14 year-olds, soccer is the game of choice ranking just behind ice hockey for boys and swimming for girls (Sport Canada 2000). Far more Canadian girls play soccer (28 per cent) than do ice hockey (6 per cent), and the growth during the 1990s has been spectacular. Of the total player registration in 2000, the number of females was 270,145, representing 37 per cent. For the past several years, females have accounted for over one-third of the new registrations each year. The vast majority of players, both male and female, are youths (under 19 years), yet there are nearly 25,000 adult women in Canada playing the game. Ontario, Quebec, British Columbia and Alberta are the provinces with the largest numbers, although the discrepancy between the numbers of males and females registered is often less in provinces with fewer players (Canadian Soccer Association 2001).

Like other Canadian sport associations, soccer did not always welcome females especially if they wanted to play on boys' teams, which many had to do before clubs, community centres, schools and universities began to initiate programmes for girls and women. To be fair, many centres encouraged boys and girls playing together and it was only when a team came under the jurisdiction of a controlling body that problems arose. For example, as late as 1992, the Ontario Soccer Association still believed it could prevent girls from playing with boys. Two female high school students had played on the local boys' team all during the year. When their team reached the quarter-finals of the Ontario championship, they were told it would be disqualified if they continued to play because they were girls in a boys' competition. A complaint was laid with the Ontario Human Rights Commission, and after an inquiry, the Ontario Soccer Association was barred from interfering with the right of female players to compete for team positions on the same basis as males ('Girls Win Soccer Tussle' 1993).

Women in top-level and professional sport

For a relatively small minority of women, Canada's top-level athletes, opportunities to compete internationally have increased significantly since the beginning of the 1990s. For example, the 1992 Summer Olympics in Barcelona offered 159 events for men, 86 for women, and 12 open to both women and men, which meant that men had double the chances to compete for a medal. The Canadian team reflected this imbalance with 189 men and 125 women (40 per cent). However, with the addition of more sports and events for women at the Olympics, such as soccer, softball, beach volleyball, water polo, triathlon, mountain biking, modern pentathlon, taekwondo, weightlifting and others, the percentage of women on the Canadian team for both 1996 and 2000 was at 50.2 per cent. Boxing, wrestling and baseball are the only sports not yet available to women at the Olympic level. Improvement at the Winter Olympics is not quite as dramatic, but the number of women on the Canadian team jumped from 26 per cent in 1992 to 42 per cent in 1998, due mainly to the inclusion of women's curling and ice hockey. Other major games, like the Commonwealth Games, Pan-American Games, World Student Games and Paralympics have also added more women's sports and events, and there are more world championships in a variety of sports for women. Overall in 1998, the representation of women athletes on Canada's national teams was 47 per cent, and according to a survey, they appear to have equal access to training, competitive environments, as well as health, medical and sport science services (Sport Canada 2001).

Advertisers eager to find a way to connect with female consumers, television and Internet producers in need of programming, and a growing pool of professional calibre athletes, all explain the recent boom in women's professional team sports in North America. The National Women's Hockey League (NWHL), for example, made its debut in 1999 as a senior women's league – a professional operation although the players are not paid. By 2001, there were ten franchises based mostly in Ontario and Quebec, but also one located in Vancouver. The long-term objective of the NWHL is the establishment of a professional league with franchises in major North American cities. The Women's Television Network (WTN) has broadcast several NWHL league games as well as their national championships. Television audiences for the women's world's championships have also risen steadily since they were first broadcast as a novelty on The Sports Network (TSN). In 1990, for example, numerous print, radio and television journalists covered the event, attended by more than 20,000 people. The television audience averaged 450,000 for the first three televised games and about 1.5 million for the gold-medal game (Etue and Williams 1996). However, TSN was still very cautious about the viability of televising women's hockey until recently. Commented one network official: 'Women's hockey has evolved from a niche sport to a jewel in terms of participants, fans, broadcasters and advertisers' (Christie 2000).

The remarkable growth of grassroots soccer among female youth during the 1990s has paid off in the development of a women's national team programme, first initiated in 1986. For most of the decade the team laboured in obscurity. They did not play in the first Women's World Cup in 1991 sanctioned by the Fédération Internationale de Football Association (FIFA), and because they came twelfth in the 1995 tournament, they did not qualify for the 1996 Atlanta Olympics, when women's soccer made its debut. Tremendous publicity surrounded the third World Cup, played in seven US cities in the summer of 1999, especially around the Mia Hamm-led team from the United States. All thirty-two games were televised live with strong ratings, and hundreds of thousands more attended the matches.

The final game played in the Rose Bowl in Pasadena, California, between the United States (who won) and China, attracted some 90,000 fans, probably the largest crowd ever to watch a women's sporting event. Unfortunately the Canadians were again not in the top eight, and hence they did not qualify for the 2000 Olympics in Sydney.

The excitement generated in the United States by their team's success in the 1999 World Cup and at the 2000 Olympics contributed to the establishment of an eight-team women's professional soccer league, which began playing in the spring of 2001. The Women's United Soccer Association (WUSA) features both top players from the United States and the best internationals from twenty different countries. Five Canadian players were signed up to play in the league. According to newspaper reports, top foreign players in the WUSA earn in the neighbourhood of $50,000 US. The main investors in the league are television and cable companies including Discovery Communications, the parent company of the Discovery Channel and the Learning Channel. CNN/*Sports Illustrated* will produce a weekly *Inside WUSA Soccer* magazine show, and matches will be broadcast nationally on TNT and CNN/*Sports Illustrated*, all in the hopes of bringing appealing sports programming to a female demographic in North America (Heath 2001; Mallett 2001).

A few Canadian players have also been drafted into the professional Women's National Basketball Association (WNBA), launched in 1997 by the men's National Basketball Association with eight teams in two conferences, and now a sixteen-team league. The WNBA expects to draw 2.5 million fans in its fourth season with millions more watching games on network television. Before the WNBA, as is still the case now, several top Canadian players went to Europe to play professional or semi-professional basketball. Bev Smith, for example, undoubtedly the finest female player Canada has ever produced and former head coach of Canada's national women's team, played and coached in the Italian league for fourteen years. Women's amateur basketball at the international level is highly competitive, and although the Canadian team does well, it is not among the top nations.

Canadian athletes, although few in numbers now, will continue to benefit from these growing opportunities in women's professional team sports. For example, Canada's ice hockey players will be attracted to a women's professional hockey league should that come about, and there is talk of a professional indoor volleyball league in the near future. An eleven-team Women's Professional Football League, playing full-contact American football, was launched in 1999 and expects to succeed where others have failed despite a chaotic first year. According to some experts, men's professional sports will continue to 'run the risk of alienating families with skyrocketing salaries and ticket prices, labour problems and players showing up on police blotters', resulting in an increased appetite for women's sports (Grange 2000: S1).

Women in sport leadership

The Canadian amateur sport system, from the local club right up to national sport organisations, requires volunteers to help run it. Traditionally, many more men have been involved in this capacity than women, but in 1998 there was an equal proportion of males and females, a change from 1992 when nearly twice as many men were sport administrators (Sport Canada 2000). Whether the increase in women as volunteer sport administrators means that they will overcome the barriers to their participation on boards of directors and committees of provincial and national sport organisations remains to be seen. In the past, approximately 25 per cent of the volunteer sector in amateur sport was female, as was the case with senior executives and technical directors in paid positions (Canadian Association for the Advancement of Women and Sport 1993; Hall et al. 1990). Most Canadian universities have an athletic programme headed by an athletic director. Within the 49 member universities of Canadian Interuniversity Sport (CIS), there are now eleven (22 per cent) women athletic directors (McGregor 2001). Similarly, in 1992 the proportion of male referees, officials and umpires outnumbered females five to one, but the gender gap had decreased to less than two to one by 1998. Fewer women (36 per cent) than men officiate at the international level even though the numbers of male and female national team athletes are about even (Sport Canada 2001).

More women are also coaching in Canadian amateur sport than was the case a few years ago. While approximately 200,000 women reported coaching in 1992, this figure had more than tripled to 766,000 by 1998. There is no longer a large difference between the percentage of coaches who are male (56 per cent) and those who are female (44 per cent). However, many of these coaches are young adults between 15 and 24 years; coaching numbers decline substantially with age (Sport Canada 2000). Many women coach at the lower levels and with younger children, which is obviously fine, but their numbers become much fewer as the level of competition increases. According to the chief executive officer (who is female) of CIS there are 559 head coaches located at some fifty universities in Canada, but only 15 per cent of these coaches are women (McGregor 2001). In 1998 there were just over 250 full and part-time coaches employed by thirty-seven federally funded national sport organisations, and of these, 17 per cent were female. Among full-time coaches at the national level, there were ten times more males than females (seventy versus seven). Women coaches were paid less than their male counterparts, even though their qualifications under the National Coaching Certification programme were similar, and in some cases higher than the males (Sport Canada 2001). For instance, when Melody Davidson (who completed Level V, the highest possible level of certification) was coach of the women's national ice hockey team in 1999, she was paid an $8,000 honorarium, supplementing her income by running a hockey school in Alberta and coaching at a college in the United States. The national men's team had two full-time coaches, each paid at least $70,000 (Robinson 1999).

Coaching, especially at the higher levels such as university or national team, is a tough profession requiring commitment, dedication, endurance, late hours and much travel, to the extent that women with families find it difficult to balance both. As Kathy Shields, a highly successful and long time university-level basketball coach pointed out:

> In Canada, coaching is a great life, but it's a tough life if you've got a family. I've had the longevity because, one, I love the game, and two, I don't have children. I admire so much women coaches who have been able to balance both. In Canada, to be able to stay in coaching with a family, to me those women are the real heroes in this country.
>
> (Robertson 2000)

There now appears to be a concerted effort, particularly among women coaches themselves, to find solutions to high levels of burnout and frustration, and to convince organisations hiring coaches that they cannot abdicate their responsibility in assisting and encouraging women (and men for that matter) who wish to combine career and family, just like everywhere else in the labour market.

Sport organisations have not always seen the need for strategies and programmes to train and promote women coaches, and allow them to gain the necessary experience to move up the ranks, especially sports that have equal numbers of male and female athletes, but have been traditionally run by men. Competitive swimming is a good case in point. Women swim coaches have long been denied the same opportunities to coach at the elite for example, Olympic – level. In preparation for the Sydney Olympics, 26-year-old Shauna Nolden was added to the six men already appointed to the team, the first time a woman was part of the Canadian swimming coaching staff at an Olympic Games. Nolden, whose qualifications were questionable, was appointed without benefit of a selection committee nor were the criteria established for such appointments. Most coaches were outraged and many felt that other women deserved the spot ahead of Nolden. Consequently, a very public and messy controversy ensued with the 900-member Canadian Swimming Coaches Association filing a complaint; her appointment was subsequently voided, but a new selection committee with different criteria reappointed her and she went to Sydney. Despite their good intentions, this was a public relations disaster for Swimming Canada and, according to other women coaches, a giant step backward for women in coaching. Following Canada's lackluster swimming performance at Sydney (one bronze medal), a positive outcome of the controversy was that woman's coaches were invited to come forward with recommendations to redefine the role of the female coach at the high-performance level.

The under-representation of women in sport leadership is not an especially Canadian problem – it is worldwide – and it is reflected in every international and national sports governing body from the International Olympic and Paralympic Committees to the international sport federations and national Olympic committees. Among the thirteen (out of 123) women members of the IOC is Canadian Charmaine Crooks, an international track athlete who participated in four Olympics and was the Canadian flag bearer at Atlanta in 1996. She is only the second woman, and the first woman of colour, from Canada to sit on the IOC. With the untimely death of Canadian Olympic Association executive Carol Anne Letheren in 2001, both the IOC and Canada lost an experienced and respected member.

Women's sport advocacy and achievements

Beginning in the 1990s, and in most areas of organisational life including sport, there was a subtle shift in the discourse of human rights in Canada and elsewhere from 'equality' to 'equity'. Equality generally meant 'equality of opportunity' and women (along with other disadvantaged groups) were identified as target groups. In sport, equal opportunity programmes were designed to increase women's overall participation by opening up opportunities for them to enjoy equal access. The shift to equity signalled a more comprehensive view where the focus was no longer exclusively on women (or any other group) but on a system, in this case sport, which needed to change to accommodate them (Hargreaves 1994). As long-time sport activist Bruce Kidd put it: 'Equality focuses on creating the same starting line for everyone; equity has the goal of providing everyone with the same finish line' (Canadian Association for the Advancement of Women and Sport and Physical Activity 1993: 4). It was stated even more clearly in a report on gender equity from the Department of Athletics and Recreation at the University of Toronto: 'An athletics programme is gender equitable when the men's programme would be pleased to accept as its own the overall participation, opportunities and resources currently allocated to the women's programme and vice versa' (Task Force on Gender Equity 1993). 'Equity is an issue of quality; excellence in sport cannot occur without equity', explains Marion Lay, a respected advocate for women's sport both nationally and internationally, who has spent more than twenty-five years working on behalf of amateur sport in Canada (Kirby 1999: 57).

The Canadian Association for the Advancement of Women and Sport and Physical Activity (CAAWS) was founded in 1981 (as an openly feminist organisation) whose purpose is to advocate on behalf of women in sport. There are also several provincial women's sport advocacy organisations although they are independent of CAAWS, which has fully endorsed this shift from equality to equity.[4] From the early 1990s onwards, its focus has primarily been on bringing gender equity within the Canadian sport system. When its leaders sought increased funding from the Fitness and Amateur

Sport Branch, after its operational budget had been cut from the Secretary of State Women's programme in 1990, it positioned itself as the only group that could work with other national sport organisations to assist them in becoming gender equity organisations (whether they wanted to was a different matter) ('CAAWS Priorities for 1991', 1991).

CAAWS also removed all references to feminism from its mission statements and goals. By 1992, its purpose was 'to ensure that girls and women in sport and physical activity have access to a complete range of opportunities and choices and have equity as participants and leaders'. A new vision was portrayed as follows:

> As the leading organisation for girls and women in sport and physical activity, CAAWS is inclusive and equitable in its philosophies and practice.
> CAAWS provides expert advice, positive solutions and support to Canada's communities. Innovative and responsive attitudes ensure that CAAWS adapts quickly to change. Policies, plans and actions are based upon these attitudes and are supported by a solid foundation of research and information.
>
> ('CAAWS Activities in 1992–93', 1992)

By 2001, the language had changed somewhat, but the mission and goals were much the same: 'CAAWS is in business to encourage girls and women to get out of the bleachers, off the sidelines, and onto the fields and rinks, into the pools, locker rooms and board rooms of Canada'; and 'CAAWS works in partnership with Sport Canada and with Canada's sport and active living communities to achieve gender equity in the sport community.'[5]

Throughout the past decade, CAAWS has gained considerable credibility within the amateur sport community in Canada, and indeed elsewhere in the world. Like any multi-sport organisation, it receives (since 1994) core funding from Sport Canada, which allows it to support an office, executive director, small staff and volunteer board of directors, and also to run its programmes. Marg McGregor, the organisation's energetic executive director from 1992 until 2000, believed that a not-for-profit organisation was no different to a business. In other words, it must fill a need, be cost effective, productive, show value, be supported by clientele, and able to market its product ('Marg a Top 40 Under 40 Winner!', 1996).

To this end, CAAWS focused on building national partnerships with recreation and active living communities, aboriginal sport groups, other multi-sport organisations, the women's health community and others. On the communications front, it established a well-designed and interesting Internet web site in both English and French, and most importantly, keeps it updated regularly. CAAWS continued to educate sport leaders and organisations about gender equity, especially by working when requested with national sport organisations by reviewing policies and publications, and providing resource materials. CAAWS was a major player in a series of national Sport Forums in the early 1990s that led to the formation of the Canadian Sport Council, a now defunct coalition of national and multi-sport organisations, where a serious effort was made to build equity, in particular gender equity, into its structure. CAAWS also contributes to the international women's sport movement by sending representatives to conferences, working with worldwide organisations like the International Working Group and WomenSport International, and helping to organise the Third World Conference on Women and Sport Conference to be held in 2002 in Montreal.

Perhaps more controversial is the partnership CAAWS established with Nike Canada Ltd. With the exception of one letter to the CAAWS newsletter, there was little concern expressed over Nike's appropriation of women's issues to suit their entrepreneurial goals (through ad campaigns like 'Just Do It' and 'If You Let Me Play'), or about the consumption of Nike products at the expense of women in developing countries where these goods are made (Lafrance 1998; Dworkin and Messner 1999). The Nike partnership allows for activities like the Girls@Play Network, a club targeted at girls and young women with a membership package, newsletter, interactive web site, on-line chats and more. Nike also helped sponsor a women and sport symposium, and continues to provide small weekly grants to deserving young women athletes.

Most recently, CAAWS has contributed to the national debate over Canada's sport system through participating in a series of regional and national conferences and proposing recommendations to the Secretary of State for Amateur Sport. These include a national strategy for girls and women in sport and physical activity, a childcare policy for the Canadian sport system and an annual Canadian conference on women in sport. It also wants governments to support gender-based research to identify the gaps and barriers to women participating and leading in sport, and enforce accountability for women and sport among funded agencies with incentives to ensure change (Canadian Association for the Advancement of Women in Sport and Physical Activity 2001).

Current and future issues

The relatively new marketing of women's sport, especially team sports, the making of female sports stars into commodities and the sexualisation of female athletic bodies and physicality is not without its problems. There has always been a 'dark side' to women's sport, just as there is in men's, but it seems magnified now through a marketing lens, which has made the stakes much higher for all concerned. Among the issues and problems are an increased use of performance enhancing drugs among women athletes, the continuing exploitation and sexual abuse of female athletes by male coaches, an often dangerously hostile environment for lesbians in sport, unhealthy practices and body abuse, and the sexualisation of female athletes strictly for marketing purposes. Again, these problems are not specific to Canada, but since we live so close to the United States – indeed, many of our top women athletes train there, at American universities – it is difficult not to expect a much more commodified approach to sport.

Through a variety of programmes and strategies, Canada has taken steps to ensure ethical conduct in sport by combating doping, harassment, abuse and violence, and at the same time promoting health, safety, and procedural fairness (Canadian Heritage 2001). The Canadian Centre for Ethics in Sport, a national non-profit organisation, manages all aspects of athlete drug testing, and works closely with athletes, coaches and sport organisations to promote and strengthen positive and rewarding values of sport (Canadian Centre for Ethics in Sport 2001). Canada is not alone in uncovering disturbing facts about exploitation, harassment and abuse within its amateur sport system because there are now a number of studies conducted in various parts of the world that confirm the magnitude of the problem. Perhaps where Canada leads at present is in the development of programmes and strategies to expose and eradicate the abuse, especially sexual harassment (Kirby *et al.* 2000).

Like all social programmes funded mainly by public monies, amateur sport in Canada must compete for limited resources. Although the federal government and most provincial/territorial governments spout the 'playground to podium' ethos, there is no question that the development of elite sport and the winning of medals take far more resources than does sport at the grassroots level. The balancing of participation on the one hand with excellence on the other is never easy. Women's ice hockey is a good example. During the past decade, there has been a radical transformation within the women's ice hockey community from a development to a performance ethos, from a volunteer leadership base to an increasingly professionalised one, and from mostly local participation to organised, high-performance competition. Of course there are many, including talented players now able to dream of the Olympics or even a professional career, who could not be happier about these dramatic changes. On the other hand, there are those who are openly critical, arguing that the skilled athlete is now privileged over other players, and that individualism, performance and advancement now characterise the women's game (Stevens 2000). Only time will tell whether the twin goals of participation and excellence will continue to coexist successfully in women's ice hockey, and indeed in all of women's sport.

Acknowledgements

Some of the material in this chapter has been condensed from Chapter 7 in M.A. Hall, *The girl and the game: A history of women's sport in Canada*, Peterborough: Broadview Press, 2002.

Notes

1   The Canadian Fitness and Lifestyle Research Institute, which regularly monitors the physical activity levels of Canadians, defines 'inactivity' as expending fewer than three kilocalories per kilogram of body weight daily, or roughly equivalent to walking an hour a day.

2   Sport is defined as an activity that involves two or more participants engaging for the purpose of competition. Sport also involves formal rules and procedures, requires tactics and strategies, specialized neuromuscular skills, a high degree of difficulty, risk and effort (Sport Canada 2000: 7).

3   It should be noted that ringette is also very popular in Canada. Invented in 1963, the game (played on ice) is a mixture of hockey and lacrosse, where players skate using a straight stick to pass, carry, and shoot a rubber ring to score goals. By 1989, player registration was at 28,000, but by 2000 it had grown to 50,000 participants, actually a few more than the numbers in girls' and women's ice hockey. Internationally, however, the game is restricted to just a few countries, mostly Finland and Sweden, as well as Canada and the United States.

4   Promotion Plus, the most active provincial association, is in British Columbia: http://www.promotionplus.org.

5   Statements found on the CAAWS web site: http://www.caaws.ca/English (April 2001).

Bibliography

'Bike riding may endanger women's sexual health' (1999) *Edmonton Journal*, 31 May: B4.

Canadian Association for the Advancement of Women in Sport and Physical Activity (1993) *Towards gender equity for women in sport*, Ottawa: CAAWS & Women's Programme Sport Canada.

Canadian Heritage (2001) 'Building Canada through sport: Towards a Canadian sport policy', *Discussion Paper for the National Summit on Sport*, Ottawa, 28–29 April.

'CAAWS Priorities for 1991' (1991) *Action: The newsmagazine of women in sport and physical activity*, 9, 2: 2–4.

'CAAWS Activities in 1992–93' (1992) *Action/CAAWS.ACAFS*, October.

Christie, J. (2000) 'Women's hockey is different', *Globe and Mail*, 8 April: S1.

Dworkin, S. and Messner, M. (1999) 'Just do…what?: Sport, bodies, gender', in M. Ferree *et al.* (eds), *Revisioning gender*, Thousand Oaks, CA: Sage.

Etue, E. and Williams, M. (1996) *On the edge: Women making hockey history*, Toronto: Second Story Press.

'Girls win soccer tussle' (1993) *Globe and Mail*, 2 November: A1.

Grange, M. (2000) 'Future looks rosy for women's pro sports', *Globe and Mail*, 17 February: S1.

Hall, M.A. (2002) *The girl and the game: A history of women's sport in Canada*, Peterborough: Broadview Press.

Hall, M.A., Cullen, D. and Slack T. (1990) 'The gender structure of national sport organizations', *Sport Canada Occasional Papers*, 2: 1, December.

Hall, M.A., Slack, T., Smith, G. and Whitson, D. (1991) *Sport in Canadian society*, Toronto: McClelland & Stewart.

Hargreaves, J. (1994) *Sporting females: Critical issues in the history and sociology of women's sports*, New York and London: Routledge.

—— (2000) *Heroines of sport: The politics of difference and identity*, London and New York: Routledge.

Heath, T. (2001) 'To market, to market', *Washington Post*, 1 April: D3.

Hoffman, A. (1995) 'Women's access to sport and physical activity', *Avante*, 1, 1: 77–92.

Humbert, L. (1995) 'Behind the smiles', *Action/CAAWS.ACAFS*, 1995 Winter: 1–3, 20–1.

Kirby, S. (1999) 'Gender equity in the Canadian Sport Council: The new voice for the sport community', in K. Blackford *et al.* (eds), *Feminist Success Stories/Célébrons nos réussites féministes*, Ottawa: University of Ottawa Press.

Kirby, S., Greaves, L. and Hankivsky, O. (2000) *The dome of silence: Sexual harassment and abuse in sport*, Halifax: Fernwood.

Kremarik, F. (2000) 'A family affair: Children's participation in sports', *Canadian Social Trends*, Autumn: 20–4.

Lafrance, M. (1998) 'Colonizing the feminine: Nike's intersections of postfeminism and hyperconsumption', in G. Rail (ed.), *Sport and postmodern times*, Albany, NY: State University of New York Press.

Lenskyj, H. (1995) 'What's sport got to do with it?', *Canadian Woman Studies / les cahiers de la femme*, 15, 4: 6–10.

Mallett, P. (2001) 'Hooper endorses women's pro loop', *Globe and Mail*, 13 April: S4.

'Marg a Top 40 Under 40 Winner!' (1996) *Action/CAAWS.ACAFS*, Spring: 11.

Olenik, L., Matthews, J. and Steadward, R. (1995) 'Women, disability and sport: Unheard voices', *Canadian Woman Studies/les cahiers de la femme*, 15, 4: 54–7.

Paraschak, V. (1995) 'Invisible but not absent: Aboriginal women in sport and recreation', *Canadian Woman Studies/les cahiers de la femme*, 15, 4: 71–2.

Picard, A. (2000) '"Couch potatoes" burden weighs in at $3.1 billion', *Globe and Mail*, 28 November: A1, A11, A18.

Robinson, L. (1999) 'Games boys play', *Canadian Forum*, October: 18–21.

Sport Canada (2000) *Sport participation in Canada*, Ottawa: Minister of Public Works and Government Services Canada.

Stevens, J. (2000) 'The declining sense of community in Canadian women's hockey', *Women in Sport and Physical Activity Journal*, 9, 2: 123–40.

Task Force on Gender Equity (1993) 'Final report to the council of the department of athletics and recreation', University of Toronto, 31 December.

Theberge, N. (2000) *Higher goals: Women's ice hockey and the politics of gender*, Albany, NY: State University of New York Press.

Vertinsky, P. (1997) 'Physical activity, sport and health for girls and women: Issues and perspectives', *Bulletin of the International Association of Physical Education and Sport for Girls and Women*, 7, 1: 1–15.

Watkinson, J. and Calzonetti, K. (1989) 'Physical activity patterns of physically disabled women in Canada', *CAHPER Journal*, 55, 6: 21–6.

Online sources

Canadian Association for the Advancement of Women in Sport and Physical Activity (2001) 'National sport policy recommendations', http://www.caaws.ca/Whats_New/apr01/Sport_policy_apr2.htm (3 April 2002).

Canadian Centre for Ethics in Sport (2001) 'About CCES', http://www.cces.ca (3 April 2002).

Canadian Fitness and Lifestyle Research Institute (2001) '1998 and 1999 physical activity monitor, http://www.cflri.ca/cflri/pa/index.html (3 April 2002).

Canadian Soccer Association (2001) '2000 demographics: Player registrations', http://www.canadasoccer.com/eng/docs/index.asp (3 April 2002).

McGregor, M. (2001) 'RE: Gender statistics', e-mail mcgregor@ciau.ca (6 June 2001).

Robertson, S. (2000) 'In their own voices: Women coaches raising a family', *Canadian Journal for Women in Coaching Online*, 1, 2, http://www.coach.ca/women/e/journal/past_issues.htm (3 April 2002).

Sport Canada (2001) 'Sport gender snap shot 1997–1998: Survey results report', http://www.pch.gc.ca/Sportcanada/Sc_e/EscH.htm (3 April 2002).

12 Brazilian women and girls in physical activities and sport

Ludmila Mourão and Sebastião Votre

Participation of Brazilian women in sport: a historical point of view

Brazil is large in size, and is the richest country among those with the biggest number of poor people.[1] Up until 1900, Brazilian women were insignificant in sport. They were absent from sports fields as well as from every other form of public life. The country, as a whole, was opposed to the emancipation of women.

Brazilian women began to participate in physical activities and sport in clubs in the 1920s. This participation has now reached special heights, since it occurs in sports clubs all over the country, regardless of whether or not these clubs have female departments. Recent figures on women's status in Brazil show that the proportion of Brazilian women participating in the nation's development increased during the 1980s. This presented a big challenge to the patriarchal system. One can find examples of this situation in different fields of human activity, including the field of sports. Women's participation in top-level sport increased during the last decades. This visibility of sports women has influenced more women to adopt more active lifestyles.

The first woman to represent Brazil at the Olympic Games was the swimmer Maria Lenk at Los Angeles in 1932 (Votre and Mourão 2001). The daughter of German immigrants and now very close to ninety years old, this eminent athlete continues to swim and to break records. Beyond her brilliant carrier as an athlete, Maria Lenk was a teacher of physical education who became involved in the organisation of female sports at the national level. In the 1960s she was the first Brazilian woman to join the National Council of Sports.

Maria Lenk was a key figure who helped bring about radical changes in federal laws which explicitly prohibited women from playing sport. For example, one law stated, 'women will not be allowed to practice sports which are considered as incompatible to their feminine nature' (Decreto-Lei 3.199, 1941). Another stated: 'women are not permitted to practice fight of any nature, as well as soccer, footsall (a kind of soccer designed for indoor space), beach soccer, polo, weightlifting and baseball' (7th Deliberation of National Council of Sports, 1965).

According to Mourão (1998), the City of São Paulo organised the first female championships for basketball in 1930. The rules for the women's matches were the same as those for men, except for the different time duration: the female competition consisted of four periods, each of ten minutes. In Brazilian society, the decade of the 1930s was marked by the women's sports movement, especially in the major urban centres of the country. Many events, apparently isolated, contributed to changing the image of Brazilian women as passive. These events helped deconstruct the myth of the 'fragile sex', thus allowing women to conquer a new social space. Although timid in its beginning, this movement was significant in that it resulted in more women becoming involved in sporting activities.

Tavares describes the proliferation of female sports events in São Paulo: 'The Women's games of the State of São Paulo, taking place in 1935, which put together 150 women in poli-sporting activities, show the enlargement of the female sports field in Brazil' (Tavares and Portela 1998: 481). The State of Rio de Janeiro was also distinguished in national terms by a long-standing event called the Spring Games. These Games started in the City of Rio de Janeiro in 1950 and, for almost two decades, contributed to the emancipation of Brazilian women and the development of their sporting activities (Mourão, 1996). This large event brought together teams from schools and clubs without any kind of discrimination. A journalist, Mário Filho, created and supported the event, motivated by a passion for physical activities and sport. Given the social importance of the Spring Games one can state, according to Mourão (1998), that they made a significant contribution to the development of opportunities for Brazilian women to participate in physical activities and sports and consequently, to the visibility of Brazilian women in sports.

Isabel, a Brazilian volleyball player, is an example of the process of change which took place. In the 1980s she proved that pregnancy was not a sickness by continuing to play during the first five months of her pregnancy. What had been thought to restrict women's participation in sport, especially during the 1940s and 1950s, was now considered a natural process which did not, any more, prevent athletes from competing, even at the Olympics.

The process of including women in sport was accelerated by the formation of women's teams in well-known clubs. Since then, women's involvement in sport has been continuously increasing, decade after decade.

Sports organisation in Brazil today

Nationally, all the different sports are controlled by confederations, federations and associations, which organise and regulate the activities of clubs. Clubs are the main cells of the entire sporting organisation and hierarchy in Brazil.

The Brazilian Sports Law (1998)

With the implementation of the 1998 Law no. 9.615 (Decreto-Lei 9.615 of 1998), the Brazilian sport system was regulated in the following way. The law establishes that the principles of sport are part of the individual rights of the Brazilian population. Three modalities of sport are described and regulated by the law: school sport, leisure sport and high-performance sport.

School sport must be made available throughout the educations system, and in all forms of education. It does not encourage elitism or highly competitive practices. The basic aim is to guarantee the overall development of the individual and his/her education for active citizenship and leisure.

Leisure sport is marked by voluntary participation and embodies the kind of sports that contribute to the integration of citizens into a full social life and promote health and education. Mainly, the development of these activities has followed the interests of men. As such, this manifestation of sport is either very weak in terms of providing opportunities for women to engage in physical activities, or women are explicitly excluded from them. In fact, leisure sport in Brazil has been traditionally dominated by the male sector. As are all aspects of social life in Brazil, women's leisure sport is considered less important than men's. This may be explained on the basis of 'cultural reproduction', as has been observed in various studies.[2]

High-performance sport consists of professional and non-professional activities. In the first case, it is regulated by formal contracts between the sports person and the sports institution (clubs and companies). In non-professional sports, it is characterised by the freedom of practice and by the absence of formal documents (as a working contract).

Sport for handicapped people

The National System of Sport includes the Brazilian Olympic Committee and the Brazilian Paralympic Committee, as well as other organisations regulating sporting activities for physically handicapped people. In this sector of sporting activity, there are almost no female participants. It is seen to be natural for boys and men to be present in these associations, both in team and individual sports. However, female paralympians are beginning to appear in Brazil. In the last Paralympic Games in Sydney, for example, Brazilian women gained medals in track and field and swimming (see Table 12.1).

Unfortunately, these achievements have not led to a policy for the development of sport for people with disabilities. It is still a stereotype in Brazilian society that handicapped women do not belong on the sportsfield.

Table 12.1 Paralympic medals at Sydney 2000*

Medal	Sport	Modality	Athlete/Team
Gold	Track and Field	100m	Ádria Santos
Gold	Track and Field	Shot Put	Roseane Ferreira
Gold	Judo	81 up to 90kg	Antônio Tenório da Silva
Gold	Track and Field	Discus Throwing	Roseane Ferreira
Gold	Swimming	50m Free	Fabiana Sugimori
Gold	Track and Field	200m	Ádria Santos
Silver	Swimming	Relay 4x50m Medley	Francisco Avelino, Adriano Lima, Luis Silva, Clodoaldo Silva
Silver	Swimming	Relay 4x50m Free	Joon Sok Soe, Clodoaldo da Silva, Adriano Gomes da Lima, Luís Silva
Silver	Swimming	50m Free	Mauro Brasil
Silver	Swimming	100m Free (S4)	Clodoaldo Silva
Silver	Swimming	100m Free (S6)	Adriano Lima
Silver	Track and Field	200m (T13)	André Luís Andrade
Silver	Track and Field	400m	Ádria Santos
Silver	Swimming	50m Butterfly	Luís Silva
Silver	Track and Field	100m	André Luíz Andrade
Bronze	Track and Field	Discus Throwing	Anderson Santos
Bronze	Swimming	50m Free (S10)	Danilo Glasser
Bronze	Swimming	50m Free	Clodoaldo Silva
Bronze	Soccer	Cerebral Paralysis	Male Team
Bronze	Swimming	50m Medley	Genezi Andrade
Bronze	Swimming	Relay 4x100 Free	Mauro Brasil, Fabiano Machado, Adriano de Lima, Danilo Glasser

Source: Brazilian Paralympic Committee 2000

Note: * Relative position of Brazil=24

Top-level sport

Top-level sport for women and men has progressed beyond the sport clubs, especially in basketball and volleyball. These are controlled by commercial companies, such as banks, industries or private teaching systems, who like to have their images associated with sport. As an illustration of this, the 2002 women's basketball State Championship in the State of São Paulo was decided between two teams supported by private organisations. The Brazilian sports system is heavily focused on clubs and professional teams controlled by educational, industrial and commercial companies.

Sport policy and the role of the State in sports development

Every year, the federal government, state and county authorities promote national, state and municipal school games. School games occur at national and regional levels. In some states, they represent the manifestation of school sport based on participation. In others, they are marked by high levels of elitism and competitiveness, and have become spectacles for high-performance sport. As a consequence, it is common for the schools to have top-level athletes in their teams, drawn from clubs. Many Brazilian schools function as clubs in terms of the way they practice sports, focusing only on competition, giving priority to elite athletes and not providing opportunities for all kind of sporting activities. University games are concentrated in private universities, which attract the best athletes. These universities are favoured over public universities because they can offer special facilities, grants and housing for students. Private middle and high schools may also organise games. School games are one of the best opportunities available for women to enter the sports field.

Girls and women in Brazilian sports

According to the figures of the Brazilian Institute of Geography and Statistics, women are solely responsible for 26 per cent of households in Brazil (Instituto Brasileiro de Geografia e Estatística 2000). They are the source of education, health, food, housing and clothing. They comprise more than 50 per cent of Brazilian paid workers. In lower-level professions, women make up the majority of the workforce. They earn less then men in the same profession and continue to be excluded from decision-making positions and opportunities for advancement in the patriarchal Brazilian society.

Girls and women-only institutions in sports

There are no women-only sports clubs or women-only sports associations in Brazil. Sportswomen in this country have become visible more through sports events than through the development of exclusive women's institutions.

Brazilian sports clubs were founded by men during the late nineteenth century and the early twentieth century. They focused on physical activities associated with men, which were predominantly to do with turf and paddle. Soccer was introduced into many paddle clubs and became identified as the male sport in Brazil. It has the status of being *the* national sport and with most prestige. It has been very systematically developed throughout the whole country, especially in the main cities.

In 1981, women were allowed to play soccer in Brazil. Since then, female participation in soccer has increased. Women have begun to find a place even in a sport from which they have traditionally been excluded. Nevertheless, male soccer has substantial support while the female version is marginalised, both by the government and by private organisations.

Some sports, such as basketball, volleyball and swimming, show signs of development for women, as many clubs have women's teams, both in basic and professional categories.

Participation of girls and women in sports outside school

Only a few Brazilian girls participate in sporting activities. This occurs mainly during their time at school. For most girls, school is the favoured, and sometimes only, place they can participate in physical activities and sport. Boys use free spaces, streets, corners of squares and every free flat space for playing ball games. At school, during the breaks and recreation times, it is common for boys to use the fields and squares, while girls tend to stay seated or, at least, are not playing or running around (Sousa and Altmann 2000).

Through the construction of public sports equipment, the provision of free spaces and the organisation of sport as a leisure/recreational activity, the government is displaying signs of a new sports initiative: sport for all. There is a proliferation of squares for many outdoor sports. Every county (of which there are more than 5,507 in Brazil) offers at least one multi-sport square in each neighbourhood. Men, however, occupy these squares in significantly larger numbers than do women. In the everyday lives of Brazilian women, physical activities and sport are far from being their routine. Ironically, the emancipatory movement which brought women into the workplace also led to them being burdened with new tasks without alleviating them from the traditional ones. The contemporary Brazilian woman who works outside the house, in the commercial sector or in any other kind of external activity, continues to be responsible for the usual, 'culturally' determined, functions of childcare and domestic work.

The majority of big stadiums in every State belong to well-known soccer clubs. These clubs have recently begun expanding their sporting businesses and many are opening their doors to women, in team sports as well as individual ones. This is true especially in the top six sports: soccer, basketball, volleyball, handball, track and field and swimming.[3]

Girls and boys interested in sporting activities see sports clubs as one of the few ways of competing in high-profile sports. For a girl to enter a club and participate in sport there, she has to become a member. This requires paying monthly taxes, which are beyond the economic means of the families of girls and boys of low socio-economic backgrounds. Therefore, the majority of girls and boys taking part in sporting activities belong to middle and upper social classes. The only way for girls of lower social classes to enter the realm of high performance sport is to 'be lucky'. If they are seen playing, and thus are found by sporting specialists, socio-economical barriers may be crossed and these girls may emerge in sport.

Academies are part of the Brazilian physical activity landscape. In commercial terms, academies are an emerging force, as private enterprises built specifically for physical training. As profit-making organisations, academies exclude the majority of the population. Gymnastic academies (fitness clubs) have developed very rapidly, especially in the last twenty years, due to the boom in physical activities and their association with aesthetics and health. In the beginning they were relatively small places, with few professional fitness trainers. Membership numbers were small too and the equipment was very limited in its sophistication. Even the kinds of physical activities on offer were very restricted, normally concentrating on muscular training and aerobic exercises.

The last ten years in Brazil have been marked by the vigorous development of big academies everywhere in the country, with very sophisticated equipment. These attract middle and upper-class people of different age levels, who can practice an innumerable range of physical activities including, among other types of exercise, different kinds of dance, combat sports and gymnastics.

Rented fields are private spaces, normally associated with soccer. Groups or teams of men who want to practice collective sport rent these spaces. Participants of games in these fields are almost exclusively men.

Mourão and Pacheco (1995: 143) showed, in a study about physical and sporting activities of boys and girls inside and outside public schools, that this very tradition is reinforced. From a total of seventy-six subjects, thirty-three boys from public schools declared that they participate in sporting activities while only three of the forty-three girls from the same schools did so. This result indicates how persistent is the idea that sport is more an activity for men/boys than for women/girls.

This tendency is derived from cultural factors, since women/girls have more passive roles than men/boys, and are charged with more tasks than are boys. In their 'free' time, girls are supposed to take care of their homes and brothers and sisters, while boys do not have to. When girls leave school in Brazil, they tend to abandon all kinds of sport and physical activity.

Access to high-performance sports

Brazilian women do become high performance athletes. To illustrate, ninety-four of the 204 Brazilian athletes at the Sydney 2000 Olympics were women and 110 were men. These figures verify women's advances in performance sport in Brazil (See Table 12.2). In comparative terms, 46 per cent of the Brazilian delegation of athletes at the Sydney Olympics were women, while the total proportion of women competing at the Games, over 199 countries and 10,382 athletes, was 38 per cent.

By comparison with male sports, female team sports in Brazil receive insufficient support from official sources and private companies, and little attention from the media. This situation reinforces misconceptions and negative attitudes towards the presence of women on our sports fields and squares. Many women athletes, with excellent sports performances, decide to abandon sport or leave Brazil to play in foreign countries, especially in the

Table 12.2   Brazilian athletes in Sydney 2000*

Sport	Athlete	Medal
Basketball	Female team	Bronze
Beach volleyball	Adriana Behar and Shelda	Silver
Beach volleyball	Adriana Samuel and Sandra	Bronze
Beach volleyball	Zé Marco and Ricardo	Silver
Horse racing team hop	Rodrigo Pessoa, Luiz Felipe de Azevedo, André Johannpeter, Álvaro de Miranda Netto	Bronze
Judo light	Tiago Camilo	Silver
Judo middle	Carlos Honorato	Silver
Swimming 4x100m free style	Fernando Scherer, Gustavo Borges, Edvaldo Valério, Carlos Jayme	Bronze
Track and field 4x100m	André Domingos, Claudinei Quirino, Édson Luciano, Vicente Lenílson	Silver
Volleyball	Female team	Bronze
Yachting laser	Robert Scheidt	Silver
Yachting star	Torben Grael and Marcelo Ferreira	Bronze

Source: Brazilian Olympic Committee
Note: * Relative position of Brazil = 52

United States where many of them join the national soccer league. They do so to continue playing and improving under better conditions than they could have in Brazil. There they may attend school and continue to play sport, with the dream of becoming a top athlete.

Because sport is associated with images of masculinity, many women and girls involved in sport challenge the gender order and experience misconceptions and stereotyping about their sexuality. This is especially so for those involved in sports which demonstrate speed, strength, and, most of all, impact.

Women in decision-making positions of organised sports

It is exceptional for women in Brazil to occupy decision-making positions in sport, especially high-performance sports, since usually men are the coaches for both male and female teams. Women coaches are insignificant in quantitative terms. Out of ten big clubs of the city of Rio de Janeiro, with hundreds of male coaches, there are only thirty-four women, the majority of whom are with basic, non-professional teams. This is a common situation in Brazil. Women are normally restricted to the basic areas of competitive sport and recreational/leisure sport. It is rare for women coaches to follow their athletes when they progress to competitive teams. It is even rarer to see them with professional teams. Most commonly, female teams (of soccer, basketball and volleyball) have men as coaches. Barriers to women's participation in this area include men's resistance to the presence of women in their terrain, and women deciding not to be involved in high-performance competition. Under present conditions, the gender order and distribution of power remains secure, since female coaches would have to conduct their teams to victory in a highly competitive context. Gender-related taboos are associated with women who aspire to being involved in high-performance sports, especially as this requires them to occupy decision-making positions.

Souza de Oliveira (2002b) addresses this topic in more detail. In her research on women who command teams of top-level sport, she highlights new tendencies and old difficulties associated with the project of modifying the heavily male-dominated world of sport. Her study demonstrates that women advance from coaches to co-ordinators of the teams they command, thus opening space for other women to work as coaches.

Brazilian women face many challenges in their progress towards more opportunities for decision-making positions in sport. The relations between men and women in this section of physical and sporting activities are more or less the same as they were a century ago.

There are no women among the fourteen members of the present Brazilian Olympic Committee, which illustrates their lack of participation in sports leadership.[4] Given the proportion of participation of women in the Olympic movement, their absence from decision-making positions requires an explanation and change.[5]

Brazil has an impressive number of women leading teams. Nevertheless, compared with the number of men, the presence of women amongst our boards of directors and coaches is far from satisfactory. Their absence from the Olympic Committee reveals that Brazilian sport is a male-dominated world.

How far does social stratification influence sports participation of girls and women? Classical social factors, such as age, ethnicity, socio-economic background and, most importantly, marital status influence women's decisions to enter or remain in the sports arena. Normally, single women abandon or reduce their participation in sport once they get married. Another common situation for girls/women involved in high-performance sport is for them to postpone marriage and sometimes decide to not have children, due to pressures coming from the sports context, particularly from professional careers. A double and interactive negative effect seems to operate in what concerns the social origin and socio-economic level of the girls and women involved in sport. In Brazil, track and field, soccer, handball and basketball seem to attract girls from lower socio-economic levels, while volleyball and swimming seem to attract women and girls from middle and upper-class backgrounds.

Programmes and action for the promotion of girls and women in sport

The number of Brazilian women competing at the last Olympic Games is no indicator that Brazilian authorities support women's sport through public policy. Women receive no encouragement to participate in sport, or to develop physical activity as a valuable habit in their everyday lives. Public policy for leisure and leisure sport activities has consistently advanced, but there is no project targeting girls who want to become top athletes, especially for those without the means to pay clubs or academies for training opportunities. Brazilian policy privileges sport, especially high performance sport. Men's teams receive more support than women's teams, who find it difficult to represent Brazil in international sporting events.

This official attitude towards women's high level sport helps us to understand why only a small number of Brazilian women have won gold medals at the Olympic Games. To commemorate the centenary of female participation in the Olympics, the Brazilian Olympic Committee chose the Brazilian beach volleyball player Sandra Pires to carry the Brazilian flag in the opening ceremony of the Sydney 2000 Games. Sandra and Jaqueline, who won the women's competition of beach volleyball at the Atlanta Olympics of 1996, entered the sport history books by being the first two women from Brazil to win an Olympic gold medal. Beach volleyball has become a popular sport on our beaches, due to the high performance level of our female athletes in the last two Olympic Games.

Official sports programmes, from both states and counties, have many projects and programmes oriented to children and older people, but none were found to specifically target women and girls. Centres and institutes involved with the promotion of sport and leisure, such as universities, academies, churches and philanthropic organisations, do not focus on women and girls in their physical activity and leisure programmes. A picture emerges showing that there are limited opportunities for Brazilian girls and women to access and become involved in sporting activities.

Other issues concerning gender and sport

The kind of sporting activities that originated inside the Brazilian national culture, such as regional folk dances, present little space for women. In this context women play the background roles, associated with the aesthetic or the erotic. Men, on the other hand, are responsible for the leading or main actions, either through gesture or precise and stylistic movements. The notable exception is capoeira, a Brazilian martial art with African roots. It is a blend of martial arts, music, dance and spirituality, nowadays very popular in every club or academy, as well as in the public squares in the country. Capoeira is divided in two styles, Angola (closest to the origins) and Regional (with features of other martial arts). Originally, it was an exclusively male activity, with its beginnings in the war efforts of black slaves in Brazil's colonial period. It originated and developed in the Brazilian colonial (1555–1808) and imperial period (1822–89). In its contemporary format, it embodies many features and gestures of an armless fight, with emphasis on leg movement. Furthermore, it is becoming popular in other countries such as the USA, Germany and France. Today, capoeira is no longer predominantly associated with males. Boys and girls enter the circle with the same levels of participation, decision-making and action.

It is also worth mentioning martial arts, such as karate, judo, tae-kwon-do and the Brazilian variant of Japanese ju-jitsu, called Gracie jiu-jitsu. These include both boys and girls, although they tend to be organised into gendered sections (i.e. girls compete with girls, boys with boys).

The number of Brazilian girls participating in individual sports is growing fast, nationally and internationally, for example, in surfing and body-boarding.[6] In these sports, athletes are consciously confronting the misconceptions about girls on surfboards. The sexist characteristics of media representations are obvious in the descriptions associated with the women's competitions, for example, in labels such as the 'sexy competition'.

Main problems of sports development in relation to women's participation

Regardless of the progress of females inside and outside the sports squares, other less visible aspects are present in Brazil. If sporting activities continue to be concentrated in clubs, with the focus on competition and professional teams, and not developed in schools, the majority of Brazilian girls (and boys) will be kept from attaining the advantages of regular sporting activities. The unique context for social order, through local and regional solidarity and national cohesion, will be lost. Schools know very well how to produce these. School authorities should be aware that part of their fundamental mission is preparing students for participation in sporting activities throughout their lives.

Regardless of requirements by law, physical education tends to favour elitism and competition, given that university-based sports have an explicitly semi-professional character. Sport in schools favours the boys, with very restrictive space for girls. This picture of discrimination against girls deepens gender inequalities and impedes women's equal citizenship in the fields of physical activities and sport. The most unfair situation concerns high-performance sport. Most men's teams receive massive public and private support, while women's teams do not have enough material resources to represent their country in international competitions.

Compared with the beginning of the past century, today there is a new and promising presence of Brazilian women in sporting activities. Brazilian women are brilliant as athletes, just as they shine in science, politics, arts and in the workplace. But their presence on the sporting fields is less obvious than in the other areas of a more democratic nation with opportunities for all. Female energies are no longer centred only on reproduction, but the home continues to be the central reference point for female life, and continues to restrict women's activities outside the home. There is a huge gap between women Olympians and the common woman on the street, who has very little opportunity to access all the advantages of citizenship and develop her potential.

The national sports context challenges educators and other sectors responsible for public policy to look for new ideas, projects and programmes, in a national movement which brings together universities and schools, churches and clubs, sports associations, government and non-government organisations. These programmes and projects should create more room for Brazilian women to experience a new reality, and more democracy and fairness in their sporting aspirations.

The analysis we have presented about the space occupied by Brazilian women in sport allows us to conclude that the power games played around the gender order in Brazilian society do not represent victory or defeat for men or women. We suggest that woman are discovering their own ways, on their own, without any kind of protection or explicit resistance from men, at least in the field of sport.

Notes

1 Here are some figures: 8,513,000 square kilometers with 169,544,443 people: 83,423,553 men, and 86,120,890 women. The country has twenty-seven states, 5,507 counties, and life expectancies of seventy-five years for men and seventy-eight years for women.

2 The topic of cultural reproduction can not be explained in more detail here. We refer to studies, e.g. Mourão *et al.* (1996): 'what has been observed in different cultures is that... since they were born, children could perceive that their mother was inferior to their father, and this fact contributed to children considering as "natural" a society in which someone used to command, and the others had to obey. Children would consider as "natural" an authoritarian, violent and excluding society' (1996: 5–6).

3 This list does not reflect the totality of Brazilian clubs, since many of them have no resources for investing in high-level teams and, henceforth, do not have enough performance to be ranked in national championships.

4 Following Maurício Capinussu's study (2002) on women involved in the organisation of sport.

5 G. Oliveira, *Social representations of women in decision-making positions in sporting teams of Rio de Janeiro*, Universidade Gama Filho, 2002. The author found that the number and importance of women in this segment of sport is more relevant than what had been established by current literature.

6 Cláudia Ferrari is one of Brazilian top athletes of body boarding.

Bibliography

Capinussu, J.M. (2002) *Mulheres na administração esportiva*, Rio de Janeiro: Mimeo.
Decreto-Lei 3.199 (1941) *Institui normas gerais sobre o desporto e dá outras providências*.
Decreto-Lei 9.615 (1998) *Institui normas gerais sobre o desporto e dá outras providências*.
Instituto Brasileiro de Geografia e Estatística (2000) *Pesquisa sobre padrões de vida 1999*, Rio de Janeiro: Government of Brazil.
Mourão, L. (1996) 'A imagem da mulher esportista nos Jogos da Primavera nos anos 50', in S. Votre (ed.), *A Representação social da mulher na Educação Física e no Esporte*, Rio de Janeiro: EDUGF.

—— (1998) *A representação social da mulher brasileira na atividade físico-desportiva: da segregação à democratização*, Tese de doutorado, Rio de Janeiro: Universidade Gama Filho.

Mourão, L. and Pacheco, G.B. (1995) 'O cotidiano da educação física escolar', in S. Votre and V.L.M. Costa (eds), *Cultura, Atividade corporal e esporte*, Rio de Janeiro: EDUGF.

Muraro, R.M. *et al*. (1996) *Sexualidade da mulher brasileira: corpo e classe social no Brasil*, Rio de Janeiro: Ed. Rosa dos Tempos.

Souza de Oliveira, G.A. (2002a) *Social representations of women in decision-making positions in sporting teams of Rio de Janeiro*, Rio de Janeiro: Universidade Gama Filho.

—— (2002b) 'Mulheres que comandam equipes esportivas de alto nível', masters thesis, Rio de Janeiro: Universidade Gama Filho.

Sousa, E.S. and Altmann, H. (2000) *Meninos e meninas: expectativas corporais e implicações na educação física escolar. Corpo e Educação*, Campinas: UNICAMP (Caderno Sedes).

Tavares, O. and Portela, F. (1998) 'Jogos Femininos do Estado de São Paulo (1935): a primeira "olimpíada" feminina do Brasil', in S. Votre (ed.), *Anais do VI Congresso Brasileiro de História do Esporte Lazer e Educação Física*, Rio de Janeiro: EDUGF.

Votre, S. and Mourão, L. (2001) 'Ignoring taboos: Maria Lenk, Latin American inspirationalist', in *Freeing the female body*, special issue of *The International Journal of the History of Sport*, 18, 1: 196–218.

13 Women in Colombian sport

A review of absence and redemption[1]

Rubiela Arboleda Gómez and Gloria Vallejo Rendón

Collaborators: Eddy Bedoya, Viviana Vargas[2]

General structure of Colombian sport

In Colombia, sports development, as part of government statutory policies does not have a firm basis. The assignment of budget allocations for the organisation of sport is low, and therefore, the law, which regulates national level sport, is left unfulfilled. In section two of the so-called Sport Law, where reference is made to basic rights, sport is acknowledged as a social right:

> Sport, recreation and leisure-time saving are fundamental education elements and a basic integral training of the individual. Sponsoring, developing and practising them are an integral part of the educational public service and constitute a social public expenditure, according to the following principles: universality, community and citizen participation, functional unification, democratisation, and sport ethics.
>
> (Ley del Deporte. Ley Nacional 181 del 18 de enero de 1995)

Despite the existence of this Law, these principles are far from being effectively applied, and especially so for women, for whom 'Universal Law' is not a reality even though Article 4 asserts that: 'The entire population of the national territory has the right to practise sport, recreation and leisure-time activity.'

On the other hand, the nature of the social infrastructure is such that sport is not regarded as a first-order priority in the lives of individuals. At primary and high school levels, minimal value is attached to sport and recreation. This is a feature, which goes hand in hand with a lack of knowledge of sport and physical education as an academic discipline. One consequence is a shortage of jobs for professionals in the area. Furthermore, sports facilities at schools do not meet the minimal required conditions, especially in those schools located in economically deprived areas.

In their research concerned with movement expressions and their relationship with the body culture and the social profile of school teenagers, aged from 14–16 years in Medellin City, Arboleda *et al.* (2000) found that there is a remarkable social status differentiation related to movement opportunities and to the resources offered by different schools: the high social status Santa María del Rosario school has a gym, swimming pool, soccer and baseball areas and other sports and playing fields and a track and field arena; the low social status Liceo la Avanzada school only has a forty-square metre yard for practising all physical activities.

In sport in general, differences between opportunities to participate and economic resources supported by the government are equally obvious: there are insufficiencies in equipment, well-trained coaches and few sport facilities in low social strata areas. Where so-called 'multi-sport play-grounds', which supposedly allow participation in different types of sport such as soccer, indoor soccer, basketball are the predominant sports facili-ties provided. However, there is a discriminatory use of them and the predilection for soccer perpetuates women's exclusion. The Northeast Zone of Medellín (Arboldea *et al.* 1996),[3] a low socio-economic status area with a population of 446,576 inhabitants, has fifty-two multi-sport play-grounds, three neighbourhood parks and two metropolitan parks, taking up a total of 1,113,967 square metres (2.5 square metres per capita). This figure includes the Parque Norte, Jardín Botánico and University of Antioquia, which are restricted public facilities belonging to the city.[4]

In contrast, high social status schools have gymnasia, sport clubs, and more recently the new import of the 'Spa', as well as a wide range of sports options within the private sector. By way of illustration there is the case of the high socio-economic status Southwest section of Medellin City, which represents only the 10.4 per cent of the population total and has 14 recog-nised physical activity sites, complemented by dancing rooms and spinning centres among others. At an organisational level, the following general structure of sport is evident in Colombia (see Figure 13.1).

The Colombian Olympic Committee's (Comité Olímpico Colombiano, COC) Constitution Act dates from 3 July 1936. The Act gave 'sport, espe-cially that of high performance, a new vision and structure for its development'. The COC encompasses organisations, athletes and others recognised by the International Olympic Committee (IOC), under whose authority they have joined and agreed to regulations of the Olympic Letter. The COC is affiliated to the following sub-regional organisations: the South American Sport Organisation (Organización Deportiva Sudamericana, ODESUR), the Central American Sport Organisation (Organización Deportiva Centroamericana, ORDECA), the Central American and Caribbean Sport Organisation (Organización Deportiva Centroamericana y del Caribe, ODECABE), the Bolivarian Sport Organisation (Organización Deportiva Bolivariana, ODEBO); and the Pacific Ocean Basin Sport Organisation (Organización Deportiva de la Cuenca del Océano Pacífico, ORDECOP).

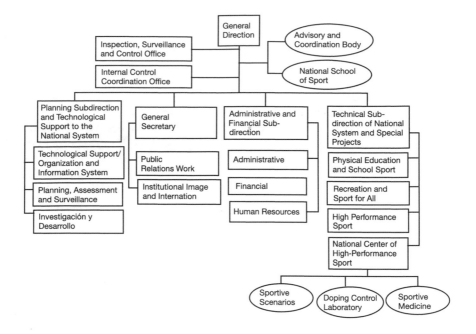

Figure 13.1 Structure of the sport system in Colombia
Source: Coldeportes.

Under-representation: Women in competitive sport

In Colombia there is no motivation culture aimed at the promotion of sport talent to ensure domestic representation in international competition. This situation, which hinders male participation, is even more disadvantageous in the case of women who are committed to the competitive sport and who engage out of personal motivation rather than from institutional, organisational support. An example here is the balance presented by the Colombian Institute for Recreation and Sports (Coldeportes) for the National Games,[5] in which the most outstanding figures from 1928–2000 are shown in Table 13.1.

Woman and sport in the past

A review of the last thirty years illustrates the female incursion in different sports. Colombian sporting culture is markedly macho and is derived from the privilege of male participation in sports, and of an equally male structural orientation. Reference is not only made to the security and internal logic of a masculine nature, inherent in sport, but also to so-called 'sport leadership'. As an example, in one Colombian state, out of 33 sport leagues, 26 are presided over by men; 22 of them have male assistants; and 25 have

Table 13.1 Best Colombian sportsmen and sportswomen with reference to the National Games

Year	Sportsman or Sportswoman	Review
1928	José Díaz Granados	Football player of Magdalena's team. Winner of the title.
1932	José Domingo Sánchez	Sprints athlete from Bolívar. He established new records.
1935	Jorge Nova	Athlete from Bogotá. Winner of the middle-distance races.
1936	Jorge Combariza	Tennis player from Bogotá. Number one at that time.
1941	Rafael Cotes	Athlete from Atlantico. He established marks of 10.4 min. in the 100m race and 21.5 in the 200m race.
1950	Efraín Forero	Cyclist from Cundinamarca. Winner of the road race.
1954	Jaime Aparicio	Athlete from Valle del Cauca. Leader in hurdling.
1960	Bernardo Caraballo	Boxer from Cartagena. Rooster-weight champion. World-category boxer.
1970	Olga Lucía de Angulo	Swimmer from Valle del Cauca. Eight gold medals.
1974	Eucaris Caicedo	Athlete from Valle del Cauca. South American record in the 200m.
1980–1985	Sandra Bohórquez	Swimmer from Antioquia. She won 19 gold medals in the two contests.
1988	Tolentino Murillo	Weight lifter.
1992	Alejandro Bermúdez	Swimmer from Antioquia. Five gold medals.
1996	María Isabel Urrutia	Weight lifter from Valle del Cauca. At the moment she is the Olympic champion in the 75 kg category.
2000	Alejandro Bermúdez	Swimmer from Antioquia, winner of eight gold medals.

Source: Coldeportes

male fiscal reviewers (Indeportes Antioquia 1999). Women's presence has only been significant since the 1980s. Before the 1980s, it is worthwhile highlighting the year 1938, when the first female representatives featured in an international event. Women's first international appearance in sport was directly related to the realisation of the First Bolivarian Sport Games (I Juegos Deportivos Bolivarianos) which took place in Bogotá in 1938: Cecilia Navarrete, Adela Jiménez, Raquel Gómez and Berta Navia participated in different athletic events.

In the 1970s, the presence of women at competitive level was scarce and sporadic: notably, Juana Mosquera participated in athletics in the Olympic Games in Munich in 1972, and Judy de Hasbun[6] participated in the World

Skittles Championships in Manila in 1979. Otherwise, there were several cases of women boxers and two women, Candelaria Rojas and Mallito 'La Sucreña', gained recognition at national level.

Since the 1980s, the number of participant women has increased and there have been more events in which some women[7] have appeared. In this period, two years in which greater participation was evident stand out: 1987 and 1989. Of the total number of participant women in the 1980–90 period, 51 per cent were in these two years (Vallejo *et al.* 2000). Although athletics continues to be the discipline of greater concurrence, there are new types of sport such as skittles, weightlifting, equestrian events, fencing, gymnastics, judo, swimming, softball, tennis, table tennis, shooting, mountain biking, golf, bridge, synchronised swimming, chess, basketball, beach volleyball and skating which have emerged. In athletics, women stand out for reaching number one positions at world level. For example, Luz Mery Tristán obtained gold and silver medals in the Pan-American Games in Indianapolis in 1987. In the same year, she was the only woman chosen in the eleven stars of Colombian sport. She also obtained the gold medal in the International Grand Prix of Buenos Aires, Argentina in 1988, the year in which she obtained fifth and sixth places in the World Skating Championships events in Grenoble, France. Her achievements contrast with the absence of any outstanding Colombian male skater at that time.

This growth in women's participation in the above mentioned sports contrasts with the traditional male practise of football, a sport ideologically associated with masculine exercise and in which whilst women diversify their scenarios, men close ranks around the game, loaded with meanings embedded within dimensions of 'initiation rite to manliness'. It is only since the middle of the 1990s that official groups have been established in Colombia that foster the game of football for women and state organisations for female football that belong to 'male leagues' have been formed. In 2000, the Colombian Corporation of Women Footballers and in 2001 the United Women for Football[8] organisations were created. At the present time, there is a Colombian Section of Young Female Football that caters for young women in the age range 12–15. Although there are examples of female football organisations in some neighbourhoods and small organisations of a private character in universities and company enterprises that include female football as one of their sports offered, there is as yet no organisational structure that has reached a representative level.

In Colombia, women's presence in football has neither been accepted by sport leaders in particular, nor by spectators in general. It is considered more a 'joke motive' by which women try to imitate men, and that, from the perspectives of techniques, tactics, strategy, capacities and abilities, they will never achieve the same level according to evidence provided by studies concerned with motor abilities and gender (Arboleda *et al.* 2000).

In our opinion, women's absence from football is explained not only by the lack of encouragement in the Columbian environment, but also because engaging in this sport means a risk for sexual identity, because most people in the country think that femininity clashes with football's inherent masculinity. This opinion is grounded in testimonial evidence given by women who have participated in this sport (Vallejo *et al.* 2000).

Competitive cycling, with fewer participants (although equal in number to men) acquired in the 1980s a sense of national identity. At an individual level, boxing gained followers and became a symbol of force, resistance, speed and tenacity, values that had been thought only possible for the masculine body. In this perspective, the sports to which Colombia has dedicated its greatest zeal, and those that it has sought to promote in the international sporting theatre, have been headed by men; that is to say, the subject of the nation's identity is the man, not the woman. Nevertheless, in the 1980s, few successes were obtained in male participation; for example, in football, only the first place in the Pre-Olympic Championship sub-group and classification in the Chilean World Championship (Youth category) were achieved.

Although from 1989 weightlifting already figured as an option for women, the number of women practitioners of this sport was, and continues to be, quite low. With respect to cycling and football, it is worthwhile recalling that in the decade of the 1980s female involvement scarcely existed.[9] During the 1990s, women also figured in sports such as athletics, beach volleyball, water skiing, karate, water polo, triathlon, mountain biking, archery, squash and cycling. Some of these women achieved important places inside and outside the country. High recognition levels were reached in the South American region and a few at world levels. This was the case for the athlete Ximena Restrepo and the tennis player Fabiola Zuluaga, who, along with the weight lifter María Isabel Urrutia, monopolised the advertising space dedicated to women in recent years.[10] Additionally, it is also important to mention that in 1993 and 1994, the second and first places respectively were gained at the Central American Softball Championships.

Given the lack of social policies directed to women's engagement in different sports, a great percentage of those who have access to these belong to a high socio-economic stratum. This is inferred from the class status associated with sports that have a female presence, as shown by various socio-economic studies (see for example Arboleda *et al.* 1996).[11] Of the twenty-nine sports in which women have figured at competitive level both nationally and internationally, nineteen (65.5 per cent) are almost exclusively the patrimony of privileged, masculine and feminine socio-economic sectors: fencing, equestrian, shooting, swimming, golf, and skating among others.

The lack of effective support for the promotion of sportswomen is verified on the one hand in the necessity for self-financing, which can only be realised by those with appropriate economic resources (this is the case of the athlete Ximena Restrepo[12]) and on the other hand, in the realisation of non-sporting activities to collect funds (raffles, sales, parties, etc.), as was the case with the Colombian synchronised swimming teamin order to participate in the World Championships in Cairo.[13] Furthermore, the desire to achieve their sport goals makes women seek refuge in other nations, under pain of representing a different country, such as the athlete Norfalia Carabalí.[14]

Paradoxically, the most significant recognition at world level has been achieved in the sport disciplines more commonly practised by individuals from low socio-economic strata. Examples are the athletics bronze medallist Ximena Restrepo in the 1992 Barcelona Olympic Games, the World Boxing Champion Flor Delgado in the same year, and the weightlifting gold medallist Maria Isabel Urrutia[15] in the 2000 Sydney Olympic Games. It is equally paradoxical that in a country where the few stimuli to sports have an essential focus in male success, it was a woman who brought Colombia the only gold medal in its history of Olympic participation and in a traditionally male sport.[16] The same year, the directives of Coldeportes honoured a female skittler with the title of: 'Promise of the sport in Colombia' in Bogotá (*El Tiempo*, Dic. 17 de 2000, Bogotá).

Women's and men's sport in Colombia: the inequalities

At present, women's participation in competitive sport has a particular feature that differentiates it from male participation: the favourite kinds of women's sports are individual sports. Of the twenty-eight sports in which women have figured, (track and field, swimming, weightlifting, skittles, equestrian events, gymnastics, judo, softball, tennis, table tennis, shooting, mountain biking, golf, bridge, synchronised swimming, chess, basketball, skating, beach volleyball, cycling, wrestling, water skiing, triathlon, karate do, squash, taekwondo, polo, volleyball) five are team sports and twenty-three are individual sports. Track and field is the kind of sport which is practiced most by women, and the one in which most successes have been achieved (Arboleda *et al.* 2000). An inventory of international representation in this individual sport from 1970–2000 shows twenty-eight women with meritorious achievements, which reflects a difference from men, who have always figured in football, a team sport (Arboleda *et al.* 2000).[17]

Women's engagement in competitive sport is mainly as direct involvement as participants of the game. Their participation in the administrative spheres,[18] in training and/or in judging, is strictly limited as shown in the following data. With reference to the participation at administrative level, of the 30 leagues in which sport in Antioquia is organised, 7 are presided over by women; of 156 directive and training charges, only 27 are women (Indeportes Antioquia, 1999). The administrative board of Coldeportes does not have any woman on its staff.

With regard to female participation in judging sporting activities, the data offered by the National Games of 2000 reflect the few opportunities for women to act as judges and their limitation to some sports. Of the total of 305 judges of the Games, only 61 were women (20 in artistic and rhythmic gymnastics, 8 in athletics, 7 in aquatic activities, 5 in equestrian, 3 in basketball, 3 in cycling, 3 in taekwondo, 3 in archery, 2 in judo, 2 in discus throwing, 1 each in fencing, karate, softball, shooting and volleyball. Moreover, in the Games there was no woman who acted as football referee; in fact, in the sporting history of Colombia only one woman has ever been a football referee: Martha Liliana Toro, who was also the first woman to fulfil this function at professional level in South America (Vallejo *et al.* 2000).

Another feature that characterises the inequities in female/male sports is related to rewards. The recognition for the same victory is inferior when the winner is a woman. Some exemplars demonstrate this inequity. In Colombia, every year the City of Medellín Half Marathon (Media Maratón Atlética, Ciudad de Medellín) takes place; the prize money for the winning man is 3,600 per cent more than that for the winning woman.[19] In the Female Cycling Tour of Colombia (Vuelta Ciclística Femenina a Colombia) the prize was 80 per cent less than that awarded to men; because of this disproportionate prize award, the event was cancelled in 1995. In the city of Medellín, a Hall of Sport Figures has been created. This is a place where homage is made to those considered as the best sports personalities; despite Olympic level performers, no woman's name appear in the hall of sport figures listed.

Sport and society – review of a redemption: recreational and sport activities

As can be inferred from the above background, competitive sport in general, and the female position in particular, are not a first-order policy strategy in the state's plans. As a consequence, people realise the need to generate spaces where they can practice games and sport activities, outside the parameters of competitiveness and productivity (Arboleda *et al.* 2000). Maybe that is the reason why women's participation in the past years has increased in movement practices of a playful, formative, prophylactic and socialising nature. All of this has meant for women the opportunity to gain access to sport facilities that some decades ago had been restricted to men only. It is in sport where the peculiarities of a culture are often overtly expressed. In the case of Colombia, sport practices might well be perceived from different points of view, as it is a country characterised by a social and economic crisis, a breakdown of ethical codes in civil life, with a gap between what is moral and what is legal, and with an increasing deepening of its political conflict. Hence, in such a context, it is necessary to address other meanings of games and sport activities, since motivations have varied according to the needs of the environment. Indeed, as can be seen in findings of several studies, both men and women look for:

- consolidation of solidarity spaces: groups that offer friendship, support, companionship, where groups with games and sport objectives are relevant (Arboleda *et al.* 1996);[20]

- solutions to problems of violence: games and sport activities are mediating elements for groups in conflict;[21]
- restructuring of identity: games and sport activities represent an alternative for the formation of values in individuals; therefore, they constitute a way to modify the image of violence and drug-addiction surrounding young people (Arboleda *et al.* 1996);[22]
- strengthening of a sense of belonging and participation in the urban/country setting: the aim is to massively consolidate the presence of people in games and sport activities that promote the idea of 'better cities', where recreational sport and civic spirit are combined.[23]

In this way, sport fulfils a more 'repairing' than competitive order, and turns out to be a social device to consolidate culture (Kendall and Cheska 1986: 146).[24] Additionally, it provides a better opportunity to release the female body.

The expectations women have in non-competitive scenarios are not those of attaining goals symbolised in medals and economic upsurge, but in a 'redemption' urge as individuals and as a group of the usual existential drama in our country (Vallejo and Restrepo 1999: 54). The above contrasts with the other expectations of the few women who adhere to competitive sport, which can be described in terms of success, risk and adventure, national and international exchange opportunities, a dream to keep abreast of their opponents, and maybe, the idea of emulation in the future of their sports performances' results (Vallejo and Restrepo 1999: 50).

As can be drawn from the above comparison, there has been a change in the expectations of the games and sport perspective towards a more social perception of the matter. This has been evidenced in the results of the movement dimension of investigations about body culture amongst adolescents, and the body culture in the population aged 10–60, where the following motivations were identified in a descending order: socialisation, health, aesthetics, recreation, and finally competition (Arboleda *et al.* 1996).

This change in the range of motivations brings with it a diversification of the practices and the inclusion of new spaces. In recent years, the traditional scenarios for games and sport activities in Colombia has transformed vertiginously. In that sense, we can find parks, squares, streets and sidewalks, among others, as the favourite places for games and sport activities, thus demonstrating a breakdown with what is formal: 'inter-street competitions', 'biking highways', 'volley-streets' and 'square-aerobics' (Informe Inder Cundinamarca, 1998). There converge traditional sports – micro-football, biking, roller skating, jogging, bars – together with non-traditional ones, where it is possible to detect how women show a more motor-volitive disposition than men, since they perform a wider range of sport practices. The re-signification of space has allowed a moderate proportion of women to go out of the house to perform movement activities in their immediate environment, while the scenarios devoted to conventional practices are restricted to men.

Thus, in the same way the peculiarities of the national context have little by little favoured the inclusion of women in the sport realm, there are other factors in the world of sports that also intervene in this situtation:

- globalisation: through mass media, life styles have spread where sport is included, as a guarantee to attain ideals of well-being; in these international models, participate female figures that are portrayed as examples of social, economic, aesthetic, physical and sport success.
- the inclusion of women in the labour force and academic life, where women have found additional alternatives to their household world; among these alternatives, appears sport as a possibility for expression and interaction.
- the breakdown of the religious paradigm: religious precepts have placed the female body in a private, banned place; as this religious ideological basis declines, women allow themselves to explore practices that were unknown to them; sport, in contrast to religion, is presented as an option of what is public, allowed, and free regarding the female body.

Archetype[25] of masculinity and femininity in sport

When investigating for the characteristics of female sport in Colombia, it is not fortuitous to find that from the types of practices, expectations and opinions that these generate, there emerges the pattern of archetypal thought in the way of collective representation that locates women in a conventional stereotype of femininity: women are still expected to be beautiful, and men to be strong. Thus, while sporting contests (especially football) are promoted for men, women are called to participate in beauty contests. Both modalities, football and beauty contests, generate huge amounts of money, which is an absurdity when compared with the lack of investment in female sport.

In other words, 'women are worth more as ornamental objects than sport subjects', as was proved in the Dimension of Sexuality (Dimensión Sexualidad) from a research project on somatic culture, where evidence was gathered in which men refer to women from their aesthetic outlook and with a 'fragmented body', while women refer to men from their personality features, and in a more integral perspective about the body (Arboleda *et al.* 2000).[26] Every year, the 'beauty contest' takes place in Colombia, an event celebrated for half a century. For this occasion, women are prepared from early childhood: they are sent to model academies, stimulating beauty contests as part of child games, whereas children with an interest in sport are sent to schools of sport initiation that are not part of the state's educational system, but rather private institutions organised by active or retired sportsmen. They are devoted only to a single sport modality. This fact, apparently embedded in vanity, marks an overwhelming distance in the relationships woman/body and man/body. From a cultural viewpoint, the corporal aesthetic attributes required for men (vigorous, strong, muscular, etc.) have been derived from the values associated with sport – *citius, altius, fortius* – in contrast with the corporal aesthetic values required for women: delicate, thin, stylised, and so on. The orientations towards motricity have that background. Exercising sport constitutes an access road to the qualities that will favour the social competition of men, while women risk that which makes them feminine; not in vain, they abstain from participating in some modalities avoiding, on the one hand, corporal modifications, and on the other, social judgement.

An illustration of what is presented is the study carried out in synchronised swimming being considered a highly feminine sport. As a special characteristic, it is noticed that the reason to carry out this sport is the search of 'beauty, harmony and art reflected with music, besides coordination, movement and agility' (Vallejo and Restrepo 1999). The follow-up concludes that the women interviewed prefer synchronised swimming because 'it is very feminine' (Vallejo and Restrepo 1999). This practice, apparently elitist, is strongly demanded in our environment, since it is associated with the conquest of basic aspects of the graceful, feminine beauty. Nevertheless, those who practise this sport belong to the high socio-economic class. It is an exclusively female sport and the number of participants is restricted, given the high costs its practice requires (Vallejo and Restrepo 1999).

In the relationship Woman–Sport–Beauty, women tend to avoid some sport activities such as soccer, boxing and rugby among others, because they consider those sports as crude and not female sports, while they prefer aerobics, hydro-gymnastics, or gymnastics of maintenance, aiming to obtain a corporal figure sometimes outside of reality. In a survey study of teenagers, the ideal top models whom the teenagers want to imitate (Claudia Schiffer, Pamela Anderson, Naomi Campbell) possess physical characteristics that are not properly representative of the Colombian phenotype (Arboleda *et al.*, 2000).

However the demand for the woman as a 'beautiful' object of the society is a universal characteristic. For women in Colombia, beauty constitutes an imperative to reach some goals such as love, acceptance and social success, because this is a country which carries out a beauty competition once per day as seen in beauty competitions such as Reinado Nacional de la Belleza (Cartagena), Coffe (Armenia), Bambuco (Ibagué), Flowers (la Candelaria, Medellín), Sugar Cane (Cali), Aguacate (Montebello), Mango (Santa Barbara) etc.[27] Idealisation of aesthetical characteristics has deepened roots in our idiosyncracy. The different dimensions in which Colombian women are present are deeply marked by this obsession; that is, Colombian women observe physical and sportive activities as a source of beauty which even invades the competition scenario.

In competition, the anxiety about a determined corporal figure often prevents these women from experiencing an adequate diet according to disciplinary requirements of the sport discipline. This fact is not common among sportsmen in Colombia, for whom an abundant diet is linked to a male condition. An example of these differences is the idiosyncratic face to the male and female; it is explained in the concept that each one has about the body. In the created categories of a study of 400 teenagers concerned with body culture among 14–16 year olds (Arboleda *et al.* 2000), there emerge definitions which relate to the collective imaginary that locates women in the maternity frame and object of aesthetic observation, and men in the land of the work force and as social agents.[28] When we classify the concept of body, it is proven that girls define it from the biological aspect, i.e. in the sense of reproductive possibility and physical appearance, as for example those aspects that make them ugly or beautiful. On the other hand, men define body from the instrumental point of view, i.e. as a form for reaching an objective, and from the mobility capacity, which is understood as the opportunity for executing an action (Arboleda *et al.* 2000).

Now, it is necessary to accept the atmosphere in which the relationship of woman sport is subscribed. In Colombia, this atmosphere is full of ambivalence and contradictions. In fact, the conquest of women of 'played forms' implies a form of liberation because it permits the exploration of the body and the appropriation of diversionary forms more accepted in all fields; it does not mean that women have abandoned their culturally assigned responsibilities. To be sportswomen means looking like they are not feminine. But this does not happen with men. This phenomenon is verified in women identified with this revision; most of them remained single during their sport and competition careers.

Finally, women from an early age are subject to different educational models offered by the female patrons for their social life; among those, sport is not a substantive element, while, as mentioned above, sport is a synonym of masculinity. From school age onwards, the process for their formation in sport activities is offered in different academic fields; however, in public schools, there is neglect in the delivery of physical education for girls and boys at the same time, whereas in private institutions educational training, the process of physical activity and sports are favoured from an early age, both for girls and boys.

Although there is a wakening conscience about the function of mobility activities with regard to female body, there is still a long way to go in order to obtain recognition and freedom for practising physical activity and sport with tenacity, desire and constancy. Few Colombian women want to be recognised in sport spheres. They still have to overcome many obstacles and many prejudices.

Notes

1 In this chapter, women's presence in sporting practices has a significant reference in the results obtained in different studies carried out in the research area of 'Body Culture', research realised at the Institute of Physical Education of the University of Antioquia, Medellín Colombia. At the same time, it has drawn from information of other research studies with gender perspectives, newspaper data, records of sports leagues and reports of sport regulatory bodies.

2 Graduated in Physical Education, Universidad de Antioquia, Medellín, Colombia.

3 In the research it is verified that this area is a very significant place of Medellín City. There live people of the lower socio-economic status who make part of almost half of the population of the city.

4 Instituto de Recreación y Deporte de Medellín (INDER), Plan de Desarrollo, 1996, p. 39.

5 This event gathers the best sportsmen and women in the country. It takes place every four years (http://www.juegosnacionales.org/default.asp).

6 More than forty years old, and with five children, she represented the country at world level.

7 Remarkable among many others, whom we cannot mention for space reasons, are Norfalia Carabalí and Zorobabelia Córdoba in athletics, Gloria Múnera in fencing, Gloria Morales in swimming, Mónica Berrío and Marta Luz Aristizabal in synchronised swimming, María Teresa Rueda in shooting, María Teresa Rueda in skittles, and Gloria Inés Corredor and Vicky Riaño in climbing the Summit of America, Aconcagua.

8 Federación Colombiana de Fútbol, Bogotá, 1998.

9 Informe de la década 1990–2000. Ligas de ciclismo del Valle, Cundinamarca y Antioquia 2000.

10 Luz Mary Tristán in skating, María Luisa Calle in cycling, Carmenza Morales in triathlon, Estella Castro in athletics, Luz Adriana Leal in skittles, Lina Mabel Zapata in skating, Mariana Table in tennis, Luz Adriana Galician in weightlifting and María Luisa Botero in water skiing are some of the sportswomen to highlight.

11 Periódico *El Colombiano*, 20 June 2000; Cátedra universitaria, Educación Física y Sexualidad Humana, Universidad de Antioquia, Medellín; Congreso Colombiano de Educación Física, Santa Marta, 1997.

12 http://www.planetadeportivo.com/olimpiadas/atletas/actuales/ximenarestrepo.htm.

13 This situation, that is more evident in the female sport, is also observed in some male sports that enjoy less popularity than football. This way, in 1999 it was possible to attend a strip-tease show, carried out by the male rugby and water polo teams, to collect funds with the purpose of representing the country at world level in Germany. This fact demonstrates the precarious condition of the sport in Colombia. Club de Actividades Subacuáticas, Boletin Mensual, Universidad de Antioquia, April 1999.

14 This athlete is nationalised in Spain; she represented the latter country in the Olympic Games of Sydney 2000.

15 María Isabel Urrutia has been the most outstanding sportswoman in the country, not only in weightlifting, but also in shot-put and discus throw.

16 This evokes the XXI South American Youth Games in Montevideo, Uruguay, 1998, where the only two medals for Colombia were won by women.

17 Arboleda *et al.* (2000) conclude that although one cannot affirm categorically that women are developing a greater motivation for activity than men, at least when referring to the variety or diversity of practices, adolescent women are reaching a superior protagonism than adolescent men; men only practice football with a significantly high index of frequency.

18 Although in the meeting of the COI in Lausanne in 1995, it was concluded that it was necessary to promote women's participation, as much in sport competitions as in the training and administrative structures, and the National Olympic Committee was urged to look for appropriate strategies so that before 2000, a minimum of 10 per cent of posi-

tions of all the structures of decision would be reserved for women, the reality in Colombia is very different because administration and training are in male hands.

19 Soon after this inequity, the Woman and Gender Group of the University of Antioquia formulated an energetic pronouncement. In consequence, the organising committee had to apologise and to reconsider the awards.

20 'I feel more at ease playing with my friends than at home.' – 'I think there isn't anything like going to the park to play basketball.'

21 As an example, a situation taking place in the Siloé neighbourhood, a poor district in the city of Cali. There, the community set out to build architectonic works, by means of 'self-construction', in order to solve problems regarding education, sport facilities, and so on. In this neighbourhood, there were two conflicting armed gangs that prevented the development of the social proposal. As a solution, the community arranged for a football match among the two gangs and set a condition of leaving their weapons away from the field of play and to avoid the use of drugs. As a result, the youngsters were able to resolve the conflict and participate in the construction of the school (Indeportes Valle 1997).

22 'We practise sport to avoid doing wrong things'. – 'Since I began to practise sport, I quit smoking pot and people look at me in a more positive way'. – 'I want my son to practise sport so he stays away from drugs'.

23 In several cities of the country, games and sport events full of civic signification are promoted, like Recobrando Caminos de Herradura (Walking Back Through the Horse Trails), Bote Paseo por el Río Medellín, (Boating along the Medellín River), Maratón Río Cali (Cali River Marathon), Media Maratón Atlética Ciudad de Bogotá (Bogotá's Halfway Athletic Marathon), and Paseo Ciclístico Ciudad de Montería (Biking Tour of Montería) (Coldeportes Nacional 2000).

24 The concept 'repairing' is used here based on Kendall Blanchard's definition, as the return or change '…if someone thinks that his current situation is dangerous, then he should look for the recovering techniques that allow him to change the behaviour of the preceding situation. "Repairing" requires a change in actions and attitudes; and game or games are means to attain that change.'

25 With the word 'archetype', reference is made to a type of architecture installed in the psychic structure, whose lines are constituted in organisers of collective action. The Eranos I circle proposes a concept that is not adjusted exactly to that of Jung's, and that introduces a more cultural aspect, for which the archetype appears essentially as images. Johmann, in close relationship with Gadamer's opinion, 'Recaptures the idea of a virtual background of a symbolic-cultural type that, by way of casting or concave mold, foreshadows or configures our conscious, latent rules: The unconscious is now a cultural unconscious, and archetypes reappear as wombs of our patterns of understanding and behaviour by way of warps underlying our structures.'

26 Man speaking: 'I love big butted women.' – 'I prefer big bumped women.' Women speaking: 'I like cute, lovely men.' – 'I feel an attraction towards strong, muscle men.'

27 Colombia La Nuestra, *Tourism Guide*, Bogotá: National Corporation of Tourism, 1996.

28 Virginia Gutierrez, anthropologist, refers to the Antioquia Complex as follows: 'There is in all of the Antioquia Region a strong highlight of female beauty with images and stereotypes. Culture requires the woman to be beautiful according to aesthetic canon, which conforms, as a personal image and realisation channel of a marriage goal. All this generates a desire to imitate the ideal aesthetic image, which is present during all her life, at the same time, religious influence complements this female image. This is extroverted on a strong internalisation of abstention values and pre-marriage sexual control.'

Bibliography

Arboleda, R. *et al.* (1996) *Usos del Cuerpo y Mitigación de la Vulnerabilidad Social en Salud.* Tesis para optar al posgrado en Problemas Sociales Contemporáneos, Medellín: Universidad de Antioquia.

—— (1998) 'Usos del Cuerpo y Mitigación de la Vulnerabilidad Social en Salud', *Revista Educación Física y Deporte* N.1, 19: 28–36.

—— (2000) *Las expresiones motrices y su relación con la Cultura Somática y el perfil social en adolescentes escolarizados de 14 a 16 años en la ciudad de Medellín*, Medellín: Universidad de Antioquia.

Coldeportes Nacional (2000): Balance de Gestión (Diego Palacios) Bogotá, 12/2000: 5–60.

El Colombiano (2000) *Todos para Todos* (Angela Piedad), 20 June: 3B.

El Tiempo (December 2000) *El Vencedor* (José Clopatosky), 17 December: 8B.

Indeportes Antioquia (1999) *Balance general* (Diego Palacio), Medellín: Gobernación de Antioquia.

Indeportes Valle (1997) *Balance de Gestión. Cali* (Carlos Alberto Lenis), Valle: Imprenta Departamental.

Instituto de Recreación y Deporte de Medellín (1996) *Plan de Desarrollo*, Medellín: Imprenta Departamental de Antioquia.

Kendall, B. and Cheska, A. (1986) *Antropología del deporte*, Barcelona: Ballesterra.

Ley del deporte (1995). Ley Nacional 181 del 18 de enero de 1995. Medellín: Secretaría para la Juventud. Gobernación de Antioquia. Asociación de Ligas Deportivas de Antioquia. Coldeportes Antioquia.

Ley General de Educación (1994). Ley 115 de 1994. Santafé de Bogotá.

Revista Confederación Suramericana de Fútbol. Noticias N.61 (1999) *La señora de negro* (Estewil Quesada Fernández), Bogotá, November: 37–9.

Revista COC (1999) *Maria Isabel Urrutia Ocoro* (Alfonso Galvis), July-August, no. 28, 19: 8.

Revista Olímpica Organo Oficial del Movimiento Olímpico (1997) *La mujer y el deporte, polaridad de sexos*, XXVI 15, June–July.

Vallejo G. and Restrepo L.J. (1999) *La actividad musical y la actividad deportiva como instrumentos del desarrollo cognoscitivo*, Medellín: Universidad de Antioquia.

Vallejo, G. *et al.* (2000) *Sistematización de la información de prensa en torno a la participación femenina en el deporte*, Medellín: Universidad de Antioquia.

Online sources

Azuero Ruiz, O. (1990) 'Juegos Nacionales de Colombia. Ganadores', http://www.juegosnacionales.org/default.asp (15 May 2001).

Barragán Correa, D. (1996) 'Juegos Nacionales de Colombia. Historia', http://www.coldeportes.gov.co

Bernal Nieto, J. (1986) 'Centro de Alto Rendimiento', http://www.planetadeportivo.com/olimpiadas/atletas/actuales/ximenarestrepo.htm (3 May 2001).

Forero Nougués, M. (1982) 'Juegos Nacionales de Colombia. Historia', http://www.juegosnacionales.org/autoridades.asp (6 June 2001).

Muñoz Aguirre, L.A. (1995) 'Coldeportes', http://www.coldeportes.com (6 May 2001).

Pombo Villar, I. (1998) 'Juegos Nacionales de Colombia. Sedes y subsides', http://www.coldeportes.gov.co/organigrama.htm (6 May 2001).

14 Women and sport in Iran

Keeping goal in the *hijab*?

Gertrud Pfister

Introduction: is there such a thing as women's sport in Iran?

Islamic women's sport appears to be a contradiction in terms – at least this is what many people in the West believe. The conviction that women in Islamic countries either cannot, will not or may not take part in sports (or at least in competitive and top-level sports) is partly borne out by the fact that Muslim immigrants in Germany, Britain and the USA scarcely take any active part in sport at all (De Knop *et al.* 1996; Pfister 2001). However, the congresses that have recently been held in Alexandria and in Tehran on the subject of women and sport go to show that Muslim women do take an interest in sport and are developing perspectives in sport.

In this respect the portrayal of the development and the current situation of women's sport in Iran is illuminating for a variety of reasons. It demonstrates both the opportunities and the limits of women in a country in which Islam and sport are not contradictions. On the one hand traditional physical cultures such as *zurkaneh* (a kind of weight training which is practised by men and has religious origins) are still carried on in Iran, while modern sport, especially football, is also very popular. On the other hand, Iranian law and the Iranian state are based on the *sharia* and Islam governs everyday life, including the opportunities and possibilities women have to practise sport.

Women's long struggle for recognition in sport

Compared with other Islamic countries, women's sport in Iran has a long history. In 1964, the Iranian Olympic Committee sent four women athletes to Tokyo to compete in two disciplines, gymnastics and track and field. (Male athletes from Iran had taken part in the Olympic Games since 1948.) At the Asian Games held in Tehran in 1974 the Iranian women's fencing team won a gold medal, the only gold medal that Iranian women athletes have ever been able to win at an international sports meeting. Subsequently, the Iranian women fencers took part in the Montreal Olympics in 1976.[1]

In the early 1970s the Federal Republic of Germany contributed funds to the construction of a sports academy in Tehran, an initiative that was given strong active support by Liselott Diem, from 1967–9 principal of the German Sports Academy in Cologne and wife of the eminent sports official Carl Diem. This college of higher education was to provide not only a four-year academic course of study but also non-academic training courses for both men and women. Liselott Diem visited Tehran frequently, taking part in discussions and organising conferences, and it was due to her untiring efforts that the seventh International Congress of the International Association for the Physical Education and Sport for Girls and Women took place in 1973 at the National University of Tehran.[2] In the following year a full-time German consultant and coach was sent to Tehran and, subsequently, numerous Iranian students, both male and female, attended training courses at the academy in Cologne. 'Investing' in sport gathered further momentum when Iran hosted the Asian Games in 1974, in preparation for which sports grounds and a swimming baths were built. The Islamic Revolution then put an end to German–Iranian cooperation for the time being. Looking back, Diem commented:

> From our point of view today, we can say that the excellent training of the Iranian teachers has not been lost. The only ones to be put at a disadvantage are the women, who are no longer able to take an active part in public life and undergo education in separate classes at the now re-opened universities.
>
> (Diem 1986: 453)

Not only sporting activities underwent a dramatic change after the overthrow of the shah; everyday life experienced upheaval too.

The situation of women in Iran today

The role of women in Islam is a subject which is heatedly debated today. Muslim feminists claim that neither the Koran nor the Hadith, the sayings of the Prophet, prescribes the wearing of veils for women or their exclusion from public life. According to them, the dominance of men in all areas of society is to be attributed instead to a mixture of Islam and patriarchal traditions. Nevertheless, it is true that, although in Islam women have the right to protection and financial support by the father, and later the husband, the price they have to pay for these advantages is that of dependence and subordination. Their lives are focused on the home, and they are largely banished from public life, which is the men's domain (see bibliography in De Knop *et al.* 1996).

The legitimisation for women's subordinate roles is sought in the Koran and the sayings of the Prophet. Thus, the introduction of Islamic law, the *sharia*, means among other things that women are disadvantaged in inheritance law and are subordinated to their husband, who is the head of the family. Moreover, divorce laws make it easy for men to repudiate their wives but virtually impossible for women to divorce their husbands. Men are entitled to marry up to four women. In the event of divorce men are invariably given custody of the children. Women, however, do have the right to financial support and to own property, as mentioned above. According to *sharia* law, certain offences are punishable by draconian measures, including whipping and – in cases of sexual offences such as adultery – death by stoning.

Since the beginning of the twentieth century, Iranian women have fought for their rights. Particularly in the course of the modernisation programme known as the 'White Revolution', girls' education was improved, the proportion of women students at universities rose to approximately one-third and in 1963 women were given the vote.[3] Women played an active and significant role in the overthrow of the shah.

In the subsequent theocracy established by Khomeini and his followers, a gender order was created based upon the essentially different 'natures' of the sexes and upon the conviction that the female sex was physically, intellectually and morally inferior; it was a gender order that defined the role of mother as the most important, perhaps even the only role of a woman's life. Further, ideology as well as everyday life were pervaded by the need to be shielded from sexual temptation in the form of women. For this reason, strict regulations for clothing were enforced, and even today the *hijab*, i.e. being correctly dressed with a head scarf, is absolutely essential outside the home. In public places women, especially those working in the public sector, must wear the so-called 'uniform' consisting of the *magneh*, a kind of hood covering the head and reaching over the shoulders, and a long, ample gown worn over trousers. Over this many women also wear the *chador* (literally 'tent'), a long black robe which hides any female curves (Brooks 1995: 17). Under the *chador* is concealed the treacherous female body, which in Islam constitutes the heavy burden of male honour.[4] While the *chador* represents the over-fulfillment of religious duty, below-knee-length coats and headscarves are the minimum requirement of correct dress that cannot be removed in shops or restaurants. Many women visitors from the West find this 'dress code' hard to accustom themselves to and so clothing is often one of the first subjects which female Western journalists raise with the Iranian women they interview (Klett 2001). Some Iranian women accept or even welcome the regulations of dress on account of their religious beliefs; others emphasise that because of the regulations they are not subjected to ideals of beauty or molestation; still others say that they have simply got used to wearing the *hijab*. However, there are also women who hate having to cover themselves up so completely before venturing out of the house. Incidentally, at home Iranian women behave and dress in much the same way as women in the West; they wear jeans or miniskirts, put on make-up and have their own hairstyles. By contrast, the men care little about the dress regulations that apply to them in Islam; they play football in shorts, for example, and many men wear tight jeans.

Correctly dressed, Iranian girls and women can move about freely in public places, attend schools and university and can also go out to work. In the early 1990s girls made up around 30 per cent of pupils at grammar schools (which are attended, however, by only a minority of young Iranians) and 28 per cent of university students. The proportion of female university students continues to grow today.[5]

Because of the low wages in Iran it is necessary for the women of many families to go out to work. In 1997 women made up around 10 per cent of the workforce. What is surprising is the high proportion of women in a number of academic professions; women, for instance, held 17 per cent (even 30 per cent according to other sources) of chairs at Iranian universities. Although the *sharia* does not allow them any powers of jurisdiction, women are nevertheless entitled to act as legal counsel. On the other hand, it must be borne in mind that a third of the female population can neither read nor write while the rate of illiteracy among men is only around 20 per cent.

The Islamic family law prevailing in Iran can be modified in the wife's favour by marriage contracts, in which issues such as modalities of divorce or the right to work can be settled. Although polygamy is not illegal in Iran, it is scarcely ever practised.

Today, Iranian women have the right to vote, there are several women members of parliament and it was women who tended to vote for the reformers in the last elections. Moreover, various women's organisations – both at home and abroad – are active in promoting the social and political interests of women. With a monthly circulation of around 40,000 copies, the intellectual feminist magazine *Zan* (Woman) is mainly addressed to female academics and students. However, it must be assumed that women differ greatly in attitudes and behaviour as well as in resources depending on social background and whether one lives in a town or in the countryside. As Klett (2001) observed on her travels through Iran, many Iranian women look optimistically into the future in spite of many limitations and problems. The students among them dream of studying in the USA or Europe and hope to embark on a rewarding career.

After my stay in Iran in the year 2000, I can wholly confirm these observations. While Iran's highest religious authority, Ayatollah Khamenei, commented in 1997 that the concept of equality between men and women was 'negative, primitive and childish' (Hughes 1998), several of the women I talked to tried to live according to this concept despite all the pressures that were put on them. Klett (2001) observed: 'Traditionally, women have always had a great deal of power, not only in the family, where nothing happens against their will, but also in social and community affairs.' She concludes: 'I have never seen so many self-confident, impressive and strong women. Neither in the Orient, nor anywhere else.'

The Prophet and women's sport

In examining the question of how sporting activities in general and girls' and women's participation in sport in particular are influenced by Islam, it must be stated first of all that there is no general prohibition of sport in Iran, and that this applies to girls' and women's sport also.[6] Islamic sport scientists, both male and female, emphasise that health and fitness are important for men and women alike and should be sustained by sporting activities. It was repeatedly pointed out in this connection that in various sayings of the Hadith, Mohammed had advocated living a healthy life and had recommended running, horse-riding, swimming and archery.[7] Leila Sfeir and others concluded from this that originally Islam was positively inclined towards women's sports. Sfeir writes:

> Islamic religion in no way tries to depreciate, much less deny sport for women. On the contrary, it attributes great significance and function to physical strength and sport activities. Islam is a constant concern with one's body, cleanliness, purification and force, with segregation of the sexes. But certain religious elements, such as Islamic fatalism and Hindu mysticism, have been dominant factors in controlling general access to sport.
>
> (Sfeir 1985: 300)

After studying Islamic sources and authorities Daiman (1995) even arrives at the conclusion that sport ought to be obligatory for women on health grounds. Nevertheless, in some countries women's sport is regarded as being irreconcilable with Islamic values and the Islamic concept of femininity, which forces women into subordination and dependence, and restricts their actions to the home and family.[8] Elnashar *et al.* comment:

> As Islamic nations struggle between inclusion and exclusion in a shrinking global community, it is to be expected that sport will take on the reflection of society which in most Islamic nations is value dominated by those empowered to interpret the words of the Koran.
>
> (Elnashar *et al.* 1996: 19)

The traditional physical cultures of Muslims, including such activities as *zurkhaneh*, are not oriented to outperforming others or breaking records; even so, modern sport of English origin also spread to Islamic countries in the course of globalisation processes, and Iranian women too were 'infected' by the general craze for sport. However, the problem arises that, whenever sport is practised, Islamic precepts must be followed, which means above all that the body must be covered and that men and women must practise sport separately since control over sexuality is not the result of internalised moral precepts but is ensured instead by separating the sexes (Bauer 1985). In order to 'defuse' the dangers inherent in women's sexuality, the entire female body must be covered by wide robes with the exception of the face, hands and feet. Men are to cover their bodies from the navel to the knees. Thus, normal sports outfits are, for all intents and purposes, taboo for men too; but they are especially, of course, for girls and women.

Apart from the 'segregation' of the sexes and the rules concerning clothing, a further factor that hinders or even precludes girls' freedom of movement and thus participation in sport is the precept of virginity in Islam. What is important here is the intense fear that the hymen might be damaged while practising sport and that a girl's whole future could be at risk because of it. Even today a young woman's chances of marriage depend on her being 'unsullied', and virginity and the sexual faithfulness of the female members are essential elements that make up a family's honour and hence its social status. Moreover, a girl's or young woman's good name is jeopardised whenever she leaves the house, especially in the evening hours, and is thus no longer under the family's supervision and control. A further obstacle preventing women from taking up sport is the fear that they might become physically and mentally 'masculinised'. Here as well as in the following, however, it must be remembered that there is a wide range of attitudes and behavioural patterns in the different Islamic cultures and that, likewise, there are great differences in the extent of interest and active participation shown by Muslim women in sport.

Sport in Iran

Today in Iran sport is 'in' and the enthusiasm surrounding sports has had a great impact. It is (men's) football in particular that has enthralled the masses and even draws women into the stadiums. Up until 1997 women were banned from the spectators' terraces. When, after their victory over Australia, the Iranian (men's) national team played in the qualifying rounds of the world championships in Tehran, 5,000 women surged into the stadium in defiance of the ban.[9] In the World Cup match between Ireland and Iran in November 2001, Iranian women were only allowed to watch the game on television while women supporters from Ireland were able to follow it live in the stadium. Women's presence is not desired at football matches because the sight of men in shorts is unbecoming for women and young girls. Besides, the authorities fear that women might learn swear words and bad behaviour there. This was not thought to be a problem for the female Irish fans since, of course, they didn't understand the language.[10]

Iran's constitution guarantees 'free education and physical training for everyone at all levels' (Art. 3/3) and physical education lessons are compulsory for girls and boys at school. The organisation of physical education and sport is shared by a Physical Education Organisation, the National Olympic Committee and the Sport Federations.

Practicing sport in the *hijab*

Aims and organisations[11]

Salam Iran's official website carries an article on the subject of women and sport, stating:

> Sports play an important role in our social life because it helps women perform their maternal duty and nurture the new generation in the best manner within the sphere of the great Islamic system. The need for and importance of women's sports and physical education is quite obvious, because women account for half of the population; specific programmes should be prepared to promote physical capabilities and sporting ability and especially to stimulate women's interest in sports.
>
> (http://www.salamiran.org)

In 1981, after the Revolution and following the principle of 'gender segregation' a separate sports authority was set up for women, whose name changed several times in the following years. At first it was called the Sports Committee for Women, then from 1985 the Directorate of Women's Sports Affairs and from 1989 onwards The Deputy of Physical Education Organization for Women Sports Affairs.

In addition, the Women's Sport Organisation (WSO) was founded in 1981, which, however, did not start to develop initiatives and activities until 1989.[12] An alliance of women sports teachers, former top-level female athletes and sportswomen as well as religiously oriented women's groups worked together in order to propagate and support physical activities and sport for girls and women. It was above all Faezeh Hashemi, daughter of Hashemi Rafsanjani and vice-president of the Iranian Olympic Committee, who had the determination, the political backing and also the right arguments to set women's sport on the agenda. In doing so, she quoted the Prophet and cited Islamic doctrine to lend weight and legitimacy to this initiative on women's sport. The crucial argument was (and is) the promotion of girl's and women's health, which would guarantee the health and the contentedness of their families.

Since the middle of the 1980s the WSO, which closely cooperates with the above-mentioned Deputy of Physical Education Organization for Women Sports Affairs within the Ministry of Education, has increasingly extended its remit and its activities. According to its official website, its goals are the promotion of 'physical and mental health', 'social relations', and 'moral, ideological and spiritual conditions' as well as the provision of leisure activities. In the area of 'sport for all', activities such as fitness training and aerobics are advocated and supported since they are 'simple, inexpensive and easy to practice at home and in indoor gymnasiums'. In the area of top-level sports, female athletes are selected and trained in various types of sport. In addition, the WSO has set itself the task of training women coaches and referees as well as 'to hold national and international competitions', 'to conduct research on women's sports' and 'to expand international relations' (http://www.salamiran.org/women).

The WSO is an umbrella organisation of various women's sports associations, but is also responsible for research and planning. Since 1980 associations have been founded in various sports, first of all in swimming, followed by badminton and gymnastics (1981), basketball, table tennis and athletics (1982), volleyball (1983), and so on. In 1997 a women's association for 'sport for all' was initiated, and in May 2000 even a football association was established.[13]

Today, in the twenty-eight provinces of the country, there are women's organisations in twenty-seven sports and one sport science association with altogether 30,000 members, more than a quarter of whom live in Tehran. Almost 40 per cent of women who take up a sport do aerobics, but other popular sports are swimming, volleyball and badminton. If one takes these figures, given in the brochure issued by the Women's Sports Organisation at the end of the 1990s, then the number of women active in sport is negligible when compared with the entire female population (approximately 30 million girls and women). However, in a television programme concerned with women's sport in Iran, quite different figures were given, namely:

> Today five million women practice sport in Iran, two million of whom take part in competitions. And – something that few people know – since the Revolution twenty years ago women's sport is booming. At that time there were nine women coaches; now there are 18,000.
>
> (ZDF *Mona Lisa*, 17 September 2000)

Even this figure is no longer valid. At the end of the year 2001 there were 23,000 qualified women coaches and 12,000 qualified women referees in Iran.[14]

Iran's National Olympic Committee has written the promotion of women's sports into its statutes (http://www.ir-iran-olympic.com). In addition, Iran's NOC supports the Islamic Countries Women Sports Federation, which was founded in 1991 and whose president is Faezeh Hashemi. The federation's main task is the organisation of the Muslim Women's Games.

Taking up sport: possibilities and limitations

In principle women have two possible ways of practicing sports: either in public, wearing the appropriate clothing, or in private rooms to which men have no access. This means that women can take part in skiing, hiking and mountaineering in public. The numerous hiking paths and skiing *pistes* in the Elburz Mountains to the north of Tehran are a particularly inviting setting for this. On public holidays the winding road up to Tocal Peak (whose summit is served by a single cable car) are black with the masses of people making their way to the top, the women in long coats and headscarves. Mountaineering is popular among women and is largely accepted. There is accordingly a Women's Mountaineering Association, whose president (a woman, of course!) even led a women's expedition to the Everest region in October 2001. Three of the climbers reached the peak of the 7,000m Mount Pumori.[15]

Let us return to Tehran. There, young people, 'decently' dressed, can play badminton, table tennis or volleyball in the parks. It can happen, however, that girls are reprimanded by stern-looking women wrapped in *chadors* if they are not suitably covered or that young men are escorted away for listening to music from portable radios or cassette players. Further sports that are possible in public are jogging and canoeing, which are made difficult by the *hijab* but not impossible. Nevertheless, there have always been (and still are) warning voices raised in conservative quarters complaining that even in spite of the *chador* too much of a women's figure is revealed when drawing back the bowstring in archery, for example, or that cycling not only allows unchaste views but also provides a greater radius of freedom, thus limiting the possibilities of control.

When women are among themselves, they can move freely and without the hindrance of long gowns and headscarves. Sport centres, swimming baths and fitness gyms are either open to only one sex, or are open to both but at different times. It must be borne in mind, however, that the sports facilities that exist only benefit a small proportion of the population, and women even less than men. 'Most sport centres are reserved for men. We don't have a tenth of the facilities they have,' complained an Iranian sportswoman in an interview.[16]

'Gender segregation', on the other hand, enables girls from traditional Muslim families to take up sport. However, many sports are considered to be 'unfeminine' even if they are practiced out of sight of the (male) public. An extremely controversial issue was allowing women to play football, the national sport. It took a lot of hard work on the part of women's sport activists, above all Fazaeh Hashemi, to convince religious leaders that playing football did no harm. In 1998 the first training session took place in Tehran. 'Schoolgirls, students and older women were there that day simply because they loved football', reported a woman coach in an interview.[17]

The chief motives for women's taking up sport are keeping fit and, above all, a slim figure. Jane Fonda's book on aerobics, for example, is available in Farsi, with the photos replaced by drawings. The ideal of a slim figure is widespread in Iran, too, and many speakers at the conference on women's sport held in Tehran in 1999 emphasized the significance of sport for a good figure – even if the shape of the body is not visible under the long coats. At home, however, women wear tight trousers and miniskirts. It must be added, though, that commercial fitness gyms and aerobic studios are only accessible to a relatively small number of well-off Iranian women.

Women and competitive sport

Iranian women take part in competitions as well as in top-level sports. One of the most popular sports in which competitions are also held is shooting – not only because Mohammed had recommended teaching children to swim and to use a bow and arrow but also because being able to shoot is of great value in a land threatened by wars and, in particular, because it can also be practiced in a *chador*. Since the early 1990s leagues have also been set up in various ball games, such as volleyball (in 1992), handball (in 1996), basketball (in 1997) and table tennis (in 1998). And in 1998 even women's football was allowed – albeit in locations inaccessible to men. Four teams were founded, women coaches and referees were trained and women's football is now becoming increasingly popular.[18] In national championships, women athletes compete in 'normal' sportswear in a 'women only' setting. The official opening ceremony and the closing celebrations, on the other hand, are held in public, sometimes in front of a large, mixed audience. Here, the women athletes wear Islamic dress.

Hashemi and her fellow activists also advocated taking part in international sports meetings, pointing out, among other things, that this might be a way of demonstrating the superiority of Islam. This was an effective argument and in 1990 six women sport shooters were able to take part in the Asian Games held in Beijing. Lida Fariman was the first Iranian woman allowed to compete in the Olympic Games after the Revolution; at the opening ceremony in Atlanta she carried the Islamic flag and appeared at the shooting contest wearing the *hijab*. She regarded herself 'as a representative of the Muslim women of my country with full consideration of the Islamic attire'.[19] This was also true of Manijeh Kazemi, who competed in the Sydney Olympics – the only woman in the Iranian delegation alongside thirty-eight men. The 26-year-old sport shooter was trained for the Games by a Chinese coach.

Thus, Iranian women have been allowed to compete in international sports meetings since the early 1990s, but only in events in which Islamic regulations on dress can be complied with. These are chess, sport shooting, horse-riding and kayak competitions, along with karate for girls. One of the most popular competitive sports among Iranian girls and women is tae kwon do. Just as in many other sports, national championships are held, but Iranian girls and women are not allowed to take part in international tae kwon do competitions. Numerous women athletes would like very much to compete in the international sports arena, a wish confirmed by the women taking part in the conference on women's sport held in Tehran in 1999. They hoped, too, that the regulations on dress would gradually be relaxed and Iranian women's freedom of movement enlarged: 'It's not just for fun', commented Silva Hanbarchian, 23, a canoeist. 'The world should know that Iranian women do everything that other women do, but with this uniform, and that we can do very well, if we have time and facilities' (*The Detroit News* 10 December 1995).

Different views, however, are voiced by women officials like Tahereh Taherian of Iran's National Olympic Committee: 'As far as international competitions are concerned', she emphasized, 'we Muslim women have decided to limit our participation to meetings and disciplines in which we can compete in our Islamic dress' (ZDF *Mona Lisa*, 17 September 2000).

Since, in the case of many sports, competitive sport is impossible wearing the *hijab*, an alternative was developed – the Muslim Women's Games, which were held in Tehran in 1993, 1997 and 2001, and from which men were barred as spectators. At these Women's Games the athletes marched into the stadium wearing the *hijab* for the official opening ceremony, watched also by male spectators. Afterwards the women competed in the various events wearing the usual sports attire but not exposed to the view of men. The women spectators, judges, journalists, doctors and coaches proved that such events can be successfully held without any men in stadiums, gyms or swimming baths.

At the first Women's Games the competitors came from nine or ten countries; however, those countries whose women athletes might have profited from a 'women only' sports meeting, like Saudi Arabia or the Gulf States, could not send teams to Tehran because there was no organised women's sport in these countries. The majority of the competitors came from countries of the former Soviet Union and so had never worn a *chador*. Most of them had already competed in international competitions and it was these athletes who won most of the medals. For all of the 122 women making up the Iranian team – with the exception of the sport shooters – this was their first international meeting and they enjoyed being in the limelight for once and competing with women athletes from other countries.

In December 1997 the Second Muslim Women's Games took place, following the same pattern. This time the competitors came from sixteen countries, and to these Games too, eight Islamic countries failed to send any athletes at all. In 2001 the Muslim Women's Games were held for the third time in Teheran.[20] Delegations from forty countries announced their participation but after 11 September 2001 and the war in Afghanistan the number of competing countries sank to twenty-seven. Nevertheless, there were over 600 competitors present, including Muslim athletes from England. It was the women from Afghanistan, however, who attracted most attention. In a statement to the press Nasrin Arbabzadeh, leader of the Afghan delegation, commented: 'We are here to say Afghan women are alive and want an active part in social life. We are here to denounce the uncivilised and anti-Islamic behaviour of the Taliban against women in the name of Islam.'[21]

The meeting began on 24 October 2001 with a torch relay and the lighting of the flame, followed by various performances and the procession of the athletes into the stadium, all dressed in compliance with the regulations on Islamic dress. A novelty of the opening ceremony was a performance given by a woman singer, since up to that time women were only allowed to sing before a female audience. During the opening ceremony there was also an appeal for solidarity with the women of Afghanistan. In 2001, too, all the work connected with the competitions was done by women who had been trained in the run-up to the Games to carry out the diverse tasks and duties. The programme was made up of fifteen events, which included tae kwon do, karate and *futsal* (indoor five-a-side football). There were also special rules for gymnastics on apparatus, where equipment was used that is not internationally recognised such as the side-horse or parallel bars. Partly on account of its superior numbers, the Iranian team of 159 athletes won the most medals.

The contests were accompanied by meetings of the host organisation, the Islamic Countries Women's Sport Federation, including an Annual General Meeting of members, at which Hashemi was re-elected president. The Games were also accompanied by an international scientific conference.

While the Women's Games were greeted in Iran as a great opportunity for women's sport and as an alternative to the Olympic Games, many athletes (and also many women and women's organisations in the West) pointed out that events of this kind would only legitimise the exclusion of women from the world of sport.[22] According to them, the holding of Women's Games only reinforced the marginalisation of women's sport. A great problem – and one that especially the athletes themselves repeatedly complain about – is the lack of spectators. Here, the lack of interest in women's sport that is familiar in the West is exacerbated by the Islamic precept of covering the body, i.e. women athletes can only be shown in photos or on film wearing the *hijab*. As a result, the reports and pictures of women's sport can in no way compete with those of men's sport. Indeed, the only publication to report regularly about women in sport, and thus perhaps motivate girls and women to take up sport, is *Zan* (Woman), the magazine mentioned earlier, which is in fact run by Faezeh Hashemi. Radio and television never report on women's sport, and this is a serious block to the development of women's sport, according to a report on women's sport by an Iranian woman journalist.[23] I cannot here go into this dispute, which is closely connected with discourses on the perspectives of values, which range from cultural relativism to universalism. One of the key issues of this dispute is whether there are universal human rights, i.e. the right of women to decide about their sport activities and, if so, who defines them. Suffice it to say that Iranian women athletes and coaches are taking advantage of the current conditions to demand more sports facilities (in small towns, too), more visits abroad and better training conditions.[24]

Using the authority of science

Women in the Iranian women's sport movement have always been aware of the significance of science in developing, steering and promoting women's sport. In 1985, a Research Committee was set up under the leadership of the psychologist Shokoh Navabi Nejad, and in the years that followed numerous projects were carried out, for example on the influence of sporting activities on women's well-being.

As shown by the detailed list printed in the WSO's official brochure, Iranian women experts began to take part in international conferences from 1990 onwards. The list includes such meetings as the World Congress of Sports Psychology held in Singapore in 1989 and a sport management course held in Thailand in 1992. Moreover, the WSO has itself hosted conferences and seminars on the subject of women and sport. And in 1999 the First Islamic Countries Women's Sport Scientific Congress was held in Tehran with over 200 participants. This congress carried on a tradition that was not confined to Iran: women's sport congresses of Arab countries had already taken place twice in Alexandria with the aim of strengthening the women's sport movement and lending it scientific legitimacy. The conference in Tehran attracted great public interest and it was reported on by all the television channels.[25] In spite of the wide range of topics presented in the papers, from hormonal changes during the menstrual cycle to anthropometrical investigations, there was general consensus among participants that women have a right to sporting activities and that the possibilities which girls and women have of practising sports should be increased and improved. Although religiously oriented speakers – recognisable by the fact that their faces were partly covered by the *chador* – advocated the spread of women's sports, citing Islam and pointing out the positive effects of sport, at the same time they spoke in favour of keeping the sexes segregated. Some speakers stressed that women not only had the obligation to look after their health but also had the right to recreation and fun in the company of others. The audience, which contained many females students, raised critical questions and put forward demands. The opinion was expressed that women's sport should be given much greater public attention since this was the only way that female athletes might become role models and the only way for the athletes to find recognition and support. Women practising sport in the privacy of their own rooms was interpreted as a deliberate show of disregard for women – and this is not surprising when one compares the invisibility of women athletes with the glorification of football idols.

The Women's Games of 2001 were accompanied by a second international congress. The 'call for papers' covered a broad spectrum of issues and the reports that have been published reveal that medical as well as technical questions and problems of sport were discussed in particular.[26] This can also be seen from the list (published by the WSO on the internet) of research studies carried out by Iranian women sport scientists, who are also concerned, however, with the situation of women's sports and the effects of doing sports.

Taking up sport and the gender order: theoretical considerations

To conclude, I would like to point to a number of interconnected issues and, thus, to a theoretical frame of reference.

It can be generally assumed that in Islamic societies, too, the gender-based division of labour and a symbolically conveyed gender duality determine social structures and everyday life as well as ways of thinking and of understanding things. In the development and the legitimisation of both the division of labour and gender duality, patterns of traditional social relationships, Western influences and religious orientations are closely interwoven.

On the basis of Norbert Elias's theory of civilisation, Waldhoff (1995) attempted to describe the specific structures and mentalities of an 'Islamic' society, taking Turkey as his example. His analysis is also partly true of Iran. Among other things, he pointed to the huge importance of the family and social networks in providing existential security for the individual. At the same time, this orientation to the family gives rise to specific psychical structures as well as attitudes towards the body. Thus, the dependence on social networks tends to demand from individuals an orientation towards rules and laws laid down from outside rather than an internalisation of moral precepts. The body is a vehicle for defined roles; the aim of exercising and 'toughening up' the body is not abstract achievement and/or trying to mark oneself off from others in individualisation processes. Consequently, staying young and keeping fit, abstract achievement and sporting success are of no particular importance in ethnic groups who rely on the cooperation of hierarchically structured families and social groups. Further, many behavioural patterns demanded by sport such as asceticism and self-discipline are generally not greatly valued in Islam (see, for example, Mihciyazgan 1996). On the other hand, traditional Iranian sports like wrestling and *zurkhaneh* (a form of weight training carried out in the 'Houses of the Strong') are physical activities whose aim is not the attainment of abstract records but the demonstration of physical strength, superiority and masculinity – and they are part of traditional Iranian culture.

This approach may be enhanced by Schiffauer's reflections on the structures of family relationships (Schiffauer 1983). In Islamic societies the strict hierarchy existing in the family plays a crucial role. Age and gender are decisive factors in defining the status of the individual in the family or community. The standing which a family has in the community depends to a considerable extent on the concept of 'honour', which is to be understood as the ability of the head, or other male members, of the family to defend it from attack or to avenge any wrong done to it. The system of relationships based on the concept of 'honour' requires those who belong to it to assume certain roles and responsibilities, while guaranteeing them at the same time the protection of the community as well as a certain standing in the wider society. Losing one's honour means exclusion from the group. Major elements of a family's honour are the sexual faithfulness of the wife and the virginity of the daughters. Any behaviour which might damage the 'good name' of the family's female members is strictly forbidden or, if the rules are broken, severely punished. In this system control over (female) sexuality is achieved not through the internalisation of moral precepts but through gender segregation. Thus, for women sporting activities in public are, if not impossible, then extremely difficult.

A brief summary

In Iran, a lively women's sports movement has developed since the 1980s which is marked by active women, a largely independent organisation, scientific accompaniment, the promotion of competitive and top-level sports and, last but not least, the support of a 'sport for all' movement. Gender segregation in sport has in some respects proved to be an advantage: to a certain degree women make the decisions, and the exclusion of men may have made it easier for some women and girls, particularly the daughters of families with traditional attitudes, to take up sport and reduce inhibitions. Nevertheless, it must not be overlooked that however difficult it may be to reconcile the *sharia* with practising sport, it is all but impossible to reconcile the *sharia* with practising sport at international level.

Numerous Iranian women, including many who are religious, hope that some of the regulations governing behaviour will be relaxed and that women's opportunities for co-determination in both sport and society will increase. This will not be easy to achieve, however, since the derestriction of gender segregation and giving up the *hijab* would shake the very foundations of Islam.

Notes

1 I thank Volker Kluge, an authority on the Olympic Games, for this information.
2 Letters and other material about the activities of Liselott Diem and the proceedings of the congress are to be found in the Carl-and Liselott-Diem-Archive in Cologne. On Liselott Diem see Hall and Pfister (1999).
3 On the situation of women in Iran, see Agha and Schuckar (1991); Minai (1991); Brooks (1995); Hughes (1998); Klett (2001).
4 Brooks (1995: 32); see also De Knop *et al.* (1996), which refers to further reading. The link between female sexuality and male honour is described in all studies on gender roles in Islam.
5 In 1993/4 312,000 men and 124,000 women studied in Iran; http://www.salamiran.org
6 On women's sport in Islam, see Lindsay *et al.* (1987); Yaldai (1988); Daiman (1995); Sfeir (1995); Walseth and Fasting (1999), which refers to further reading; De Knop *et al.* (1996).
7 Hadith constitutes the sayings of the Prophet handed down by his followers. The meaning and the importance attached to the individual sayings is a matter of interpretation.
8 Sfeir (1985); Daiman (1995).
9 Siavosh Ghazi, journalist in Teheran; http://www.unesco.org/courier/1999_04/uk/dossier/txt12.htm

10 CBBC/BBC Newsround, 7 November 2001; http://www.news.bbc.co.uk
11 According to information by the NOC of the I.R. of Iran, the two main responsible bodies for physical education and sport in Iran are I.R. Iran Physical Education Organisation (PEO) and I.R. Iran National Olympic Committee (I.R. Iran NOC). The sport for women's division is governed by the Deputy of Physical Education Organisation for Women Sports Affairs which functions under the umbrella of PEO. However, there are two other organizations which are the subcategories of this Deputy: one is Directorate of Sport Associations that is responsible for general women sports in different provinces and the other one is the Womens Sport Organisation (WSOs) that include national governing bodies, responsible for each sport on national level (source: e-mail by Mr. Bahram Afsharzadeh, National Olympic Committee of the Islamic Republic of Iran, February 2002).
12 http://www.salamiran.org/women/organisations/wso.html On this webpage the aims of this organisation are published. WSO is one of Iran's Governmental Women's Organisations.
13 Cf. the brochure 'The Status of Women's Sport in the Islamic Republic of Iran'; on the football association, see DAWN the INTERNET, 29 May 2000; http://www.dawn.com.
14 Haleh Anvari, the *Guardian*'s Newsunlimited, 26 October 2001; http://www.guardian.co.uk/religion/story/0,2763,581205,00.html
15 Payvand's *Iran News*, 27 October 2001; http://www.payvand.com
16 Siavosh Ghazi, journalist in Teheran; http://www.unesco.org/courier/1999_04/uk/dossier/txt12.htm
17 Siavosh Ghazi, journalist in Teheran; http://www.unesco.org/courier/1999_04/uk/dossier/txt12.htm
18 The *Iranian Times*, 12 March 1998, Esfand 21, 1376, No. 433.
19 *Muslim News UK*, December 1996.
20 Cf. the website of the Islamic Countries Women Sport Federation; http://www.icwsf.org. See also newspaper reports, e.g. *Der Tagesspiegel*, 27 October 2001.
21 MSNBC News, 24 October 2001; http://www.stacks.msnbc.com/news/647540.asp
22 The most important initiatives seeking the admission of Islamic women to the Olympic Games were started by the Atlanta Plus group, founded by French feminists. See Atlanta Plus (1996); 'An Open Letter to Juan Antonio Samaranch on his Birthday'; http://www.feminist.org/other/olympic/juan.html
23 Siavosh Ghazi, journalist in Teheran; http://www.unesco.org/courier/1999_04/uk/dossier/txt12.htm
24 ICWSF News; http://www.icwsf.org
25 I took part in this congress and spoke to numerous women about their situation as well as about women's sport.
26 ICWSF News; http://www.icwsf.org

Bibliography

Agha, T. and Schuckar, M. (1991) *Frauen im Iran*, Berlin: Parabolis.
Bauer, J.L. (1985) 'Sexuality and the moral "construction" of women in an Islamic society', *Anthropological Quarterly*, 58, 3: 120–9.
Bröskamp, B. and Alkemeyer, T. (eds) (1996) *Fremdheit und Rassismus im Sport: Tagung der Dvs-Sektion Sportphilosophie vom 9.–10.9.1994 in Berlin*, Sankt Augustin: Academia.
Brooks, G. (1995) *Nine parts of desire: The hidden world of Islamic women*, New York: Doubleday.
Daiman, S. (1995) 'Women in sport in Islam', *ICHPER-SD Journal* 32, 1: 18–21.
De Knop, P. *et al.* (1996) 'Implications of Iran on Muslim girl's sport participation in Western Europe', *Sport, Education and Society*, 1, 2: 147–64.
Diem, L. (1986) *Leben als Herausforderung. Autobiographie 1906–1986*, Köln: Academia.

Elnashar, A.M., Krotee, M.L. and Daiman, S. (1996) 'Keeping in stride with the games: An Islamic impression', *ICHPER Journal*, 32, 4: 17–21.

Hall, A. and Pfister, G. (1999) *Honoring the legacy: Fifty years of the International Association of Physical Education and Sport for Girls and Women*, Nanaimo: North Isle Printers.

Hargreaves, J. (1994) *Sporting females: Critical issues in the history and sociology of women's sports*, London and New York: Routledge.

Hughes, D. (1998) 'Khatami and the status of women in Iran', *Z Magazine*, October: 22–4.

König, K. (1989) *Tschador, Ehre und Kulturkonflik*, Frankfurt: Verlag für Kommunikation.

Klett, R. (2001) 'Befreien die Frauen den Iran?', *Emma*, July/August: 80–3.

Lindsay, K., McEwen, S. and Knight, J. (1987) 'Islamic principles and physical education', *Unicorn*, 13, 2: 75–8.

Midol, N. (1998) 'Hassiba Boulmerka and Islamic green', in G. Rail (ed.), *Sport and postmodern times*, New York: State University of New York Press.

Mihciyazgan, U. (1996) 'Türkische Mädchen im Sportunterricht', in B. Bröskamp and T. Alkemeyer (eds), *Fremdheit und Rassismus im Sport*, Sankt Augustin: Academia.

Minai, N. (1991) *Schwestern unterm Halbmond*, München: Deutscher Taschenbuch Verlag.

Pfister, G. (1997) 'Frauen und Sport in der Türkei', in M. Klein and J. Kothy (eds), *Ethnisch-kulturelle Konflikte im Sport*, Hamburg: Czwalina.

—— (2001) 'Doing sport in a headscarf? German sport and Turkish females', *Journal of Sport History, Special Issue: Ethnicity, Gender and Sport in Diverse Historical Contexts*, 27: 497–525.

Schiffauer, W. (1983) *Die Gewalt der Ehre*, Frankfurt: Suhrkamp.

—— (1989) 'Vom schweren Los, ein Mann zu werden', *Geo Special: Die Türkei* 1998: 24–32.

Sfeir, L. (1995) 'The status of Muslim women in sport: Conflict between cultural tradition and modernization', *International Review for the Sociology of Sport* 1995, 30: 283–306.

Waldhoff, H.-P. (1995) *Fremde und Zivilisierung: Wissenssoziologische Studien über das Verarbeiten von Gefühlen der Fremdheit. Probleme der modernen Peripherie-Zentrums-Migration am türkisch-deutschen Beispiel*, Frankfurt a.M.: Suhrkamp.

Walseth, K. and Fasting, K. (1999) 'Islam: Women and sport', paper presented at Women's Worlds 99, 7th International Interdisciplinary Congress on Women, Tromsoe, Norway, 20–26 June.

Yaldai, S. (1988) 'Frauensport im Islam', in P. Jakobi and H.-E. Rösch (eds), *Frauen und Mädchen im Sport*, Mainz: Matthias-Grünewald-Verlag.

ZDF (German television's second channel) (2000): *Mona Lisa*, 17 September 2000.

Online sources

http://www.dawn.com
http://www.feminist.org/other/olympic/juan.html
http://www.guardian.co.uk/religion/story/0,2763,581205,00.html
http://www.icwsf.org
http://www.ir-iran-olympic.com
http://www.ir-ws.com
http://www.news.bbc.co.uk
http://www.salamiran.org
http://www.salamiran.org/women
http://www.salamiran.org/women/organisations/wso.html
http://www.stacks.msnbc.com/news/647540.asp
http://www.unesco.org/courier/1999_04/uk/dossier/txt12.htm
http://www.zmag.org

15 Women's sport in the People's Republic of China

Body, politics and the unfinished revolution

Fan Hong

Introduction

After 1 October 1949 the Chinese Communist Party (CCP) finally won national power and established the People's Republic of China (PRC). The Communists promised that it would be a New China embracing gender equality. Have women received full equality now as the Party promised? What sort of changes has the Communist Party brought to Chinese women's sport and their social position? Why has Chinese women's sport achieved so much in such a comparatively short time in a country of such deeply-rooted feudal tradition? What has been the political impact on sport in Communist China and what influence has it had in turn on women in Chinese society? What is the basis for the contradiction between political rhetoric and grass-roots reality? To answer these questions, we have to put women's sport in the context of the change of political objectives, gender relationships, sports ideologies and management systems from 1949 to the present.

Women's bodies: a political issue for the re-construction and defence of the New China (1949–56)

Throughout history, in every society and in every culture men and women have been regarded as different in biology, psychology and behaviour. The focus of gender differentiation is the body. The body itself is a natural product, but it is socially constructed and historically reconstituted in the interest of society. Therefore, feminism sees the body as central to an understanding of women's oppression. De Lauretis argues that 'the stakes, for women, are rooted in the body' (De Lauretis 1987: 57). 'Your body is a battleground' (Cole 1994: 13). In traditional China, by controlling women's bodies, men controlled women's lives. The practise of footbinding not only bound women's feet, but their freedom (Hong 1997: 45–8). The practice of the Confucian doctrine of obedience to father before marriage, to husband during marriage and to son(s) after the death of the husband defined women's behaviour and provided the opportunity for men to exercise their power over them. In Communist China, women's bodies were liberated from the feudal practice of footbinding and from constraints of Confucianism; instead they were appropriated as a political symbol for the Party and the nation.

As soon as the People's Republic was founded, a new sports culture was formed. The Common Programme *inter alia* advocated that 'the Government promote physical exercise and sport among the people' (cited in Guan 1996: 165) in anticipation of the setting up of the All China Sports Federation in October 1950, supervised by the Communist Youth League, a tradition carried over from the Red Sports Movement in the past (Hong 1997: 165–8). However, the functional potential of sport was increasingly recognised by the government, especially after the 1952 Helsinki Olympic Games, and the State Council decided to set up a new governmental body to control sport. On 15 November 1952 the State Physical Education and Sports Commission (hereafter Sports Ministry) was established (see Table 15.1 and Table 15.2).[1]

Since women were an important force in both the re-construction and defence of the New China their bodies became an important political issue. Feng Wenbin, the first Chairman of the All China Sports Federation claimed in March 1950 that Chinese sport should involve young and old, men *and* women. One of the main aims of the sports movement was to encourage more women to participate in physical exercise (Feng 1950: 5).

Xin tiyu (New Sport), the mouthpiece of the Sports Ministry and Government, published an editorial entitled 'On the Development of Women's Sport' in October 1950. It stated:

> Women of the New China not only require immense patriotic enthusiasm, scientific knowledge and work skill, but also healthy bodies. Only when they have healthy bodies can women be able to participate in economic, cultural and military work and be able to produce and nurture a new and healthy generation.
>
> (Editorial 1950: 10)

Physical education became a compulsory course in schools' curricula. Girls and boys were required to have three PE classes a week plus one hour

Table 15.1 Centralised Chinese Sports Ministry before 1980

Pre-1980 *Administrative Structure of Chinese Sport, State Council* *Chinese Sports Ministry*	
Personnel Department	Three Sports Competition Departments
Political Department	Sports Training Department
Propaganda Department	Physical Education Department
Planning & Finance Department	Sports Research Department
International Liaison Department	Mass Sports Department

Source: Adapted from Fan Hong (1997a) and from Fan Hong's interview with the China State Administration Committee of Sports in September 2001 in Beijing

Table 15.2 Reformed Chinese Sports Ministry after 1980

Post-1980 Administration System of Chinese Sport, State Council China State Administration Committee of Sport (Former Chinese Sports Ministry)	
RETAINED AND CHANGED	
Personnel Department	Sports Training Department
Political Department	Physical Education Department
Propaganda Department	Mass Sports Department
Planning & Finance Department	Policy & Law Department
International Liaison Department	
CHANGED FROM THE PREVIOUS THREE COMPETITION DEPARTMENTS	
Athletics Training and Management Centre	Gymnastics Training and Management Centre
Football Training and Management Centre	Cycling Training and Management Centre
Basketball Training and Management Centre	Shooting Sports Training and Management Centre
Volleyball Training and Management Centre	Weightlifting Training and Management Centre
Swimming Training and Management Centre	Chess Training and Management Centre
Water Sports Training and Management Centre	Winter sports Training and Management Centre
Table Tennis & Badminton Training and Management Centre	Tennis and Hockey Training and Management Centre
ADDITIONS	
Sports information Centre	Sports Travel Agency
Sports Museum & Exhibition Centre	National Olympic Centre
Sports Equipment & Costume Dept.	Sports Service Company (hotels, restaurants and health clubs)

Source: Adapted from Fan Hong (1997a), and from Fan Hong's interview with the China State Administration Committee of Sports in September 2001 in Beijing

physical activities and games out of school. To meet the need for physical education teachers and instructors, six physical education institutes were established between 1952–6. There were 2,699 students (one-fifth of them female) studying in those institutes. At the same time, female peasants, workers and students were encouraged to participate in organised sports activities. For example, women competed at events in Shanghai (approximately 4,000 in ten events), Wuhan (900 athletes and over 50,000 spectators), Beijing, Shengyang, Jinan, Guishui, Hangzhou, Nanjing and Nanzhou. Female workers and peasants received particular attention: at the sports meeting in Shengyan city on 14 May 1950, women workers Wang Cuiyin and Han Xueyai became shot put and 50-metre sprint champions respectively (*Xin tiyu* 1950 no.1: 33). At the First Heinongjiang Provincial Sports Meeting, Yang Suzhen, a peasant woman, became the winner of the 60-metre and the 100-metre sprint. Her success as the first peasant woman to win at a big sports event in the New China was hailed as a demonstration of sports potential among worker and peasant women and that working class women need sport (Editorial 1951: 10). The Chairwoman of the Sports Organisation Committee, who was also the Chairwoman of the Wuhan Women's Federation, claimed that the sports meeting portrayed the new image of women and their competitive spirit. They were deemed to be 'healthy and strong and ... ready to devote themselves to the cause of socialist construction' (*Xin tiyu* 1950, no.1: 33).

At the beginning of the PRC the focus of Communist sports culture was to provide a basis for rationalising physical exercise and improving productivity in response to a state eager to use all possible means to build the new country rapidly. Competitive sport was not the immediate concern of the Party. Mass sport was the concern. As women formed one of the most underdeveloped of China's resources, women's bodies became one of the crucial elements in the cause of the revolution. Mass campaigns for women's exercise began. Sporting women became visible human beings and entered onto the stage of New China.

Training bodies for the Socialist Revolution: politics and elite sport (1956–66)

During the period 1956–66, which included the Great Leap Forward (GLF) campaign and the pre-Cultural Revolution period, the Chinese elite sports system developed and was consolidated. In 1956 the Sports Ministry issued 'The Competitive Sports System of the PRC'. A competitive sports system was formally set up: forty-three sports were officially recognised as competitive sports; rules and regulations were implemented; professional teams were set up at provincial and national levels and they would compete each other at regional and national championships. The national Games would take place every four years. In order to train and advance talented athletes from a young age, the Soviet Union's spare-time sport school model (*Yeyu tixiao*) was copied. The Sports Ministry issued 'The Regulations of the Youth Sparetime Sports Schools' in 1956. By September 1958, there were 16,000 spare-time sports schools with 770,000 students throughout the country (Wu 1999: 102).

This elite sports system was further developed during and after the GLF from 1957 to 1962. The GLF officially started in 1957. Its task was to speed up economic development and social progress in order to overtake Great Britain economically within seven years and the USA fifteen years. In response to the Party's call, the Sports Ministry initiated the Sports Great Leap Forward campaign from 1957 to 1962. Its ambition was to catch up with the world's best competitive sports countries in ten years. It was planned that by 1967, China's basketball, volleyball, football, table tennis, athletics, gymnastics, weightlifting, swimming, shooting and skating performers were to be among the very best in the world. China would produce 15,000 professional athletes. At the same time, in order to meet the needs of a healthy labour force, mass sport was also promoted throughout the country. The Soviet model, 'Preparation for Labour and Defence' (*Laoweizhi*), was adopted. Two hundred million men and women were expected to pass the fitness grade of *Laoweizhi*, 1,720,000 sports teams would be formed among 40,000,000 urban workers and 3,000,000 sports teams among peasants by 1967. It was expected that Chinese sport would develop under the 'two legs walking system': elite and mass sports developing simultaneously (Wu 1999: 102–6). However, the failure of the GLF and the Great Famine in 1960 changed the direction.[2]

The Sports Ministry changed its policy to produce elite sports stars in 1961. The government determined to use the best of limited resources to give special and intensive training to potential athletes in a particular sport so that they could compete in the international sports stage. Consequently, professional sports teams increased from three in 1951 to more than fifty in 1961. The Sports Ministry also issued the 'Regulations of Outstanding Athletes and Team' in 1963 to improve the system. Under the instruction of the Ministry, a search for talented young athletes took place in every province (Zhengyanshi 1982: 102). Meanwhile, ten key sports were selected from the previous forty-three.[3] The development of traditional Chinese Communist sports policy and practice marked a major historical change: a new era of elite sports, especially female elite sports began.

The Party started to pay special attention to the promotion of female elite athletes in the 1960s. In 1961 the Sports Ministry pointed out that the level of women's sports performance was lower than the rest of the world, and that emphasis should be placed on the development of women's sport (Zhengyanshi 1982: 71). In 1962, the Sports Ministry re-emphasised that all professional teams should pay particular attention to recruit and train women athletes. More female cadres should be sent to women's teams to solve their problems so that female athletes could concentrate on their training (Zhengyanshi 1982: 71, 88). The reasons for the emphasis on development of female elite athletes were, first, there was potential to develop women's sport so that the whole standard of Chinese competitive sport could be improved, and second, it would be evidence of gender equality in the New China. For the Party, the sports women should be superwomen: they were selected, tested, and graded during a long process and period from millions of young girls.

The sport of table tennis offers an illustrative example of this. Following the success of Rong Guotuan, who won the 25th World Table Tennis Championship in 1959, a campaign of producing young female table tennis stars began in the early 1960s. The Sports Ministry, Education Ministry and the Youth League all worked together to systematically produce talented female athletes. Table tennis training courses for girls were offered in and out of schools. School and out-of-school competitions were held in almost every city (Zhengyanshi 1982: 330). Additionally, multi-city festivals such as the Spring Festival and the Sixteen Cities Girls' Table Tennis Competition in Beijing were utilised to draft talented girls into professional teams. Chen Yin, Vice-Prime Minister of the State, encouraged female athletes:

> Sport is not just playing ball. It reflects our country's image, force, spirit and the superiority of our socialist construction. The achievements in sports are the glory of our country and people. But the glory cannot be achieved without hard training.
>
> (Cited in *Xin tiyu* 1963 no.5: 12)

Army intensive training and practice methods were adopted in 1963. Old training methods, which emphasised scientific training and rest alternately, were criticised as bourgeois. In 1964, the hard, disciplined military-type training was re-aligned to include qualities of hardship, difficulty and injury, and toughness of spirit, body, skill, training and competition.

In the four-year period from 1961–5, female athletes won three world championships and broke world records forty times. This was significant progress on the previous four-year period (1956–60) when no world championship victories were recorded by Chinese women and world records were only broken eighteen times (Wu 1999: 558).

In conclusion, this period witnessed the development of the Chinese elite sports system and practice. The Party concentrated all the resources on a few elite athletes in order to produce high performances on the international sports stage. It was a turning point in Chinese sport ideology and the system, which was changed from 'two legs' to 'one leg' – to elite sport. In the country, women athletes became icons of women's liberation and symbols of gender equality. However, this equality was defined by the state's political interest. Female athletes were treated as instrumental to political solidarity. Nevertheless, the elite sports system came under attack during the Cultural Revolution.

Women can hold up half the sky: iron bodies and sport (1966–76)

The Great Proletarian Cultural Revolution began in 1966 and ended with the death of Mao Zedong in 1976. It was one of the greatest political and social upheavals of modern history. The goal of the Cultural Revolution was to re-establish the ideological purity of communism threatened by the revisionists and capitalists over the previous eighteen years and to recreate unpolluted 'Mao Zedong Thought'.

The Cultural Revolution represented, among other things, attempts to promote an equal society. Therefore, on the one hand, elite education and sports systems were criticised as bourgeois and revisionist, and, on the other, sex equality was vigorously promoted. The Party claimed that so far in China it had been impossible to completely eliminate the remnants of the Confucian ideology advocating male supremacy and the persistence of old habits and customs underlying discrimination against women. If women were determined to identify and criticise the influence of Confucianism they would be able to emancipate their minds, do away with all fetishes and superstitions and press ahead despite the difficulties.

Women were called upon to 'Learn from *Dazhai*' and 'Learn from *Daqin*'. '*Dazhai*' was a model production brigade in a rural Shangxi province; '*Daqin*' was an oil industry company in north China. In both cases, women played an active role in their political and productive existence. They organised their own 'iron girls' shock brigade' and 'iron women's team' to compete with male peasants and workers. Women in China, therefore, were encouraged to learn from them and practise Mao's famous words that 'the time has changed'. Anything men can do, women can do'. Since both rural and industrial work was mainly physical, women had to demonstrate their physical strength to prove equality. 'Iron' bodies were required, for which sport and exercise were useful instruments. Thus, mass sport was promoted among girls and women in urban and rural settings and numerous peasant women participated in different activities in rural areas. Media attention highlighted the scale of participation: for example, in 1973 in Xiaofanzhuan Brigade, Nanyao County, Hebei province 70 per cent of women participated in physical activities. Women in Daxin Brigade, Zhangtai County, Fujian province challenged the custom that women could not swim in the river (*Xin tiyu* 1973 no. 9: 4–5). Even in the most backward tribal area, the Kucong stockade village in Yunnan province, which had never had any organised sports activity in its history, women were playing basketball (Kucong Village 1975: 13–14). In the cities, almost every large factory enterprise and work unit had women's basketball or volleyball teams. They competed against each other every weekend as a major entertainment for the factory workers and citizens. 'Friendship first, competition second' became a popular slogan.

In line with the new ideological emphasis on women's emancipation, local and national government and sports bodies provided equal opportunities, in terms of finance, coaching and training, to young girls who had sports talent and a worker-peasant-soldier background, for which Hunan provincial women's gymnastics team provides a good example. The team was established in 1971 to improve the sports performance level in Hunan. Eleven girls (ages 9–13), selected from sports schools, came from worker-peasant families. The team leaders and coaches lived on campus and looked after them; the sports authority provided all facilities and financial and managerial support. After two years training, the team became a top gymnastic team in the country (*Xin tiyu* 1973 no.10: 14–17). From then on Hunan became the base for training top female gymnasts in China. Some 60 per cent of members of the national team in the 1980 and 1990s came from Hunan including Lu Li, the Olympic champion in 1992.

Zen Guiying, a national swimming heroine, came from a worker's family. As a young girl, she trained in a spare-time sports school. After secondary school graduation, she went to the countryside for two years, but her family background and swimming talent ensured her return to the city and she joined the Jiangsu provincial team in 1970. At the national swimming championships in the spring of 1973 she broke four national records and became the top swimmer of the year (Jin 1973: 10–11). Another national heroine was Pan Duo, the female mountain climber. She came from a slave family in Tibet. In 1959 she became one of the first Chinese female climbers. In 1975 she and eight males climbed the summit of Mount Everest. She claimed: 'In our new society Chairman Mao supports women. We shall not let him down. So I determined to conquer the mountain and to prove the fallacies of Confucius that men are superior to women' (*Xin tiyu* 1975 no. 8: 22–4). When the Third Sports Meeting of the People's Liberation Army and the Third National Games took place in 1975 more women athletes became national heroines. They received most of the media coverage (*Xin tiyu* 1975). In the same year, the Women's Table Tennis Team became world champions. In short, women played a significant part in sport during the Cultural Revolution at national and local levels. It was a continuation of the work of the Communist Party to break down the barriers between sexes and to establish a new sports culture.

The massive development of women's sport during the Cultural Revolution helped pave the way and to lay down stepping-stones for the success of women athletes after the Revolution when China came back fully on to the international sports stage in the 1980s. Once the bodies were trained, the gold medals were not far behind. From 1977 to 1981 China won forty-six world championships; among them, women athletes won twenty-three championships in gymnastics, acrobatic gymnastics, shooting, diving, badminton, table tennis and volleyball (Ma 1990: 296–7).

An intensive effort by the Party to eliminate men's privileged status and establish full cultural, social, legal and economic equality for women by the 1970s produced considerable progress in women's sport and women's emancipation. Elizabeth Croll observed in 1978:

> Whatever the twists and turns in the history of the women's movement the image and expectations of women have altered beyond all recognition. Women in China were deeply committed to their present opportunities, the scope of which was unimaginable in the past. Gone are the days when women likened their secluded and confined existence to that of a 'frog in a well'.
>
> (Croll 1978: 331)

In conclusion, while there is a great danger of over-emphasising the role of sport in the Cultural Revolution, arguably, sport provided an opportunity for women to challenge the masculine world. The Cultural Revolution on the one hand advocated equality between sexes, and on the other hand created opportunities for thousands of girls and women to enable them to develop their sporting talents. Women took advantage of the political circumstances and successfully confronted traditional beliefs about women's physical and psychological abilities. They took their physical liberation a step further into the world of competitive physical activity largely considered a masculine world. In time their identity became embodied in ideology and action. Their competitive experiences became an authentic reflection of how women could be, and were now in society. Sport gave a powerful thrust to women's liberation in China.

The heavy gold medals: victors and victims (1977–2000)

Mao's death in 1976 ended the Cultural Revolution. It was Deng Xiaoping who took up the Party reins and initiated profound economic reformation in 1981. His ambitions were to accelerate China's development and to catch up with the Western capitalist world through 'controlled emulation'. He demanded an altogether new style of intercourse with the world. The success of the Chinese athletes at the 1979 World Volleyball Championships, the 1982 Asian Games and the 1984 Olympics brought the buzzword 'Competition' to the Chinese. Competition was believed to 'promote activism'. It could stimulate the nation's enthusiasm and motivate people to strive for excellence. The famous slogan 'friendship first, competition second' disappeared.[4] The principle of modern sport was competition. The Sports Ministry devised its Olympic strategy. Its aim was to become a leading sports power by the end of the twentieth century. To achieve this goal, the government channelled the best of limited resources to give special and intensive training to potential gold medallists.

Female sports stars played a major role in this Olympic strategy, benefited from this special treatment and achieved very satisfactory results. From 1985–93 China had 404 top sportswomen at international level, accounting for 51 per cent of all Chinese athletes at that rank. At the 25th Olympic Games held in 1992, Chinese women athletes won twelve gold medals, three-quarters of China's gold medals. In 1998 China won eighty-three world championships and broke thirty-one world records sixty-eight times. Of these, women won fifty championships and they broke twenty-eight world records sixty-five times. In fact, in almost every sport women have done better in international competitions than men. Hu Yiaobang, the General Secretary of the Party, pointed out that the indomitable and tenacious character displayed by Chinese women athletes embodied the new Chinese nation and brought it to the notice of the whole world (Hu 1988). In 1981 the State Council announced that the whole nation should learn from women athletes and use their spirit in sport to create the new face of socialist modernisation and reconstruction (Rong 1987: 199). Women athletes are not only models for new Chinese women but also for new Chinese men! In 1983 the National Women's Congress used women athletes as an illustration of women's superiority over men. The Sports Ministry announced proudly in 1990 that women athletes had established a new inspirational femininity. A survey in 1993 showed that female athletes were role models for the Chinese (Feng 1993: 24).

Nevertheless, on the whole gender inequality has persisted and has even increased in the 1990s. While women are said to have equal opportunity to work, many have to take lower-paid and less challenging jobs. Leadership positions are dominated by men, or given to women simply as window-dressing. In 1995, there were twelve female vice-ministers among the 200 male vice-ministers, and only ten women were provincial vice-governors, compared to about fifty men at this level. The Politburo of the CCP Central Committee had no women member at all (Li 1995: 408). Modernisation has brought technological reform and freedom from labour intensive work. Consequently, female unemployment is rising. In cities female workers are sent home to await work while male workers retain their jobs. In rural areas, since men with machines can do field work by themselves, women are instructed to return to their homes to concentrate on household work. Women do not receive equal pay for equal work. In urban areas they receive only 77.4 per cent of the pay given to men, in rural areas the figure is 81.4 per cent. In the 1980s and 1990s female graduates from college found it more difficult to obtain a suitable job than men. About 8 per cent of children who dropped out of school in rural areas were girls. Concubinage and prostitution, which the CCP fought hard to eliminate in the revolutionary years and which largely vanished after 1949, have reappeared. Women themselves and society question the belief that women 'can hold up half the sky'. A survey in 1991 showed that more than half of the respondents (both men and women) believed that men were superior to women (Wang 1992: 24–5). Women in China have thus failed to 'hold up half the sky', as Chairman Mao promised they would do if they simply embraced a communist 'New China'. Nevertheless, there seems to be one exception: women in sport. A frequent topic for discussion in 1990s was why 'the Phoenix (the symbol for women) can fly higher than the dragon (the symbol for men)'. Women certainly did themselves and the nation proud in international sports areas.

However, the heavy gold medals not only carried happiness, fame and glory, but also pain, suffering and humiliation. The ambitions of the government, the medal craze of the nation and the rewards available to athletes have placed officials, coaches and athletes under enormous pressure and have made drug use almost irresistible (Cao and Zhang 1998: 2). Since 1988, some fifty-two international Chinese athletes have tested positive for anabolic steroids. They include twenty-three women swimmers in the last decade (1992–2002). The Chinese were humiliated by rival nations and condemned as a team of 'cheats and liars' (Lord 1998: 44). Some coaches and the Western media have claimed that the Chinese systematically drug their athletes, especially young females (Lonsbrough 1998: 36).

Since the 1960s, women athletes have been trained under cruel and inhumane circumstances. The situation has not changed, and in some cases it has deteriorated. In the 1990s, Chinese women runners emerged as the dominant performers in middle and long-distance races in international competitions. The person credited with this success was their coach, Ma Junren. The team's success was attributed to the use of traditional Chinese herbal medicine and his rigorous training methods. However, the writer Zhao Yu revealed in his book *The Investigation of the Ma's Army* the dark side of the story. Ma Junren acted not as a modern athletics coach, but as an ancient gladiator trainer. Girls under his training had to run 220km a week or almost a marathon a day. He beat them at will. Wang Junxia, the holder of world records from 1,500m to 10,000m and recipient of the prestigious Jesse Owens Trophy in 1994, the world's highest athletic honour, was beaten by Ma every week for her 'inappropriate behaviour'. In fact, all girls suffered his verbal and physical abuse regularly (Zhao 1998: 127–61). Although Ma's cruelty and inhumanity were partially revealed and criticised by the media, Ma was not punished but promoted from a coach to a vice director of Liaoning Provincial Sports Commission and a member of the Chinese People's Political Consultative Conference for his contribution to winning the gold medals.

An irony here is that Chinese women have fought hard to free their bodies through sport over centuries but now some of them allow drugs and male dominant force like Coach Ma to abuse their bodies. It is vital for Chinese athletes to realise that they should not subordinate their bodies to politics, drugs and traditional male dominant culture. They should stand up for their own rights and to improve their image in the sports field.

There has been a debate since the 1990s on whether millions should be spent on a female Olympic medal or on the improvement of women's physical education, fitness, leisure activities and other welfare at grassroots level. The following facts usefully illustrate the worries of the scholars as well as the general public.

In terms of funding, female elite sports are emphasised and fanatically sponsored by the state, girls and women's physical exercise and leisure activities are ignored. Therefore, while a professional athlete's training cost 14 thousand yuan a year in 1990, the annual sport funds for an average primary school in Beijing only amounted to 800 yuan. More sadly, in 1990 the per capita sports fund in China in 1990 was 0.4 yuan per person and for a primary school pupil was only 0.3 yuan.[5]

In terms of sports facilities, after 1949, the government built a large number of stadia and gymnasia and purchased a great deal of sports equipment and apparatus. Most has been allocated to professional training. The

Chinese people have an average of 0.62 square metres of sporting space per person (Xie 1999: 8). Only about one hundred or so of all the 2,566 county towns own stadia, swimming pools or gymnasia. Many schools do not even have enough space for physical education classes. Yuan Weimin, the Vice-Sports Minister, pointed out in 1998 that physical education in schools had not developed as well as it used to in the 1950s and 1960s (Wang 1998). Between Chinese men and women, according to statistics for 1999, the proportion of men's participation in physical exercise and leisure activities was 62.13 per cent and women 37.87 per cent, because of lack of time, financial support and suitable facilities (Lu 1998: 183–4).

In terms of equal opportunity in sport, there were 18,173 coaches in China in 1990, of whom female coaches numbered only 3,527 (19.4 per cent). Most of the major administrative positions at every level were held by men. At the highest level there are five sports ministers, all men. While top male football players received a monthly income of 160,000 yuan (£13,000), top women football players received an income per month of 1,000 yuan (£100) even though they have won second place at the World Cup and won Asian Cup and Asian Games ten times (Xiang 1997: 74–6).

Conclusion

When the People's Republic was established in 1949, the Communists promised gender equality for both men and women. The years between 1949 and 2000 were an era of gender revolution and reconstruction. The period witnessed an unprecedented growth in Chinese women's sport. Chinese government leaders, as Marxists, believed in the superiority of their socialist system, and they were ideologically committed to the principle of female equality in society as part of the superiority of their system. For this reason, women's sport at a representative level had a major role, attracted attention from the government, and was financially and administratively endorsed. This has produced satisfactory results. However, women were, and are, still strongly discriminated against at the elite level and grassroots level. Women's participation in sport – the product of political change – has, to a certain extent, changed the traditional image of women and improved their social status – for some (like sports heroines), but not for all. The revolution has not yet finished.

Notes

1   The sports system structured in the late 1950s and consolidated during the 1960s and changed in the 1980s. A brief demonstration is given in Tables 15.1 and 15.2. The sports system has undergone dramatic changes. A look at the change in the structure of the Chinese Sports Ministry makes this point clear (see Table 15.1). The changes to the sports administrative structure, shown in Table 15.2, have clear competitive sports focus. The additions, shown in Table 15.2, all have explicit commercialism and customer focus.

2   The failure of the GLF brought economic disaster. Heavy industrial production was halved and the government cut back on all state investment. Twenty million workers lost

their jobs, and most of these were women. The government claimed that women's work in the next ten years was to manage a household and bring up young children. Gender equality subordinated to the government's political objectives and to a male dominant culture and a male dominant system.
3   They were: athletics, gymnastics, swimming, football, basketball, table tennis, shooting, weightlifting and skiing.
4   The last time it appeared in an official document of the Sports Ministry was in 1980.
5   The rate of exchange is 1US$=8 Chinese yuan (RMB).

Bibliography

Cao, Y. and Zhang, L. (1998) 'Aoyun jinpai yao chenbao daowei' (Setting Olympic medal targets), *Tiyubao* (Sports Daily), 8 January.

Cole, C.L. (1994) 'Resisting the canon: Feminist cultural studies, sport and technologies of the body', in S. Birrell and C.L. Cole (eds), *Women, sport and culture*, Champaign, IL: Human Kinetics.

Croll, E. (1978) *Feminism and socialism in China*, London: Routledge & Kegan Paul.

De Lauretis, T. (1987) *Technologies of gender: Essays on theory, film and practice*, Bloomington, IN: Indiana University Press.

Dong, J. (2001) 'Women, sport and society in the early years of the new China', *The International Journal of the History of Sport*, 2: 1–27.

Dong, N. (1989) 'Wangu changqin de shiyi' (Evergreen Cause), *Tiyu wenshi* (The Journal of Sport Culture and History), 4: 6–13.

Editorial (1950) 'Kaizan funu de tiyu yundong' (On the development of women's sport), *Xin tiyu* (New Sport), 3: 10.

—— (1951) 'Lun funu tiyu de fazan (On the development of women's sport), *Xin tiyu* (New Sport), 8: 10.

—— (1974) 'Rang shuoyou de funu dou zanqilai' (Let all women rise up), *Renmin ribao* (People's Daily), 2 February.

Feng, W. (1950) 'Quanyu kaizan renmin tiyu de jige wenti' (On the development of the people's sport), *Xin tiyu* (New Sport) 3: 5–6.

Feng, X. (1993) 'The changing images of women – An analysis of the contents of the magazine Chinese Women', *Chinese Education and Society*, 26, 3: 16–32.

Guan, W. *et al.* (1996) *Tiyu shi* (Sports History), Beijing: Gaodeng jiaoyu chubanshe.

He, B. (1988) *Shanao sheng de Zhongguo* (Contemporary Chinese Issues and Problems), Guiyang: Guizhou chubanshe.

Hong, F. (1997) *Footbinding, feminism and freedom: The liberation of women's bodies in modern China*, London: Cass.

Hu, Y. (1988) 'Dui tiyu zhanxian de tongzimen de jianhua' (The Speech to the Sports Ministry), unpublished document, Beijing: Zhongguo tiyu buwuguan.

Jin, C. (1973) 'Zai Fenglang zhong duanlian chengzhang' (Growing up in the stormy waves), *Xin tiyu* (New Sport), 8: 10–11.

Kucong Village (1975) 'Hongtaiyang de guanhui zhaoliang le Kucong sanzai' (The Red Sun Brightens the Kucong Village), *Xin tiyu* (New Sport), 8: 13–14.

Li, X. (1995) 'Gender inequality in China and cultural relativism', in M.C. Nussbaum and J. Glover (eds), *Women, culture and development*, Oxford: Clarendon Press.

Lonsbrough, A. (1998) 'Australian coach wants total ban on China's liars', *Daily Telegraph*, 15 January.

Lord, C. (1998) 'Expulsion calls after four more Chinese test positive', *The Times*, 15 January.

Lu, Y. (1998) 'Woguo tiyu renkou xianzhuan fenxi' (The analysis of sports population in our country), in Ketizu (ed.), *Zhongguo qunzong tiyu xianzhuan diaoca yu yanjiu* (The investigation and research of the situation of Chinese mass sport), Beijing: Beijing tiyu daxue chubanshe.

Ma, N. (1990) 'Zhongguo titan Niangzijun' (The sports women detachment), in Zhengfasi (eds), *Zhongguo titan sishi chun* (Chinese sports achievements in 40 years), Beijing: Renmin tiyu chubanshe.

Reporter (anonymous) (1950) 'Gedi baodao' (Reports from the country), *Xin tiyu* (New Sport), 1: 30–4.

—— (1987) 'China's best winning year', *China Daily*, 28 December, Beijing.

Rong, G. *et al.* (eds) (1987) *Dangdai Zhongguo tiyu* (Contemporary Chinese sports), Beijing: Zhongguo shehui kexue chubanshe.

Wang, D. (1998) 'Zhongguo tiyu guanjian zaiyu pinhen fazan' (Chinese sport needs balance), *Renmin ribao* (People's Daily), 4 Febuary, Beijing.

Wang, J. (1992) '40,000 diaocabiao xiansi zhongguo funu de shehui diwei' (Data illustration of the social status of Chinese women: the investigation of 40,000 questionnaires), *Zhongguo funu* (Chinese Women), 1: 24–5

Wolf, M. (1987) *Revolution postponed: Women in contemporary China*, London: Methuen.

Wu, S. *et al.* (eds) (1999) *Zhonghua renmin gongheguo tiyushi 1949–1999* (Sports History of the People's Republic of China 1949–1999), Beijing: Zhongguo suji chubanshe.

WuDunn, S. (1991) 'Feudal China's evil revived: Wives for sale', *New York Times*, 3 August: 7.

Xiang, A. (1997) 'Zhongguo titan de oldisan shijie' (The Third World in the Chinese sports world), *Xinshiji* (The New World) 1: 74–6.

Xie, Y. (1999) 'Qunzhong tiyu yu jingji tiyu suqingquzong' (Which is more important: Mass sport or competitive sport), *Tiyu wenshi* (The Journal of Sport Culture and History), 2: 7–9.

Xin tiyu (New Sport) (1950), 1: 30–4.

—— (1963), 5: 12.

—— (1973), 9: 4–5 and 10: 14–17.

—— (1975), 1–12: passim.

Zhao, Y. (1998) 'Majiajun diaoca' (The Investigation of Ma's Army), *Zhongguo zuojia* (Chinese Writers), 3: 1–217.

Zhengyanshi (ed.) (1982) *Tiyu yundong wenjia xuanbian 1949–1981* (The collection of sports policy documents 1984–1981), Beijing: Renmin tiyu chubanshe.

16 Gender relations in Japanese sports organisation and sport involvement

Machiko Kimura

Introduction: sports development in Japan

Organisational structure of sport in Japan

The core of the Japanese sport system is the Japanese Amateur Sports Association (JASA), a non-governmental organisation. JASA was established when Japan took part in the 1912 Olympics for the purpose of promoting national sports and to raise international competitive ability. Its current activities include responsibility for staging the national athletics meeting (since 1946), the biggest competitive event in the country, and training sports coaches, promoting sports clubs and conducting sports programmes, etc. JASA is, in conjunction with the Japanese Olympic Committee (JOC), also responsible for the selection and development of athletes for international competition. Government departments such as the Ministry of Education, Culture, Sports, Science and Technology support these activities as public benefits, and the JOC grants a subsidy to the JASA.

At regional level, JASA is structurally organised into 47 prefectures, in addition to which there are local municipal (city) organisations. The Department of Physical Education and Sports, a division of the Board of Education which has branches in each prefecture and city, subsidizes amateur sports association activities for the benefit of the general public benefit.

Sports clubs are usually organised at junior high school, high school and university levels,[1] as well as company enterprises. The clubs are organised on a sport-specific basis and students can choose the club they wish to join. The coach is usually a teacher at the school, but in some cases where success in competitive sport is a priority, specialist coaches are employed. Company enterprises support sports clubs for their potential benefits to employees' health and in order to enhance corporate image through promotion of elite athletes, the latter being more a feature of established and successful companies. Within the education system there are sports associations at junior high schools (JHSSA), high schools (HSSA) and universities (USA). A corresponding association, the Companies Sports Association (CSA) co-ordinates company sports clubs. Cross-sectional agencies cooperate to organise sports events. For example, the Prefectural High School sports meeting is held in cooperation with the Regional Amateur Sports Association, the Regional Board of Education and the HSSA; the Junior High School sports meeting that is held in each city is staged in cooperation with the Local Amateur Sports Association, the Local Board of Education and the JHSSA. Sports meetings at national level for high school, university and company enterprises are organised jointly by JASA and the Ministry of Education, Culture, Sports, Science and Technology, and the prefecture in which the site of the meeting is located.

Most sports clubs within the structure of the JASA belong to schools and universities. Needless to say, schools and universities are within the jurisdiction of the Ministry of Education, Culture, Sports, Science and Technology. Despite its status as a non-governmental organisation, JASA is also subject to government control, thus epitomising a weak voluntary sector network, for there is no umbrella organisation to co-ordinate the sports activities for residents at local levels in Japan. This means that voluntary sports organisations for people who do not belong to a school, university or company sports club (infants, elementary school students, housewives, senior citizens and other non-club affiliated individuals) do not yet exist in Japan. This 'gap' is only partially filled (in the pursuit of life-long sporting engagement promotion) by the sports programmes for local residents jointly provided by the Department of Physical Education and Sports (Board of Education) and the Amateur Sports Association. The Nara City Amateur Sports Association in co-operation with the Nara City Board of Education (Nara City 1996: 62),

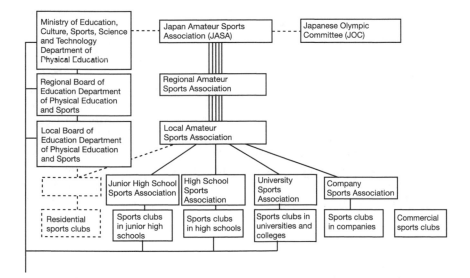

Figure 16.1 Structure of the sport system in Japan

for example, provides programmes in health gymnastics, badminton, volleyball, tennis, table tennis, track and field, swimming, kendo, judo, naginata (Japanese halberd) and kyudo (Japanese archery). In September 1999, the Ministry of Education, Culture, Sports, Science and Technology issued its 'Sports Promotion Basic Plan', whereby it is proposed that local residents organise sports clubs with the overall goal of promoting competitive sport and life-long participation in recreational sport in an attempt to change the traditional sports system by shifting emphasis away from the core component in structural organisation.

Other than this, commercial/private sports clubs provide for people who are not in membership of sports clubs in schools, universities and companies and there are swimming clubs for infants, elementary schools and housewives as well as fitness clubs for the workforce for which the respective customers pay for the service experienced.

At present, there are no data to compare the quality and volume of public sports services with commercial sports services. However, Nara City with a population of 350,000 provides an example of swimming pools supply by way of reference. In 2001, the city had only two public heated pools compared with ten commercial heated pools (NTT Media Scope 2000: 126). Notwithstanding this, non-heated outdoor 25-metre swimming pools are provided in every elementary, junior high and high school.

Characteristically in Japan, school sports clubs have a significant presence in the sports system, which is grounded in historical determinants. In the middle of the nineteenth century, when the European colonial period was extended to East Asia, Japan underwent a crisis of change culminating in a new form of government in 1867 that embarked upon rapid modernisation. The model for modernisation was Western. Hence, Japanese universities employed Western teachers and devoted themselves to absorbing Western science, technology and culture in a process of Westernisation, which included the introduction of modern forms of sport such as baseball, tennis, track and field, gymnastics and soccer as club activities (Kinoshita 1970: 13–24). The process of Westernisation, however, initially impacted only on university students, who were few in number, and elite society in the latter part of the nineteenth century. University students who became high school teachers took with them the sports they had enjoyed at university, and so with time helped to spread these imported modern sports throughout the school education system. School sports clubs were a logical development.[2] Today all schools have sports clubs and sport has become part of school culture in Japan. The Japanese word *taiiku* was translated from the English 'physical education' in 1876 (Kishino 1973: 22), but *taiiku* in Japanese later came to embrace 'sports' as well as 'physical education' without distinguishing between the two terms. Interestingly, the translation in Japanese of the 'Japan Amateur Sports Association' is 'Nippon *Taiiku* Kyokai'.

Organisations for girls and women only in the sport sector

The first national organisation to promote women's sport was the Japanese Women's Sports Federation (JWSF), which was established in 1926. Men headed the Federation, with Dr Tousaku Kinoshita as Chairperson. JWSF's essential purpose was to foster *kenbo* through the promotion of sport for young women in general but for high school girls in particular. *Kenbo* means a mother who bears a healthy child who will become a leader in the next generation. In co-operation with the Fédération Sportive Feminine Internationale, JWSF has concentrated on sending women athletes to international meetings. The track and field 800m athlete Kinue Hitomi, who won a silver medal in the ninth Olympic Games (Amsterdam 1928), was supported by this organisation. The JWSF ceased to exist in the period around 1936–7 when it was absorbed by the Japanese Amateur Athletic Federation (Raita 1999: 120–34). After a gap of two decades, the Japanese Association of Physical Education for Women (JAPEW) was formed in 1954. The Association is affiliated to the International Association of Physical Education and Sports for Girls and Women (IAPESGW). The main focal area of activity of the JAPEW is on dance education in schools; thus, apart from dance, since the demise of the JWSF there has been virtually no other body to promote women's sport for over 60 years (Raita 1999). A more recently established organisation, the Japanese Association for Women in Sport (JWS), which is a non-profit organisation and which aims at 'men and women jointly participating in society' (http://www.jws.or.jp, 8 April 2002) offers greater expectations for women's sport than hitherto.

Participation of girls and women in school sports

Curricular sports activities and physical education

The Japanese Constitution and the Fundamental Law of Education (based on the Constitution) was promulgated in 1947 with an expressed principle of the equality of the sexes. However, contrary to this principle was a differentiated school physical education programme for boys and girls over a long period of time. For example, 'Budo'[3] was designated for boys and 'dance' for girls in Junior High and High Schools. Boys have more physical education lessons than girls in High School (for boys, 11 credits, for girls 7–9 credits); moreover, home economics features only for girls (Itani *et al.*2001: 194).

The school teaching curriculum guidelines introduced in 1989 constituted a landmark from the gender point of view. Home economics became a compulsory subject for boys and girls; and in the physical education curriculum both boys and girls were given the opportunity to choose 'budo' or 'dance'. Therefore, equality of the sexes was achieved formally, at least in the school curriculum content matter. However, this did not result in actual equality of the sexes. According to the findings of a survey of 156 Osaka prefecture public high schools, conducted by the Osaka Prefectural Board of Education in 1999, ten years on from the revision of school teaching curriculum guidelines, only 13 schools (8.3 per cent) permitted the choice 'budo' or 'dance' (Itani *et al.* 2001, 199). The other schools either designated 'budo' for boys and 'dance' for girls, as was traditionally the case, or removed both 'budo' and 'dance' from the curriculum. Any realisation of actual equality of the sexes in school physical education at school is a subject of the future.

Extra-curricular activities: school sports clubs

As mentioned in the introduction, school sports clubs are well established in Japan. School sports clubs affiliate to the Junior High School Sports Association (JHSSA) or High School Sports Association (HSSA) on a sport-specific basis. The only exception is high school baseball clubs, which do not join the HSSA, but are organised in the High School Baseball Association (HSBA).[4] The HSBA does not allow girl's baseball teams to join.

The number of HSSA members has declined in recent years due to the reduction in the number of children. Boy members number 814,931 and girls 531,518 – 65 per cent of the number of boys (Itani *et al.* 2001, 206). There are different kinds of sports preferred by each sex. The HSSA membership statistics (High School Sports Association 1999) reveal that the preferred top five sports for boys or male adolescents according to membership are:

1   basketball (approx. 105,000 male members)
2   track and field (approx. 65,000 male members)
3   volleyball (approx. 52,000 male members)
4   tennis (approx. 51,000 male members)
5   table tennis (approx. 44,000 male members)

Girls and female adolescent members, on the other hand, prefer:

1   volleyball (approx. 73,000 female members)
2   basketball (approx. 68,000 female members)
3   badminton (approx. 53,000 female members)
4   soft-tennis (approx. 46,000 members)
5   tennis (approx. 44,000 female members

(see Itani *et al.* 2001: 207)

From a gender comparative perspective, more girls participate in softball, volleyball and badminton, whereas more boys participate in judo, table tennis, track and field, and basketball. There is little difference between boys' and girls' participation in tennis and swimming.

There were thirty-one kinds of sport in HSSA in 1997. The exclusively male sports were soccer, rugby, sumo wrestling, wrestling, cycling, boxing and weightlifting. The number of exclusively male sports increases to eight if we add baseball under the HSBA to the thirty-one. The only sport exclusively for girls was naginata (Japanese halberd; see Itani *et al.* 2001: 208).[5]

The difference in participation patterns of boys and girls, mainly in High School, mentioned above, demonstrates a strong gender bias. Research by the Tokyo Women's Foundation backs this up at the conscious level. In this research, the questions 'whether active activity' is appropriate for boys and girls and who is more 'enthusiastic about sport' were posed to junior high and high school students. The answer 'I can't say which' accounted for around half of the responses, but 'suitable for boys' was overwhelmingly larger in responses than 'suitable for girls'; more boys than girls tended to answer in this way (Itani *et al.* 2001: 185).

Furthermore the existence of active 'women managers' in high school and university clubs is a radical gender issue, especially in sports clubs. The word 'manager' originally related to a person who takes charge, however 'woman manager' means a woman member who performs chores such as recording matches, cleaning rooms, washing uniforms, serving drinks during practice, picking up balls and so on. Because these people do not usually register as club members, nationwide research is not available. According to recent research by Hatakeyama (2000) conducted in high schools in Kanagawa prefecture, 97 per cent of men's sports club have 'women managers' (Hatakeyama 2000: 90). According to a study by Matsumoto (2001) conducted on 150 'women managers' of university sports clubs, 'women managers' in men's sports clubs show an overwhelming majority (84.6 per cent) compared with 'woman managers' in women's sports clubs. Furthermore, though the role of women managers in women's sports clubs is close to the original meaning of management, women managers of men's sports clubs undertake chores far from the original meaning of management (Matsumoto 2001: 32). However, about 70 per cent of 'women managers' do not regard the job as a chore and think of it as both invaluable in cultivating the club 'spirit' and in personal development (Matsumoto 2001: 50). This is a very similar role to the *okamisan* of the traditional Japanese sport, sumo. In the case of a professional sumo wrestler who attains the highest rank, *yokozuna*, he can become a 'stable master' who then trains the next generation of wrestlers. At the same time, the wife becomes *okamisan* and looks after the young sumo wrestler's daily life and acts as a personal counsellor. Sumo wrestlers adore *okamisan* as an actual mother (Oinuma 1994: 84–6). Assuming that this picture of *okamisan* is the ideal image of a woman, even though 'women managers' do only chores in their visible role, they believe that they provide discrete mental support through the chores.

Participation of women in out-of-school sporting activities

Leisure sport and gender difference

According to research on people aged twenty years and older, only 24.1 per cent of the men and 34.5 per cent of the women do not participate in sport. But of those who do participate in sport for more than thirty minutes, twice a week, the proportions are closer: 33.9 per cent are men and 32.1 per cent are women (Itani *et al.* 2001, 91). With regard to sports participation rates of active women by age, the proportion of those who engage in a sport activity for over thirty minutes, more than twice a week, decreases from 15.9 per cent (of all twenty-year-old women respondents) to 11.3 per cent in the thirties, increasing rapidly to 19.9 per cent in the forties, peaking with 21.7 per cent in the fifties, and then decreasing to 15.6 per cent (amongst sixty-year-olds) and to 12.7 per cent of women aged seventy and older (Itani *et al.* 2001: 92).

The adult membership rate for sports clubs is about 18 per cent for women and 25 per cent for men (SSF 2000: 109). By age group, the membership figure for women in their twenties and thirties is especially low, with the peak in the fifties. There is little difference between men in this age group (see Figure 16.2). This finding concurs with the tendencies referring to the sports participation rates for active women by age mentioned above.

Clubs mainly for local residents have the largest proportions in membership for both men and women (men 46.8 per cent; women 63.8 per cent); second are private/commercial sports clubs (men 14.9 per cent; women 22.9 per cent). Club membership for employees is 2.9 per cent for women against a much higher 20.9 per cent for men (Itani *et al.* 2001: 98).

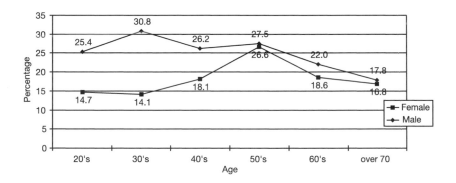

Figure 16.2 Admission rates to Japanese sports clubs (by sex and age)
Source: Itani *et al.* 2001: 95

Activities where the rate of women's participation is higher than that for men in the top twenty ranking of sport-related activities during the last year are walking and 'strolling', health gymnastics, swimming, hiking and badminton. Activities in which only women participated are skipping rope, 'aqua exercise', volleyball, aerobics dance and tennis, while events in which only men participated are playing golf, practising golf, baseball, softball and ground golf (Itani *et al*. 2001: 94).

Access to high-performance sport/top-level sport

No data exist at present to show whether there is equal support for men and women in elite sport. This may be due to the fact that the philosophy of the amateur sport movement in Japan is strong – as demonstrated in the name of the Japanese Amateur Sports Association. Top amateur athletes who perform at high level are less well known by the public than a professional with regard to opportunities of meetings, rewards, incentives, evaluation, sponsorship or promotion. For example, the right to an athlete's portrait is owned by the Japan Olympic Committee (JOC) in Japan and any money earned was pooled in the JOC and used as a fund for training other athletes. Therefore the earnings and expenses of the individual athlete are completely unknown when accounts of the organisation are made public. The 'Professionalisation Declaration' of Yuko Arimori, a marathon athlete, was sensational in the JOC and the Japanese Amateur Sports Federation. Some athletes may now directly receive monies earned through their performance in commercials, albeit under strict conditions, since 1996 (Asahi Press 1997: 2).

From other less scholarly-derived data, the ratio of men to women amongst Japanese athletes who took part in the Nagano Winter Olympics of 1998 and the Sydney Olympics in 2000 was 59.7 per cent to 40.3 per cent. There were only two activities in which women alone competed: softball and beach volleyball; for men only, there were six activities: baseball, soccer, bobsledding, wrestling, equestrian events and boxing. The difference in the number of participants by gender was small, but there was a big difference in number of events (Itani *et al*. 2001: 64).

Women in decision-making positions in organised sports

The proportion of men to women who participated as officials in the Nagano Winter Olympics in 1998 and the Sydney Olympics in 2000 was for 92.5 per cent for men and 7.5 per cent for women (Itani *et al*. 2001: 62). The ratio of women sent as officials who coach or manage athletes is low compared with the ratio of female athletes: softball 33 per cent, gymnastics 25 per cent, swimming 22 per cent, skating and curling 14 per cent and other sports less than10 per cent (Itani *et al*. 2001: 65).

Officials, other than those belonging to sports associations, who were sent to the Sydney Olympics under the JOC included only four women (8 per cent) out of a total of forty-nine. All executive officials such as leader and vice-leader were men (Itani *et al.* 2001, 70). In any case, generally the number of women officials is extremely low and decision making for sports organisations is, in most cases, conducted by men.

Social structure and its influence on sports participation in respect to girls and women

Under the Constitution of the Japanese Empire (established in 1889) prior to the Second World War, the equality of the sexes was not widely accepted with women not only excluded from politics but also holding a lower position in both home and society. In those days the image of the ideal woman was 'a good wife, a wise and healthy mother', and women had to bear and raise healthy children following the husband's wishes in the house. Men were to work hard outside of the home, while men who were involved in housekeeping and child care were seen as objects of contempt (Tanaka 1975: 131–2).

Approval of fundamental human rights and the philosophy of equality of the sexes was written into the Japanese Constitution and enforced after the Second World War in 1947. In this way, the equality of the sexes was guaranteed under the Constitution and the ideas of different roles of the sexes have decreased little by little. People who agree with the notion of 'the husband is at work, the wife is in the house' were given at 83.2 per cent of women and 83.8 per cent of men in 1972, but changed to 51.9 per cent of women and 64.9 per cent of men in 1997 (Inubushi *et al.* 2000: 42).

However, there is little or no evidence of action change in keeping with the level of consciousness change. Comparing the average time spent on housekeeping in a week in a dual income family, the husband spends only twenty minutes, whereas the wife spends four hours and thirty-three minutes. The average time spent on housekeeping by the husband in a family where only the husband works is twenty-seven minutes; the time spent on housekeeping by the husband does not increase if the wife goes out to work. As for the total time spent on housekeeping and work in a day, the wife in a dual income family spends nine hours and three minutes, or more than one hour longer than the seven hours and forty-six minutes of the husband (Inubushi *et al.* 2000: 40). According to fundamental social life research conducted by the Management and Coordination Agency, housekeeping time amongst single men is eighteen minutes and married men twenty-eight minutes, so marriage only brings an increase of ten minutes. In the case of women, single women spend fifty-nine minutes, a figure which increases with marriage by four hours ten minutes to a total of five hours nine minutes (Inubushi *et al.* 2000: 40). These figures show that the housekeeping burden on women increases considerably.

For working rate of Japanese by age, a high working rate of more than 95 per cent is shown in the case of men between 25 and 55 years old; in the case of women, the graph has a letter 'M' shape with 73.4 per cent as the maximum (20–24 years old), a decrease to 55.8 per cent (30–34 years old), and then a further gradual increase (Inubushi *et al.* 2000: 33). Such data reveal the normal lifestyle of Japanese women in that most women work after graduating from school, but almost all women quit working with marriage and arrival of children and return to work part time after completing child care commitments. This letter 'M' shape and the high working rate of men generate a difference between the overall working rate of men and women in Japanese. Furthermore, 89 per cent of men work on a full-time basis, compared with only 55 per cent of women, very many of whom work part time (Inubushi *et al.* 2000: 33).

The letter 'M' shape can also be seen in the sports conduct rate of Japanese active women as described above. It is inferred that in the typical sports life style of Japanese women, many women are unable to practise sport after marriage and simultaneously with childcare responsibilities in their later twenties and thirties; they return to sports from their forties after completing childcare. There is a clear difference between the sports lifestyle of men and women in Japan. There are more men who play sport in clubs mainly for employees than women.

Differences between men and women occur most conspicuously within marriage in Japan. What social cultural background generates this situation? Nakane, a social anthropologist, characterised Japanese society as a society built through vertical human relationships (Nakane 1967: 25–114).[6]

The place in which mutual activity is conducted through direct contact is regarded as important in Japan and people are required to devote their whole life to this place. This applies to the company enterprise. For example, in Japan there is little sense of 'contract', and thus human relationships form a village-like community, or family, in the company rather than a contract, though the 'contract' made between the company and its workers is regarded as important in the USA. Devotion of their whole life to the company is required rather than simply requiring the worker to carry out tasks in line with a contract. Superiors are good to subordinates and subordinates are loyal to superiors. Sometimes superiors are involved in a subordinate's private life (e.g. marriage). Subordinates try to obey these superiors even if it is difficult. Japanese companies have adopted a lifetime employment system from this foundation of human relationships. The reason Japanese office workers work long hours is to maintain human relationships rather than carrying out a contract. This tangible human relationship is important and is manifested in after-work collective social drinking until late at night. Within such a social system, uptake of paid vacation is low as prolonged absence is perceived as disadvantageous. As for the labour unions, it is usual that craft unions in such countries as the USA are formed, whereas in Japan, it is usual for them to be formed by company as a sense of unity with the employees, who communicate directly every day. A full-scale labour dispute seldom happens as familiar human relationships are formed between the employer and employee within the same company (Nakane 1967: 69–114).

In the case of a foundation of vertical human relationship at work, if both partners in a marriage work full time, they are both absorbed in the company and the family may become a lifeless shell. Moreover, it is almost impossible for both of them to keep working under equal conditions in the case of responsibility for childcare. The result of this situation is that responsibility is divided; work outside and staying at home. In almost every case, the former role is accorded to the husband and the latter to the wife. If the wife works outside, she never can neglect her job of housekeeping.

In vertical human relationships, to be absent from the place becomes greatly disadvantageous in building a career as the place where tangible human relationships are developed is regarded as important. As a reason why so few women take leadership and are involved in decision making in organisational sport, it is considered that many leave sports organisation because of marriage and childcare. How long the person stays active in the organisation is more important than the actual ability to obtain status. In case of selection of athletes for the Olympics, regardless of the length of the term the person belongs to the sports association, ability is evaluated. However, in the case of selection of officials, the term during which the person has established human relationships within the organisation tends to be more important than ability or personality as an officer. So it is disadvantageous to women.

Thus, although the Constitution refers to equal status of men and women, the actual situation is that this is still not reflected in conscience and action. In particular, the role of men and women is divided clearly by marriage. Female participation in sport is repressed in Japanese society where it has the foundation of vertical human relationships.

Recently, there has been a trend amongst independent women not to marry as they do not want to take a socially disadvantaged position through the burden of housekeeping and childcare. One consequence is that late marriage has increased and the birth rate is decreasing rapidly.[7] In times when it was difficult for women to be financially independent, marriage was a 'place of life security' for women and, as getting married and raising children were regarded as the standard lifestyle of women, research on women's sports activity has been conducted as if all women are the same. But more differentiated research corresponding to various lifestyles of women and research into categories like that of single women, married women, mother, widow, or working or not, will be required in the future.

Evaluation of the main problems of sports development in relation to women's participation

In summary from the above discussion on issues surrounding Japanese women's sports participation:

- The difference between men and women in school physical education curriculum disappeared in 1989.
- However, differences between males and females are often still apparent in the physical education class in every school at present.
- Women participate in school sports clubs at the rate of 65 per cent of men and there are many sports activities that women cannot engage in such as baseball, and soccer amongst others. Students tend to think of sport being more suitable for men.
- There are women managers who only do chores in school sports clubs, and most of them believe this to be their job.
- In adults over 20 years of age, women exceed men in the number who do not participate in sport (24.1 per cent men; 34.5 per cent women).
- There is little difference between the participation of men and women adults who do some sports activity for over thirty minutes more than twice in a week.
- Women in their late twenties to early thirties show a decrease in sports activity due to the role of men and women at that age being clearly divided, with women responsible for housekeeping and child-care.
- Women have been promoted as top-class athletes, but women hardly participate in decision-making processes.

Over fifty years have elapsed since equality of the sexes was articulated in the Japanese Constitution after the end of the Second World War. However, equality of the sexes in sports participation has not been achieved yet, neither in consciousness nor action. In particular, the role of men and women is divided very clearly after marriage in Japan. The institution of marriage has a considerable influence on the extent of sports participation by women. It leads to a reduction in sports participation by women who are engaged in childcare and it causes a situation, whereby women hardly have an opportunity to be involved in decision making in sports organisations. The image of the role of men and women after marriage is filtered down to young people, with the image being condensed in the existence of 'women managers' in the school sports club.

The issue of polarisation of the roles of men and women after marriage has its foundation in the vertical human relationships that make up Japanese society. Therefore, it is difficult to resolve. However, recently Japanese companies have had to abandon the lifetime employment system and the seniority system due to globalisation. It is also a fact that it is becoming more difficult to regard vertical human relationship as a criterion. The number of women who do not include marriage and having children in their life plan has increased. The Japanese social structure is undergoing change. This change may well produce a gender-free society, and gender-free sports participation.

Notes

1   Nine years in total; six years in elementary school and three years in junior high school is compulsory education, followed by three years in high school and four years in university.
2   Strictly speaking, though the school system before the Second World War differs from the present system, I will use the current names 'high school' and 'junior high school' here to avoid confusion.
3   The general term for Japanese competitive sports such as judo and kendo.
4   This historical background is omitted here for a lack of space.
5   Naginata was developed in the Edo era (1603–1868) as women of *samurai* family's self-defence art, so it is played by mainly women at present. Naginata was installed in the curriculum and played well before the Second World War; however it disappeared from the curriculum after the war, so the population that play naginata is now small. Present membership of naginata in the HSSA is 1,850, 2.5 per cent of volleyball's 73,000 (High School Sports Association 1999: 34).
6   Her book had been translated into several languages.
7   The rate of single women was around 20 per cent at 20–29 years of age in 1970, but it increased to around 50 per cent in 1995 (Inoue and Ehara 1999: 15). 'Total birth rate', the number of children born per woman, has declined to 1.34 in 1999 from 2.13 in 1970 (Inubushi *et al.* 2000, 12).

Bibliography

Asahi Press (1997) *Arimori sennsyu no Proka-sengen?* (Arimori of athletes's professionalisation declaration?), Tokyo: Asahi Press, 26 January.
Hatakeyama, S. (2000) 'Clubkatsudo ni okeru Seitekiyakuwaribungyo' (Division of role between men and women in the club activity), in H. Kameda and K. Tachi (eds), *Gakko o Gender Free ni* (Making school gender free), Tokyo: Akashisyoten.
High School Sports Association (1999) *Data book of high school sports clubs*, Tokyo: HSSA Press.
Inoue, T. and Ehara, Y. (1999) *Josei no Data Book* (Women's Data Book), Tokyo:Yuhikaku.
Inubushi Y., Mukuno, M. and Muraki, A. (2000) *Joseigaku Key Numbers* (Key numbers of women's studies), Tokyo: Yuhikaku.
Itani, K., Tahara, J. and Raita, K. (2001) *Me de miru Josei Sports Hakusho* (Visual data book of women's sport), Tokyo: Taisyukanshoten.
Japan Amateur Sports Association (2002) 'Organigram and information on the Japan Amateur Sports Association (JASA)', http://www.japan-sports.or.jp (8 April 2002).
Japan Association for Women in Sports (2002) 'Information on the Japan Association for Women in Sports, http://www.jws.or.jp (8 April 2002).
Kinoshita, H. (1970) *Sports no Kindai Nihonshi* (Modern Japanese history of sports), Tokyo: Kyorinshoin.
Kishino, Y. (1973) *Taiikushi* (Theory of sports history), Tokyo: Taishukansyoten.
Matsumoto, S. (2001) 'Daigaku Undo-bu niokeru Joshi-manager nikansuru Kenkyu' (Research for women managers in university sports clubs), unpublished graduation thesis, University of Education, Nara.
Nakane, C. (1967) *Tateshakai no Ningenkannkei* (Human relationship of vertical society), Tokyo: Kodanshagendaishinsho.
Nara City (1996) *Nara Kurashi no Benricyo* (Handbook of living in Nara City), Nara: Nara City Press.
NTT Media Scope (2000) *Town Guide Nara*, Osaka: Yoshidachizu.
Oinuma, Y. (1994) *Sumoshakai no Kenkyu* (Study of Sumo society), Tokyo: Fumaidoshuppan.

Raita, K. (1999) 'The movement for the promotion of competitive women's sport in Japan', *The International Journal of the History of Sport* 16, 3: 120–34.

Sasagawa Sports Federation (2000) *Data of sports life 2000*, Tokyo: SSF Press.

Tanaka, S. (1975) *Joseikaiho no Shiso to Kodo Senzenhen* (Thought and action of women's liberation), Tokyo: Jijitsushinsya.

17 Women and sport in New Zealand

Shona M. Thompson

Sports development in New Zealand

Sport in New Zealand developed in ways peculiar to it being a small, young, geographically isolated country colonised by Britain. Women's experiences of sport in this country were greatly influenced by these characteristics, and by a social history that came from pioneering in a male-dominated, agriculturally based capitalist economy. Under these conditions, a society emerged that was strongly marked by gender, in which women's and men's sports tended to evolve separately and, in some cases, distinctly differently.

British colonisation of New Zealand began in the 1840s, with immigrants coming to a land that was already well settled by Maori. Although race relations have been far from smooth, the Maori took avidly to the sports introduced by their colonisers, who brought from their homelands the traditions, skills and equipment of the sports they had played there. The earliest sports to be established in New Zealand, therefore, were those popular amongst the middle classes in Britain, such as cricket, tennis, golf, lawn bowls, rugby, rowing, polo and horse racing (Stothart 2000). Being so far from Europe, colonial settlers were forced to rely heavily on their own resources. As a result, they developed a strong 'do it yourself' approach to leisure, adapting to the new geographical and social conditions in ways that were often unique.

During the peak of early colonisation (1840–80), the migrants to New Zealand were disproportionately men, most of whom were dispersed into isolated all-male work camps to clear rugged, densely forested land and build the infrastructure necessary for a new society. This situation, as Phillips (1987) explains, gave rise to the popularity of rugby, a sport well suited to the physical and social conditions that prevailed and which became strongly associated with the country's emerging national identity. More than any other, it shaped New Zealanders' views and values about sport, which are particularly androcentric. As Coney commented,

> New Zealand has been called 'a man's country' and nowhere has this been more true than in sport. Sporting contest has been a male proving

ground, sport a source of national identity and pride. Traditionally, the nation's heroes have won their colours either on the battlefield or the sports field.

(Coney 1993: 238)

Women in New Zealand, therefore, struggled against ideological beliefs deeming sport an extremely highly valued male terrain in which rugby has been paramount.

While early colonial women were restricted in all their endeavours by family and church (Lynch and Simpson 1983), the frontier-like environment did nevertheless provide them with opportunities for physical recreation which were not readily available to them in Victorian England. As pioneers, many women worked alongside their menfolk in partnerships that required, often for their survival, that they be strong, courageous and unencumbered by restrictive conventions. Furthermore, unmarried women were not super-fluous to the workforce in this young colony. Here there was a desperate shortage of labour and paid work provided these women with a certain enti-tlement to leisure.

As in other parts of the world, the introduction to New Zealand of the safety bicycle was the impetus in a few short years for an extraordinary level of emancipation for women, who were cycling in large numbers by the late 1880s, preferring to do so in all-women clubs (Simpson 1995: 22). Direct links can be made between women's cycling clubs and the suffrage move-ment. Women in New Zealand gained the right to vote in 1893, being the first in any world nation-state to do so. Commemorating that event, Coney commented:

For women to enter the sporting arena has not been easy, but New Zealand women are nothing if not intrepid. In the 1890s they estab-lished cycle clubs, formed a rugby team, took up shooting, played hockey and rowed in regattas. The New Woman wanted more than her political rights, she wanted her sporting rights as well.

(Coney 1993: 238)

From the start, some sports were considered far more acceptable for women than others. Their attempts to play rugby and cricket, for example, were the most fiercely resisted, these being the sports most popular with New Zealand men and most symbolic of the Victorian cult of manliness (Coney 1993). A proposal in 1891 for a women's rugby team to tour the country was met with such a 'public roar of outrage' the idea was quickly scrapped (Crawford 1987: 169). One hundred years passed before women's rugby became acceptable and recognised. By contrast, field hockey did not present the same threat and was promoted as robust and invigorating, epito-mising 'healthy girls'. It became the first major team sport played by women outside of schools. Also less problematic were those sports that had traditionally been mixed, such as tennis, croquet and golf. Clubs for these sports were well established for middle-class women by 1890, particularly amongst married women for whom golf was described as '"a heaven-sent boon" for the middle-aged mother of a grown-up family who had more time on her hands' (Coney 1993: 239).

Organisation of the sport systems

Sports in New Zealand developed in ways reflecting both the 'do it yourself' approach to leisure and the gendered divisions in social life. It became organised through a system of sport-specific clubs, created and voluntarily administered by groups of enthusiasts to facilitate their own participation in that sport. It is estimated that there are 1.3 million people who are members of sports clubs in New Zealand today, approximately one-third of the country's total population of 3.8 million (see Figure 17.1). These community-based clubs are affiliated to regional sport associations, whose major roles are to organise the local competitions, and to national sport organisations (NSOs) that govern institutionalised codes of practice and connect with international sports networks and authorities. With recent expectations

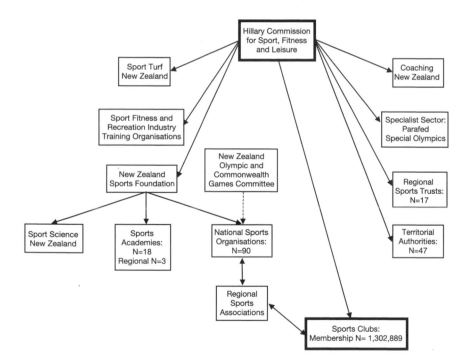

Figure 17.1 Structure of the sport system in New Zealand

Source: Haye and Gunson 1999; Stothart 2000.

that these NSOs conduct their business in more professional ways, paid executive positions now exist in the larger sports but generally the organisation of sport in New Zealand remains within the voluntary sector.

Today, most sports have one amalgamated NSO catering for both men and women but this has not always been so. The sports in which women participate have traditionally been organised in one of three ways. The largest number of them developed in mixed-sex clubs, giving rise to a single administration in which women and men compete separately, such as the case for athletics, badminton, gymnastics, softball, swimming and tennis. Others, such as cricket, field hockey, golf and lawn bowls, developed separately in ways best described as an 'unbalanced parallel' (Macdonald 1993: 407). For example, when women were not admitted to men's golf clubs, they formed their own and negotiated a variety of terms for access to courses and facilities. These terms were rarely equitable. Women's play was usually restricted to mid-week days, suiting only middle-class women who were not in full-time paid employment and privileging men's participation during weekends.

In other sports, women deliberately sought independence from the men's organisations in order to control the quality of their sporting experiences. The Auckland Ladies Hockey Association was formed in 1921 because, as described by the then chairwoman, 'We got sick of being ordered around by the men. The men always gave us a ground out in the back blocks...We got the dirty end of the stick all the time' (Coney 1986: 176). The amalgamation of men's and women's sporting organisations began in the 1970s. Today, only golf and netball retain gender-separate NSOs.

In the third category are sports in which, traditionally, only females competed. Of these, netball remains the most significant and will be discussed in more detail later. Until very recently it has been controlled exclusively by women through deliberate policies that excluded men (Nauright and Broomhall 1994).

State involvement and policies

New Zealand's central government became formally involved in sport in 1937 with the passing of the Physical Welfare and Recreation Act. This helped establish parks, swimming pools and community halls throughout the country, and vast areas of land were set aside for sports-grounds, providing public space for field sports and places where clubrooms could be built (Hindson *et al.* 1994). These facilities, however, catered more to the needs of men than women, although women's physical welfare officers, established under this legislation, were very important resources for the development of women's sports (Macdonald 1993).

The 1973 Recreation and Sport Act of Parliament established a governmental ministerial office and an autonomous advisory council, responding to pressure from sports leaders for resources to be provided to help achieve greater international sporting success. While the well-established, mostly men's sports criticised this initiative for excessive government interference in the private realm of people's leisure (Hindson *et al.* 1994), women's sport generally benefited, lacking alternative sources for funding such as gate and bar sales or large sponsorships (Macdonald 1993). Women were appointed to the new Council for Recreation and Sport (NZCRS) from its beginning. At this time, social developments were greatly influenced by feminism, with women challenging the traditional sexual divisions in sport and recreation and being more forthright in demanding equal recognition and access to participation.

In 1987 the Ministry and the NZCRS were replaced by the Hillary Commission for Recreation and Sport (HC) and the state-controlled 'Lotto' was introduced to help fund it and other community projects. New recreation initiatives were developed, such as KiwiSport for children and programmes specifically targeted for women, Maori, older adults and people with disabilities (Collins and Stuart 1994). Since then, the exact name and emphasis of the HC has changed several times. Although these changes have not always been in women's best interests (Bell and Hayes 1994), the HC has nevertheless remained the main sports funding organisation, pivotal to the development, control and state support of amateur sport in New Zealand (see Figure 17.1). A recent ministerial review of amateur sport, set in the aftermath of the 2000 Sydney Olympics (Sport, Fitness and Leisure Ministerial Task Force 2001), has recommended major structural changes and the HC and associated supporting organisations are currently in transition.

Participation of girls and women

The first national representative survey of recreation preferences in New Zealand (Robb and Howarth 1977) challenged the cherished notion New Zealand had of itself as a nation of people who passionately participated in sport by revealing the gendered bias of that belief. While results showed this tended to be true for men, boys and girls, it was not so for adult women. Sport declined rapidly as a chosen leisure activity for women from aged twenty onwards. While a high proportion of women (18 per cent) did nominate sport as their most favoured leisure activity, this was almost half the figure for men (34.6 per cent) and second to activities categorised as 'home science and home maintenance' (22.4 per cent) such as gardening, culinary crafts and handicrafts (Robb and Howarth 1977).

In a later survey of New Zealander's physical activity levels (Hopkins *et al.* 1991), women again reported less involvement in sporting activities than men, being more frequent participants than men in only two: aerobics and netball. The survey encompassed participation ranging from casual, noncompetitive leisure activities to formal, highly competitive experiences, and found that women's participation was highest in swimming (28 per cent), aerobics (17 per cent), cycling (17 per cent) and tennis (12 per cent) (Hopkins *et al.* 1991). More recently the Hillary Commission (1997) found

Table 17.1 Sport and Physical Activity National Survey 1997 (New Zealand)

	Women	Men
Took part in at least one sporting activity over a year	74%	82%
Average number of activities	4.0	4.5
Took part in competitive sport	25%	43%
Belong to at least one sport club	24%	35%

Source: Hillary Commission (1997)
Note: N = 3,259 adults over eighteen years of age

that the most popular physical activities done by New Zealand women were casual and non-competitive, such as walking (88 per cent of the women surveyed), gardening (63 per cent) and exercising at home (33 per cent). Table 17.1 shows some results of this survey, in which women's involvement in competitive sport is consistently less than men's.

While the results of these two surveys indicate that New Zealand women are relatively less active in organised sports, their numbers in specific sports tell a different story. Macdonald's (1993) history of women's organisations highlights the central place that sport has occupied in the lives of a very large number of New Zealand women, noting that the three most popular sports for women, netball, golf and lawn bowls, had at that time 106,000, 35,000 and 30,000 women members respectively. Since the mid-1970s there has been rapid growth in women's soccer, and in 2001 there were 21,000 girls and women playing field hockey (Hillary Commission 2001).

Hopkins *et al.* (1991) also found that Maori women participated more frequently than other New Zealand women in virtually all sports. From the earliest days of white settlement, Maori women took enthusiastically to competitive physical activity and introduced sports. They had fought along-side their men in the 1860s New Zealand Land Wars, and came from a culture where age and rank often mattered more than gender. Dated photographs show Maori women horse racing (riding astride) in 1905 and cycling in 'reform' dress in 1906 (Coney 1993). They particularly enjoyed team sports and took avidly to field hockey and netball. The first New Zealand women's national representative sport team, selected in 1914 to play field hockey against a visiting team from England, contained at least two Maori women. When Melnick (1996) surveyed the senior netball union teams at the 1992 national netball championships, he found that Maori women comprised 30.9 per cent of the total players, which is double the proportion of Maori in the general population.

Women's own sport: netball

Netball was introduced to New Zealand as 'outdoor basketball' at about the turn of the twentieth century, brought from Britain where it had been adapted from basketball in the USA. It was promoted as an activity especially suitable for females, being 'more acceptable than hockey because it was less aggressive and more graceful. And, as men didn't play it, no male sensibilities were offended by women taking it up' (Coney 1993: 242). It was also considered ideal for the restricted playground space available to girls, an important consideration in view of the colossal disparities in available playground space between the separate boys' and girls' public high schools. Ten of the earliest boys' high schools in New Zealand had, on average, 23 more acres of land available to them than their counterpart girls' school (Fry 1985).

Neither competing with men for space, nor challenging dominant constructions of masculinity or femininity, netball players were simply let get on with the game and it flourished. The NSO was first formed in 1924, with 127 affiliated teams. By 1992 this had grown to 11,000 teams, with more clubs than any other sport in the country and an estimated 10 per cent of the entire female population playing the game (Nauright and Broomhall 1994). Today, it has the highest participation rate of any sport, men's or women's. Official participation figures for 2001 report 120,440 girls and women in netball clubs throughout the country. This participation rate is second only to golf (128,860 women *and* men). Soccer rates third with 105,023 players, then rugby union with 98,543, both predominantly male sports (Hillary Commission 2001). The few other parts of the world where netball is played are almost all ex-colonies of Britain, but only Australia has greater numbers of netball participants than New Zealand.

While the media have traditionally ignored or denigrated women's sport in New Zealand (McGregor and Fountaine 1997), netball has received relatively good television coverage and commands a huge local spectator following. This was initially facilitated by the national television network (NZTV) designating netball as one of four sports, and the only women's sport, to be broadcast free-to-air. Fuelling its spectator popularity is the intense rivalry in netball between New Zealand and Australia. This has made compelling viewing, providing a watershed moment in 1999 when the New Zealand team lost to Australia by one goal in the last few moments of the final match of the Netball World Cup. This event drew the highest public viewing ratings ever recorded on New Zealand television, higher than any previous Olympics or rugby match coverage (Henley 2001). Armed with these figures, NNZ negotiated an unprecedented contract with NZTV for exclusive coverage of a national netball league competition, the Coca Cola Cup, becoming the first women's team sport able to sell television rights.

The Netball Coca Cola Cup is much heralded as 'proof' of New Zealand women's equality in sport, being the first and highly profiled example of a 'professional' women's team sport. In fact, the budget is tiny, the team franchises must raise their own operational funds through business and community sponsorship, and players themselves receive very little, if any, direct financial reward. Most hold down regular jobs but are nevertheless expected to perform as if fully contracted professional athletes. Regardless, the contract between NZTV and NNZ which produced the Coca Cola Cup has been extremely successful in boosting the profile of the sport, increasing both participation numbers and viewing audiences, and tapping into traditional regional community identification with sports teams in ways that rugby has been accused of abandoning. One netball franchise in particular, the Southern Sting, has become an unprecedented cultural phenomenon, such is the level of support in its home town of Invercargill (pop. 53,000). Here, the largest indoor sport stadium in the country has been purpose-built for netball and season tickets sell out within hours to fans of all ages, men and women (Butcher 2000).

High-performance sport

High-performance athletes in New Zealand receive financial assistance and support via the New Zealand Sports Foundation (NZSF) (see Figure 17.1), allocated through a system similar to practices in Australia and Canada whereby athletes are 'carded' according to their competitive standing in national and international competition. Figures for 2001 show that, of the total 1,023 carded New Zealand athletes across thirty-seven different sports, 47 per cent are women (New Zealand Academy of Sport 2001).

Athletes may be allocated carded status at one of four possible levels. Level 1 is generally for those who are ranked within the top ten of world competition in their sport. Of the total of 168 New Zealand athletes carded at this level, 107 (63.7 per cent) are women. The rationale given for this gender imbalance is that, worldwide, women's sport is not seen as having the same competitive depth as men's and therefore elite women athletes are considered to have a better chance of ranking well internationally. Additionally, New Zealand women rugby and cricket players are carded at the highest level while the men in these sports are not. This is because the male codes of rugby and cricket are professional, multi-million dollar businesses deemed well capable of supporting their own. No women's sport is similarly situated. New Zealand women are currently ranked at Level 1 in sixteen sports. These are athletics, cricket, cycling, downhill skiing, equestrian, field hockey, judo, lawn bowls, netball, paralympics, rowing, rugby, softball, squash, weightlifting and yachting (New Zealand Academy of Sport 2001).

Women in decision-making positions

Most major team sports in New Zealand are coached by men. Skilton's (1994) study revealed that only 19 per cent of coaches of high-performance sports in New Zealand were women and a later study showed similar results (Hillary Commission 1999a). Commenting on this lack of progress over five years Cameron (2000) noted that, with the increased status of women's sport, men have moved into coaching women's teams, subsequently decreasing the opportunities for women coaches.

Women are also under-represented in the management of New Zealand sport. Cameron's (1996) study found that, while about one-third of all New Zealand women play sport, only one-fifth of those who manage it at the national level are women, a figure which she noted was comparable to Australia (18–20 per cent) and Canada (21–25 per cent). In New Zealand, men made up 79 per cent of paid executive officers, 89 per cent of elected directors (chairs) and 80 per cent of national board members. These men, Cameron (1996) noted, were primarily well educated, with high incomes and high status occupation. Furthermore, 97 per cent were Pakeha (New Zealanders of European extraction).

Like the men, the women in management positions were also predominantly Pakeha, middle-aged, well-educated, in high-status occupations and with (for women) high incomes. However, they differed markedly from the men in significant ways regarding marital and family status. The women were disproportionately either not married or, if married, had no dependants. Very few had both a partner *and* dependent children. By comparison, the men who had dependants also had a partner. In other words, 'They have someone else to manage the family and, importantly, to manage the marriage as well as the household' (Cameron 2000:180). Given the characteristics of the women in senior sport management, the potential pool from which women can be drawn for these positions is very small, and certainly smaller than that from which the men are drawn.

Cameron (1996) profiled seven women who had 'made it to the top' of the volunteer sector of sport management in New Zealand as executives and chairs of national boards. While these women tended to deny having experienced barriers to their progress in sport administration, or impediments to their ability to do the job, their stories revealed a litany of practises and structures that 'help reinforce the masculinity of sport' (Cameron 2000: 181). These included such practices as clinging to traditional constitutions and by-laws which reinforce the formal, pseudo-democratic procedural ways that men have always managed sport, alienating women and denying the sorts of consensual decision-making processes that women tend to favour. The women spoke of having to deal with the common masculine practice of talking business in urinals and bars – practices that either exclude women or are foreign to them. They reported sexual harassment in their roles as sport managers and of being assigned tasks assumed to be women's 'proper' roles, such as being responsible for tea, food, clothing or children's teams.

Policies and programmes

Following the political and social turbulence surrounding sport in New Zealand resulting from the 1981 Springbok Rugby Tour (Thompson 1988), the newly elected Minister of Recreation and Sport in 1984 commissioned a general inquiry into sport which identified women as a special sector group (Ministry of Recreation and Sport 1985). The inquiry recommended the establishment of a limited term Woman's Sport Promotion Unit and a full investigation into the level of financial and structural support for women's sport. As a result, a Task Force on Women in Physical Recreation and Sport produced a policy document which identified key issues presenting barriers to women's participation (Hillary Commission 1989). It included policy statements requiring sport organisations to review equitable criteria, and suggested that financial support would be reviewed if such bodies were 'found to be inequitable' (Hillary Commission 1989: 6–7). The amalgamation of women's and men's NSOs was similarly encouraged through financial incentives.

The focus of this policy document was clearly on structural barriers to women's participation and the accountability of sport and recreation organisations to address gender equity issues. By 1993, however, the focus had shifted to women themselves, not as a collective force for changes in sport but as individuals who could succeed in the present system. At the HC-sponsored 'Women in Action' Conference held that year, the emphasis was on leadership, role models, motivation and marketing, suggesting that women simply needed to get out there and 'do it for themselves'. This shift matched trends McKay (1997) documented also in Australia and Canada, arguing that the 'corporate push' in amateur sport was subtly subverting affirmative actions projects aimed at assisting women's collective interests.

After the International Conference on Women in Sport held in England in 1994, a Women's Advisory Group was established to adapt the resulting 'Brighton Declaration' for the New Zealand context. The outcome was the 'Winning Women Charter', launched as the 'public face' of the HC's strategies for women and sport, setting down sporting rights for women and girls and providing guidelines for gender equity in sporting organisations (Hillary Commission 1999b). When the leaders of New Zealand NSOs were brought together in 1995 to launch the Charter, the first woman president of the NZ Softball Association was amongst them. She noted, with irony, that she was the only woman signatory, saying 'all the rest were men, [for] the Winning *Women's* Charter' (Cameron 1996: 34, original emphasis). Nevertheless, the 'Winning Women Charter' has been a catalyst for a range of initiatives at the national and regional level. These have included leadership and media skills training, advocacy within NSOs, and pilot projects to increase the number of women in coaching and officiating roles. Additionally, a Harassment-Free Sport Policy was developed with separate guidelines written for athletes and coaches.

While the emphasis is still mainly on empowering and supporting individual women, there is also recognition of the structural impediments outside women's control. This is reflected in the *Women in Coaching* report (Hillary Commission 1999a), which notes the changes between 1994 and 1999 of reported barriers to women coaches. Gone are the 'individual woman' problems (lack of experience, lack of confidence, lack of women role models, lack of mentors); remaining are the structural and patriarchal problems (male networking, biased selection processes, lack of administrative support for women, preferences for male coaches, cost of childcare, time commitments).

'Girls on the Go' is the HC's brand name for its initiatives targeting young female New Zealanders. This links with co-educational programmes delivered in schools, such as KiwiSport and Sportfit. The HC sees evidence of the success of these programmes in the 14.8 per cent increase from 1992 to 1997 of girls in secondary schools taking part in sport and physical activity (Hillary Commission 1999b). While netball is still played by more schoolgirls than any other sport, it is followed in popularity by field hockey, basketball, volleyball, athletics, soccer and touch sevens rugby. Recently the growth in girls' sports has been in codes that have traditionally been the realm of males, such as rugby union, rugby league, touch sevens and soccer. The number of girls and women playing club rugby, for example, increased by 40 per cent in 1999 (Hillary Commission 2001).

Issues

One of the obstacles for New Zealand sportswomen has always been New Zealand's geographical isolation. For example, our first woman Olympian, Violet Walrond, who competed in swimming events at the 1920 Olympics, spent nine weeks travelling to Antwerp, most of which was spent at sea with minimal opportunity to train (Coney 1993). Jet travel has solved most of these problems, but the logistics of distance and the cost of travel remain huge obstacles for New Zealand athletes in an increasingly globalised sporting world. Many spend large amounts of time and money based overseas in an attempt to remain internationally competitive. Today, what is considered to be the single most important issue on the Liberal agenda for women's sport is money, principally for promoting women athletes to perform in international competition as New Zealand struggles to maintain its ideological vision of itself as a successful sporting nation.

While it has been suggested that high-performance New Zealand women athletes are receiving more State-sponsored support than their male counterparts, men are still commanding a great deal more of the corporate dollar through commercial sponsorship, endorsements and professional contracts. However, a strong instrumental undercurrent to the State support of elite sportswomen is emerging, which feeds into New Zealand's traditionally strong construction of national identity through sport. Sources within the administration of high-performance sport talk about sportswomen as being a better 'bang for the buck'. In other words, through the financial support of female athletes there is a greater chance of achieving national glory and recognition with their greater likelihood of winning world championships or, more importantly, Olympic and Commonwealth Games medals. Furthermore, it is considered that a better 'return' for the investment can be gained by supporting individual women competitors rather than teams, particularly if those individual women can compete in multiple medal winning events such as is possible in swimming or cycling.

A stronger mix of media and corporate interests has recently developed around women's sport in New Zealand and with it, a narrower definition of dominant corporeal femininity is being asserted. The national organisations of high-profile women's sport teams are carefully controlling the 'image' of these teams, paying particular attention to the team name, clothing design and the players' grooming, behaviour and diet. In their study of women soccer players, Cox and Thompson (2000) recorded the extent to which these women were increasingly aware of needing to present themselves in conventional heterosexually feminine ways. Wholesome 'girl-next-door' personalities or heterosexy, fair-skinned blondes appear to have the most marketable power, as has been recently seen through the commercial success of the national filed hockey team (Corbett 2001).

Achievements and problems

As with any nation-state, New Zealand's social history has led to some specific ways in which women's sport has developed. Some aspects of that history have limited their participation, others have provided unique and extensive opportunities. Being geographically tucked away in the far south of the globe has not meant that we escaped the problems associated with patriarchal traditions in sport. In fact, our own version of those traditions produced a sporting ideology that is very strongly male-dominated and masculinist, in which men's rugby is still believed to embody our national identity. In the past, women's solution has been to develop their own separate sports and organisations and simply get on with the play, often in large numbers. Today, gender relations within commercialised sport are far more complex. While women's participation numbers continue to grow, challenges arise from a new corporate focus on sportswomen as commodified bodies for national performance goals and consumer audiences. In New Zealand this is particularly problematic because of the strength of Maori and Pacific Island women in our sports, who gravitate to team sports, who are more readily excluded within narrowing, Anglo-oriented definitions of marketable femininity and who frequently feel culturally compromised by instrumental and corporate agendas in sport (Thompson *et al.* 2000).

A further challenge concerns netball. While this has traditionally been, and remains, the most widely played sport by New Zealand women, its future in a corporatised, globalised world looks uncertain because it is played by so few other nations. Without the resources to foster development of the sport in other countries, a common practice in men's sport, or the power to influence international decision-makers in sport, we wonder if its long-term fate is to become an endangered 'ethnic' game.

Overall, we see the control of women's sport further slipping from women's hands. While young sportswomen reaping benefits from corporatised sport may not be lamenting this, their personal control, safety and autonomy in sport can not be guaranteed, nor can their passage to future coaching or managerial positions.

Bibliography

Bell, M. and Hayes, L. (1994) 'From programming to partnerships: "Managing" active women? National policy shifts in women in sport programmes in Aotearoa/New Zealand', paper presented at the 10th Commonwealth Scientific Congress, Victoria, Canada.

Butcher, M. (2000) 'Southland's Southern Sting: The dream team', *North & South*, June: 42–9.

Cameron, J. (1996) *Trail blazers: Women who manage New Zealand sport*, Christchurch: Sports Inclined.

—— (2000) 'The issue of gender in sport: "No bloody room for sheilas…"', in C. Collins (ed.), *Sport in New Zealand society*, Palmerston North: Dunmore Press.

Collins, C. and Stuart, M. (1994) 'Politics and sport in New Zealand', in L. Trenberth and C. Collins (eds), *Sport management in New Zealand*, Palmerston North: Dunmore Press.

Coney, S. (1986) *Every girl: A social history of women and the YWCA in Auckland*, Auckland: Auckland YWCA.

—— (1993) *Standing in the sunshine: A history of New Zealand Women since they won the vote*, Auckland: Penguin Books.

Corbett, J. (2001) 'Hot property', *Weekend Herald* 20–1 January: 14.

Cox, B. and Thompson, S. (2000) 'Multiple bodies: Sportswomen, soccer and sexuality', *International Review for the Sociology of Sport*, 35, 1: 5–20.

Crawford, S.A.G.M. (1987) '"One's nerves and courage are in very different order out in New Zealand": Recreational and sporting opportunities for women in a remote colonial setting', in J.A. Mangan and R. J. Park (eds), *From 'fair sex' to feminism*, London: Frank Cass.

Fry, R. (1985) *It's different for daughters*, Wellington: New Zealand Council for Educational Research.

Hayes, L. and Gunson, L. (1999) 'The structure of sport and its management in New Zealand', in L. Trenberth and C. Collins (eds), *Sport business management in New Zealand*, Palmerston North: Dunmore Press.

Henley, M. (2001) 'Emotional despair, ratings magic: Television and World Cup netball', paper presented in the Department of Sport and Exercise Science Seminar Series, University of Auckland.

Hillary Commission for Recreation and Sport (1989) *National policy for women in physical recreation and sport*, Wellington: Hillary Commission for Recreation and Sport.

Hillary Commission for Sport, Fitness and Leisure (1997) *Active lifestyles: A profile of New Zealanders at play*, Wellington: Hillary Commission for Sport, Fitness and Leisure.

—— (1999a) *Women in coaching*, Wellington: Hillary Commission for Sport, Fitness and Leisure.

—— (1999b) *Winning Women Charter: Resource document*, Wellington: Hillary Commission for Sport, Fitness and Leisure.

—— (2001) 'Sportfacts', http://www.hillarysport.org.nz/sportfacts/members/shtml (4 August 2001).

Hindson, A., Cushman, G. and Gidlow, B. (1994) 'Historical and social perspectives in sport in New Zealand', in L. Trenberth and C. Collins (eds), *Sport Management in New Zealand*, Palmerston North: Dunmore Press.

Hopkins, W., Wilson, N., Russell, D. and Herbison, P. (1991) *Life in New Zealand Commission Report: Physical activity*, Wellington: Hillary Commission for Sport, Fitness and Leisure.

Lynch, P. and Simpson, C. (1983) 'Gender and leisure', in H. Perkins and G. Cushman (eds), *Leisure, recreation and tourism*, Auckland: Longman Paul.

Macdonald, C. (1993) 'Organisations in sport, recreation and leisure', in A. Else (ed.), *Women together*, Wellington: Daphne Brasell Associates Press.

McGregor, J. and Fountaine, S. (1997) 'Gender equity in retreat: The declining representation of women's sport in the New Zealand print media', *Metro*, 112: 38–44.

McKay, J. (1997) *Managing gender: Affirmative action and organisational power in Australian, Canadian and New Zealand sport*, Albany, NY: State University of New York Press.

Melnick, M.J. (1996) 'Maori women and positional segregation in New Zealand netball: Another test of the anglocentric hypothesis', *Sociology of Sport Journal*, 13: 259–73.

Ministry of Recreation and Sport (1985) *Sport on the move*, Wellington: Ministry of Recreation and Sport.

Nauright, J. and Broomhall, J. (1994) 'A woman's game: The development of netball and a female sporting culture in New Zealand, 1906–70', *The International Journal of the History of Sport* 11, 3: 387–407.

New Zealand Academy of Sport (2001) *Athletes for NZAS Carding System*, Auckland: Academy of Sport Northern Region.

Phillips, J. (1987) *A Man's Country?*, Auckland: Penguin.

Robb, M. and Howarth, H. (1977) *New Zealand Recreation Survey*, Wellington: New Zealand Council for Recreation and Sport.

Simpson, C. (1995) 'The development of women's cycling in late nineteenth century New Zealand', in J. Nauright (ed.), *Sport, power and society in New Zealand: Historical and contemporary perspectives*, Sydney: Australian Society for Sports History.

Skilton, J. (1994) 'Taking the lead – Women in coaching in New Zealand', *The New Zealand Coach*, Summer: 21–3.

Sport, Fitness and Leisure Ministerial Task Force (2001) *Getting set for an active nation*, Wellington: Ministry for Sport, Fitness and Leisure.

Stothart, B. (2000) 'The development of sport administration in New Zealand: From kitchen table to computer', in C. Collins (ed.), *Sport in New Zealand society*, Palmerston North: Dunmore Press.

Thompson, S.M. (1988) 'Challenging the hegemony: New Zealand women's opposition to rugby and the reproduction of a capitalist patriarchy', *International Review for the Sociology of Sport*, 23, 3: 205–12.

Thompson, S., Rewi, P. and Wrathall, D. (2000) 'Maori experiences in sport and physical activity: Research and initiatives', in C. Collins (ed.), *Sport in New Zealand Society*, Palmerston North: Dunmore Press.

18 Women's inclusion in sport

International and comparative findings

Ilse Hartmann-Tews and Gertrud Pfister

The preceding chapters have presented numerous, mainly descriptive information on sports developments over the past decades with a particular focus on the inclusion of women in sixteen countries from all parts of the world and representing a range of socio-economic, political and cultural settings: Norway, Great Britain, Germany, France, Spain, Czech Republic, USA, Canada, Brazil, Columbia, Iran, Tanzania, South Africa, China, Japan and New Zealand. Readers who are primarily interested in basic facts, or descriptions of trends and developments in specific countries, will probably have found the information they are seeking in the relevant chapters. The insights of indigenous scholars and foreign nationals with cultural expertise characterise each chapter and make them of special value .

From the outset, the content of the book aimed at providing base-line information on a variety of social issues in the domain of women and sport by sharing a common framework and analytical goals in order to identify more general propositions about gender, sport, policy and the state. The shared conceptual framework should help to discern similarities and variations as well as any differences between the countries. This concluding chapter addresses more general findings with the central questions of whether there are any cross-cultural trends and common phenomena of inclusion and/or exclusion of women in sport described in the sixteen contributions and whether there are any variations or idiosyncratic developments. The answers should provide us with some additional understanding about the influences of the socio-cultural context and the gendered structures and processes in society.

As was argued in the introduction to this book, we cannot directly compare the quantitative data in the various descriptions of the countries because the methods of collection and measurement vary from country to country and even within most countries, surveys are neither standardised nor are they designed to produce comparative data over a defined period of time. At the same time we cannot directly compare most of the qualitative data, as our approach was not intended to take a 'most similar system approach' and unearth the complex causal connections between cultural contexts, gender and sports development and the state. However, out of the diverse countrywide descriptions, it is possible to identify at least some general, probably worldwide trends, and many others that seem to be more regional in nature and tied up with specific cultures. In this sense the book should provide the foundations and first steps in the feminist comparative study cycle of sports policy.

Historical background of the involvement of women in sport

Not all contributors of this book provide an insight into the historical development of physical activity and sport in the eighteenth and nineteenth centuries. These contributions which take a historical point of view, identify manifold mechanisms by which physical exercise and sport have been defined as a male domain. Views and values about sport have been androcentric right from the start, creating connotations of physical strength, muscularity, competition and masculinity. In addition the instrumentalisation of physical education for military service in some countries gave way to define sport as a male activity that educated boys to become men. In the nineteenth century in Germany and France, patriotic goals and emphasis on military preparedness made the exclusion of women self-evident and nobody bothered to explain or justify it. Modern sport with its orientation toward competition and records was developed in England and spread all over the world at the end of nineteenth century. The embedded ideology of a natural gendered order was proliferated as well. In New Zealand, as Thompson in this book intimates, the disproportionately male pioneers were striving to build up a nation state and 'the nation's heroes...won their colours either on the battlefield or the sports field'.

Everywhere, the exclusion of girls and women has been embedded in moral, medical and aesthetic arguments. In many countries participation of girls and women in sport was considered dangerous, because women were not seen to have the physical potential to face competition in sport and most of the medicines argued against physical activities and sport for women and girls. Participation of women in most of the sports or physical exercises in the nineteenth century was seen as useless, dangerous to health status and to public morals. Furthermore, female participation constituted an element of immorality. In many countries physical exercises of girls and women were restricted by their clothing, which in turn was the expression of moral and aesthetic values – tight corsets, for example, in the eighteenth and nineteenth centuries. In some countries laws explicitly prohibit(ed) women from playing sport. This was true for Brazil during the 1940s when women were not permitted to practise sports, which were considered as incompatible with their 'feminine nature' and even in the 1960s and 1970s single activities were explicitly banned. This systematic and explicit exclusion of women from sports, and its gradual repeal in recent decades, becomes obvious when looking at the participation patterns in the Olympic Games.

Despite the generally discouraging atmosphere for the development of girls' and women's participation in physical activities and sport in the past, some positive niches can be identified. In some countries there were some medical practitioners who advised women to practise gymnastics because strength and healthy well-being were necessary qualities for good motherhood. Actually, there was a strong belief that physical education would be the best way to give women, whose primary function was seen to be procreation, a solid constitution for a more fertile life and a healthier maternity. When women took up sports other than gymnastics (like upper class women in Great Britain in the nineteenth century engaging in archery and croquet), this always had to be done in a way which did not undermine or challenge traditional ideologies of 'femininity'. Sportswomen were expected to behave in an exemplary fashion and display feminine traits. Obviously from the start, some sports were considered far more acceptable for women than others. It seems to be a truism that those sports most popular with men and most symbolic of the cult of manliness have been the most fiercely resistant; rugby and soccer being two examples often cited in the contributions.

However, some idiosyncrasies can be identified in the contributions, too. In New Zealand for example field hockey was promoted as robust and invigorating, epitomising 'healthy girls'. It became the first major team sport played by women outside of schools. As field hockey was not a male domain and not so vigorously pursued in providing manliness, the inclusion did not present a strong threat. In Norway in the 1930s, as another example, handball was a popular team sport with girls and women, whereas in other countries it has been a strong male domain activity. These two examples provide an excellent insight into the constructive basis of exclusion and inclusion politics and gender ideology as they demonstrate that the gendered images of some sports are different in different countries and cultures. There are examples, too, showing that the gendered image of individual sports may change over time as is the case with capoeira. It originated from military affairs in the sixteenth century in Brazil and has a long tradition of being a male domain. Today, participation rates of boys and girls have levelled out.

The organisation of sport and physical activities: space for girls and women?

All over the world there is a mix of governmental, quasi-governmental, and non-governmental voluntary and/or commercial organisations that are concerned with sport policy, development and provision of opportunities to play sports and participate in physical activities. In addition, in all countries people take part in physical activities and sport without any institutionalised organisational frame. The development and differentiation of these types of sport provision and involvement in physical activities seem to occur everywhere, albeit with different starting points, focal points, paths and rates of speed. The core of almost all sport systems are public offerings, primarily in schools and institutions of higher education, and voluntary organised offerings in sports clubs.

From the perspective of participation and opportunities to become involved in physical activities and sport, the following frames can be distinguished and the ideological underpinning of these types of sport and physical activities has to be considered when evaluating their inclusiveness:

1   physical activities and sport without any institutionalised form of frame (e.g. jogging, cycling, volleyball at the beach during holidays);
2   organised physical activities within the education system (physical education at all levels of the school system, university teams);
3   organised sport within voluntary sector clubs and associations (generally all kinds of amateur competitive sports but also a huge variety of leisure sport activities);
4   physical activities and sport within commercially led private centres (primarily fitness training or racket sports as squash and tennis).

Local authorities very often provide leisure facilities and services although this is a statutory requirement only in some of the countries discussed in this book. Performance development is provided primarily through voluntary sector clubs and its amalgamations into regional/county associations affiliated to national governing bodies/federations and in the education system via athletic teams at high school and colleges. Sporting excellence (some would argue elite sport) is nurtured primarily by the governing bodies (NGBs), which are, for this part of the sport development, mostly funded by the state. The introduction of new sources of public funding (as for example the introduction of a National Lottery) always has had a significant impact on the support for elite sportswomen and men.

Although there is no complete picture on the development and state of physical education at school (we did not include this aspect of sports development in the framework), there appears to be a long tradition of sex-segregation in all countries. Not only the children were taught different activities in different classes but also men and women physical education teachers were trained separately in sex segregated colleges. Those contributors who discussed the development of school education made it clear that the physical education curriculum is crucial in the socialisation of gendered bodies and that it still tends to reflect a traditional gendered approach, with predominantly sex segregated classes, cultures of femininity and masculinity, that pervades the way physical education is taught. In some industrialised countries today, we see a trend to co-education, although in others where co-education has been the norm for some years, there are signs of 'turning the clock back'.

As indicated by the historical data all over the book, female sport developed on the fringes of male sport. The development of organised women's sport generally follows two different sets of strategies and ideologies. In most countries, the largest number of sports developed in mixed-sex clubs and associations giving rise to a single administration in which women and men take part in physical activities and compete separately. In some countries and in a few number of sports, women deliberately sought independence from men's organisations in order to control the quality of their sporting experiences. In those industrialised countries where single-sex organisations were established in the last century (like in England), we can discern a trend towards mixed provision and organisational structures and only very few sports still have gender-separate associations or NGOs. The general pattern emerging is that women have sacrificed autonomy and control over their sport, but gained financial advantages and access to facilities, coaching and sponsorship.

Inclusion of girls and women into physical activities and sport

In order to identify the extent of inclusion of girls and women into sports as a feature, we need reliable and systematically gathered observations and data. At first glance, the contributions reveal large variations in the availability and quality of such data. In some countries, national surveys have been/are undertaken on a regular and standardised basis as in Great Britain's National Household Survey. In most of the countries this is not the case, and information about the number of people who are involved in physical activities and sport can only be derived from small case studies. There appears to be a correlation between the availability of data on participation and the state's or sport system's interest in the inclusion of people. Awareness of the benefits of regular physical activity and sport for the population is closely connected with the amount of interest to increase knowledge about health and social welfare of people, which in turn very often seems to lead to some sort of social policy intending to increase the number of people involved in physical activity and sport.

The most often used indications for inclusion are self-reported participation as is documented in survey data and membership in voluntary sport associations. There are several well-known methodological reservations concerning the reliability and validity of survey data as well as of membership figures, and some of our contributors stress that even national surveys show inconsistent results. This must be kept in mind when trying to identify trends, similarities and differences. Comparative analyses on single country studies of participation in sport only allow for some empirically based assumptions, which seem to raise more questions than provide answers.

Participation in physical activities and sport

Participation in recreational physical activities and sport has been rising throughout the 1980s, while the 1990s are characterised by a more diversified development with rising, stagnating and even decreasing rates of participation. The diversified and heterogeneous developments in participation in the 1990s are mirrored by data informing us about parallel or contrary tendencies of males' and females' participation in the countries included in this book. In some countries there is an overall increase in the percentage of males and females participating regularly in physical activities and sport, which is higher amongst girls and women than amongst boys and men (Germany) or vice versa, higher amongst men than amongst women (Spain). In some countries there is an increase in the percentage of girls' and women's involvement and at the same time a stagnation or even decrease of men's involvement (UK, France) or an overall decrease in sports involvement irrespective of sex (Canada).

However, across the countries discussed in this book (and probably worldwide), girls and women are less likely to participate in physical activities and sport than boys and men. In cases where there are as many girls and boys participating in sport, boys seem to exercise more often than girls and, after leaving school, generally more girls than boys tend to withdraw from regular participation in physical activities. Whereas most reports confirm the general gender-gap in participation over the last few decades, some recent data reveal interesting variations concerning gender and age, indicating that this gender gap narrows with age.

Another indicator of inclusion of people into the sport system is membership in sports clubs or membership in high school/college athletic teams. Membership rates vary from country to country but the overall membership of girls and women used to be lower than of boys and men. This gender gap in sports clubs membership is reported to be higher than it is in general and overall participation data. In those countries with a long tradition of sports clubs as in some Western European countries, there was a trend towards rising male and female membership in the 1980s followed by stagnation and/or decreases in the 1990s.

The reasons why girls and women are less likely to be members of a sports club are multifarious. A major reason is that sports clubs were, right from the start, traditionally male domains, founded and led by males focusing primarily on competition and competitive sports. Additionally sports clubs offer predominantly traditional (team) sports requiring regular participation and commitment to training sessions. It seems to be a general finding that the bigger the club is, the higher is its female membership. Of course clubs that are big in size are more likely located in urban areas, which in turn tend to reflect less traditional gender roles. The most important reason for a higher female membership in bigger clubs seems to be the range of sports, physical activities and facilities offered.

There is a tendency towards a higher participation rate of girls and women in fitness and health centres in those countries which are more industrialised. However, in these cases social stratification plays a central role as these centres are part of the commercial sector and are rather expensive in comparison with public amenities and sports clubs.

Motives to participate vary with age and gender. They shift from 'fun' (relevant with young people) through 'stress reduction, need for fitness' (middle aged) to 'health concern' (relevant for the elderly). Women generally score higher on motives such as health concern, keeping down weight and other aesthetic concerns. Men generally score higher on motives related to competition, excitement, challenge and adventure.

All levels of inclusion, unorganised and organised sport, leisure and high-performance, are strongly mediated by socio-economic status and ethnicity. The lower the class, the less physically active are people and this effect seems to be stronger amongst girls and women than amongst boys and men. Despite an expansion of facilities for outdoor and indoor sport (at different levels but worldwide) and the overall increase in participation, social class remains a persistent factor in women's sport participation. The overall participation rate for ethnic minority groups is less compared with the national average for both men and women, but there are wide variations concerning different ethnic groups in some countries. In addition the issue of religion plays a vital role in understanding participation of girls and women in sport. This holds true for countries with dominant religious cultures like Islam in Iran or Catholic roots in Spain and Latin America, but this issue is pertinent to immigrant groups in, for example, Germany, France and the UK. In many cases the dominance of men is attributed to a mixture of religious beliefs and patriarchal traditions, where women's lives are focused on the home, and they are largely banished from public life. In some countries, as for example Columbia, the erosion of the religious paradigm, gives way to a more liberal framework to take part in physical activities and sport – especially for women.

Most contributions of western industrialised countries give the impression that jogging, swimming and cycling are the most preferred physical activities. Although girls and women have lower participation rates these activities, which are mostly informally performed without an institutionalised frame, are always found in the top three activities of both sexes. Trying to identify in a comparative perspective typically male or female activities is a rather difficult task. Two views can be taken: either the overall number of girls/women and boys/men taking part in physical activities and sports or the relative proportions to be found looking at all single-sport participants. The latter perspective confirms some of our stereotype perceptions of sports activities such as boxing and rugby as male domains and gymnastic/aerobics and netball as female domains. But the analysis of the data also evokes results quite contrary to our perceptions as the reader may well have noticed in some of the contributions.

Soccer for example is very popular all over the world and generally associated as the boys' game. A closer look at membership data reveals its increasing popularity with girls and women and the loss of its traditional image of a male domain. Resistance over this development seems to be 'natural' and is reported in several countries. Girls and women have long been denied participation, membership, playing areas and facilities and, last but not least, admission to competition. Like other sport associations, soccer did not always welcome females especially if they wanted to play in boys' teams, which many had to do before clubs, community centres, schools and higher education institutions began to open their 'doors' and initiate programmes for girls and women. Many countries show the increasing willingness of clubs to allow female membership and the founding of female teams, but there are examples, as is the case in New Zealand, that demonstrate strong androcentric resistance.

Shooting is another example. In many countries shooting is a male preserve with far more boys and men in membership of sports clubs than girls and women. By way of a contrast, one of the most popular sports for women in Iran is shooting and they have access to competitions as well. Girls and women favour this sport as it is a culturally accepted physical activity for both sexes. This is mainly due to the fact that the Prophet, Mohammed, had recommended teaching children to use a bow and arrow but also because it assists in training for defence of a nation under threat of war.

Access to playing grounds

The availability of public play areas seems to be a crucial factor in overall participation rates and it plays a major role in relation to involvement of girls and boys. Several contributors observe that boys are much more active in the use of open free spaces, streets, and corners for playing ball games whereas girls tend to remain sedentary and inactive. This finding may well on the one hand be interpreted as reflecting the natural differences between boys and girls, but on the other hand, it may give some insight into the political dimension of this issue.

A closer comparative look reveals that the availability of playgrounds and spaces is higher for boys and men than it is for girls and women. In some countries especially those with traditional and rigidly implemented gender roles, there are (almost) no public places for girls and women to engage in sport, testimony to which are the situations in Iran and Tanzania respectively. The role of the political and religious order in providing places for games and sport is well documented in Columbia, too. Alongside severe economic and political crises, formal and traditional scenarios for sport and games give way to new sport practices and a redesignation of space that allow women to take part in physical activities sport and games.

Access to play areas is also a direct political issue in other countries. In New Zealand, for example, the introduction and promotion of netball for girls was facilitated by the fact that the game needed little space and there has always been restricted playground and space available to girls. In addition there are some findings indicating considerable disparities in available playground space between the separate boys' and girls' public secondary schools as examples from Great Britain and New Zealand show.

Access to high-performance sports

Pierre de Coubertin, President of the International Olympic Committee for a considerable amount of time, demanded that the Olympics should never admit women to competition. Alongside this ideology, sports organisations and clubs in France and elsewhere were adamant in their refusal to accept women and many experts (primarily medical practitioners) had strong reservations about competitive sport for women. It took some time before these reservations were withdrawn and gave way to equal access for men and women to top class sport. The 1992 Summer Olympics in Barcelona offered 159 events for men and 86 for women with 12 open to both men and women. In the Summer Olympics 2000 in Sydney, only three sports (boxing, wrestling and baseball) were not available for women at this level. However, more events are still offered for men than for women (due to variations in weight classes and differentiation within sports, for example in track and field).

The proportion of female athletes in Olympic team delegations has varied substantially over the years and countries but has generally been lower than the proportion of male athletes. Some countries report a stable gender imbalance and low proportion of female delegates, whilst other countries indicate increasing numbers of female athletes. The Canadian Olympic team seems to be a 'good practice' model as it comprised 50 per cent women in 1996 and 2000. Some countries report that the success quota of female athletes has been (much) better than that of male athletes.

There is a tendency throughout the countries that talented males are more likely to be identified as potential top athletes than talented females and, therefore, more male elite athletes are likely to have access to public funding and support than female elite athletes. Moreover, most contributions give the impression that women and women's teams do not receive the same attention and support as men and the men's teams as far as media coverage, reimbursement of expenses, lodging and team-building conditions and medical follow-up are concerned. Nevertheless, there are examples of good practice in some countries: according to a Canadian survey, women have equal access to training and competitive environments as well as health, medical and sport science services, but then this general feature holds true for most of the countries discussed in this book.

Despite progress that has been made, women's top-level sport is generally the history of a constant struggle to attain equality with men. In general, female elite athletes have had to, and in some instances still have to, overcome prejudices, obstacles that hitherto denied them access to top-level sport. The problem becomes even more acute in those sports regarded as male. In general terms, if a club is short of money the first to suffer are women's teams and athletes and priority of support is given to men. The lack of recognition and sometimes disrespect shown to female elite sportswomen have significant consequences for the career of athletes.

Against this general background of gender imbalance, two contrasting examples of funding and supporting strategies are quite interesting. In the UK on the one hand, more male athletes receive financial support than female athletes. Officials explain this away by the greater number of sports, events and competitions available to men, and the better development opportunities for boys and men to put them in the 'potential medal winner' category. In New Zealand, on the other hand, there are far more women than men granted a status that ranks them within the top ten of world competition in their sport and makes them eligible for comprehensive support. This is explained by the fact that worldwide, women's sport is not seen as having the same competitive depth as men's and, therefore, elite women athletes are considered to have a better chance of ranking well internationally.

The rationale given for this gender imbalance in the UK and New Zealand is that there seems to be a greater chance of winning world championships or Olympic or Commonwealth Games medals. Both countries argue on the basis of a better 'return' for their investment that can be gained by supporting either male athletes as is the case in the UK or female athletes as is the case in New Zealand, but the outcomes of their arguments are quite different. Although the 'status quo' and facts to be taken into consideration and the starting point of arguments are the same, both countries derive contrasting funding strategies. The example seems to be an interesting case study of the degree and manner in which state and sport system policies are a cause and/or a solution to persistent gender hierarchies and women's low status in society.

Women in decision-making positions

All contributions report a markedly low level of representation of women in decision-making positions in organised sport in the public and voluntary sectors. Women are grossly under-represented in the management of sport, as paid executive officers, as board members and elected chairs, and as referees and coaches. With a few notable exceptions, most senior positions in the national governing bodies across all the countries analysed in this book are held by men and there is no general tendency towards any increase, rather in some countries, female representation is even on the decrease. Some contributions give the impression that a greater involvement of women is found at public policy level and in quasi-governmental institutions, where equal opportunity has been on the agenda for some time. In addition to the gender gap, all levels of inclusion in sport leadership are strongly mediated by socioeconomic status and ethnicity.

Most major team sports are coached by men and only in very few countries is the female proportion of coaches of high-performance sport higher than 10 per cent. There seems to have been little progress over the years, and some contributors even note that with the increased status of women's sport, men have moved into coaching women's teams (like in the USA), concomitantly decreasing opportunities for women coaches.

Sports development and inclusive strategies

Sport for All

In most of the countries, awareness of women and sport issues has grown in more recent years. Throughout the countries discussed in this book, sports development has been changing from exclusive to inclusive and it seems that modernisation and globalisation have spread the idea of sport for all. 'Sport for All' is a rather young idea in modern society. The European Sport for All Charter, ratified in 1975, relates to a comprehensive sports policy, which attempts to extend the beneficial effects of sport on health, social, educational and cultural development to all sections of the community. The European Council Charter expresses the belief that all of its member states should foster inclusion of people into the sports system. The idea(l) of inclusiveness implemented in the 'Sport for All' movement has spread to many countries and encompasses two dimensions: (i) a factual or pertinent inclusiveness as regards the activities that are meant by sport; sport is no longer confined to competitive games and sport 'proper', presupposing special abilities and regular training within an organisational frame, but it now includes physical activities with the proviso that they demand some effort; and (ii) a social inclusiveness as regards the people taking part in sport and physical activities; participation in sport should no longer be the sole domain of young male people from the upper classes but it should be accessible to all people irrespective of their age, colour or ethnicity, sex and ability.

However, the spread of the idea of sport for all does not necessarily imply the implementation of gender equality in sport. In the Czech Republic, for example, the official implementation of 'Sport for All' particularly focuses on children and youth, but there is no special recognition of girls and women! In Iran, as another example, the institutional guarantees of sport and physical activities for everyone at all levels is embedded in strong patriarchal and Islamic traditions that restrict open access to all activities for girls and women.

Many contributions give the impression that the spread of the idea of sport for all has been articulated in words but has not necessarily been realised in actions. White papers, educational programmes and federations' statutes have realised the lack of inclusiveness and gender imbalance in sport. Women and girls are identified as special interest groups alongside senior citizens, people with disabilities or from different ethnic origins etc. Much documentation refers to gender equality and the right of women to participate in sport as of paramount importance and prevails upon public authorities and sports associations to devise training and development programmes to facilitate the participation of women in sport. They also refer to the removal of barriers, which prevent women from participation in physical activities and sport, from pursuing careers in training, administration coaching and management. Nonetheless, very often such rhetoric, programmes and statutes fail to offer any concrete programme, any concrete action or the effectiveness of programmes is not evaluated. In some countries, findings of evaluation or monitoring studies show, that although the policy provided written encouragement about efforts on behalf of women's sport promotion and special programmes, the policy objectives have not been implemented effectively. The reasons are multifarious but lack of money is the most prominent one. This observation is just as true in Western European countries as it is in other countries and continents all over the world.

Women's sport advocacy and achievements

Those explicit initiatives that have been taken to promote sport for women and girls fall into three broad categories: (i) special programmes for developing women's and girls' sport; (ii) the implementation of national and international women's advocacy organisations; and (iii) mainstreaming gender equity within sports development programmes. These initiatives have been pursued in most of the countries – but not in all!

Special programmes

The most frequently recorded initiatives are special measures and programmes for developing women and girl's sport. These are very often integrated in programmes, which focus on marginalised groups, among them girls and women. Programmes to increase and enhance female participation in sport embrace the promotion of physical activities, special courses for women only as well as special training opportunities, courses in leadership management for women only and the establishment of women's sport associations. The UK has a tradition in sports policy targeting special groups and recently innovative projects have been established in partnership with a variety of agencies designed to develop new ways of working with target groups; women being one. There is no doubt that support programmes for special disadvantaged groups have (had) their positive effects in all countries that made use of these programmes.

Women's advocacy organisations

The implementation of women's advocacy agencies plays a vital role in some countries. The organisational status, size and impact vary from country to country. They are either (a) standing committees within voluntary sport associations and their national governing bodies or umbrella organisation, (b) 'quasi-governmental' foundations or associations for the advancement of women and sport and physical activity based on mixed funding of voluntary and public sectors, or (c) 'women and sport' departments or working groups of national ministries and their regional public departments. Although their organisational status varies their origins are more or less the same. Most of them were initiated by a group of women (women sports teachers, sportswomen, feminists, scientists), who were concerned about the male domination, discrimination and inequalities faced by women. Their purpose is to advocate on behalf of women in sport and to bring gender equity within the sport system, especially in voluntary sector sports clubs and public amenity provision. Their mission is to develop physical activities and sport for girls and women and to ensure that girls and women have equal access to opportunities and support at all levels of sport.

Many contributions reveal that national women's advocacy agencies have acted as catalysts in three ways. First of all they have acted as agencies which fostered and sometimes realised the implementation of gender equality programmes that have been set on the agenda years ago. Secondly they have initiated their own programmes and actions, and thirdly, these organisational units have often been followed by the establishment of committees or at least the implementation of a women's contact network at all levels of the sport system thus giving rise to regional and local groups. For example, the US Women's Sport Foundation, formed in 1974, has helped other countries (including the UK and Japan) to form their own Women's Sport Foundation.

In addition to these national institutions, European and international bodies of women's advocacy in sport have to be acknowledged, as there is the European Working Group on Women and Sport (EWS; http://www.ews-online.com) and the International Working Group on Women and Sport (IWGWS; http://www.iwg-gti.org). Both are informal, co-ordinating bodies consisting of government and key non-government organisations with the objectives of promoting and facilitating the development of opportunities for girls and women in sport and physical activities. The first international conference on women and sport, which brought together policy and decision makers in sport at both national and international level took place in Brighton, UK in 1994. It was organised by the British Sports Council and supported by the IOC. The agreed outcome of the conference, the so-called 'Brighton Declaration' addressed the issue how to accelerate the process of change that would redress the imbalances women face in their participation and involvement in sport. The follow up conference in Windhoek in 1998 and the respective declaration on 'Action' recognised the need for linkages into existing international instruments on the elimination of discrimination. The main task of the IWGWS is to monitor the adoption and implementation of the Brighton and Windhoek Declarations by government and national and international organisations worldwide. In 2002 the third conference took place in Montreal, Canada.

Gender mainstreaming

In the recognition of the need of a more effective way of implementing equal opportunities, another more recent initiative in industrialised Western countries is mainstreaming gender equity within sports development programmes by attempting to change existing practice within existing structures. The general policy of gender mainstreaming was introduced in 1985 at the World Conference of the United Nations but was not implemented until 1995 in the UN organisations and 1996 in the European Union. The focus of this policy in sport is clearly on structural barriers to girls' and women's participation and the accountability of sport and recreation organisations in addressing gender equity issues. The argument here is that the organisations/associations as a whole should be responsible for the development of women's sport with full gender integration defined as a cross-sectional task. This approach has been adopted by policy agencies in a variety of countries. Some reservations were expressed as advocacy and persuasion alone will not be sufficient to change structures and long established male domains. Some countries, namely the UK and New Zealand, go a step further and combine this advocacy policy with a rigorous strategy, i.e. public funding is made dependent on the compliance of the applicant with equity conditions. In France, too, the approval of a sports association and prerequisite of funding is in particular based on the existence of statutory regulations that guarantee, amongst other things, equal access of women and men to its leading positions.

In this context the example of the US Title IX, the educational amendment to Civil Rights legislation, is of relevance. According to a variety of studies the participation of women in sports has increased continuously since its implementation in 1972. Even though it is difficult to prove any direct causal correlation, it is obvious that this law has fostered equal opportunities and has helped girls and women seeking equal access to playing fields and resources to fight their case against gender-based discrimination. There have been discussions most recently around President Bush's plans to announce the suspension of Title IX regulations. The US Department of Education has formed a Commission on Opportunities in Athletics to study the effects of Title IX on college sports.

Another advocacy measure introduced by several countries is that of quota regulations, whereby both sexes should be represented on sports associations' committees. In this context the 1988 resolution of the International Olympic Committee (IOC), which recommended that all National Olympic Committees and national sports organisations should have women's committees and increase the numbers of women representatives on their boards seems to have had an impact all over the world. Even those countries with rigid and traditional gender segregation and hierarchies have started or intensified their gender equality programmes.

In general there are two focuses of women advocacy policy, which seem to alternate in their relevance by time and by country. On the one hand the focus of the policy is on the women themselves, not as a collective force for changes in sport but as individuals. The 'individual woman' problems like lack of experience, lack of confidence, lack of women role models, lack of mentors are targeted with individual support programmes. The emphasis here is on motivation and marketing, role models and leadership, suggesting that women simply need to become aware of the benefits of physical activities, of the opportunities to become involved in sport and just do it. On the other hand, the focus of the policy is clearly on structural and cultural barriers to women's participation and on the accountability of sport and recreation organisations to address gender equity issues. These barriers are effects and part of a traditional gender order and become obvious in the semantics of 'sport' and 'women's sport'. Sport has been male sport right from the start and exclusiveness has been implemented by men as reflected in preferences for male coaches, lack of administrative and financial support for women's sport, and so on.

In Anglo-American countries, we see a subtle shift in the discourse of human rights from equality to equity in the early 1990s. *Equality* generally meant equality of opportunity and women (along with other disadvantaged groups) were identified as target groups. Equal opportunity programmes were designed to increase women's overall participation by opening up opportunities for them to enjoy equal access. Gender continued to be equated with women and gender inequality remained a 'woman's problem', her experience and hers to transform. The shift to *equity* meant a more comprehensive view and is a quality issue. The focus is no longer on singled out target groups but on the system, which needed to change in order to accommodate them. Accordingly women's advocacy policies are becoming twofold. While the emphasis is still mainly on empowering and supporting individual women, there is also recognition of the structural impediments outside women's control.

The gender order

Discussing the case studies in a comparative perspective reveals that the gender order and its hierarchical structures persist in all societies and in sport systems as well.

The level of awareness and the invention of tools to implement gender equity in contrast varies enormously, being high in the Nordic countries and North America and low in (economically) developing countries. As an effect of equal rights politics in general, girls and women have much better chances and opportunities to participate in physical activities and sport and Norway, Canada and the USA may be taken as good practices for gender mainstreaming in sport. It will take a lot of work to change the gender order, to change attitudes and bring about fundamental change to the sport culture. The role of the media has been mentioned in many contributions and seems to be crucial in the process of permanent affirmation of traditional gendered images of sports or of conveying new images.

However, a mixture of special measures and mainstreaming is probably the best way to challenge the existing gender order that continues to place men's sport above women's sport and to give men greater opportunities than women to become involved in sport. There is cause for some optimism: the challenges to the gender order through the increasing participation of women in traditionally male sports is one; the fact that some strong-minded women, both in the sports and the political systems, are becoming increasingly influential and respected by the male establishment is another.

Overall the challenge remains to accelerate the process of change to a more inclusive culture of sport.

Index